The American Craftsman and the European Tradition
1620–1820

The American Craftsman and the European Tradition
1620–1820

Edited by Francis J. Puig
and Michael Conforti

The Minneapolis Institute of Arts

Distributed by University Press of New England
Hanover and London

This book was produced in conjunction with the exhibition *The American Craftsman and the European Tradition, 1620–1820.*

The Minneapolis Institute of Arts
September 23–December 31, 1989

The Carnegie Institute, Pittsburgh
April 14–June 10, 1990

© 1989 by The Minneapolis Institute of Arts
2400 Third Avenue South
Minneapolis, Minnesota 55404

All rights reserved. Except for brief quotation in critical articles or reviews, this book, or parts thereof, must not be reproduced in any form without permission in writing from the publisher. For further information contact University Press of New England, Hanover, NH 03755.

Printed in the United States of America
∞

5 4 3 2 1

Distributed by University Press of New England
17½ Lebanon Street
Hanover, New Hampshire 03755

Library of Congress Catalog Card Number 89-61718
ISBN (cloth): 0-912964-38-3
ISBN (paper): 0-912964-37-5

Major funding for this publication was provided by the National Endowment for the Humanities, a federal agency.

Cover illustrations:
(foreground) *High chest of drawers*, American, Philadelphia, Pa., 1762–75, The Metropolitan Museum of Art, New York, John Stewart Kennedy Fund, 1918, 18.110.4
(background) *Desk and bookcase design* (detail), Thomas Chippendale, *The Gentleman and Cabinet-Maker's Director* (London, 1762), plate CVIII, The Metropolitan Museum of Art, New York, The Elisha Whittelsey Collection, The Elisha Whittelsey Fund, 1982, 1982.1133

Frontispiece:
Side chair, American, Philadelphia, Pa., 1762–75, possibly by Thomas Affleck, The Philadelphia Museum of Art, given by Mrs. William Macpherson Hornor, 46-87-1

Contents

Lenders to the Exhibition / vii

Foreword / ix

Acknowledgments / xi

Michael Conforti
Introduction: The Transfer and Adaptation of European Culture in North America / xiii

Gary B. Nash
A Historical Perspective on Early American Artisans / 1

Barbara McLean Ward
The European Tradition and the Shaping of the American Artisan / 14

Robert F. Trent
The Symonds Shops of Essex County, Massachusetts / 23

Wallace B. Gusler
The Anthony Hay Shop and the English Tradition / 42

Barbara McLean Ward
The Edwards Family and the Silversmithing Trade in Boston, 1692–1762 / 66

Morrison H. Heckscher
Philadelphia Furniture, 1760–90: Native-Born and London-Trained Craftsmen / 92

Robert F. Trent
The Colchester School of Cabinetmaking, 1750–1800 / 112

Gerald W. R. Ward
The Dutch and English Traditions in American Silver: Cornelius Kierstede / 136

Francis J. Puig
The Early Furniture of the Mississippi River Valley, 1760–1820 / 152

Donna L. Pierce
New Mexican Furniture and Its Spanish and Mexican Prototypes / 179

Arlene Palmer
"To the Good of the Province and Country": Henry William Stiegel and American Flint Glass / 202

Graham Hood
The American China / 240

Gregory R. Weidman
Baltimore Federal Furniture: In the English Tradition / 256

Contributors to the Catalogue / 283

Index / 285

Photograph Credits / 297

Lenders to the Exhibition

The Art Institute of Chicago
The Baltimore Museum of Art
The Brooklyn Museum of Art
The Carnegie Museum of Art, Pittsburgh
Cincinnati Art Museum
Richard Cleland
The Colonial Williamsburg Foundation, Williamsburg, Virginia
The Connecticut Historical Society, Hartford
The Corning Museum of Glass, Corning, New York
H. Richard Dietrich, Jr.
Essex Institute, Salem, Massachusetts
Mr. and Mrs. Benjamin Ginsburg
Groninger Museum, Groningen, Netherlands
John Hardy
Hershey Museum of American Life, Hershey, Pennsylvania
Historisch Museum, Rotterdam
The Jack Holden family
Lancaster County Historical Society, Lancaster, Pennsylvania
David Lindquist and Associates, Whitehall Shop, Chapel Hill, North Carolina
Los Angeles County Museum of Art
Mr. and Mrs. Robert McNeil, Jr.
Maryland Historical Society, Baltimore
The Metropolitan Museum of Art, New York
Millicent Rogers Museum, Taos, New Mexico
Shirley and Ward Alan Minge
The Minneapolis Institute of Arts

Missouri Historical Society, St. Louis
The Montreal Museum of Fine Arts
Museum of Art, Rhode Island School of Design, Providence
Museum of Fine Arts, Boston
The Museum of Fine Arts, Houston, The Bayou Bend Collection
Museum of New Mexico, Museum of International Folk Art, Santa Fe
Philadelphia Museum of Art
Dr. and Mrs. Richard Robichaux
The St. Louis Art Museum
School of American Research, Santa Fe
Anthony Scornovacco
Robert E. Smith, Au Vieux Paris Antiques, Breaux Bridge, Louisiana
Society for the Preservation of New England Antiquities, Boston
The J. B. Speed Art Museum, Louisville, Kentucky
Lynne Stair
Mr. and Mrs. J. Paul Taylor
Victoria and Albert Museum, London
Wadsworth Atheneum, Hartford, Connecticut
The Henry Francis du Pont Winterthur Museum, Winterthur, Delaware
Worcester Art Museum, Worcester, Massachusetts
David Wojchiechowski
Yale University Art Gallery, New Haven, Connecticut
Anonymous lenders

Foreword

Just as political theorists and writers such as Tocqueville and Dickens have been trying to identify and explain the unique qualities of American culture and politics since the eighteenth century, so art historians have wrestled with the question of what is American about American art. Since the early twentieth century, scholars in various fields have attempted to define the peculiarly American quality of art produced in this country mostly through comparisons with the European prototypes in which so many of our traditions have their roots. "The American Craftsman and the European Tradition, 1620–1820" follows this line of scholarship but is the first major exhibition to compare European and American decorative arts in a way that highlights their differences as well as their similarities.

The organizers of the exhibition have worked with preeminent scholars of American material culture to produce a broad view of the development of domestic American furniture, glass, silver, and ceramics. Their approach is to trace the growth of these arts within complex social and political environments instead of from a purely stylistic standpoint. Both the exhibition and this catalogue place our nation's material culture in a larger context that reveals its unique qualities as well as its relationships to European traditions that served as either models or foils for its development.

The Minneapolis Institute of Arts owes a great debt of gratitude to Francis J. Puig and Michael Conforti for their joint efforts in organizing this exhibition and catalogue, which will add so much to our knowledge of this complex and compelling field of study. We are also very grateful to the many scholars who contributed their time and expertise to this publication. The National Endowment for the Humanities has supported all phases of this project from its inception, and we are deeply grateful for their commitment.

EVAN M. MAURER
Director

Acknowledgments

In November 1981, Michael Conforti and I organized a meeting at Winterthur to discuss the possibility of a comparative exhibition of American and European decorative arts. The meeting was hosted by the late Benno Forman and virtually all of the scholars who have written for this catalogue participated there or in subsequent gatherings held in 1984 and 1987 in Boston and Williamsburg. Others who made valuable contributions to these early discussions were Jane Nylander, Wendy Cooper, John Bivins, and Brad Raushenberg. Many of the discussions had the benefit of John Kirk's special perspective and experience, and he helped greatly in the early stages of this project. William Heidrich also contributed significantly to the initial definition and articulation of the show's theme.

I thank the authors for their patience and support through the duration and evolution of this project. Their willingness to propose and explore different points of view, and their scholarly interest in presenting new research in this publication, were fundamental to the exhibition's realization. I am also grateful to the numerous private and public lenders to this exhibition, whose generosity has made the project possible. Without the financial support of the National Endowment for the Humanities, this exhibition might have taken a less ambitious form.

For generously assisting in many different ways, Michael Conforti and I would like to thank the following: James Ackerman, Svetlana Alpers, Luke Beckerdite, Leslie A. Bellais, John Bivins, Leslie Greene Bowman, Richard Brilliant, Lynn Brittner, Michael Brown, Pamela Cartledge, Dr. Thomas E. Chavez, Karel A. Citroen, Nicole Cloutier, Edward Cooke, Wendy Cooper, Jonathan Coxe, Susan Gray Detweiler, James J. Didier, Frits Duparc, Robert Egleston, Anita Ellis, Jonathan Fairbanks, Robin Farwell, Sally Freitag, Beatrice Garvan, Robin Farwell Gavin, Christopher Gilbert, Henry Glassie, Claire Graham, Carol Grazier, Liza Gusler, Teetee Holle, Frank Horton, William Hosley, Diane Hudgins, Ronald L. Hurst, Mark Jacoby, Simon Jervis, Brock Jobe, Phillip Johnston, C. J. A. Jorg, Patricia Kane, George Kubler, Dean Lahikainen, Dwight Lanmon, Irving Lavin, Clair Le Corbellier, Hans Lorenz, Peter Marzio, DeCourcy McIntosh, Kristan McKinsey, Jessie McNab, A. M. Meyerman, Thomas Michie, Christopher Monkhouse, Jeffrey Munger, Christina Nelson, James Parker, Dianne Pilgrim, Charles Pittenger, Jessie Poesch, Anne Poulet, Sumpter Priddy, Jules Prown, Olga Raggio, Deborah McCracken Rebuck, Thomas Reese, William Rieder, Dr. Richard Rudisill, Beatrix Rumford, Rachel Russell, Frances Gruber Safford, Robert Blair St. George, Nora Schadee, Magdalyn Sebastian, Anna Sim, Katheryn Smith, Debra D. Smith, Randall Rankin Snyder, Jane Shadel Spillman, Lynn Springer-Roberts, Linda Stanley, Kevin Stayton, Colin Streeter, Laurie Suber, Shelby Tisdale, Celestina Ucciferri, Dell Upton, Alan C. Vedder, Olivia White, Joan Parks Whitlow, and Philip Zimmerman.

Members of the staff at The Minneapolis Institute of Arts have been intimately involved with various aspects of this show over the past eight years: Marilyn Bjorklund, Gwen Bitz, and Karen Duncan in the Registrar's Office; Harold Peterson, librarian; Gary Mortensen and Robert Fogt, photographers; Karen Ridgon, Jack Becker, and Ann Kohls, interns in the Decorative Arts Department; Katherine Hedberg, Jodi Auvin, Carolynn Scholz, Jane Satkowski, and Theckla Williams, administrative assistants in the department, have helped with this project at many stages; Beth Desnick and Mary Mancuso, exhibition coordinators, provided invaluable help in the submission of grant applications; Elisabeth Sövik, Sandra Lipshultz, and Louise Lincoln edited the catalogue; and Roxy Ballard was the designer for the exhibition in Minneapolis. I am especially grateful to

Ann Kohls, recently appointed assistant curator of decorative arts and sculpture, who has coordinated all the details of this exhibition with intelligence, efficiency, care, and patience.

To Samuel Sachs, Alan Shestack, and Evan Maurer, successive directors of the Institute while this project was in progress, and to the membership of the museum's Decorative Arts Council, especially Bouky Labhard, its president, I express my sincerest gratitude for years of support. I wish to extend special thanks to Michael Conforti, chief curator and Bell Memorial Curator of Decorative Arts and Sculpture, for his help in sharpening the focus of this exhibition and catalogue, and for carrying the project through after my departure from The Minneapolis Institute of Arts in February 1989.

Lastly to my wife, Eileen Toolin, I am deeply grateful for years of support and patience.

FRANCIS J. PUIG

Michael Conforti

Introduction
The Transfer and Adaptation of European Culture in North America

We Americans see ourselves as a nation of immigrants, as an amalgamation of people who migrated here in quest or in captivity from much of the rest of the world. Yet despite our diverse ethnic roots, the ideas and objects that we prize and that we take for granted separate us from our forebears and from today's citizens of the countries our forebears called home. Many of the values of the past have succumbed to time, geography, and a different cultural milieu. Along the way language has probably been lost, social customs have been adapted, and the original meanings of former rituals have been almost or completely forgotten. Slowly the progeny of an immigrant past have come to represent their American region, class, or hyphenated subculture more than the society of their forebears: a homogeneous people maybe never, but a distinct nation nonetheless.

The process of confrontation and change, and the adaptation people must make to a different environment, were as significant for early Europeans in North America as they are for the most recent immigrants today. The factors determining assimilation in the past were different, however. Certainly, physical and climatic issues represented the most overwhelming obstacles to the first settlers. But as these newcomers established their colonies in as close imitation of their homelands as their memories and new environments would allow, the inherent conservatism of a colonial society would be altered by time, distance, and a greater familiarity with their surroundings. Other causes of change were the differing perspectives, aspirations, and behavioral patterns of new generations and immigrant groups. The evolution of this colonial culture was manifested in its changing attitudes and assumptions, and these, in turn, found expression in the language and texts it used, in the buildings and objects it made.

Early America is best understood as a colonial enterprise: an extension of European culture, at times a blending of European cultures, slowly altered by changing conditions over time. The reality of America's origins as a European outpost and of its slow evolution to separateness was never fully appreciated in the nationalist mood that dominated historiography in the late nineteenth century. The glorification of the American experience in popular literature and the press stimulated a quest for an American individuality. At the same time descendants of early Anglo-Saxon settlers elevated colonial history to counter the waves of new immigrants from different cultural backgrounds. A patriotic antiquarianism arose, and new values were attached to the surviving artifacts of the colonial period, artifacts that now were employed to support a romantic vision of a heroic American identity. This antiquarian sentiment eventually inspired the earliest scholarship in the field and came to influence programs in academic institutions and the formation of museum collections.

Over the past two decades, scholars have slowly been undoing this romantic chauvinism. Writers have used perspectives developed from the fields of history and anthropology, or have redirected earlier positivist approaches, to drive out remnants of an idealized past from most journals and many museums. In time, the sentimental patriotism on which the study of American decorative arts was founded will be completely erased from the institutional and museological programs it fostered.

It is in this context of the rejection of old historical ideologies that "The American Craftsman and the European Tradition, 1620–1820" has been organized.[1] The show parallels other contemporary scholarly endeavors in its reexamination of the intellectual and material components of the European colonial societies that coalesced in the late eighteenth century to form our early nation. Our approach to the subject is somewhat different from that of other recent studies, however. We are using the exhibition format as a laboratory for the comparative study of artifacts, a study that will provide the foundation for a discussion of cultural continuity and change from the earliest colonial period to the first years of the Republic.

In undertaking this exhibition we endorse the view that some of the most significant assumptions of culture are never verbalized. Artifacts can represent keys to cultural understanding; they are particular expressions of the perspectives and values of the society that generated their creation and their formal evolution. We believe that diachronic studies such as ours have a unique ability both to create possibilities and to set limits in historical analysis. In a comparison that involves the transfer of culture to a colonial situation, one finds that old assumptions and traditional attitudes continue to be manifested in the form and structure of artifacts produced in a colony. Tradition is maintained as a positive acknowledgment of the colonial society's continuing ties to home. In the cultural adaptation that must occur in a different environment, however, new perspectives slowly infiltrate artifactual vocabularies, creating changes that have their root in differing needs and ambitions, resulting from altered geographical and social conditions.

Borrowings imply more than artistic influence. Changes reflect more than the development of form. Colonial societies were places where borrowings were endemic, where space and time made tradition operate under special conditions, and where culture evolved slowly. The causes for the continuing vitality of old forms were culturally specific, however. The conservatism of colonial society represented an affirmation of the traditional values of the mother culture, and the meaning of artifacts in the new society often paralleled that in the old. In the cultural disjunction experienced in a colonial environment, however, some forms came to be preferred over others, often acquiring different associations. At the same time, peripheral cultures could be centers of formal innovation, places where changing conditions resulted in different perspectives that had material consequences. Away from the cultural centers with their set rules, theories, and critical norms, individuals were allowed the opportunity to choose, the independence to combine, the freedom to introduce new ideas into a system. Experimentation could flourish as tradition became useless in a new context.[2]

Early America was a combination of both conditions of the periphery: the colonial society as preserver of the values of the center and the colonial society as a changing culture with a slowly developing separateness, the site of sometimes tentative, sometimes innovative exercises undertaken to adapt to a new situation. Early American life was modeled on the regional European existence of the earliest settlers, but differences eventually manifested themselves. These differences were determined by the altered conditions of the early colonies: their new material possibilities, the synthesis of ethnic traditions that mixed on these shores, different economic determinants, and a changing political and social value system developed in geographical isolation from Europe.

When we began this exhibition based on comparative analysis of artifacts some years ago, we focused on objects we felt were "typical" of the production of the American craftsman over a two-hundred-year period. We soon abandoned this method of selecting data, because inappropriately chosen works could easily have distorted our study. We substituted for it a method less susceptible to contemporary attitudes regarding the representative nature of examples from the past. We chose eleven regions, craftshops, or manufacturers to study in depth. These eleven subjects span the period from the first years of settlement to the early nineteenth century. The traditionalism of our time frame was intentional—this is the period most studied by scholars. We also wished to focus on the preindustrial era, when craftsmen operated as individuals representative of the material needs and aspirations of their societies, when manufacturing was still experimental, and when stylistic vocabularies were little affected by historical revivals. We chose our subjects to be paradigmatic of differing American situations—to reflect varying temporal, geographical, and technical conditions. Topics also had to interest scholars ready to provide new information or a new perspective. Our choice included shops and regions that followed precedent closely and those with greater tendencies to change. We were anxious to examine the non-Anglo tradition, and thus included Dutch, German, French, and Spanish colonial topics in our analysis.[3]

To establish some consistency in investigating similarities and differences in artifacts, we asked each author (1) to analyze American and European objects according to type, three-dimensional elements (scale, proportion, etc.), surface treatment (motif, color, pattern), materials, and construction; (2) to clarify the means of transfer of design and craftsmanship through an analysis of the ethnic origins of artisans, immigration patterns, the importation of objects into a region, and the use of pattern books; and (3) to interpret the similarities and differences in terms of both internal and external factors that could have affected the craftsman in his maintenance and change of form and structure, that is, the availability of materials, differing technologies, training, economic restraint or opportunity, social customs, climate, geography, religion, politics, and behavior. Authors also had to consider objects as a possible blend of ethnic traditions in America or as the result of the transfer of a transformed style within North America. Last, we encouraged speculation on what the similarities and differences might suggest about early American culture as a whole.

In focusing on the development of forms over time and space, these studies support principles of diffusionism, that is, the spread of culture from one geographical area or people to another. It is important to add, however, that our diffusionist assumptions are cultural, not social.[4] They are not qualitative, not generated by "top-down" theories, and we have placed no special value on inventive versus repetitive behavior. In spite of this, we do not feel we have abnegated our aesthetic responsibility as an art museum. We are conscious of our role as arbiter, as well as preserver, of our culture's collective aesthetic values. We are also aware, however, of the relativity of aesthetic judgments. History proves that attitudes toward quality in works of art—indeed, the very definition of "art" itself—change over time.[5] In a period like ours, in which objects increasingly are interpreted for their cultural value and signification, clarification of the complex cultural nature of an object only enhances the possibility of its aesthetic nature being identified and appreciated.[6]

Furthermore, it is not for aesthetic reasons that we have included elite as well as vernacular objects in our exhibition. Nor have we included them simply to chronicle the changing aspirations of the leaders of society. We feel that the objects most appropriate and representative for a study such as ours are in no sense confined to vernacular material, because all artifacts are fashioned by craftsmen representative of their culture and its collective constraints. In undertaking this project we assume a greater coherence in culture than do many historians working today. Cultures have underlying systems of thought as well as underlying conditions and values that transcend class lines. We believe an emphasis on class differences can often encumber cultural insights.

Many of these studies have a decided morphological orientation in which individual elements of form, structure, and decoration are often separated in analysis. By considering morphologies, in focusing on artifactual grammar, we do not mean to undermine the unity of form and intent in objects; we intend rather to understand the wholeness of an object by concentrating on its parts. This was the approach of the two earliest historians of ornament, Gottfried Semper and Alois Riegl, and it has represented a strong tradition within linguistic scholarship since its development in the nineteenth century.[7] Our project descends from Riegl's behavioral and diffusionist aspirations as well, from his consideration of peripheral cultures and their relationship to the transfer of forms over time and space.[8] Riegl's consideration of the conditions of the periphery was given application in folk art by Henri Focillon, whose own student, George Kubler, incorporated certain anthropological perspectives in his consideration of colonial societies.[9] In spite of his distrust of determinist objectives in art historical writing, Kubler's work remains the most significant intellectual foundation for this project.[10]

There is a determinism, an assumption of causality, in our morphological comparisons, but the determinants we propose must be tentative. An object's form, its structure, its actual and implied intention are tightly intertwined in an intricate fabric which only the imaginative questioning of a historian can begin to unravel. The objectives of interpretation in material culture studies will change with subsequent generations, and future empirical successes will shade any present conclusion. It is important to add, too, that in our search for causality we do not deny the role of the creative behavior of the individual, the application of human skill, effort, and imagination in the evolution and articulation of formal language. Artisans can both accommodate clients with a work easily understood and tempt markets with something never before created. Through both a repetitive and an inventive nature, the craftsman speaks for his environment, its collective restraints and possibilities, as he fulfills the material expectations and aspirations of his society. The craftsman is the intermediary through which material is chosen, technique is utilized, and function is actualized. In this process both culture and creativity receive expression in utilitarian form.[11]

The American Craftsman and the European Tradition, then, is a study of the American artisan's expression of personal and collective needs as he worked within the limits of a society both tied to and removed from its sources, a colonial culture slowly evolving toward independence of mind and material. Our examination of early America may have implications for the study of other colonial or peripheral cultures in transition, but we do not have a structuralist agenda in pursuing this work. Neither do we claim to be comprehensive. We are, in the simplest sense, presenting paradigmatic discussions of the possible meaning behind maintenance and change in artifacts in a North American context. In so doing we hope to undermine lingering notions of a romanticized American identity. We posit instead a set of assumptions more consistent with the transplanted European character of our colonial past and its slow and undramatic evolution to separateness.

While the goals of this exhibition are manifested in the interpretive discussions generated by each object comparison, much of its scholarship reflects the present need for empirical analysis. The foundations of each discussion are the formal comparisons between European and American objects along with new information on each shop or region, often drawn from primary sources. Both the formal comparisons and the new scholarship will have a continuing value to historians. Many of the visual juxtapositions, however, remain to be refined. For example, we would have liked to identify European objects documented to North American areas where a craftsman lived, but this was nearly impossible in the cases presented. Further, the study of regional furniture is just beginning in Europe and a large sampling of comparative pieces was not easily available.

The means of transfer of stylistic vocabularies from cultural center to cultural periphery are well established in these studies. Imported objects, particularly smaller objects made of glass or ceramic, were a barometer of European stylistic norms. The desire to duplicate such wares in America led to the establishment of the Bonnin and Morris porcelain factory and to Stiegel's earliest experiments in useful glasswares. Pattern books, too, provided a constant reference for maintaining the domestic symbols of European culture. As these books proliferated in the late eighteenth century, American cities with a strong desire to uphold their English identity, such as Williamsburg, had an easy vehicle for setting standards. Other urban centers, like Philadelphia, copied the latest motifs from English design books but incorporated them into what already had become traditional regional forms.

It was ethnic tradition as reflected in the native training of immigrant craftsmen, however, that was the greatest single means of transferring European material practices to North America. This is particularly evident in first-generation societies. John Symonds moved his shop from East Anglia in England to Essex County in Massachusetts, bringing his workshop practices to this continent more or less intact. Except for initial technical limitations, the regional traditions of his Norwich birthplace were not compromised in his new environment. Colonists had little meaningful contact with the native population, and the American Indians of the northeast had a limited woodworking tradition in any case. The patrons who constituted Symonds's market in the New World were similar to those who had been his clients in England, and they supported his shop as they would have in England.

Ethnic tradition as reflected in native training rarely expressed itself as simply as it did in first-generation New England, however. Often the combination of a craftsman's own background with the different cultural traditions of his clients resulted in the creation of objects unlike anything made before. The work of non-English immigrant silversmiths in early eighteenth-century Boston had to conform to the tastes of their largely English patrons, but it still occasionally exhibited formal characteristics of continental European styles. Henry Hurst incorporated Scandinavian handle-tip designs in his tankards, and the fashion for this motif endured in New England for years. A similar combination of English and Continental elements is characteristic of the work of the Dutch craftsman Cornelius Kierstede. In his early career he produced silver modeled after Dutch or English precedents for his clients of different ethnic backgrounds, but later he applied traditional Continental motifs to objects of English form, as is evidenced in many of his tankards.

At the beginning of the industrial era, the German immigrant Henry William Stiegel hired German glassblowers for his factory, glassblowers who were well schooled in Continental glassmaking traditions. The objects they produced had to conform to the English tastes

Michael Conforti

of his patrons, however. Although adaptations were made to meet market demands, certain German characteristics were maintained in form and technique.

A similar blending of ethnic traditions could also occur in more technologically simple situations. French traditions in furniture making were maintained by early settlers in the Mississippi River valley, but the furniture forms produced were subsequently altered by English immigrants and, to some extent, by later Spanish arrivals. Was it the immigration of new craftsmen or the demands of a different market that created the curious features of the armoire (cat. no. 70)? In an unprecedented way it combines a French form, as interpreted first by Quebec and later Louisiana craftsmen, with English-inspired floral inlay, as developed by cabinetmakers in the East.

As is evident, the combination of ethnic traditions was often made more complex by the movement of cultures within North America, variations in form and decoration evolving at different places and at different times. The archetypal Spanish joined chest was the precedent for similar chests made by first-generation craftsmen in Mexico. In later years, however, many of these Mexican chests would be decorated in imitation of painted oriental ones imported to the New World. The combination of European and oriental elements, brought together in a new form, served as precedent for a group of painted chests made in New Mexico some years later.

There are many other examples of ethnic traditions blending in successive geographical locations. For example, the French immigrants who moved into the Mississippi River valley from Canada were already conditioned to Anglo culture through contact with the English in the north. This relationship resulted in early alterations to traditional French provincial forms in places like Quebec. A more pronounced anglicization would occur in the lower Mississippi valley, however, as shifting political alliances brought new waves of immigration to this region in the late eighteenth century.

We see, therefore, that the ethnic background of a craftsman could combine with the social pressures of a colonial society and the demands of the marketplace in a variety of ways. The pressures could either help to maintain old forms or contribute to change in formal traditions. English standards of culture were entrenched in most of its colonies in spite of political animosity toward the mother country, which intensified as the eighteenth century progressed. Emulation could be absolute in regions like Virginia, where a homogeneous culture of landed English gentry saw itself as socially and economically closer to London than to any American regional center. Furniture had to imitate English design and craftsmanship as much as possible. In ethnically diverse early nineteenth-century Baltimore, English tradition also prevailed. But here market mechanisms were driven by the social aspirations of patrons rather than by social traditions. No matter what the ethnic origin of a craftsman or client, Anglo culture was now the culture of choice. With the beginning of industrial manufacturing and more rapid communication, one can clearly detect an Anglo-centricity in Baltimore's aspiring middle- and upper-class culture that has continued in America to the present day.

An appreciation for English standards was also evidenced in late eighteenth-century urban centers like Philadelphia. In spite of the sophisticated English orientation of its society, however, a distinct regional style in furniture developed in Philadelphia. The so-called highboy became a conventional symbol of elegance in elite bedrooms and parlors of the city. Descending from English chests-on-stands as transformed by Boston cabinetmakers, it incorporated unique motifs of floral carving on its lower drawers and upper cornice. The Philadelphia high chest-on-stand owes its individuality to the confident mercantile society of one of the largest cities in the English-speaking world. It was a society willing, on the one hand, to support the skill of recently immigrated English carvers in executing such floral ornamentation and, on the other, to maintain distinctive but retardataire forms as symbols of domestic elegance within its own regional culture despite the availability of more current London styles from printed sources. As was true in contemporary Dublin and Edinburgh, Philadelphians created and supported a regional style that was English in origin but confidently independent as well.

Economic and social forces could work in unusual ways to maintain the popularity of certain forms. Boston suffered economic difficulties in the early eighteenth century. This soon resulted in a decrease in the number of immigrant silversmiths from England, craftsmen who might have brought more recent stylistic ideas to the colony. For twenty years, economic stagnation fixed traditional silver forms in the popular consciousness, and during that time these forms came to be preferred by patrons as a whole. Thus, porringers and flat-top tankards remained popular in America long after they ceased to be fashionable in England. Their prevalence and persistence encouraged many early antiquarians to see them as icons of our colonial society.

Social and economic forces also played a role in the development of novel decorative embellishments on colonial furniture. The eccentricity of the work of the Colchester furniture maker Benjamin Burnham is not fully explained by his Philadelphia training or by his understanding of Boston and Newport precedents, which together represented the stylistic foundation for Colchester's local school of cabinetmaking. It was the post-Revolutionary economic boom that pushed Burnham to extend his ornamental vocabulary with innovative additions of his own. Burnham fulfilled his patrons' desire for ostentatious display by creating unprecedented designs appropriate for eastern Connecticut's competitive and newly rich society.

Indirectly, the political consequences of the American Revolution were behind the economic success of eastern Connecticut's agricultural elite. In the areas under study, political issues seldom affected artifacts directly. In one example, however, the ongoing fight for hegemony in North America brought a wave of immigration to the Mississippi River valley that eventually created an ethnically diverse population. The influx of differing populations was generated by political conflicts in Canada and the Caribbean as well as by the regular use of the Mississippi region as a pawn at European treaty tables.

Nowhere, however, were political issues more influential and direct than in the establishment of two of this country's earliest manufacturers. The Stiegel glassworks and the Bonnin and Morris porcelain factory grew out of the nonimportation agreements that were begun by the Stamp Act of 1765 and strengthened by the Townsend Acts of 1767. The repeal of those acts in 1770 led to the demise of these companies, though not until Stiegel had given this country its first "buy American" campaign. Both companies appealed to the Pennsylvania legislature for loans, urging the importance of supporting local commercial endeavors, but their requests were denied. The Stiegel and Bonnin and Morris factories could not overcome marketing obstacles, particularly the public perception that imported wares were better and cheaper.

Different material restraints and possibilities in North America, as well as the technical limitations of a small and young society, contributed to the appearance of American-made objects. In village or rural environments, where markets were neither large nor rich enough to import wood for furniture making, materials that were only occasionally employed in Europe became popular. Mahogany and other imported woods were prohibitively expensive, and cherry, maple, and softer native woods were used instead. Pecan was sometimes chosen for tables in the Mississippi River valley, where furniture was often constructed by housewrights who also functioned as cabinetmakers. In New Mexico, Ponderosa pine, the only readily available wood, was the favored material—it was also easy to carve, which contributed to its utility. Metal was scarce in the Southwest, and tools were crude. In seventeenth-century New England, John Symonds and other cabinetmakers nearly duplicated the appearance of their native East Anglian furniture; but with labor expensive and materials plentiful, they developed the quick but wasteful technique of riving to fashion logs down to manageable size. Evidence of this practice can be seen in many of Symonds's works.

Contributors to the catalogue have not emphasized climate as a factor in the maintenance and change of form. Geography is considered largely in terms of the distance between America and the cultural centers of Europe, which contributed to the continuation of traditional forms over time. This continuation was particularly evident in the more isolated regions of the Mississippi River valley and in New Mexico. Religious beliefs, the catalyst for much early immigration to this continent, did not affect the appearance of objects directly in the studies undertaken. Quakerism is discounted as a reason for the simplicity of certain forms in Philadelphia. Instead, simple uncarved chairs, cabinets, and tables, often executed by native-born craftsmen, were used in the less public rooms of middle- and upper-class homes. The religious background of patrons in Baltimore may have directed them to a particular cabinetmaker, but it does not seem to have affected what they chose from the English pattern books that inspired so much of their furniture in the early nineteenth century.

The studies presented in this catalogue clarify many of the complex factors that influenced the appearance of objects used functionally or symbolically in early American environments. In the process, we are presented with specific explanations for the longevity of stylistic vocabularies in a colonial society ("la longue durée" of Fernand Braudel, the "slow change" of George Kubler). For example, the economic depression in eighteenth-century Boston contributed to the maintenance of traditional silver forms there. Because of the geographical isolation of western settlements, traditional French forms and Spanish prototypes were remembered by craftsmen and clients as an affirmation of cultural roots long after they had ceased to be popular in European cultural centers. In these essays, too, the eccentricities of design in objects created in cultural peripheries are not simply treated as aberrations. Philadelphia furniture, which can appear unusual in the context of high-style London work, is seen as the preferred form of a regional society capable of following the prevailing fashions of London but usually unwilling to do so. The furniture tradition of eastern Connecticut is placed in the context of the economic opportunities and pressures of a newly rich rural society. Unusual and distinctively decorated furniture resulted from this combination of tradition, training, and market demands. This study might serve as a model for the consideration of normative variations in other situations, variations that occur with great frequency in peripheral societies.

In the following essays, early American life is interpreted through the nonverbal evidence of its furniture, glass, silver, and ceramics and their European precedents. In considering these studies as a whole, one is impressed by the consistent, sometimes overwhelming, evidence of assimilationist behavior among the earliest populations of this country. Assimilation is something we take for granted in our own time, but its pervasiveness in these histories is somewhat startling. We see in the blending and occasional annihilation of many early ethnic traditions the roots of a standardization, as well as an anglicization, of culture that continued into the nineteenth and twentieth centuries. Social pressure stemming from colonial ties to England was enforced through politics and language, as well as through the example and success of the earliest English settlers. These (and no doubt other subtle factors) contributed to the perception of Anglo culture, and later of Anglo-American culture, as the accepted norm for new arrivals.

While it is unclear when concern regarding the assimilation of non-Anglo immigrants began, it was certainly expressed openly by colonial leaders as early as the mid-eighteenth century.[12] The pressure to assimilate was used to advantage when the ethnically diverse country needed to establish a more unified identity as a nation. Assimilation pressure, therefore, began long before the late nineteenth-century wave of immigration fostered the revival of colonial Anglo values by descendants of early English settlers. The trend to unify and to conform began in the maintenance of English systems in Virginia, in the subtle blending, and eventual overwhelming, of ethnic traditions in the Northeast. It continued as the reality of Anglo dominance and the belief in the superiority of Anglo standards moved to the West, to the Mississippi River valley, and to the former Spanish territories in the Southwest.

No indelible pattern can be observed here, for America was to vary the literalness of its social ties to English society in numerous ways, in ways far more dramatic than is evidenced by the archaeology of Connecticut, Philadelphia, or New Orleans furniture, by Boston silver, or by Bonnin and Morris porcelain. But as America developed a social value system of its own, Anglo-American traditions remained a reference point in breaking up the cultural patterns of new arrivals. While ethnicity remains in our culture, it exists most markedly in the rural byways not subject to the pressure of change—in the Scandinavian farming communities of the Midwest, in the French villages of Louisiana—or in urban neighborhoods composed of immigrants so recently arrived that their culture has not yet been fractured by a perceived need to alter its norms. For most non-first- and non-second-generation Americans today, ethnicity is maintained in the repetition of family rituals and the occasional celebration of national and religious festivals, activities in which the remembrance of ethnic roots is often more in evidence than the reality of their original meaning.

In this manner, a group of colonies formed a separate society in constant reflection of and variation from the European societies that had spawned it. This new society accepted many different people, but from its begining there was pressure to conform to an ever-evolving standard. The traditions of the new land may have been forced on the earliest immigrants by economic necessity as established through social patterns articulated in the marketplace, but the societal consciousness of future generations would be regulated in the practices and beliefs taught in schools and preserved in institutions.

Through the occasional acceptance of new traditions and the ready enforcement of existing ones, the shared beliefs needed to establish an identity as a different society, as a separate country, were achieved: homogeneous maybe never, but a distinct nation nonetheless.

NOTES

1. Exhibitions that have represented this change in attitude have concentrated on seventeenth-century subjects and include Robert F. Trent, *Hearts and Crowns* (New Haven, Conn.: New Haven Colony Historical Society, 1977); Robert Blair St. George, *The Wrought Covenant: Source Material for the Study of Craftsmen and Community in Southeast New England, 1620–1700* (Brockton, Mass.: Brockton Art Center–Fuller Memorial, 1979); Edward Cook, *Fiddleback and Crookback Chairs* (Waterbury, Conn.: Mattatuck Historical Society, 1982); Jonathan Fairbanks et al., *New England Begins* (Boston: Museum of Fine Arts, 1982) (for its most significant review see John Demos, "Words and Things," *The William and Mary Quarterly* 40, no. 4 [October 1983]: 584–97). John T. Kirk's important book, *American Furniture and the British Tradition to 1830* (New York: Alfred A. Knopf, 1982), also symbolizes a fundamental change of attitude in the profession toward the consideration of American decorative arts in the context of European tradition. For a bibliography of the many articles reflecting revised perspectives in the field of American material culture see Thomas J. Schlereth, comp. and ed., *Material Culture Studies in America*, Nashville, Tenn.: American Association for State and Local History, 1982; and Thomas J. Schlereth, ed., *Material Culture: A Research Guide* (Lawrence: University Press of Kansas, 1985).

2. For the most recent perspectives on art from the cultural periphery see Jan Bialostoski, "Some Values of Artistic Periphery," and Richard Brilliant, "Resistance and Receptivity to Greco-Roman Art," in *World Art: Themes of Unity in Diversity*, Acts of the 26th International Congress of the History of Art, Washington, D.C., 1986, ed. Irving Lavin (University Park, Pa.: Pennsylvania State University Press, 1989). For a consideration of the processes that governed maintenance and change of form in a colonial society see Thomas Reese, "Colonial Transformations of Spanish Art: Sixteenth Century Mexico" (unpublished manuscript). In drawing comparisons with Spanish colonies, however, one must remember that the Protestant mercantile colonies of North America were more independent of their cultural centers than were Spanish colonies to the south. There was also little interchange with the native population in the non-Spanish colonies of the New World. For a recent discussion of the relationship between New Spain and Europe, see Octavio Paz, *Sor Juana; or, The Traps of Faith*, trans. Margaret S. Peden (Cambridge, Mass.: Harvard University Press, 1988), especially pp. 11–23. On the politics of domination that governs writing on the art of peripheral societies, see Enrico Castelnuovo and Carlo Ginzburg, "Domination symbolique et géographie artistique dans l'histoire de l'art italien," *Actes de la recherche en sciences sociales*, no. 40 (November 1981): 51–72.

3. The lack of historical material from black culture has kept us from studying slave society.

4. For a distinction between cultural and social diffusion in writing on art (and a critique of the latter) see Dell Upton, "Toward a Performance Theory of Vernacular Architecture," *Folklore Forum* 12 (1979): 173–95.

5. Compare Wanda Corn, "Coming of Age: Historical Scholarship in American Art," *Art Bulletin* 70, no. 2 (June 1988): 205.

6. These views are consistent with certain trends in art history. On the equal treatment of vernacular and elite material in an art historical context see Irving Lavin, "The Art of Art History," *Art News*, October 1983, pp. 96–101; and Svetlana Alpers, "Is Art History?" *Daedalus* 1 (Summer 1977): 3. For the most articulate expression of the artist's relationship to society in a fine arts context see T. J. Clark, *Image of the People: Gustave Courbet and the 1848 Revolution* (Princeton, N.J.: Princeton University Press, 1982), pp. 10–13. These perspectives in art history should be contrasted to Schlereth's description of the field in *Material Culture Studies in America* (p. 401), where its objectives are described as being limited to "creator worship," "primary fascination" (or "first instances"), and "normative evaluation." Margaretta Lovell has already challenged the narrowness of Schlereth's perspective in *Winterthur Portfolio* 19, no. 4 (Winter 1984): 287–89.

7. Gottfried Semper developed an evolutionary model for forms determined by cultural and social factors, geography, climate, and material availability. This was formulated in his famous two-volume work of 1861, *Der Stil*. For Semper's perspectives on the applied arts see Harry F. Mallgrave, "The Idea of Style: Gottfried Semper in London" (Ph.D. diss., University of Pennsylvania, Philadelphia, 1983), especially pp. 168, 177, 257; also, "London Lecture of November 11, 1853" (by Gottfried Semper), ed. H. F. Mallgrave, preface by J. Rykwert, *Res* 6, Autumn 1983, pp. 5–31; and Gottfried Semper, *The Four Elements of Architecture and Other Writings*, ed. and trans. H. F. Mallgrave and W. Herrmann (Cambridge: Cambridge University Press, 1989).

For a recent consideration of the implications of Riegl's thought in twentieth-century art history see Rolf Winkes's foreword in Alois Riegl, *Late Roman Art Industry*, trans. Rolf Winkes (1901; Rome: G. Bertschneider, 1985), pp. xi–xxiv. Also, Henri Zerner, "Alois Riegl: Art, Value and Historicism," *Daedalus* 105, no. 1 (Winter 1976): 177–88; and Margaret Rose Olin, "Alois Riegl and the Crisis of Representation in Art Theory, 1880-1905" (Ph.D. diss., University of Chicago, 1982).

8. Riegl, *Late Roman Art Industry*, and Alois Riegl, *Stilfragen* (Berlin, 1893; republished, Munich: Maeander, 1985). For an interpretation of *Stilfragen* see E. H. Gombrich, *The Sense of Order: A Study in the Psychology of Decorative Art* (Ithaca, N.Y.: Cornell University Press, 1979), pp. 180–90.

Early behavioral and diffusionist concerns in art history had a parallel manifestation in late nineteenth-century anthropology. For a review of diffusionism in anthropology see Alice B. Kehoe, "The Dominance of Diffusion and Its Decline in American Anthropology," in *Diffusion and Migration: Their Roles in Cultural Development*, ed. P. G. Duke et al. (Calgary: University of Calgary, 1978), pp. 6–13 (I thank Thomas Reese for this information). For a discussion of diffusionist anthropologists Friedrich Ratzel and Franz Boas's influence in early material culture and folklore studies see Simon J. Bronner, *American Folklore Studies: An Intellectual History* (Lawrence: University Press of Kansas, 1986), pp. 65–74.

9. For a translation of and a commentary on Focillon's 1931 article "Art Populaire" and a discussion of Focillon's ideas in relation to material culture, see Trent, *Hearts and Crowns*, pp. 10–20. For a summation of George Kubler's perspectives on the nature of colonial culture, see "Time's Perfection and Colonial Art," in *Spanish, French, and English Traditions in the Colonial Silver of North America*, Fourteenth Annual Winterthur Conference, 1968 (Winterthur, Del.: Henry Francis du Pont Winterthur Museum, 1969), p. 7; also George Kubler, *The Shape of Time: Remarks on the History of Things* (New Haven, Conn.: Yale University Press, 1962). A discussion of Kubler's intellectual development is included in Thomas Reese, *Studies in Ancient American and European Art: The Collected Essays of George Kubler* (New Haven, Conn.: Yale University Press, 1985), pp. xvii–xxxvi, and Thomas Reese, "George Kubler: An Intellectual Biography" (unpublished manuscript).

10. For Kubler's most direct consideration of determinist objectives in art history see George Kubler, "History—or Anthropology—of Art," *Critical Inquiry* 1, no. 1 (1975): 157–67. For recent, and different, perspectives on causality in history and art, see Theodore K. Rabb and Jonathan Brown, "The Evidence of Art: Images and Meaning in History," *Journal of Interdisciplinary History* 17 (Summer 1986): 3.

It is important to note that while Kubler saw his theory of form development outlined in *The Shape of Time* as applicable to all human works, he regularly differentiated between applied and fine arts in defining a work of art, for example, "We are in the presence of a work of art only when it has no preponderant instrumental use, and when its technical and national foundations are not preeminent" (*Shape of Time*, p. 16; see also pp. 26, 38, 46–47). His distrust of determinist interpretations of works of art, therefore, may not apply to objects with a definite utilitarian purpose.

11. Barbara McLean Ward's essay in this catalogue, "European Tradition and the Shaping of the American Artisan," defines the parameters that determined the creative behavior of artisans in a colonial society.

12. See Benjamin Franklin, *A Memorial of the Case of the German Emigrants Settled in the British Colonies . . .* (London, 1754); L. W. Larabee, ed., *The Papers of Benjamin Franklin* (New Haven and London: Yale University Press, 1962), pp. 158–60; Martin A. Larsen, *Jefferson: Magnificent Populist* (New York and Washington, D.C.: Robert B. Luce, 1981), pp. 48–49; and Philip S. Foner, *Basic Writings of Thomas Jefferson* (New York: Willey Book Co., 1944), pp. 219–21.

Gary B. Nash

A Historical Perspective on Early American Artisans

The artisans of colonial America and the early republic were a large and diverse group essential to the functioning of their communities, whether these were agricultural villages, seaports, or large plantations.[1] In the commercial towns, upon which this essay focuses, artisans usually made up half or more of the taxpaying heads of household. They belonged to several social ranks because they were members of two overlapping hierarchies: first, the traditional three-level craft hierarchy of apprentice, journeyman, and master; and second, the hierarchy of trades in which shoemakers, coopers, soapboilers, and tailors were generally found at the bottom, construction craftsmen (carpenters, glaziers, shipwrights, mastmakers, bricklayers) in the middle, and metalworkers (goldsmiths, watchmakers) at the top, with dozens of other trades variously positioned.[2]

It is important to understand the social and political milieu in which the craftsmen labored and to try to apprehend their political consciousness. Not a single piece of furniture was joined, nor a boot cobbled, nor a weathervane smithied, nor a pot turned except by a man wielding his tools in a social and political context. The distance between workbench and street was very small. The relationship of craftsmen to their clientele had political and social dimensions, and, as American society developed, craftsmen became more and more involved in life beyond their shop doors. This essay will look at artisans as participants in the social, economic, and political changes that took place in their towns from the early seventeenth to the early nineteenth century.

During the colonial period, two seemingly contrary developments occurred among American craftsmen. On the one hand, occupations became more specialized in all of the growing port towns and inland agricultural villages and market centers. As Boston, New York, Philadelphia, and Charleston became commercial centers, with populations of fifteen thousand to thirty-five thousand on the eve of the Revolution, they supported a great variety of artisans, some of whom practiced highly specialized crafts. After four generations or so in these expanding urban economies, artisans represented a broad spectrum of wealth and social position, and this tended to split them into groups along lines of wealth and status. On the other hand, with each generation their political involvement increased. During a series of eighteenth-century wars, they witnessed wealth becoming concentrated in the hands of merchants and large property owners and saw periods of growth and recession becoming more pronounced. This tended to strengthen their sense of a common interest and to reshape their understanding of their political rights and responsibilities.

Among the values informing the lives of these early American artisans none was more important than a belief in the utility and dignity of labor—particularly skilled labor for the purpose of creating a crafted product. The dignity inhering in craft labor had its basis not only in the Protestant concept of calling, which held that in God's eyes the mason was as worthy as the merchant, but also in the notion that no community could exist without the products of its dexterous artisans. Craft skill represented indispensable knowledge, and upon that knowledge rested a claim to a certain authority in the community. Moreover, skill was a form of capital, nonmaterial to be sure, but at least as important as cash or real estate. Artisanal skill was invested in products, and those products, to the craftsman's way of thinking, always bore his personal stamp and therefore, in an indirect way, were his possessions.[3]

Conditions in America fostered a corollary attitude that intensified this belief in the dignity of labor. In America, the incentives for industriousness went beyond a search for "a decent competency" because the availability of land and the persistent shortage of labor produced a more fluid social structure, and that encouraged unremitting labor. Crèvecoeur wrote, perhaps a bit optimistically, of the European immigrant, "He very suddenly alters his scale; . . . and embarks in designs he never would have thought of in his own country."[4] But it was true that in America rising to the status of master was easier and often swifter than in the German Palatinate, Ulster, or even East Anglia.[5] In such an environment the attitude toward industriousness changed. One of the revealing results was the abandonment in America of "St. Monday," the English artisan's habit of taking Monday as well as Sunday off from work. If more work meant only lower daily wages, as was often the case in England, where a surplus of labor existed, then a shorter work week made perfect sense. But in the seaboard towns of colonial America, where labor was often (though not always) in short supply, "St. Monday" fell victim to the conviction that laboring people, by the steady application of their skills, could raise themselves above the ruck.[6]

The supreme justification of this new outlook occurred in Philadelphia in the first half-century after it was founded. Not everyone succeeded in the early decades; but except for a depression in the mid-1720s, the city experienced steady growth and general prosperity from 1681 to the late 1740s, with many artisans achieving great material success. One gets a sense of the opportunities open to them by tracing the early careers of some of the men who had become the city's leading merchants by the end of Queen Anne's War in 1713. Lionel Brittain began as a blacksmith but advanced to shopkeeper and then to merchant by the 1720s. Thomas Coates moved from brickmaking to shopkeeping and then to importing and exporting. John Palmer started humbly as a bricklayer in the 1690s but by the early eighteenth century was a carter and finished his career as an important merchant. John Warder was pipemaker, then hatter, then haberdasher, and finally merchant. The city to which Franklin came as a printer's apprentice in 1725 was filled with ambitious young artisans, and a number of his early friends rose to prominence, if not quite so spectacularly as "Poor Richard." Success for so many in the first two generations of Philadelphians naturally encouraged high aspirations in newcomers. No wonder, then, that Franklin became the hero of the city's leather-apron men and that his little book, variously entitled *Father Abraham's Speech*, *The Way to Wealth*, and *The Art of Making Money Plenty in Every Man's Pocket*, became a best-seller.[7]

As greater opportunities led to greater industriousness, efficient use of time became vital. Franklin filled his almanacs with aphorisms about not wasting time: "The Industrious know how to employ every Piece of Time"; "Time is Money"; "The Treasure of Time, once lost, can never be recovered."[8] This advice, however, made economic sense only for the self-employed. Apprentices and journeymen could not increase their income by working harder or longer, and they were probably slower to accept such precepts than the master craftsmen. Yet while most English artisans reduced their working hours to ten per day in the early eighteenth century, apprentices and journeyman artisans in eighteenth-century America kept toiling from first light to last.[9]

Believing in the dignity of labor, holding that an investment of knowledge and skill in a product represented an expenditure of capital in labor, and witnessing the success of many artisans in the cities, the colonial craftsman desired to be respected in the community. The sober, industrious artisan, regardless of social rank, thought himself entitled to respect. However, respect from those above him in the social order usually came only when the artisan achieved an autonomous position—when he controlled his own property and tools and the capital invested in his enterprise and employed others to assist him. Reaching this stage of self-employment took time; "the mysteries of the craft" were not learned overnight and sufficient capital was seldom accumulated quickly.

Apprenticeship was the traditional means by which craft skills were transmitted to the young, and even when lengthy this status was not unrespectable. How involved an apprentice could become in the master's business, and the extent to which masters often entrusted their affairs to their apprentices, can be gathered from the words of Joseph Richardson, Jr., a third-generation Philadelphia silversmith, to a prospective apprentice: "I shall expect thy steady attention to my Business in supplying my place in the Work Shop . . . and occasionally to attend the front Shop in case of my absence, etc., and in short, use thy best endeavors to promote my Interest as tho it were thy own."[10]

If apprentices were often charged with important responsibilities, it is no wonder that the status of journeyman was entirely respectable. This was the middle rung of a three-step ladder, essential to the honing of craft skills and the acquisition of capital and clientele prerequisite to status as an independent master craftsman. In America, a journeyman was accorded more respect than in Europe because he was more likely to complete the ascent to master craftsman in a decade or less. Even among the cordwainers and tailors, whose occupations were among the least profitable, the chances were favorable. In Philadelphia, 38 percent of the journeyman tailors and shoemakers in 1756 had become masters within a decade.[11]

The ultimate goal was to be one's own master, an independent producer-proprietor who could hang a sign outside a shop of his own built on land that he himself owned. In no era, in no city or village, could every journeyman set up shop for himself, and it was certainly possible to have self-esteem and the respect of the community without doing so. Nonetheless, few were the young craftsmen who did not aspire to the greater freedom and control of workplace and work pace that came with achieving the status of master.

The craftsman's goal of independence, however, was framed by a broader outlook. Belonging to a trade implied a view of cooperative workshop labor in which master craftsman, journeyman, and apprentice toiled together in service to themselves, each other, and the community. A man was not simply a chairmaker in Newport or a pewterer in Savannah, striving independently to make "a competence." He was also part of a collective body that, with other collective bodies representing the various trades, made up the laboring part of the community. Men certainly aspired individually — Franklin could not brook the role of apprentice or journeyman and competed fiercely with his fellow printers in Philadelphia once he established his own shop — but their striving was curbed by a collective trade identity that carried with it obligations to the community.

How important independence was for artisans can be better understood by looking at its opposite — dependence. The extreme form of dependence was the recourse to charity or public poor relief, signifying that a man could not provide for his family. In some cities, such as New York, municipal authorities made sure that the shame of poor relief sunk marrow deep by making all recipients wear a yellow badge on their shoulder. "The ability to maintain oneself by one's labour without recourse to such things as charity," writes I. J. Prothero of the preindustrial English artisan, was "a crucial material and psychological dividing-line," and this applied also in Boston, Braintree, or Baltimore.[12]

In their quest for respectability, colonial American artisans had to surmount certain deep-lying problems. A series of wars from the 1670s through the 1760s caused wrenching economic dislocations; their early stages usually created a hefty demand for goods and services but later, at war's end, came slack times with unemployment and material want.[13] Another impediment that craftsmen had to overcome was the attitude of upper-class urbanites who regarded men who worked with their hands as inferior. Colonial craftsmen believed that their skill, judgment, and attachment to community warranted respect from those above them in the social order. "The humblest workman thinks nobly of his trade" was a French saying in the eighteenth century, and it applied no less in America than in Europe. In America, as in England, craft pride and a sense of contributing to the community were "an alternative to wealth as a criterion for social judgement."[14] Franklin was the foremost exemplar of this pride in craft and the accompanying entitlement to respect that artisans felt.

Some of this pride comes through in the rare portraits of eighteenth-century artisans. When Paul Revere sat for John Singleton Copley about 1769, he wanted to be depicted in the workingman's simple linen body shirt and vest, his sand-filled leather pad and engraving tools before him on the work table, an unfinished silver teapot he had fashioned cradled in one hand. Joseph G. Cole's painting of the ninety-three-year-old Boston shoemaker George Robert Twelves Hewes, the last surviving member of the Boston Tea Party, portrays Hewes in 1835 with a countenance displaying "the pride of a citizen, of one who 'would not take his hat off to any man.'"[15] Charles Willson Peale's portrait of John Strangeways Hutton, the Philadelphia mariner who after thirty years at sea became a notable silversmith who could still turn out a silver tumbler at age ninety-four, similarly displays the face of a man with strong self-esteem.[16]

In a society that was relatively fluid and yet was presided over by a wealthy elite who often decried the frequent crossing of status lines, craftsmen occupied a sometimes awkward and anomalous position. They did not always receive the respect they felt was their due; those in the lower ranks were viewed by loftier town dwellers as "mere mechanicks." Yet social betterment and involvement in community affairs often brought charges of inappropriate striving and misplaced self-importance from those in the upper echelon, who wanted an orderly society in which their own leadership was unquestioned. Since most craftsmen derived their living from "bespoke" work—articles made to order for a shopkeeper, merchant, doctor, lawyer, or official—artisans sometimes found themselves in the uneasy situation of having social and political aspirations that ran counter to their clients' elitist notions of how they should behave.

This was especially true when it came to political involvement. Craftsmen from the very beginning of settlement saw themselves as having civic interests and responsibilities. They moved from their shop benches to the streets whenever their interests, or those of the community as they perceived it, were threatened. Many artisans joined the crowd that attacked the grain-loaded ships and the warehouses of Andrew Belcher in 1710 and 1713, when that wealthy Boston merchant threatened bread shortages in the Bay Colony's capital by attempting to ship much of the year's wheat harvest out of the colony. A grand jury (which included artisans) returned a writ of ignoramus rather than indict the rioters, because they saw this foray as protecting the citizenry's right to be fed.[17] In Philadelphia a decade later, artisans responded to a severe recession and to the ruling elite's indifference to the plight of craftsmen by flocking to a Leather Apron Club organized by the populist governor William Keith. This political artisans' group, probably the first of its sort in colonial America, pressured legislators and swung votes behind those responsive to artisans' needs.[18]

Such activities aroused the indignation of those in the upper stratum of urban society, and some withdrawal of patronage undoubtedly resulted. To the wealthy merchant Isaac Norris, whose account books show dealings with a large number of artisan neighbors, the activities of the Leather Apron clubmen of the 1720s in Philadelphia proved that "the people head and foot run mad.... All seems topside Turvy." Government had been taken out of the hands of "the Wise, the Rich [and] the learned," the shocked Norris lamented, and given over to "Rabble Butchers, porters & Ragtags" so that social hierarchy was obliterated and government by the multitude became the fashion.[19] Several decades later, the aristocratic Dr. Thomas Cadwalader imagined that the legislature had been taken over by "mechanicks and ignorant wretches; obstinate to the last degree." In Boston in the 1730s, the Massachusetts-born governor called the craftsmen's political leader, Elisha Cooke, Jr., "head of the scum" and "idol of the mob."[20]

In these early decades of the eighteenth century, craftsmen often entered the political arena gingerly, struggling to overcome a tendency to defer to their betters. But this reticence had its limits, for artisans prided themselves on being the inheritors of the rights of freeborn Englishmen with habits of mind that abhorred subservient behavior. "Constant Trueman," addressing craftsmen in Philadelphia in 1735, stated the lesson clearly. "Let me tell you, Friends," he wrote,

if you can once be frightened by the Threats or Frowns of great Men, from speaking your Minds freely you will certainly be taught in a very little Time, that you have no liberty to act freely, but just as they shall think proper to Command or Direct; that is, that you are no longer freemen, but Slaves, Beasts of Burden, and you must quietly submit your Necks to the Yoke, receive the Lash patiently ... and carry all the Loads they think proper to clap on your Backs.[21]

In sermonizing this way, Constant Trueman revealed that many craftsmen had indeed been "frightened by the Threats or Frowns of great Men." In small towns, where craftsmen and their customers often met face-to-face, this was probably common. But as towns grew and politics became more contentious, the reluctance to offend began to disappear.

Episodic in the early eighteenth century, the intrusion of artisans into urban politics became more sustained when the midcentury wars brought economic dislocation and hard times to all the cities. The most politically involved craftsmen, at least those who took to the streets, probably belonged mostly to the lower artisanry—the shoemakers, tailors, ship caulkers, coopers, bricklayers, and others whose material rewards were less and whose economic security was precarious. Acutely aware of the changes that affected their well-being, artisans began abandoning their customary deference in relations with their social superiors and gradually gained a new sense of their place in society.

In Boston, where since the early eighteenth century economic disruptions had caused more suffering than in any other port town, craftsmen joined mariners and laborers by the hundreds in 1747 to stymie Commodore Charles Knowles of the royal navy when he started dragooning shipbuilders and other artisans, as well as mariners and laborers, to man his fleet. Knowles provoked the largest disturbance that had so far occurred in a colonial city. Few chairs were fashioned or pewter bowls hammered during the tumultuous days of November when laboring men, protesting Knowles's press-gangs, took control of the town. Boston's leading citizens tried to downplay the opposition of respectable artisans to the dragnet by claiming that the "riotous, tumultuous assembly" was composed of "foreign seamen, servants, Negroes, and other Persons of Mean and vile Condition"; but privately it was admitted that "men of all orders" had been involved.[22]

As they struggled to protect their own interests, the craftsmen of the colonial towns often saw themselves as the true protectors of the community's interests—in sharp contrast to patrician tendencies to regard them as a "herd of Mechanicks" or "mobbish Tradesmen" when they assumed a political stance. Benjamin Franklin appealed to this deep and widespread feeling among craftsmen when he rallied Philadelphia artisans to the defense of their community in 1747. During the War of the Austrian Succession, when a French attack on Philadelphia seemed imminent and the assembly balked at mobilizing the militia, Franklin turned to the producing class. They had always been civic-minded, he averred, and now they must step forward to solve a problem which their social betters (upper-class merchants, lawyers, and large property holders) cravenly evaded. The result was the formation of the Associators, a voluntary militia that became symbolic of artisan strength, respectability, and community-mindedness. In the Seven Years' War that followed in the 1750s, Franklin again played on the idea that craftsmen were the most civic-minded members of the community. In his clever "XYZ Dialogue," a fictional debate among three Philadelphians about the volunteer Militia Act, X, an artisan, got the better of his patrician neighbors Y and Z. Having thus "prepared the public mind," Franklin organized a general election for militia officers in each of the city's wards. He then staged an elaborate parade: a thousand men, most of them artisans, rallied to the colors of his private army, created because the legislature would not sanction a public army. As in the previous war, Franklin spread the message that the craftsmen of Philadelphia were the city's bone and sinew.[23]

Before the Seven Years' War, the upper artisanry that served the fashion trades may have hesitated to involve themselves in street politics that could anger their upper-class patrons. Indeed, in many cases their rise to middling status and even affluence made them identify more with those above them than with those below, for upward mobility always weakens working-class consciousness. But in the depression that followed the departure of the British forces in 1760, most craftsmen, including many who were economically secure, saw little choice but to leave the sidelines and participate in contentious politics.

The economic downturn in the major port cities of colonial America after 1760 signaled an increasingly volatile market economy and brought home the lesson that those who took risks in good times sometimes suffered egregiously in bad times.[24] The case of Hugh Hughes of New York City is illustrative. In the 1740s Hughes had moved to New York from Philadelphia, where his older brother John was a successful baker and a political ally of Benjamin Franklin. Striking out on his own, he became a successful tanner and currier in the 1750s. But Hughes suffered severe credit problems in the early 1760s and was "in a state of ruin" by 1765. Pursued by his creditors, he narrowly escaped imprisonment for debt. Hughes was soon involved in the politics of radical protest against English policies, leading one of Franklin's confidants in New York to observe caustically that "those who have little or nothing to lose are the greatest Sons of Liberty."[25]

Already artisans had taken part in public affairs, both in the streets during moments of crisis and in ordinary times as town officials (overseer of the poor, tax assessor, fireward, or constable). But the fracturing of relations with the mother country that began in 1763 brought them into the political arena as never before.

The severity of the post-1760 depression explains this new political consciousness of craftsmen high and low. The rapid growth of a large class of indigents in all the major seaport towns challenged people's assumptions about what it took to succeed, shook artisans' confidence in the economic system, and intensified class feeling. Printer Ben had always advised fellow artisans that "he that gets all he can honestly, and saves all he gets (necessary Expenses excepted) will certainly become RICH."[26] The rupture of this system of moral economics became plain in the 1760s, when scores of honest and industrious artisans went bankrupt and indigency overtook many in the laboring ranks, not simply the aged and infirm.

In the tumultuous 1760s and 1770s, artisans entered the public arena with mixed feelings about the relation of the individual to the community. The traditional outlook, emphasizing the mutuality of relations between craftsmen at different ranks within a trade and the responsibility of the trade itself toward the community, had been challenged from the early eighteenth century by a laissez-faire ethos that promoted entrepreneurial, competitive, and accumulative activity. In the older view, every form of economic activity was social in nature insomuch as it to some extent affected the community as well as the individual. For example, the craftsman, along with the baker and the merchant, was bound by customary (and sometimes legislated) rules about fair prices and just wages. As one group of Philadelphia artisans put it in 1779, "Every man [is] accountable to the community for such parts of his conduct by which the public welfare appears to be injured or dishonoured, and for which no legal remedies can be obtained."[27] But the newer outlook legitimized unrestrained economic activity: like shopkeepers and merchants, craftsmen were entitled to charge as much as the market would bear for their products or their labor.

It is impossible to measure precisely the advance of the capitalistic mentality and the receding of the older communalistic ethos. For many craftsmen the two were fused into a kind of collective individualism in which the values of community-oriented workshop production commingled with newer notions of economic rationality and the pursuit of self-interest.[28] In times of prosperity the new bourgeois orientation was probably dominant, particularly among artisans in the more profitable trades, where opportunity for advancement was greatest. In times of economic stress, however, which usually coincided with wartime dislocations such as food shortages or with postwar economic slumps, the allegiance to the older outlook revived, especially among the lower artisanry, whose opportunities were more circumscribed and who lived on the knife-edge of economic security. Over and above this dialectic was the tendency within many crafts for the bonds of mutuality to fray between masters and journeymen.

Thus suspended or vacillating between two views of economic life, craftsmen in the Revolutionary era entered politics with a passion. From their benches, anvils, sawhorses, and counters, from Portsmouth, New Hampshire, to Savannah, Georgia, they became a fount of revolutionary energy. In all towns, many of them joined the Sons of Liberty, and in some places they dominated these centers of revolutionary ferment. Most striking, craftsmen began to exert themselves as a separate political entity in the protests of the 1760s and early 1770s, spurring foot-dragging merchants to comply with nonimportation agreements, sometimes calling public meetings to discuss strategies of protest, publishing newspaper appeals for community-wide action, and organizing secondary boycotts of merchants who continued to import British goods. For example, from Boston in 1774 came this report: "Those worthy members of society, the tradesmen, we depend on, under God, to form the resolution of the other ranks of citizens, in Philadelphia and New York. They are certainly carrying all before them here. . . . This will insure a non-importation in this province, whether messieurs les marchands, will be graciously pleased to come into it or not."[29]

The political strength possible through cross-craft union, anticipated by Franklin a quarter century before, was being realized. The mechanics in their separate crafts, Franklin had counseled, "are like separate Filaments of Flax before the Thread is form'd, without Strength because without Connection, but the UNION would make us strong and formidable," even when opposed by "the *Great* . . . from some mean views of Their Own."[30] Now they found their political voice. In the early 1770s, Philadelphia artisans began reducing their reliance on upper-class leadership, nominating men from their own ranks for local and provincial offices. Conservatives within the merchant elite could sputter, "The Mechanics . . . have no Right to *Speak* or *Think* for themselves." But in spite of "Many Threats, Reflections, Sarcasms, and Burlesques" against the craftsmen, they could not be deterred.[31] By the early 1770s in all the port cities, craftsmen had become numerous on the committees that were assuming de facto powers of government, most conspicuously in enforcing community covenants for the boycotting of British goods. The replacement of the Sons of Liberty in New York by the Mechanics Committee in 1774 denoted "a maturing artisan self-confidence in political affairs," and the same can be said of each of the other seaboard cities.[32]

The decade preceding the Revolution brought the fashion tradesmen, with whom the essays in this book are mostly concerned, into the political arena in unprecedented numbers. Nobody could avoid the weighty issues that arose from the argument with England, and, furthermore, nonimportation agreements, by stopping the influx of British goods at the water's edge, were the biggest boon to home manufacturing in the history of the colonies. In the first nonimportation movement, in 1765, furniture makers were deeply involved. In Philadelphia, joiners supporting nonimportation remonstrated with wealthy men such as Dr. John Morgan, insisting that their products were as cheap and well made as English imports; thus, as Carl Bridenbaugh puts it, "did political conditions favor the emergence of the Philadelphia Chippendale style."[33] After the partial repeal of the Townshend duties in early 1770, merchants jumped to end the boycotts and replenish their shrunken inventories through new importations. When craftsmen resisted, street melees occurred in several cities between importers and nonimporters, and craftsmen rejected merchants' exhortations to withdraw from politics. "Nothing can be more flagrantly wrong," they read in a New York newspaper, "than the Assertion of some of our Mercantile Dons that the Mechanics have no Right to give their Sentiments about the Importation of British Commodities. . . . What particular Class among us has an exclusive Right to decide a Question of General Concern?"[34] Philadelphians who wore leather aprons felt a satisfaction beyond pride in their city when their fellow tradesman Timothy Matlack matched his prize cock against the bird of the haughty Tory aristocrat James Delancey of New York, and Matlack's bird won.[35]

Whereas before 1760 the upper artisanry's involvement in contentious politics was limited by a close reliance on the patronage of the elite, in the years preceding the Revolution this changed. When the elite divided on the issue of how forcefully to protest Britain's attempts to bring the colonies under stricter control, some of the fashion tradesmen, who depended on mercantile clients, may have felt obliged to trim their political sails accordingly. But the momentousness of the issues led some of them to leave expediency behind. Many of the upper artisans became Revolutionary leaders: John Laughton, Edward Weyman, and Joshua Lockwood, Charlestown coachmaker, upholsterer, and watchmaker, respectively; wigmaker David Philipse and silversmith Abraham Brasher in New York; upholsterer Plunkett Fleeson, instrument maker David Rittenhouse, cabinetmaker Thomas Affleck, watchmaker Owen Biddle, and painter and former saddlemaker Charles Willson Peale in Philadelphia; silversmith Paul Revere and jeweler George Trott in Boston; and many others. Their political activity may have cost each of them customers, clients who shifted business to someone with more conservative views. But new customers might also come through the door because of a craftsman's emergence as a resolute political leader, a man of courage and commitment to community in parlous times. In Boston, a thousand workingmen were said to be dependent on the patronage of John Hancock; therefore, the protest politics of a large segment of the artisanry in the Bay Colony's capital posed no threat to business.[36]

Some artisans not only served as committeemen and street marshals during demonstrations but also became fervent propagandists for the patriot cause. In Boston, Revere began combining silversmithing with Whig politics in 1768 by fashioning a 45-gill punch bowl, weighing 45 ounces, to celebrate John Wilkes's notorious *North Briton*, number 45, in which Wilkes had viciously attacked King George as a corrupt monarch. When British troops occupied Boston later that year, Revere drew a frontispiece for the *North-American Almanack* depicting the allegorical female figures Britannia and America facing off with liberty pike and cap. Revere's most famous graphic contribution came two years later with his publication of *The Fruits of Arbitrary Power; or, The Bloody Massacre*, an engraving of the Boston Massacre. Beneath the grim winter night's scene in King Street runs a scathing verse on the brutish nature of the British soldiers: ". . . fierce Barbarians grinning o'er their Prey, Approve the Carnage and enjoy the Day."[37]

The silversmith John Leacock of Philadelphia was another craftsman who used art as well as artisanry in the American cause. Although associated with the Sons of Liberty, Leacock was never elected to one of the city's radical committees. But he made his contribution in "a rousingly audacious" play published as the Second Continental Congress took the final steps toward independence in the late spring of 1776. Widely advertised in the Philadelphia papers, Leacock's *Fall of British Tyranny; or, American Liberty Triumphant* had a diverse cast of characters who spoke "everything from Negro dialect to sailor's bawdry to Roman oratory" in a succession of "rapid-fire vignettes conceived in exultant bitterness and crackling with violence."[38]

While the coming of the Revolution drew craftsmen into politics, the stresses of war and the dislocations of the wartime economy pitted them against each other.

The tension between the traditional ethic and the new individualistic ethos reached a crisis in almost every American town when the inflation of the late 1770s, combined with profiteering by some merchants, brought intense pressure for price and wage controls.

In general, the lower artisans were hardest hit by currency depreciation and food shortages. For example, in Philadelphia, with bread in short supply in 1779 because profiteering merchants were monopolizing the grain supply and selling it out of the city, the shipwrights determined to stop the vessels of the wealthy Robert Morris from carrying away the community's daily bread. Trying to rally the citizenry, the shipbuilders invoked the old notion that property was social in origin and claimed that they, as the builders of Morris's vessels, were entitled to keep him from using the ships in ways inimical to the community. The shipwrights "and the state in general have a right in the service of the vessel," they argued, "because it constituted a considerable part of the advantage they hoped to derive from their labors."[39] Here was the old argument that craft skill was a form of capital, invested in particular products and not completely alienated from those products by their sale to another party.

The concept of skill as a form of property, not to be regulated in the same way as cash transactions, was in a way the craftsman's last defense against a laissez-faire economy. An invocation of the law of equity, craftsmen set it against the laws of the market. But opposed to price regulation were tanners and shoemakers. Some of the older ethic of limited aspirations and commitment to the community and to the rule of equity resonated in their public appeal. "The prices of skins, leather, and shoes were so proportioned to each other as to leave the tradesmen a bare living profit," they claimed. "Our professions rendered us useful and necessary members of the community; proud of that rank, we aspired no higher."[40] But such references to traditional craft life and a prebourgeois mentality were followed by an argument against regulated prices that clearly echoed the merchants' view that "trade should be free as air, uninterrupted as the tide."[41]

Arguments such as that between the Philadelphia merchants, shipbuilders, and shoemakers could not be resolved by the Revolution and were carried into the postwar period. Overlapping those disputes were others that arose not from the stresses of a wartime economy but from other, long-term causes. During the era from independence into the early nineteenth century, the eastern commercial centers grew rapidly; seaport towns with populations of 15,000 to 30,000 in 1775 had become major cities of 90,000 to 200,000 by 1830. The beginnings of manufacturing and the development of regional and national markets connected by improved transportation produced this transformation. But expansion was accompanied by greater disparities in wealth, the decline of slave and indentured servant labor, the bastardization of apprenticeship, the subdivision of craft labor and the increasing use of semiskilled workers, and the hardening of the distinction between journeymen and masters, with many of the latter becoming entrepreneurs and leaving their former workshop role to foremen.

The debasement of the apprentice phase of craftsmanship and the separation of journeymen and masters were still in the early stages. However, where previously there had been no division between labor and capital, now they were becoming separated. Heretofore, the master craftsman had performed many different functions: he purchased materials, designed the product, fabricated it while supervising the work of others, and marketed it. But in the early nineteenth century, production dominated by self-employed artisans began to be supplanted by production dominated by nonlaboring entrepreneurs. The mutuality of the master-apprentice and master-journeyman relation turned into an "economically defined contractual relationship."[42] The eventual effects included the separation of household from shop, gradual residential segregation by class, and the withdrawal of masters from manual labor.

Evident in all cities by the early nineteenth century, this momentous transformation was remarked upon by many. "When I was a boy," wrote one Philadelphian in the early nineteenth century, "there was no such thing as [masters] conducting their business in the present wholesale manner, and by efforts at monopoly. No masters were seen exempted from personal labor in any branch of business—living on the profits derived from many hired journeymen." Nor, this chronicler recalled, was the artisan's road upward to master craftsman blocked as it was becoming in this era. In earlier times,

almost every apprentice, when of age, ran his equal chance for his share of business in his neighbourhood, by setting up for himself, and, with an apprentice or two, getting into a cheap location, and by dint of application and good work,

Gary B. Nash

recommending himself to his neighbourhood. Thus, every shoemaker or tailor was a man for himself. . . . In those days, if they did not aspire to much, they were more sure of the end—a decent competency in old age.[43]

In New York in 1820, coachmaker Abraham Quick noted that the crafts were coming under the sway of a new set of entrepreneurs, who operated "without any regards for their reputation or respect for their Creditors" in order to produce cut-rate goods for rapid sale.[44]

This was by no means the case with all craftsmen, of course. The changes occurred most rapidly in shoemaking, tailoring, and other crafts for which large export markets developed, fostered by rapid westward expansion and better transportation links. In these trades, masters might set up large shops crowded with apprentice labor or hire outwork journeymen and parcel out piecework to women and children in the production of slop goods. To be sure, some of those who enlarged the scale of their operations in order to serve an export market maintained the tradition of exquisite craftsmanship. The cabinetmaker Duncan Phyfe, who came penniless to New York from Scotland in 1792 and by 1815 was operating three shops, is an example. He employed scores of journeymen who produced handsomely crafted regency-style furniture that could be found in elegant homes in every seaboard city.[45] But the Phyfes of the cities became ever more uncommon as the nineteenth century progressed.

The gradual reorganization of craft production in the post-Revolutionary era created permanent fissures in the structure of the mechanical arts, and from the 1790s on, almost all craft products were made in an atmosphere of unstable labor relations. By the early nineteenth century, New York City newspapers contained public notices deploring "the increasing evils . . . of the disputes between the masters and the Journeymen Mechanics."[46] By the end of the War of 1812, journeymen were increasingly propertyless, increasingly unlikely to achieve the status of master, and increasingly likely to live in rented rooms rather than in the master's home as before. For example, in Boston, where master housewrights had outnumbered journeymen by more than four to one in 1790, journeymen made up nearly two-thirds of all such artisans in 1825. Nearly three-quarters of all house carpenters in Boston owned real property in 1790, but this proportion decreased to less than 40 percent by 1825.[47]

In every eastern city, journeymen's benevolent societies and unions, which had made their first appearance just before the Revolution, sprang up. Beyond dispensing aid gathered from dues, they became quasi-political organizations that shaped group consciousness and planned and carried out strikes. In 1791, journeymen carpenters in Philadelphia organized the first strike for a ten-hour day (6 A.M. to 6 P.M., with two hours off for morning and afternoon meals), which brought from the patrician class the signal comment, "They will work from six to six—how absurd."[48] In New York, where only three journeymen's strikes are known before 1788, about twenty-five occurred between 1795 and 1825, and it is evident in the sharp language of journeymen's protests—with masters often being indicted as "haughty" aristocrats and "merciless tyrants"—that the harmony of the crafts was being lost.[49]

The problems in the master-journeyman relationship that began to appear in the era of early industrialization are illustrated by the Philadelphia carpenters' demand for a ten-hour working day in 1791—a demand that initiated a two-generation struggle for reduced hours which ultimately succeeded in the antebellum period. By the 1790s, Philadelphia's master carpenters were withdrawing from manual labor to devote themselves to purchasing materials, bidding on contracts, and superintending journeymen and their helpers. For their part, journeymen were becoming permanent wage laborers, more and more blocked from attaining the status of master craftsman. In this situation, "work-time peculiarly defined the lines of conflict."[50] Rather than receiving the traditional four-fifths of the price at which the master artisan had contracted a job, journeymen in Philadelphia were now usually paid by the day. And masters became more insistent on concentrating work in the summer season, when there were more daylight hours and hence longer workdays for the hired journeymen. The "*main* object," declared the wage carpenters in 1791, "[is] to have it a matter entirely at *our* option, whether we will begin our work before, or continue it after, six in the morning, and the same hour in the evening. If we labor early and late, as has been the case heretofore, we shall expect compensation *extraordinary* for the time each day's work exceeds the hours before mentioned."[51] As David Brody points out, "Six-to-six the year round would deprive the masters of the advantage they found in the seasonally variable work day." If masters refused to measure the value of journeymen's work according to each specific task—what the carpenters called "mensuration"—then the wage artisan's only protection was to insist on measuring work by units of time. This "remarkable shift in industrial consciousness," initiated in 1791 in the carpenters' trade, would spread to other trades and become a focus for debate in the first half of the nineteenth century.[52]

Although changes in craft organization divided artisans of different ranks, masters and journeymen could often still claim a common allegiance to a political ideology inherited from the Revolution. However, freeing themselves from patrician control and taking an active role in popular politics during the war years had not guaranteed them a permanent public role after independence. In fact, a revival of elitist political power in the late 1780s forced craftsmen to struggle to validate the egalitarian political tradition of the Revolution.

Examples of the patrician determination to reverse the democratizing process of the Revolutionary era could be found in every city. In Philadelphia in 1783, the aristocratic merchant Samuel Meredith complained that no matter how early he rose to buy a "good turkey" at the market he came home disappointed because "the Tradesmen run away with them all." Tradesmen had too much money to suit Meredith. After complaining of his plight "in a Thousand different ways," he proposed to the legislature, according to a fellow Philadelphian, that craftsmen be prohibited from eating turkey.[53] On a more serious note, in New York in 1785 merchants completely blocked the attempt of craftsmen to incorporate the General Society of Mechanics and Tradesmen in order to create a loan fund. Fearing that incorporation would enable the artisans to raise their wages and would confer upon them greater political power, merchants on the Council of Revision vetoed the incorporation bill. One old Son of Liberty asked bitterly "whether these gentlemen . . . would consider themselves endanger'd by a Combination of the Mechanicks to extinguish the Flames of their Houses, were they on fire . . . ? And are not those honest Men [the mechanics], the very Persons, who *principally* extinguish all Fires, and, in Conjunction with the Country, have saved the State?"[54] Much of the old distrust of high flyers and "Torified" upper-class merchants and lawyers, and much of the old sense, dating back to the early eighteenth century, that honest, industrious working men were more capable of discharging the public trust, comes through in a New York City electoral appeal in 1786:

Men who have spent the prime and vigour of their days in reading and contemplating the rise, progress and declension of states and empires;—men who study Grotius, Puffendorf, Montesquieu and Blackstone. . . . Away with such legislators! we will neither be able to comprehend the laws they make, nor to practice them when they are made. But the laws of the mechanics, like the makers of them, will be simple and unperplexed. . . . Therefore let us have mechanics, and mechanics only for our legislature.[55]

Two years after this comment appeared, artisans in New York City, and in every other city, overwhelmingly supported the Constitution. A dozen years before, one of their heroes, Tom Paine, had written in *Common Sense*, "The continental belt is too loosely buckled," and this thought became all the more important as Great Britain flooded the new American states with manufactured goods after the signing of the peace treaty in 1783. Only a more powerful central government could offer tariff protection for home manufactures, and for that reason alone a large majority of craftsmen favored ratification of the Constitution. This solid support of federalism lasted only a few years, however, because the merchant-mechanic coalition was, in fact, an unnatural one for most craftsmen and could never really transcend a common desire for protectionism. When the Democratic-Republican opposition arose, coinciding with and crystallized by the French Revolution, large numbers of craftsmen drifted into the rising urban Jeffersonian party. It was this camp that upheld views more congenial to their position: antiaristocratic, protariff, Anglophobic, more egalitarian in interpreting the American Revolution, and emphasizing the special virtue of productive labor. "Less respect to the consuming speculator, who wallows in luxury, than to the productive mechanic, who struggles with indigence," rang one toast of a young pro-Jeffersonian artisans' society in New York in 1795.[56]

In the 1790s, a decade of passionate political debate and a time when the French Revolution divided Americans by obliging them to define their political ideology more sharply, artisans tried to defend and extend their hard-won gains of the Revolutionary era against Federalist desires for less democratic political processes. They still cleaved to the old ideology of productive labor, as can be seen in the emblems they adopted for the mechanics societies they formed. In Charleston and New York City their motto was "By Hammer & hand, all Arts do stand," and the emblem showed a brawny arm holding aloft a hammer. In Baltimore, craftsmen struggled to put through a democratic city charter of incorporation, with a unicameral council, broad suffrage, and direct elections.[57] It took New York mechanics until 1804 to secure the suffrage in municipal elections for those who were not property holders—what their spokesman called a "Second Declaration of Independence to the Citizens of New York."[58] By that time Federalists had already been obliged, in order to win elections, to include artisans on their municipal tickets; indeed, in the heated election of 1800 in New York City, Hamilton had arranged a Federalist ticket entirely filled with artisans in hopes of capturing the mechanics' vote.[59]

Craftsmen in all cities had not only become a potent political force, with their vote recruited by both political parties, they had also advanced to occupy high political office themselves. The election of a craftsman as mayor or Congressman would have been unheard of before the Revolution. It occasioned little surprise, however, when Baltimore voters elected a stonecutter, Robert Steuart, to the Maryland assembly in 1806 and sent Peter Little, a watchmaker, to Washington in 1810. In 1821, the mayor's office in New York was occupied by Stephen Allen, a sailmaker.[60]

The early nineteenth century was a time of shifting allegiances for craftsmen in politics because the Napoleonic wars led to embargoes and nonintercourse acts that hamstrung urban economies, leaving artisans caught between a natural affinity for the more democratic Jeffersonian persuasion and the appeal of Federalists to their pocketbooks. In all cities, Federalists made inroads into the strong mechanic allegiance to the Jeffersonian party, partly because of the difficult times and partly because Federalists learned that to secure artisans' votes they had to mix with men of lower status "on terms of equality and fraternity."[61] The Federalist appeal was most successful among masters, especially in the luxury and shipbuilding trades, which had the strongest ties to wealthy mercantile interests. For example, in the Washington Benevolent Society of New York, designed to lure craftsmen into the Federalist fold, the Federalists had their greatest success among chair- and cabinetmakers, riggers, shipwrights, sailmakers, and watchmakers.[62] Thus did political divisions among the craftsmen of the seaboard communities roughly follow the divisions that had appeared in the reorganization of the crafts themselves.

In the spectacular parades held in many cities in 1788 and 1789 to celebrate the ratification of the Constitution, craftsmen turned out in large numbers, each trade sporting banners and insignia and marching alongside hand- or horse-drawn floats that carried symbolic displays of their handiwork. In one city, bakers accompanied a gigantic "Federal Loaf"; in several instances shipwrights exhibited a fully rigged, if scaled down, "Ship of State"; upholsterers marched with a huge "Chair of State." Other craftsmen plied their trades atop floats: printers turned out broadsides, coopers hooped thirteen staves into a federal barrel, tailors sewed garments, potters turned pots at their kick wheels. In most cities, the order of march was either alphabetical or fixed by lot, showing a democratic desire to avoid any appearance of a hierarchy of crafts. The entire parade, as Alfred Young puts it, was "a magnificent *summa* of the mechanic consciousness that had welled up in the revolutionary era; pride of craft, producer consciousness, awareness of mechanic interest, above all pride of citizenship—together constituting artisan republicanism." Perhaps the bricklayers of Philadelphia expressed it best with their banner: "Both buildings and rulers are the work of our hands."[63]

The parading craftsmen of 1788 could not know that they marched on the eve of momentous changes that would bring the restructuring of their daily work, the reorganization of their crafts and their relations to capital, the dilution of craft skills, and the loss of the very tools they held in their hands. That would not happen in a decade or a generation. Even when industrial production had turned the sons and grandsons of thousands of craftsmen into factory wage laborers, the crafts survived. They are still a part (though a very small part) of the economy today. But sometime in the early decades of the nineteenth century, the craftsman's role in making those things the community found indispensable began to diminish. His prominence as a citizen active in political affairs nearly coincided with the beginning of his decline as a creative producer of essential goods.

NOTES

1. For the use of the terms *artisan, craftsman, tradesman,* and *mechanic* see Thomas J. Schlereth, "Artisans and Craftsmen: A His-

torical Perspective," in *The Craftsman in Early America*, ed. Ian M. G. Quimby (New York: W. W. Norton & Co., 1984), p. 37.

2. Schlereth provides a useful discussion of the artisanal occupational hierarchy and the economic and social status of craftsmen in "Artisans and Craftsmen," pp. 37–39.

3. Robert B. St. George illuminates the notion of skill as property in "The Decentralization of Skill in New England Society, 1620–1820" (Paper presented at the Institute of Early American History and Culture Conference on the Social World of Britain and America, 1600–1820, September, 1985).

4. Hector St. John de Crèvecoeur, *Letters from an American Farmer* (1782; London: J. M. Dent & Sons, 1912), p. 58.

5. I have discussed the accumulation of wealth among urban artisans in *The Urban Crucible: Social Change, Political Consciousness, and the Origins of the American Revolution* (Cambridge, Mass.: Harvard University Press, 1979), pp. 17–19, 114–23, 258–60, and Appendix, table 5.

6. On St. Monday in England see E. P. Thompson, "Time, Work-Discipline, and Industrial Capitalism," *Past and Present*, no. 38 (1967): 56–97.

7. Gary B. Nash, "Up from the Bottom in Franklin's Philadelphia," *Past and Present*, no. 77 (1977): 60–61.

8. *Poor Richard Improved: Being an Almanack and Ephemeris . . . for the Year of our Lord 1751 . . .* (Philadelphia, 1757), in *The Papers of Benjamin Franklin*, ed. Leonard W. Labaree, William B. Willcox et al., 27 vols. to date (New Haven, Conn.: Yale University Press, 1959–), 4:87.

9. On working hours for craftsmen in England see M. A. Bienefeld, *Working Hours in British Industry: An Economic History* (London: Weidenfeld and Nicolson, 1972), chaps. 1, 2; David Brody, "Time and Work during Early American Industrialism," *Labor History*, forthcoming.

10. Quoted in Martha Gandy Fales, *Joseph Richardson and Family: Philadelphia Silversmiths* (Middletown, Conn.: Wesleyan University Press, 1974), p. 157. On the changing nature of apprenticeship, see W. J. Rorabaugh, *The Craft Apprentice from Franklin to the Machine Age in America* (New York: Oxford University Press, 1986).

11. Billy G. Smith, "The Material Lives of Laboring Philadelphians, 1750–1800," *William and Mary Quarterly*, 3d ser., 38 (1981): 197–200.

12. I. J. Prothero, *Artisans and Politics in Early Nineteenth-Century London: John Gast and His Times* (Folkstone: Dawson, 1979), p. 26.

13. These economic fluctuations and their effects on urban artisans are discussed at length in Nash, *Urban Crucible*.

14. Geoffrey Crossick, *An Artisan Elite in Victorian Society: Kentish London, 1840–1880* (Totowa, N.J.: Rowman & Littlefield, 1978), p. 135.

15. Alfred F. Young, "George Robert Twelves Hewes (1742–1840): A Boston Shoemaker and the Memory of the American Revolution," *William and Mary Quarterly*, 3d ser., 38 (1981): 622.

16. Peale's account of Hutton is in *American Museum* 12 (September 1792): 184–85.

17. Nash, *Urban Crucible*, pp. 76–80.

18. Ibid., pp. 148–54.

19. Isaac Norris to Stephen DeLancey, February 12, 1722/23; Norris to Jonathan Scarth, October 21, 1726, Norris Letter Book, 1716–30, Historical Society of Pennsylvania, quoted in Nash, *Urban Crucible*, pp. 151, 153.

20. Cadwalader is quoted in Carl Bridenbaugh, *The Colonial Craftsman* (Chicago: University of Chicago Press, 1961), p. 155; Governor Jonathan Belcher's comment on Cooke is in Belcher to Richard Waldron, July 12, 1733, Massachusetts Historical Society *Collections*, 6th ser., vol. 6 (Boston, 1893), pp. 324, 438.

21. Constant Trueman, *Advice to the Free-Holders and Electors of Pennsylvania* (Philadelphia, 1739), pp. 1–2. I have discussed the question of artisan deference to those in the upper echelon in "Artisans and Politics in Eighteenth-Century Philadelphia," in *The Origins of Anglo-American Radicalism*, ed. Margaret Jacob and James Jacob (London: George Allen & Unwin, 1984), pp. 168–69.

22. Nash, *Urban Crucible*, pp. 221–23.

23. *Papers of Franklin* 6:296–306.

24. Nash, *Urban Crucible*, chap. 9.

25. James Parker to Benjamin Franklin, November 11, 1765, quoted in Bernard Friedman, "Hugh Hughes, A Study in Revolutionary Idealism," *New York History* 64 (1983): 236.

26. *Papers of Franklin* 3:308.

27. *Pennsylvania Packet*, June 29, 1779.

28. For the new economic thought see Joyce Appleby, "The Social Origins of American Revolutionary Ideology," *Journal of American History* 64 (1978): 935–58.

29. Thomas Young to John Lamb, June 19, 1774, quoted in Staughton Lynd, "The Mechanics in New York Politics, 1774–1785," in Lynd, *Class Conflict, Slavery, and the United States Constitution* (Indianapolis: Bobbs-Merrill Company, 1967), p. 90.

30. Franklin's statement is in *Plain Truth: or, Serious Considerations on the Present State of the City of Philadelphia . . .* , in *Papers of Franklin* 3:202.

31. *Pennsylvania Gazette*, September 27, 1770; Samuel Coates to William Logan, December 10, 1770, quoted in Charles Olton, *Artisans for Independence: Philadelphia Mechanics and the American Revolution* (Syracuse, N.Y.: Syracuse University Press, 1975), p. 53.

32. Lynd, "Mechanics in New York Politics," pp. 88–97; Sean Wilentz, *Chants Democratic: New York and the Rise of the American Working Class, 1788–1850* (New York: Oxford University Press, 1984), p. 66.

33. Bridenbaugh, *Colonial Craftsman*, p. 179.

34. Broadside signed "Brutus," New York Public Library, quoted in Arthur M. Schlesinger, *The Colonial Merchants and the American Revolution, 1763–1776* (1918; reprint, New York: Atheneum, 1968), p. 220.

35. Steven Rosswurm, *Arms, Country, and Class: The Philadelphia Militia and the "Lower Sort" during the American Revolution* (New Brunswick, N.J.: Rutgers University Press, 1987), p. 37.

36. The literature on artisans in politics in the Revolutionary era has been much enriched in the last three decades. Jesse Lemisch's "The American Revolution Seen from the Bottom Up," in *Towards a New Past: Dissenting Essays in American History*, ed. Barton J. Bernstein (New York: Vintage Books, 1968), pp. 3–45, provided a new conceptual model that many have followed. In addition to works already cited, the main contributions have been Richard Walsh, *Charleston's Sons of Liberty: A Study of the Artisans, 1763–1789* (Columbia: University of South Carolina Press, 1959); Roger L. Champagne, "Liberty Boys and Mechanics of New York City, 1764–1774," *Labor History* 8 (1967): 115–35; Alfred F. Young, *The Democratic-Republicans of New York: The Origins, 1763–1797* (Chapel Hill: University of North Carolina Press, 1967); Jesse Lemisch and John K. Alexander, "The White Oaks, Jack Tar, and the Concept of the 'Inarticulate,'" *William and Mary Quarterly*, 3d ser., 29 (1972): 109–34; Philip S. Foner, *Labor and the American Revolution* (Westport, Conn.: Greenwood Press, 1976); Eric Foner, *Tom Paine and Revolutionary America* (New York: Oxford University Press, 1976); Dirk Hoerder, *Crowd Action in Revolutionary Massachusetts, 1765–1780* (New York: Academic Press, 1977); Richard Alan Ryerson, *The Revolution Is Now Begun: The Radical Committees of Philadelphia, 1765–1776* (Philadelphia: University of Pennsylvania Press, 1978); Howard B. Rock, *Artisans of the New Republic: The Tradesmen of New York City in the Age of Jefferson* (New York: New York University Press, 1979); Edward Countryman, *A People in Revolution: The American Revolution and Political Society in New York, 1760–1790* (Baltimore: Johns Hopkins University Press, 1981); Marcus Rediker, "Good Hands, Stout Hearts, and Fast Feet: The History and Culture of Working People in Early America," *Labour/Le Travailleur* 10 (1982): 123–44; Charles G. Steffen, *The Mechanics of Baltimore: Workers and Politics in the Age of Revolution, 1763–1812* (Urbana: University of Illinois Press,

1984); Alfred Y. Young, "English Plebeian Culture and Eighteenth-Century American Radicalism," in Jacob and Jacob, eds., *The Origins of Anglo-American Radicalism*, pp. 185–212; Graham Russell Hodges, *New York City Cartmen, 1667–1850* (New York: New York University Press, 1986); and Paul A. Gilje, *The Road to Mobocracy: Popular Disorder in New York City, 1763–1834* (Chapel Hill: University of North Carolina Press, 1987).

37. Kenneth Silverman, *A Cultural History of the American Revolution* (New York: Thomas Y. Crowell Company, 1976), pp. 122, 141, 147–48.

38. Ibid., pp. 310–11; on Leacock's career and political involvement see Francis James Dallet, Jr., "John Leacock and *The Fall of British Tyranny*," *Pennsylvania Magazine of History and Biography* 78 (1954): 456–75, and Carla Mulford, ed., *John Leacock's "The First Book of the American Chronicles of the Times," 1774–1775* (Newark: University of Delaware Press, 1987), pp. 11–17.

39. The incident is recounted and analyzed in Rosswurm, *Arms, Country, and Class*, pp. 184–99; the quotation, from *Pennsylvania Packet*, September 10, 1779, is on p. 195.

40. *To the Inhabitants of Pennsylvania in General, and particularly Those of the City and Neighbourhood of Philadelphia* (Philadelphia, 1779).

41. Peletiah Webster, *Political Essays on the Nature and Operation of Money, Public Finance, and Other Subjects* (Philadelphia, 1791), quoted in Rosswurm, *Arms, Country, and Class*, p. 197.

42. Brody, "Time and Work," p. 29.

43. John Fanning Watson, *Annals of Philadelphia, and Pennsylvania, in the Olden Time . . .* , 3 vols. (Philadelphia: Edwin S. Stuart, 1887), 1:220–21.

44. Wilentz, *Chants Democratic*, p. 34.

45. Ibid., pp. 36–37.

46. Quoted in Brody, "Time and Work," p. 30.

47. Lisa Beth Lubow, "Artisans in Transition: Early Capitalist Development and the Carpenters of Boston, 1787–1837" (Ph.D. diss., University of California, Los Angeles, 1987), p. 208, table 6; p. 292, table 16.

48. *Federal Gazette*, May 11, 1791, quoted in Brody, "Time and Work," p. 1.

49. Wilentz, *Chants Democratic*, pp. 56–58.

50. Brody, "Time and Work," p. 48.

51. *Dunlap's American Daily Advertiser*, May 11, 1791.

52. Brody, "Time and Work," pp. 47–56, analyzes this crucial change in the measurement of time and wages.

53. Peter S. DuPonceau to R. R. Livingston, October 15, 1783, quoted in Rosswurm, *Arms, Country, and Class*, p. 256.

54. Hugh Hughes to Charles Tillinghast, March 7, 1785, quoted in Lynd, "Mechanics in New York Politics," p. 105.

55. *New York Daily Advertiser*, April 5, 1786, quoted in Lynd, "Mechanics in New York Politics," p. 107.

56. Quoted in Wilentz, *Chants Democratic*, p. 71.

57. Steffens, *Mechanics of Baltimore*, chap. 6.

58. Rock, *Tradesmen of New York City*, p. 51.

59. Ibid., p. 59.

60. Steffens, *Mechanics of Baltimore*, pp. 171–72, 189; Rock, *Tradesmen of New York City*, p. 71.

61. Rock, *Tradesmen of New York City*, p. 84.

62. Ibid., pp. 85–88.

63. Young, "Plebeian Culture," pp. 201–2; Whitfield J. Bell, Jr., "The Federal Processions of 1788," *New-York Historical Society Quarterly* 46 (1962): 5–39.

Barbara McLean Ward

The European Tradition and the Shaping of the American Artisan

The American artisan in the colonial period existed within a larger western European context which determined the type of work that he did, the way he learned his craft, the organization of his workplace, and the look and form of the objects he made. Differences among artisans were recognized; some were producers, making items for sale, while others were engaged in services of various kinds; or, as in the building of houses or ships, worked as part of a team. The type of work an individual performed defined him or her as a craftsman, and it is therefore the nature of the work itself, the skills it required, and the amount of creativity that it demanded, that are the subject of this essay. In the catalogue that follows, various authors have dealt with the impact of the European tradition on colonial artisans, focusing attention on the social and cultural forces which shaped their efforts to adapt the skills of their homelands to the needs of the new society. Here I will examine the nature of learning and creative behavior in order to understand the common forces that shaped the colonial experience and transcended local economic or environmental conditions.

In the seventeenth and eighteenth centuries, as now, conventions about social hierarchy were widely accepted. Royalty was followed by the clergy, clergy by the aristocracy, and below were those people who were engaged in professional, mercantile, or manual labor. In 1747 an Englishman named Campbell attempted to categorize the various types of work in a book entitled *The London Tradesman*.

Campbell wrote his book for rural parents whose sons and daughters were ready to be apprenticed to a trade. Because many of the trades practiced in London were unfamiliar in the countryside, he outlined the requirements and expectations of each craft in some detail.

Campbell divided the callings useful to society into three basic categories: the learned professions or sciences, the liberal arts, and the mechanical arts. His categorization of work was essentially functional and grouped together tradesmen who interacted on a regular basis.[1] The learned professions included theology, medicine, and law. The crafts which he regarded as falling under the liberal arts began with music and proceeded to painting, "sculpture and statuary," and finally architecture. Painting included all trades for which drawing was essential: house and sign painting, engraving, gilding, printing, and bookselling, as well as historical and portrait painting. Sculpture and statuary included goldsmithing and silversmithing, jewelry making, and lacemaking, as well as sculpting in metal, clay, plaster, or wax. Architecture, by which he meant domestic building, involved carpenters and housewrights, bricklayers and stonemasons, joiners, and plasterers. Next, he turned his attention to the artisans who specialized in finishing and furnishing these houses. The most important of these was the "upholder," or upholsterer. The cabinetmaker, chair carver, glass grinder, glass frame maker, glass frame carver, appraiser, screenmaker, buckram maker, spring curtain maker, bellhanger, and narrow weaver all worked in conjunction with the upholsterer in producing the items necessary to decorate a house.

The mechanic arts were those that required less judgment or creativity. Butchers, leatherdressers, bakers, hatters, cutlers, coopers, dyers, soapboilers, and distillers were all tradesmen required to have a "mechanic head" but no great degree of education. Finally, Campbell introduced the merchant, whom he saw as the individual with the greatest potential for producing wealth. His entire system gave greater esteem to crafts and professions in which judgment was employed, where rules were not hard and fast, and where the exercise of one's intelligence was needed to assess situations and to make appropriate decisions.[2]

This conceptual division of professionals from merchants, merchants from artisans, and one type of artisan from another was not unique to Campbell, nor to England. The eighteenth-century Frenchman who wrote the *Etat et description de la ville de Montpellier fait en 1768* divided the artisan class into several branches, those "who worked with their minds as well as their hands (*artistes*), those who worked in mechanical trades (*métiers mécaniques*), day laborers and agricultural laborers," and finally domestic servants and the unemployed poor. For the writer of the *Etat* the basic source of prestige was wealth, but wealth from established traditional sources: land, offices, rents, and trade, not from manufacturing or other entrepreneurial activity. In fact, the author was proud that manufacturing played only a minor role in Montpellier's economy and suggested that factories brought more evil than good to a city. He believed that agricultural work was more beneficial to society than factory work because the former supplied necessities while the latter only increased the taste for needless luxuries. Idleness was the greatest sin, all members of society should be engaged in useful pursuits, and work was honorable.[3]

There are few documents surviving that help us ascertain how Americans conceptualized the relationship between the trades—both in the intellectual and economic sense provided by Campbell's framework and in the social sense provided by the author of the *Etat*. In the year 1788, however, major cities celebrated the ratification of the United States Constitution with processions of the leading citizens, and the trades were systematically represented in these processions. In many towns these events became part of the annual celebration of Independence Day, and their organization both reflected and reinforced local attitudes about the proper "order" of society.

In 1789 the city of Boston held a procession to honor a visit from President George Washington. At its head were town officials, followed by French and Dutch consuls and officers of the squadron, and by clergymen. After the clergy came physicians, lawyers, merchants, and traders. The significance of maritime trade to the town was represented by the members of the Marine Society, followed by masters of vessels and by revenue officers. At the end of the first section of the procession "strangers, who may wish to attend" were to march. Next were artisans, in alphabetical order. Seamen followed along at the very end of the parade, and a member of the Marine Society was charged with organizing and accompanying this potentially unruly group.[4]

In Boston, as in London, trades that involved reason as well as skill—the professions of physician and lawyer—were placed apart from the other trades. Participation by artisans was important because they, rather than merchants, were seen as the creators of wealth. Furthermore, as Gary Nash points out in his essay in this volume, artisans also had made a major contribution to the Revolutionary cause. In Boston, seamen, the harvesters of the wealth of the oceans and the gatherers of the wealth from trade, formed the bedrock of the city's existence. In other cities, such as New York, farmers played an equally important role.[5]

The artisan, particularly one who produced goods for trade, played a key role in the early American economic system. His ownership of skill made him independent, his ability to add to the wealth of his community made him useful, and his dedication to a simple life of hard work made him noble.[6] Work itself was an essential element in his character, a significant factor in setting him apart from his fellow citizens. Although historians have focused a good deal of attention on the political lives of artisans, the actual process by which they learned and exercised their skills has attracted relatively little attention.[7] In order to understand how craftsmen learned their trade, and how they absorbed new information, it is necessary to examine the nature of artisanal work.

We have already noted the variety and hierarchy of craftwork in the seventeenth and eighteenth centuries. For the purposes of this analysis we will bypass those craftsmen who sold labor only and those who sold a particular skill applied to a specific material or group of materials. Instead we will concentrate on those who sold a particular skill, along with a talent for artifice, and a tangible and durable end product. Of particular interest are artisans whose trade required that they possess the talent to fabricate objects in the latest fashion, and the judgment to create new designs of their own.

Such an artisan differed from his fellow craftsmen because of the nature of the work he performed and the degree of skill and education required for the exercise of his trade. Campbell expressed the importance of these factors in his description of the successful cabinetmaker:

A Youth who designs to make a Figure in this Branch must learn to Draw; for upon this depends the Invention of new Fashions, and on the Success of his Business: He who first hits upon any new Whim is sure to make by the Invention before it becomes common in the Trade; but he that must always wait for a new Fashion till it comes from *Paris*, or is hit upon by his Neighbour, is never likely to grow rich or eminent in his Way.[8]

The nature of one's work dictated the kind of training and the measure of creativity needed to succeed.

The colonial American artisan's education began with basic schooling and the acquisition of verbal skills such as reading and writing and also of cognitive skills such as simple arithmetic. Following this basic education the young person, usually at the age of fourteen or fifteen, was bound apprentice to a master of a craft. In this context he was able to observe at first hand the proper repetition of the motor skills basic to the trade. His master, who was committed to teaching the craft to his apprentice, would from time to time verbalize the processes carried on in the shop, and would allow the novice the opportunity to practice each discrete operation. It was the job of the master and his journeymen to make sure that the apprentice was practicing the skill properly and to provide both positive and negative reinforcement.

Modern theorists describe motor learning as a two-stage process.[9] In the first stage the learner repeats the same skills over and over again. Through practice, and through positive reinforcement provided by a teacher, these actions become automatic. Once students can, through memory trace, recognize that they are repeating the action correctly, it is time to allow them to put skills together into a continuous operation.[10] In the case of the craft apprentice, the first skills learned would probably have been simple ones in which repetition served as a powerful means of practice, such as planing or hammering. Later skills would have been more complex, requiring a great deal of dexterity and the ability to control several factors at once: carving a chair leg or engraving a tankard. Ultimately the apprentice would have been allowed to fabricate an entire object.

Once the performance of basic skills becomes automatic, the learner enters the second, or autonomous phase, in which his technical skill enables him to devise new and more efficient ways of working. In the crafts, this process takes place when artisans find themselves confronted with new problems. Although their first response may depend upon previously learned behaviors or habits, if those are inadequate to a new situation, artisans attempt a different approach, sometimes in consultation with co-workers.[11]

Taking these principles of learning into account can help us to understand the way Americans adapted European designs. What was the inheritance that the American artisan received from the "European tradition"? His actual functioning within the shop on a day-to-day basis probably differed little, perhaps only in the scale of operation, from what he would have known in Europe. Furthermore, the process by which he learned of new designs, and created his own versions of those designs, was fundamentally the same. But added to this inheritance were conditions essentially different from those with which he was familiar. Labor was scarce, not plentiful, and therefore his pay was higher and his opportunities for advancement greater than in England or Europe. The absence of a hereditary aristocracy meant that his patrons were less extravagant in their commissions, but it also meant that he was regarded with greater esteem and that his judgment on points of fashion was considered more important. Both he and his clients were limited in their exposure to new designs in a way that they were not in England and Europe.

The authors writing for this catalogue, in their discussion of the process of stylistic transfer, have observed that new design ideas reached the colonies by three principal carriers: people, objects, and printed sources. It is a basic principle of learning that "regardless of our intentions, we learn something about those things to which we are exposed."[12] The type of learning, however, differs according to its source. Within the workshop people might share ideas and techniques when a particular problem needed to be solved. Unusual objects of unfamiliar design brought to the shop for polishing or repair might excite the curiosity of workers, causing them to study their attributes with care, and perhaps to preserve them in drawings or commit them to memory. Printed sources might be borrowed either wholly or piecemeal, or might provide inspiration to the artisan.

In the first type of contact, that between individuals, the possibility of conceptual transfer is great. Not only can one worker observe another performing a task, but there is also the possibility of demonstration of a technique by one, followed by practice, with comments and corrections from the initial teacher. Feedback is a necessary component of proper motor skills learning, and

Fig. 1. *Drawing for carved decoration for sternboard of ship.* American, Salem, Mass., 1795–1811. Samuel McIntire. Samuel McIntire Papers, Essex Institute, Salem, Mass.

without it, little actual learning takes place.[13] Thus, a situation in which both perception of a new idea and feedback concerning its proper execution can occur provides the greatest opportunity for transfer of ideas and skills.

When artisans have a model object from which to work, the process differs. The craftsman's perception of that object is governed by his ability or inability to respond to all of its attributes. Although continued exposure to objects with rococo-style repoussé decoration might allow the artisan to grasp all the nuances of the style—form, decoration, stance—he might at first perceive only individual decorative motifs rather than the whole formal system by which they were designed. This phenomenon has in fact been noted frequently in the study of colonial and provincial art. Thomas Reese contends that the originality of Mexican art comes from the act of "decomposition." In his view colonists saw various Spanish styles merely as storehouses of forms and ideas, and did not seek to comprehend the "coherent stylistic system" from which they were derived.[14] In this way observation of an imported object could only provide messages without context. It was up to the observer, the colonial artisan, to process these messages and to fit them into a conceptual framework of his own.

Printed sources provided even less contextual information. Although the provincial architect might read the works of Gibbs, most American buildings demonstrate that he wasted little time poring over the meaning of the classical orders. Instead, as so many architectural historians have noted, he borrowed the elements that suited him, often without understanding the full stylistic system. One particularly graphic illustration of the way in which an architect might appropriate printed images for his work appears in two drawings by Samuel McIntire of Salem, Massachusetts. One is a drawing for a parlor interior, the other a drawing of the carved decoration planned for a sternboard of a ship (fig. 1). Both

Fig. 2. *Tankard*. American, Boston, Mass., about 1700. Henry Hurst (1665–1717). Silver. H. 7 in (17.8 cm), Diam. (lip) 4⅜ in (11.1 cm), Diam. (base) 5³⁄₁₆ in (13.2 cm). Museum of Fine Arts, Boston, gift of Mr. and Mrs. Dudley Leavitt Pickman, 31.228.

have small decorative elements that have been cut out of larger prints and pasted near the edge of the drawing. The architect appropriated a single element from another work and skillfully incorporated it into his own decorative scheme, one that had been worked out through experience and had reached the level of habitual behavior. Nonetheless, in searching for the novelty apparently desired by his clients, he was able to incorporate new elements from other sources without changing his overall system of decoration.

Although direct interaction with persons trained in another stylistic system potentially offers the greatest opportunity for learning, instances of exact replication of foreign style systems are relatively rare in America. During the first years of settlement, direct transfer was common. New immigrants sought to recreate the material culture of the society they had left behind. Nonetheless certain selections were made, and certain forms began to develop along lines independent of those in the mother country. Once these independent traditions became established, although we may find the names of London-trained joiners and cabinetmakers in the records, most newcomers adapted their skills to the needs of the community within which they found themselves.

One example of this is Henry Hurst, a silversmith born and trained in Sweden, who emigrated from London to Boston in 1699. His Swedish training is evident in a tankard with an embossed handle (fig. 2) similar in decoration to Swedish examples. The handle design is grafted onto an otherwise typical English form, one which Hurst had doubtless learned to make in London and which continued to find favor in Boston. His elaborate handles must have created little interest among Bostonians, for only one example exists, and there is ambiguous documentary evidence of another.[15] His handles were never widely adapted or copied by other Boston silversmiths. Their customers did not demand such objects and therefore they were not compelled to adopt the design in order to compete in the marketplace.

One of the best-known instances of transfer from one colonial style center to another is to be found in the work of Eliphalet Chapin, a cabinet- and chairmaker who began his career in Connecticut. Fleeing a paternity suit, he moved to Philadelphia, where he soon learned to construct furniture in the local manner. In spite of the habits developed in his youth, he was able to become fully conversant with the new techniques and thus presumably with the stylistic system prevalent in

Philadelphia as well. When he returned home, however, he reverted to the system which was familiar to his customers and fellow woodworkers, although he retained some of the technical expertise that he had learned while away and he modified some designs to accommodate his new knowledge.[16] His later chairs, for instance, although in the overall outline of their backs they display the rectilinear quality distinctive to New England, have seat rails constructed in the Philadelphia manner. Most Philadelphia chairs of this period did not have stretchers between the legs, although these supports were commonly found on New England examples. Chapin omitted stretchers on most of his chairs, thus producing a lighter and more curvilinear form. In transferring his skill from one context to another, Chapin made certain concessions to local taste. He, like other craftsmen, hesitated to respond to his new situation until he had an opportunity to see if his habitual behavior would be accepted.[17] Although the full Philadelphia style was not readily acceptable, the new synthesis that marked Chapin's work became popular and influential in central Connecticut.

How do we define the individual artisan's creativity? Although most art-historical inquiry focuses on the question of design sources, this orientation takes us away from a consideration of how the artisan uses the information he receives from outside stimuli. The nature of craftwork itself is fundamental to this process. David Pye, one of the most influential theorists on the subject, has divided workmanship into two basic categories: the workmanship of risk and the workmanship of certainty.[18] Workmanship of risk involves those parts of the creative process that can vary each time an object is made. Thus a glassblower, for example, cannot completely determine what the final appearance of a freeblown pitcher will be. The design of the pitcher may actually evolve during the process of fabrication and new design solutions may occur accidentally. George Kubler has observed that since every act occurs at a unique time and place, no two acts can ever be the same. Therefore, no two objects can ever be exactly the same, even if duplication is the maker's intention.[19] This principle is observable when objects are made by workmanship of risk because exact duplication of the antecedent object is impossible. In order to reduce the risk factor, and increase the chances of producing matching pitchers, the glassblower might ask a machinist to make a mold into which the glass could be blown. The mold, although it does not completely ensure that the pitchers will be alike, increases the probability of uniform production. Blowing glass into a mold is an instance of the workmanship of certainty, that is, workmanship in which a regulating tool has been introduced to provide at least the appearance of uniformity.

The special talent of the inventor, or innovator, is that he is able to see previously unobserved connections between things. As Pye expresses it, the inventor has the ability "to discern similarities between the particular result which he is envisaging and some other actual result which he has seen and stored in his memory."[20] Although Pye sees the designer as merely the instrument by which the inventor's vision is transferred into reality, we can observe Pye's principle at work in the way the colonial artisan made connections between what he saw and what he intended to produce. A small spout cup by John Edwards (cat. no. 18) demonstrates this point. Edwards evidently wanted to produce a spout cup monumental enough to be a worthy gift for a noted minister. He drew an analogy between the form he was trying to produce and a somewhat similar form, a chocolate pot, which he had seen in the shop of another silversmith. Although the resulting object was not widely reproduced by other silversmiths, it was esteemed enough by its recipient to be preserved and passed on to his descendants.

In his consideration of the issue of invention, George Kubler has observed that the inventor is "the first to perceive a connection among elements to which the key piece [has] only just come into view." Nonetheless our ability to accept new knowledge of this type, he contends, is circumscribed by what we already know. If a particular invention cannot be realized in its own time, it may remain a mere curiosity.[21] The steamboat's first inventor was unable to make society accept his creation; Leonardo's flying machines remained only ideas on paper. Invention and creativity are possible at any time, but society's willingness to accept innovation varies greatly.

Within the American context, we find varying attitudes toward invention and innovation in the decorative arts. In one context the artisan might find that the most valued objects were those which most closely duplicated English and European prototypes. Certainly Gregory Weidman's work on federal-period Baltimore demonstrates that in that city, at that time, close replication of English forms was extremely desirable. In another context, the artisan might find that invention and innovation were more highly esteemed than copy work. In our own time, for instance, copies of old master paintings, so highly valued in the early nineteenth century, are regarded as virtually worthless. We show little or no interest in the virtuosity displayed by the copyist. Instead, we prefer the work of innovative artists who have developed their own distinctive techniques, themes, compositions, and use of color.

While certain design innovations may occur unintentionally within the workmanship of risk, the act of designing a mold—such as the glassblower's mold for a pitcher discussed above—involves active thought about design, and implies that the ability to replicate the same design indefinitely is valued. Therefore, the desire to ensure uniform availability and reuse of a mold over time has the effect of limiting creativity until competition or influence from outside stimuli motivates the glassblower to have another mold produced. The same process occurred in the pewterer's business. Because of the difficulty of obtaining them, molds tended to lessen the impact of new design ideas. Unless the pewterer was motivated to find a new solution to the problem of creating a salable teapot, he would continue to rely on the same molds he had already found useful.

This brings us to the issue of motivation and creativity. In the American context the degree of motivation experienced by a particular craftsman may have been significantly increased by competition from other craftsmen and by response to external stimuli. While creative geniuses may have labored in isolation, from what we can observe, competition, either economic or social, was probably a significant factor in the creation of local artistic expressions. In a recent article Gerald L. Pocius has explored the creative process in furniture making in a small Newfoundland village. A folklorist, Pocius expected to find that the inhabitants of a town with a population of only 125 would produce furniture within a distinctive local folk tradition. Instead, he found that in the town of Keels furniture making had become a competitive activity, with several makers vying to produce the most creative, and the most useful, adaptations of furniture designs gleaned from trade catalogues. His work suggests that isolation from major design centers can result in heightened, rather than diminished, creativity.[22]

Societies in which members perceive themselves as distinct from their close neighbors sometimes intentionally foster a special artistic identity which does not rely for its validity on the criteria reserved for assessing high-style urban objects. Here we should examine the furniture made by the Dunlaps of south central New Hampshire (fig. 3), which, although it may be said to derive originally from Scottish traditional furniture, clearly developed independently in New Hampshire, without any significant input from external designs. Major John Dunlap (1746–92) is known to have made frequent trips to Boston for various reasons, and yet his work seems to have been largely unaffected by the experience.[23] The basic form of the chest-on-chest may have been based on things he had seen, but he freely developed his own idea of how it should be decorated, and his ideas found local acceptance. In contrast, his sons' work suggests a change in the local criteria for judging cabinetwork. Now clients demanded objects in the new neoclassical designs introduced after the war. The brothers accordingly made card tables that look very much like Boston card tables, except that they used straight-grained maple and applied inlay of their own manufacture.[24] In the face of competition, these rural craftsmen responded by altering their designs. As long as their own independent manipulation of older design ideas remained acceptable to their customers, however, they saw no reason to change. And, in fact, their own distinctive style actually assured them the continued patronage of the local gentry.

The basic question remains whether we, as twentieth-century historians analyzing the colonial experience, value American demonstrations of virtuosity or American demonstrations of innovation. Since the beginning of the study of American history, the debate over the "Americanness" of our political and social institutions, and of our art, has raged without resolution. We seek evidence of American genius or exceptionalism in all aspects of our history, but very often we fail to see that the process by which we became a separate nation, with a distinctive art and a distinctive culture, is a process similar to that by which all colonial societies have matured.

As we examine that process we should not forget the distinct ways in which America differed from European societies. For example, we cannot lose sight of the importance of the laborers and mechanics in early American society, nor should we remain unaware of the significant difference in status and privilege that these persons experienced in America as opposed to the position that they occupied in most European societies. The writer of the Montpellier *Etat*, for example, was frankly contemptuous of this lower sort, whom he characterized as unseemly rabble. Visitors to the colonies, and critics of the mobs who fueled the fires of revolution in America, often noted that "low and mean" mechanics served in high offices in America, which they interpreted as evidence of the degenerate character of American government.[25]

This is not to say that distinctions among artisans did not exist in America. Divisions occurred not according to the nature of one's craft, but rather according to one's place within a craft. That is, early mechanic associations drew one or two master craftsmen from each of the trades. Rivaling these in numbers and intensity, if not in wealth, were organizations of journeymen, struggling to maintain their status as skilled artisans in the face of competition from unskilled or partially trained workers. Without a strong system of organization for each craft, like the guild system of England and Europe, the development of close craft identity was not nearly as important in America as it had been in the mother country. Master artisans did not exercise clear control over their journeymen as they could under the guild system, and they had no organizations to help foster a feeling of brotherhood among the laborers in a particular craft.

The representation of artisans in the federal processions thus seems to stand as a symbolic effort to maintain craft identity in the face of its disintegration. Within the community the major importance of the artisan class was its role in producing wealth. As the organization of production changed toward the end of the eighteenth century, however, ownership of skill ceased to provide economic security. The emergence of economic classes meant an end to the corporate community in which individuals understood the obligations that accompanied their social status — the reciprocal relationships which have been explored by historians such as E. P. Thompson in his work on English eighteenth-century patricians and plebians.[26] A new capitalist mentality was slowly eroding the old notions of station and deference. Ranking in processions makes it evident that while Americans saw this change as evidence of a new democratic spirit in which all men were regarded as potentially equal, they were also aware that it marked the erosion of the traditional order they had inherited from Europe.

This exhibition and catalogue attempt to assess American material expression in terms of the expectations of its producers. We do not deny creativity, but rather seek

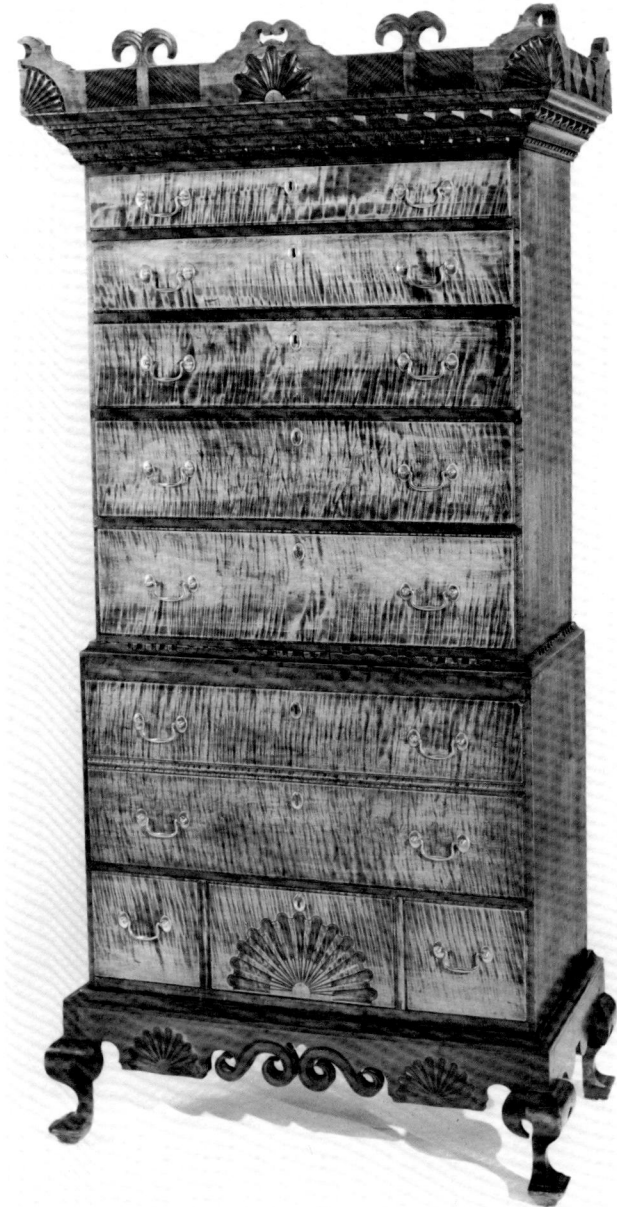

Fig. 3. *Chest-on-chest-on-frame*. American, Bedford, Henniker, or Salisbury, N.H., about 1785. Dunlap family. Tiger maple; white pine. H. 82⅝ in (209.8 cm), W. 36 in (91.44 cm), D. 16⅞ in (42.62 cm). The Currier Gallery of Art, Manchester, N.H., 1959.3.

The Shaping of the American Artisan   21

to understand how it was shaped by the colonial context. We try not only to see objects in their relationship to European models, but also to look at their indigenous context and assess them as independent design solutions rather than judging them on the basis of foreign style systems. As we examine the colonial system, how it adapted and borrowed rather than copied from European sources, we come to have a fuller appreciation of the real contribution of colonial art.

NOTES

1. R. Campbell, *The London Tradesman* (1747; reprint, Newton Abbot, England: David and Charles, 1969), pp. 1–241.

2. Campbell, *London Tradesman*. On the professions, see pp. 24–88; on liberal arts, pp. 88–176; on mechanic arts, pp. 177–282, on retailing, pp. 282–92, and on maritime trades, pp. 293–301.

3. Robert Darnton, "A Bourgeois Puts His World in Order," in *The Great Cat Massacre and Other Episodes in French Cultural History* (New York: Basic Books, 1984), pp. 107–43.

4. For a reprint of the broadside announcing the procession, see Jonathan L. Fairbanks and Wendy A. Cooper, eds., *Paul Revere's Boston, 1735–1818* (Boston: Museum of Fine Arts, 1975), p. 142.

5. Charles G. Steffen, *The Mechanics of Baltimore: Workers and Politics in the Age of Revolution, 1763–1812* (Urbana: University of Illinois Press, 1984), p. 242; and Thomas E. V. Smith, *The City of New York in the Year of Washington's Inauguration, 1789* (Riverside, Conn.: Chatham Press, 1972), pp. 214–44.

6. For further discussion of the significance of skill ownership, see Barbara McLean Ward, "Hierarchy and Wealth Distribution in the Boston Goldsmithing Trade, 1690–1760" (Paper presented at the Conference of New England History, Salem State College, Salem, Massachusetts, October 30, 1984).

7. Carl Bridenbaugh, *The Colonial Craftsman* (1950; reprint, Chicago: University of Chicago Press, 1966), p. 1, notes the distortion of facts resulting from a romantic view of the craftsman. This view continues to be perpetuated by such works as Clay Anderson et al., *The Craftsman in America* (Washington, D.C.: National Geographic Society, 1975). In recent years the literature on preindustrial artisans has been divided between works that treat the political consciousness of a rising proletariat and those that seek to provide a broader understanding of the world view of the artisan. Among the former are Steffen, *Mechanics of Baltimore*; Howard B. Rock, *Artisans of the New Republic: The Tradesmen of New York City in the Age of Jefferson* (New York: New York University Press, 1979); Alan Dawley, *Class and Community: The Industrial Revolution in Lynn* (Cambridge, Mass.: Harvard University Press, 1976); Charles S. Olton, *Artisans for Independence: Philadelphia Mechanics and the American Revolution* (Syracuse, N.Y.: Syracuse University Press, 1975); and Richard Walsh, *Charleston's Sons of Liberty: A Study of the Artisans, 1763–1789* (Columbia: University of South Carolina Press, 1959). Publications providing a larger context for the study of preindustrial artisans and the shift in artisan consciousness at the beginning of the nineteenth century include Sean Wilentz, *Chants Democratic: New York City and the Rise of the American Working Class, 1788–1850* (New York: Oxford University Press, 1984) and Susan E. Hirsch, *Roots of the American Working Class: The Industrialization of the Crafts in Newark, 1800–1860* (Philadelphia: University of Pennsylvania Press, 1978). Even these, however, have focused more attention on the artisan's leisure than on his work. For a study of one man's work and its seasonal rhythms see Barbara McLean Ward, "The Joiner of Mill Creek Hundred," in *After Ratification: Material Life in Delaware, 1798–1820*, ed. J. Richie Garrison, Bernard L. Herman, and Barbara McLean Ward (Newark, Del.: Museum Studies Program, University of Delaware, 1988), pp. 79–97.

8. Campbell, *London Tradesman*, p. 171.

9. The basic concepts used in the following discussion of the learning process can be found in Henry C. Ellis, *Fundamentals of Human Learning and Cognition* (Dubuque, Iowa: William C. Brown Company, 1972). For an attempt to relate stylistic variation in material artifacts to interaction during the craft learning process, see Brian Hayden and Aubrey Cannon, "Interaction Inferences in Archaeology and Learning Frameworks of the Maya," *Journal of Anthropological Archaeology* 3 (1984): 325–67. I wish to thank Robert Guffin for bringing this article to my attention.

10. The process is similar to what an athlete experiences in acquiring a new skill. A diver learns to "feel" whether or not he or she has entered the water correctly, a skater learns to "feel" if a jump has gone well; a football player learns the "feel" of a successful block.

11. Ellis, *Learning and Cognition*, pp. 74–75.

12. Ibid.

13. Ibid., pp. 197–98. See also Ina McD. Bilodeau, "Information Feedback," in *Principles of Skill Acquisition*, ed. E. A. Bilodeau (New York: Academic Press, 1969), pp. 255–85.

14. Thomas S. Reese, "Colonial Transformations of Spanish Art: Sixteenth Century Mexico" (Unpublished paper, June 1978), p. 11.

15. Barbara McLean Ward, "Boston Goldsmiths, 1690–1730," in *The Craftsman in Early America*, ed. Ian M. G. Quimby (New York: W. W. Norton, 1984), pp. 142–44.

16. Philip Zea, "Furniture," in *The Great River: Art and Society of the Connecticut Valley, 1635–1820*, ed. William N. Hosley and Gerald W. R. Ward (Hartford, Conn.: Wadsworth Atheneum, 1985), pp. 228–34.

17. Most of us have had the experience of testing acceptable behavior in a new situation. This might include determining the appropriate dress for an unfamiliar occasion, or how other motorists will respond to a yellow light at an intersection.

18. David Pye, *The Nature and Art of Workmanship* (Cambridge: Cambridge University Press, 1968), pp. 4–8.

19. George Kubler, *The Shape of Time: Remarks on the History of Things* (New Haven, Conn.: Yale University Press, 1962), p. 67.

20. David Pye, *The Nature and Aesthetics of Design* (New York: Van Nostrand Reinhold, 1978), p. 60.

21. Kubler, *The Shape of Time*, p. 63. See also George Kubler, "Time's Perfection and Colonial Art," in *Spanish, French, and English Traditions in the Colonial Silver of North America*, Fourteenth Annual Winterthur Conference Report, 1968 (Winterthur, Del.: Henry Francis du Pont Winterthur Museum, 1969), pp. 7–18. For a discussion of the relationship between invention and the useful arts see Cyril Stanley Smith, "Art, Invention, and Technology," in *A Search for Structure: Selected Essays on Science, Art, and History* (Cambridge, Mass.: MIT Press, 1981), pp. 325–31.

22. Gerald L. Pocius, "Gossip, Rhetoric, and Objects: A Sociolinguistic Approach to Newfoundland Furniture," in *Perspectives on American Furniture*, ed. Gerald W. R. Ward (New York: W. W. Norton, 1988), pp. 303–45.

23. Charles S. Parsons, "The Dunlaps of New Hampshire and Their Furniture," in *Country Cabinetwork and Simple City Furniture*, ed. John D. Morse (Charlottesville: University Press of Virginia, 1970), pp. 109–50. For a brief discussion of the possible Scottish antecedents of Dunlap furniture see Philip D. Zimmerman, "Regionalism in American Furniture, in *Perspectives on American Furniture*, pp. 33–38.

24. See, for instance, the card table illustrated in Benjamin A. Hewitt, Patricia E. Kane, and Gerald W. R. Ward, *The Work of Many Hands: Card Tables in Federal America, 1790–1820* (New Haven, Conn.: Yale University Art Gallery, 1982), p. 119.

25. Dirk Hoerder, *Crowd Action in Revolutionary Massachusetts, 1765–1780* (New York: Academic Press, 1977).

26. E. P. Thompson, "Patrician Society, Plebian Culture," *Journal of Social History* (Summer 1974): 382–405; and "The Moral Economy of the English Crowd in the Eighteenth Century," *Past and Present*, no. 50 (February 1971): 77–136.

Robert F. Trent

The Symonds Shops of Essex County, Massachusetts

This day was buried Mr John Symonds, a Batchelor, from his House near the ferry. With the loss of this man the appearance of the last & the beginning of this Century is lost. His father died a few years since at 100, & John died at 74. The children all lived in single life till they were advanced, & only one ever entered into married life & she after 70. . . . The windows of this house [the Symonds house] are of the small glass with lead in diamonds & open upon hinges. The Doors open with wooden latches. The Chairs are the upright high arm chairs, & the common chairs are the short backed. The tables small & oval, the chest of drawers with knobs, & short swelled legs. The large fire place, & the iron for the lamp. The blocks of wood in the corner [the corner posts]. The Press for pewter plates with round holes over the door of it. Large stones rolled before the door for steps. Old Dutch maps and map mondes highly colored above a Century old. The beds very low, & the curtains hung upon the walls. The woolen caps worn by the men, & the small linen caps tied under the chin by the women.[1]

So wrote the Reverend William Bentley (1759–1819), Salem's indefatigable antiquarian and minister, in 1796 when describing what he thought represented the end of both an artisan dynasty and the seventeenth-century traditions that nurtured it. In a way, Bentley was right. The Symonds family of Essex County, Massachusetts, had been capable joiners and turners who dominated the Salem furniture trade throughout the 1600s and well into the first half of the eighteenth century. Sidney Perley, Salem's great nineteenth-century historian, remembered them as having "assisted in a great degree in the life and development of the town and city. Men with professions have been rare among them, and the larger number of its men have been city and bank officials and mechanics and traders."[2] If Perley had been less charitable, he might have called the Symondses "townies." They are only remembered today because of the diligent research of a few scholars who have identified several regional furniture styles and the individual craftsmen who practiced them.[3]

In fact, the Symonds family and their works illustrate the transmission of an English regional school to the New World. The patriarch of the group passed on his expertise to his sons and apprentices virtually unchanged, but the second generation, often exposed to new influences, subtly altered those traditions.

Since the 1890s, average Americans have had some very curious notions about the first colonists and the environment in which they lived. Not only was it believed that settlers underwent dramatic changes during the voyage across the Atlantic but that a nebulous entity called "the frontier" impacted them in even more surprising ways. In the wilderness, centuries-old craft traditions are thought to have crumbled in the rush to build and furnish the first shelters. A natural extension of this theory makes every man his own carpenter and joiner, constructing his house of logs and fashioning tables and benches out of immense wooden slabs fitted with stake feet. Pioneer Village in Salem, a 1930 reconstruction of the first huts and wigwams complete with slab tables and half-log benches, epitomizes this myth.

While there is some truth to the idea that the settlers constructed a variety of temporary dwellings and rough furniture of some sort, these kinds of things were temporary, and many of them may have been derived from traditional English field crafts. The frontier theory, however, postulates that such crude or nonprofessional workmanship characterized the entire seventeenth century.

On the contrary, professional woodworkers began to make expert products almost immediately. John Symonds (1595?–1671), the founder of the Symonds shop tradition, arrived in Salem from Great Yarmouth, Norfolk, in 1636, a good ten years after the settlement of Naumkeag. If he reverted to a primitive level of design and workmanship in America, then we must believe that during the crossing he lost his tools, forgot almost all his training, and despaired of ever trying to work as he had in England. What is more, we must then suppose that he willingly used laborious and wasteful ways to split whole tree trunks, methods that were thoroughly incompatible with his previous woodworking techniques. And finally, we must think that all of Symonds's fellow craftsmen rejected their professional training and decided to invent the furniture trade *de nuovo*. This thinking is patently unacceptable. Symonds experienced no technical or psychological deprivation. His training, in fact, enabled him to set up shop and begin making furniture like he had in Great Yarmouth.

Great Yarmouth, Norfolk, was a prosperous market town and seaport near Norwich. As an East Anglian entrepôt, Norwich supported a large population of Netherlandish refugees, who had fled to Protestant England to escape religious persecution in the Lowlands during the 1560s. Many of them came from Antwerp, an artistic and crafts center, and the skilled joiners among them brought to Norwich an avant-garde strain of Mannerist carving and applied ornamentation.[4]

An excellent example of this style is a room of paneling formerly in the Star Hotel in Great Yarmouth (figs. 1, 2), dated 1595 to 1600, about the time John Symonds began serving his apprenticeship there. To those unacquainted with metropolitan English joinery of this period, the room might come as something of a surprise. It consists of two stories, with a lower order of Corinthian pilasters and a strapwork frieze, and an upper one of caryatids and atlantes separated by niches and heavy panels of mitered work, which support a plainer frieze. Unfortunately, as presently installed in the Metropolitan Museum of Art, the room has lost its plaster cove of intertwined and foliated S scrolls and its shallow Gothic stone ribs, but otherwise is in superb condition.[5]

The sources for these Mannerist compositions and decorative motifs can be found in the architectural prints of such famed Amsterdam and Antwerp designers as Hans Vredeman de Vries (1527–1604). But the joiners fashioning the Star Hotel paneling would have referred to different plates for their designs, freely choosing the capitals or strapwork friezes from one image and the detailing of the mitered work or lion's head bosses from another. However, this method was generally only used at the highest levels of craftsmanship and patronage. For most workmen, the business of planning and embellishing a chest or a cabinet was accomplished by repeating certain established, often simplified, formulas. In all likelihood, John Symonds worked in this way, with a repertoire of designs that he had memorized and could construct with little more than a rule and a pair of compasses. Such swift and economical replication of a set pattern, in fact, was at the heart of the preindustrial age.

Although settlement patterns of woodworkers in the English colonies were extremely complex, it is true that joiners who were most successful in such emerging cities as Boston or Salem also originated in urban areas of England. By remaining in Salem, instead of moving to a settlement in the interior, Symonds consciously chose an economic and social environment much like the one he had come from, albeit on a reduced scale.

Salem was built on a peninsula surrounded by natural harbors and irrigated by many shallow rivers and creeks. With abundant marshes, wooded uplands, and a level plain by the waterside, the town was recognized as a potential port in the 1620s and remained second only to Boston and Charlestown as such throughout the seventeenth century.[6] As both the county seat and a trading center, the town was also quick to develop the fishing, shipping, and lumber industries, and to vie with the Dutch for trade with English colonies in the South and the Caribbean.[7] In such an environment a joiner like John Symonds could reasonably expect to support himself on his craft alone. Others who moved into agricultural communities, for example, could only survive by spending at least half their time farming. But as a city dweller, Symonds's principal concern was to establish himself on a street with access to water portage for lumber. And although he may have taken part in land speculation, his estate inventory reveals that he was only moderately prosperous at the time of his death. This inventory, however, dated September 1671, contains some all-important references to tools that help establish the identity of works made in his shop:

> Joyners Tools Benches and lare, 5 li. 5s. 6d.
> 2 Bedsteds almost finished, 3 li.
> 3 stools and one halfe of a Box, 12s. 6d.
> 1–2 Grindstone & windlass & a small
>   grindstone, 5s.
> Timber, planke & board, 5 li. 12s.
> an apprentice of 17 years old [that]
> hath 3 year and 9 monneths and 2 weekes
> to serve.[8]

First, the listing includes a "lare," or lathe, thus proving that Symonds could execute both joined and turned

24   Robert F. Trent

Fig. 1. *Carved oak room from the William Crowe house.* English, Great Yarmouth, Norfolk, about 1600. The Metropolitan Museum of Art, New York, The Edward Pearce Casey Fund, 65.182.1.

furniture. While it was common for later eighteenth-century cabinetmakers to practice both techniques, it was unusual for a seventeenth-century joiner to use turning. Joiners trained in London, where guilds protected the exclusivity of the trades, rarely knew how to turn, whereas joiners from provincial areas often possessed a wide range of skills, including joinery, turning, cooperage, house carpentry, and shipbuilding. Those joiners who could do turning did not have to subcontract for turned ornaments and could not only sell these services, but a host of turned products like sieves, hogshead pumps, oars, architectural elements, and turned chairs. Case pieces from the shop of such a versatile joiner, in fact, display turnings with a consistency of appearance that provide an important index for identifying their work.

Comparison between the Star Hotel paneling and chests, cupboards, and cabinets made by the Symonds shops can help to establish which decorative forms were based on English traditions. The most elaborate carvings on the Star Hotel paneling, notably the Corinthian capitals, caryatids, lion's heads, and corbels with acanthus leaves, were not made in the New World, most likely because they were too expensive for most of Symonds's customers. However, a surprising amount of the rest of the decoration is echoed in Symonds case pieces. Among these are horizontal moldings; corbels, keystones, or triglyphs; elaborate mitered moldings in panels, especially octagonal sunbursts; and, in the case of three known cabinets, strapwork carving on the sides. The architectural character of these works is particularly crucial. John Symonds taught his sons and apprentices basic rules about classical proportion, ornamentation, and composition, which they could apply to any furniture form or interior fixture. They may not have had the opportunity to exercise these skills on a com-

Fig. 2. *Detail of paneling from the William Crowe house.* From M. Jourdain, *English Decoration and Furniture of the Early Renaissance (1500–1650)*, first published in 1924.

mission as elaborate as the Star Hotel paneling, but they certainly could examine an unfamiliar furniture form and formulate a version of it in accordance with the shop's tradition.

There is also the question of who carried on John Symonds's influence after his death. Symonds trained two of his sons, James Symonds (1633–1714) and Samuel Symonds (1638–1722). James Symonds remained with his father after completing his apprenticeship and undoubtedly had assumed active responsibility for the shop well before his father's death in 1671; he also completed the training of the apprentice John Pease (1654–1734), who moved to Enfield, Connecticut, in 1681 and founded a major woodworking shop there of his own. Another apprentice trained by John Symonds was Nathaniel Silsbee (1650?–1717/18) of Salem. James Symonds, in turn, trained two of his sons, John Symonds (1666–1728/29) and Thomas Symonds (1677–1758). The other second-generation joiner of the family, Samuel, moved to Rowley Village and trained three apprentices, William Brown (1655?–90), Joshua Bisson (1652–1750), and Nathaniel Capen (1695–1749). (Capen, or perhaps the elder Samuel Symonds, made a glass case front later found in the Capen house in Topsfield that is the only surviving example of this once common furniture form.) This large group of workmen practiced the Symonds style well into the eighteenth century and extended its influence from southern Essex County north and even to the far-off Connecticut River valley.[9]

A late seventeenth-century fad among the gentry of Essex County for inscribing case pieces made for marriages, however, allows us to date the high point of Symonds production quite exactly, between 1676 and 1701.[10] And although the Symondses were not the only joiners in Salem, their leading role there probably resulted from their ability to provide turning services to other joiners.[11] Indeed, ten joiners not affiliated with their shops through apprenticeship or marriage did work in Salem between 1636 and 1700. Most of these joiners, however, moved in and out of Salem during their careers. By the 1670s, in fact, many of them were living in one particular neighborhood, a section of present-day Essex Street that was then only two hundred yards from the wharves where timber and plank could be unloaded from coastal vessels.

While the Symonds family can thus be seen as having in some way outproduced or simply outlasted their rivals, they also founded a woodworking dynasty of their own, and a wide variety of objects survives from their shops, including chests with one drawer, chests of drawers, cupboards, cabinets, chamber (or dressing) tables, square tables, upholstered chair frames, and glass cases. Some of these forms are familiar, while others elude our modern ideas about how a piece of furniture functions. Nor can we assume that all these types of furniture were made as early as the first working years of John Symonds's shop. On the contrary, the dated pieces are all associated with the second generation of the shop, and some of these furniture forms neither existed nor were made in Salem when John Symonds arrived there. Furthermore, a few of the objects display turnings that are readily identified as being in the Symonds style, but have joinery that is not, suggesting the sale of turned ornaments by the shop to outside furniture makers.

Probate inventories from Salem's first thirty years reveal that houses there were sparsely furnished. Most residents appear to have been rich in land, livestock, and shipping, but cash poor. They limited their furniture to storage pieces like chests, along with tables and a few stools and chairs. John Symonds most likely supplied many of these objects, but from their relatively low appraised value, this furniture was probably quite rudimentary and not heavily decorated. By the 1660s, the town's residents began to include a number of prosperous merchants, mariners (as ship captains were known), artisans, and farmers who had enough surplus wealth to begin investing a substantial amount of it in more elegant furnishings.

The increased commercialization of New England coincided with the spread of new social practices there and the attendant furnishing schemes that were developing throughout Europe under the influence of Louis XIV's court. These trends began to have an impact on the kinds of joinery the Symonds shops were providing. London merchants, who enjoyed significant exposure to the practices of the English court and aristocracy, served as models for these new kinds of comportment. Through their contacts with New England merchants and mariners, European practices were spread to such places as Boston and Salem.[12]

Any new fashion in costume or the decorative arts could be brought to the New World in three ways. First, a New England resident could import or bring back examples of a new fashion and thus make it available for emulation. Second, designs or patterns for such a new product could be imported by an American patron or artisan. And third, an English artisan acquainted with the latest style could arrive in New England and begin making products based on it for local patrons.

In the case of Salem, the first two ways—importation and new designs—seem the most plausible, while the arrival of an English-trained competitor there who began producing new furniture forms seems unlikely. However, when we view Salem in the context of the entire Massachusetts Bay Colony, Boston's influence—as the capital and dominant port of the area—comes into play. From the 1630s on, Boston enjoyed significantly higher levels of wealth and far more contact with England. Thus, its inhabitants were in an advantageous position insofar as new fashions were concerned. Moreover, the dominant joinery shops of Boston had been founded in the 1630s by two London-trained joiners, Ralph Mason and Henry Messinger. They quickly reestablished an urban tradition in Boston that appealed to the London merchants who settled there, businessmen who enjoyed a prestigious reputation as discriminating and fashion-conscious individuals. And ownership of a London-style case piece made in Boston came to be a sign of urbanity in outlying towns, even in Salem which sought to compete with Boston as a commercial center.[13]

All these factors affected the second generation of Symonds joiners. By the late 1660s and early 1670s, the transition away from utilitarian house furnishings toward more complex, urbane patterns seems to have been accomplished. By then, many merchants had amassed great fortunes in colonial trade, and their sons and daughters deliberately intermarried in order to heighten their social prestige. This second generation began to reject the furnishings that had dominated their parents' houses: the joined, board-seated chairs and stools; the great joined tables fixed in the center of rooms; and the cupboards used only for display. Instead, their ideal included sets of upholstered chairs; great oval-leafed tables that could be folded up and placed against the wall when not in use; and chests of drawers that functioned as both display surfaces and as storage for expensive textiles.[14]

This shift in furnishing practices started to become apparent in the probate inventories of Salem residents in the early 1670s. That of the merchant Nathaniel Grafton, for example, who died in 1671 at the age of twenty-nine, contains a number of furniture forms that differ markedly from those found in earlier listings. And in view of Grafton's age, the objects were likely to have been less than five years old. Grafton owned a fairly large house near his warehouse and wharf, with a parlor, hall, and kitchen on the ground floor and chambers over them; the house may also have had a porch, or an enclosed entry, at the front with a room over it. His inventory, in fact, is the first to mention a set of twelve leather chairs valued at £4, or about 6s 7d each. These were expensive chairs, probably new, and most likely made in Boston, where upholsterers had been working since the early 1660s.[15] Ephraim Skerry, another mariner who died in 1676, possessed a chest of drawers, the first listed in a Salem inventory.[16] Chests of drawers, as opposed to chests with one or two drawers under a storage compartment with a lid, were an advanced furniture form that was not likely to have been constructed anywhere else in New England except Boston, where Mason and Messinger had been making them since the 1630s.[17]

Perhaps the most important inventory that brings a number of disparate trends into focus is that of Hilliard

Veren, a wealthy merchant who died in Salem in 1680. In Veren's parlor were twelve expensive Turkey work chairs worth 9s apiece, along with two square tables worth 12s each. His hall was furnished with six leather chairs, four rush-bottomed chairs, and six joint stools, all probably old. Also in the hall were six serge chairs, two leather-covered trunks, and a chest of drawers, where expensive sets of linen napkins, towels, and tablecloths were undoubtedly kept. Previously, textiles were stored in great chests that concealed and protected them; chests of drawers, on the other hand, not only made their contents more accessible, but flaunted the quantity of textiles therein. Altogether, Veren's impressive inventory signals a new level of investment in both upholstered chairs and chests of drawers, and if the 1680 estate inventory of the rich Salem merchant John Turner had listed his furnishings in detail, we might now possess an even more complete record of this new furnishing style. (Veren's estate was worth a total of £969, while Turner's, who resided in what is now known as the House of the Seven Gables, was valued at £6,788!)[18] As it is, no record exists of a great oval-leafed table having been owned in Salem during the 1670s, although they were in Boston by 1670.[19]

Of the surviving objects attributed to the Symonds shops, only chests, cupboards, cabinets, and perhaps glass cases reasonably date to the working career of John Symonds. Chests of drawers, upholstered chairs, and chamber tables are more problematical. As noted, chests of drawers were a labor-intensive product with distinct London and Boston associations, and it is doubtful that James Symonds made one much before the first appearance of such a furniture form in a 1676 Salem inventory. Upholstered chairs only began to be produced in Boston when English upholsterers arrived there in the 1660s, and while it is conceivable that John Symonds may have constructed frames that he sent to Boston to be stuffed and covered, it does not seem very likely, because a buyer who could afford such expensive chairs could easily have ordered them directly from Boston. Chamber tables were also luxury items that are only found listed in inventories of the wealthy from the 1670s onward.[20] It appears, then, that while John Symonds brought a distinctly English regional style to Salem in the 1630s, his sons and apprentices had to formulate new designs for the furniture forms that became popular in the 1670s.

Equally significant on all Symonds case pieces are turned ornaments of a consistent fineness and detail. Half spindles, which function as columns on facades, are composed of pillars and urns connected by reeded reels. A variation of this motif on other Symonds case pieces, copied from a Boston work with London-inspired half spindles, displays a Tuscan Doric column that is flanked top and bottom by sharp-edged reels and capped by an urn. Multiple reels on the base molding of another Symonds cabinet can be related directly to the massive gadroon moldings seen on certain of the mitered panels in the Star Hotel paneling.

Three of the furniture forms introduced from Boston in the 1670s or 1680s also provide proof that the Symondses were selling turned ornaments to other joiners. Chamber tables, upholstered chair frames, and certain square tables from Salem have turnings that are patently by the hand of a Symonds workman, probably James Symonds. The chamber tables, however, have stopped-mitered panels (on their facades) and drawers that are inconsistent with documented works from the Symonds shop. In the case of upholstered chair frames, one example may have been fashioned entirely in the Symonds shop, but two others exist that have radically different, somewhat cruder frames and must have been made by another joiner. All Salem upholstered chair frames date from 1685 to 1695, when the upholsterer George Herrick was working there.[21] A variety of rectangular and square tables have joinery by perhaps three different shop traditions, but all were turned in the Symonds shops. Regrettably, no turned chair that is indisputably a Symonds product has been identified. And yet another hybridized Symonds work from this period is a chest of drawers with graduated drawers and powerful Boston-style moldings.

Although Salem was environmentally similar to Great Yarmouth, certain conditions there did affect the products and techniques of the Symonds shop. While wood was scarce and labor plentiful in England, the reverse was true in New England,[22] and this impacted the use of materials in Salem. By the 1670s, the Symonds shops bought imported lumber from New Hampshire and Maine, for the great stands of trees that once stood in the vicinity of Salem had long since been cut for houses, fencing, shipbuilding, smithing, and firewood. Even so, lumber was so cheap that the Symonds joiners habitually prepared their oak boards through a swift but extremely wasteful technique known as riving. The entire trunk of the tree was split radially into smaller and smaller wedge-shaped pieces, which were then trimmed and squared. The interiors of Symonds case pieces display the characteristic torn wood fibers associated with this process, because any surface that was not immediately visible did not have to be planed. Conversely, English joinery almost never displays evidence of riving, for wood was so expensive and scarce that riving was out of the question. Instead, English joiners subcontracted their logs to sawyers, who worked in pairs with great pit saws. After the trunks were reduced to manageable balks, the lumber was further trimmed by a joiner with a frame saw, and it was manipulated in every direction possible to secure the greatest amount of lumber. The interior surfaces of English case pieces invariably show the irregular saw kerfs produced by this method, known as frame sawing. When the Symonds shops used pine boards, they are usually found to have the regularly spaced, consistent saw kerfs produced by sawmills, which operated on practically every New England river and stream large enough to drive a waterwheel. In England, sawyers protested against the introduction of sawmills well into the eighteenth century, sometimes even resorting to riots or destroying the mills themselves. No such protection of hand labor was ever considered in New England, because too much forest needed to be felled and not enough artisans were available to do it.[23]

The primacy of the Symonds shops in Salem's furniture trade began to be challenged by new fashions in the mid-1690s. A new kind of woodworker called a cabinetmaker began to immigrate to Boston. These cabinetmakers made cases constructed from dovetailed boards and covered with thin sheets of figured veneer. While some Boston and Charlestown joiners apparently learned the technology to produce such new cabinetry, many provincial joiners did not. Symonds apprentices of the third generation did not meet this challenge. Instead, they took up turned chairmaking or carpentry and the construction of joined paneling for interiors. The last member of the family to be associated with cabinetmaking, in fact, was Joseph Symonds (1721–69), son of Thomas Symonds, a third-generation member of the shop.[24]

The John Symonds whose death William Bentley lamented in 1796 was born in 1727. (His father, John Symonds (1692–1791/92), had been a farmer and fisherman, and his grandfather, another John Symonds (1666–1728/29), a joiner.) Undoubtedly, few others in Salem noticed the passing of the last John Symonds, and even Bentley seems to have been unaware that the furniture he was looking at in the Symonds household had been made by previous generations of the family. By the late nineteenth century when Sidney Perley wrote his three-volume history of Salem, he noted the professions of various members of the Symonds family in a detailed genealogy appended to his text, but he never realized that the ancient furniture he so proudly illustrated was made by them as well. The Trask family chest, the Osborne family chest, and the Putnam cupboard—all Symonds products—were thought (by descendants of the original owners) to have been English, perhaps because of the widespread Victorian idea that anything that old and refined could not possibly have been American. Not until the 1960s, when Benno M. Forman reexamined this entire group of furniture, were these objects attributed to the Symonds shop tradition, and since that time new pieces, made wholly or in part, by the Symonds joiners have been identified and added to the published canon of early American joinery. With a better understanding of how American furniture from the first century after settlement looked, we know that most of it closely resembled English prototypes and differed only in the techniques employed to reduce the lumber to usable forms. And by the late seventeenth century when new English fashions and practices began to impinge on colonial traditions, even those innovations followed English precedents. Indeed, until America developed discernible regional economies and cultures in the eighteenth century, little that is distinctly American can be said to have been made here.

NOTES

1. *The Diary of William Bentley, D. D.* (Salem: The Essex Institute, 1905–14), vol. 2, p. 172.
2. Sidney Perley, *The History of Salem, Massachusetts* (Salem, 1924–28), vol. 1, pp. 392–401; see footnote 4 on p. 392 for a genealogy; the quote regarding the Symonds family is found on pp. 394–97.
3. Benno M. Forman, "The Seventeenth Century Case Furniture of Essex County, Massachusetts and Its Makers," (M.A. thesis, University of Delaware, 1968); Benno M. Forman, "The Osborne Family Chest Rediscovered," *Historical New Hampshire* 26 (Spring 1971): 26–30; Robert F. Trent, "Two Seventeenth-Century Salem Upholstered Chairs," *Essex Institute Historical Collections* 116 (January 1980): 34–40; Robert F. Trent, "The Symonds Joinery Shops of Salem and Their Works," *Peabody Museum of Salem Antiques Show* (Salem, Mass.: Peabody Museum, 1981), pp. 33–36.

4. William White, *History, Gazetteer, and Directory of Norfolk, and the City and County of Norwich* (Sheffield, Va.: Robert Leader, 1845), pp. 232–52. See p. 246, which reads: "In 1574, the town was so full of *Protestant refugees* from France and the Netherlands, that the bailiffs published an edict forbidding the influx of any more of these foreigners, many of whom were ingenius artisans, and by settling in Norwich and its neighborhood, greatly improved the staple manufactures of this county."

5. The plaster frieze and vaults are illustrated in Margaret Jourdain, *English Decoration and Furniture of the Early Renaissance, 1500–1660* (London: B. T. Batsford, 1924), p. 52, fig. 58.

6. See Perley's *History of Salem* and his series of articles entitled "Salem in 1700," in *Essex Institute Historical Collections*, vols. 48 (1912), 55 (1919).

7. Bernard Bailyn, *The New England Merchants in the Seventeenth Century* (1955; reprint, New York: Harper and Row, 1964).

8. *The Probate Records of Essex County, Massachusetts* (Salem: Essex Institute, 1916–20), vol. 2, pp. 247–50.

9. Forman, "The Seventeenth Century Case Furniture of Essex County," pp. 42–46.

10. Robert F. Trent, "The Emery Attributions," *Essex Institute Historical Collections* 121 (July 1985): 215–16.

11. Forman, "The Seventeenth Century Case Furniture of Essex County," pp. 46–50.

12. Robert F. Trent, *Historic Furnishings Report: Saugus Iron Works National Historic Site, Saugus, Massachusetts* (Harper's Ferry, W. Va.: National Park Service, 1982), pp. 38–74.

13. Bailyn, *New England Merchants in the Seventeenth Century*, pp. 75–111.

14. Trent, *Historic Furnishings Report*, pp. 51–61.

15. *The Probate Records of Essex County*, vol. 2, pp. 225–26.

16. Ibid., vol. 3, pp. 105–06.

17. Benno M. Forman, "The Chest of Drawers in America, 1635–1730: The Origins of the Joined Chest of Drawers," *Winterthur Portfolio* 20 (Spring 1985): 1–30.

18. *The Probate Records of Essex County*, vol. 3, pp. 362–65, 399–401.

19. Trent, *Historic Furnishings Report*, pp. 60–61.

20. Andrew Passeri and Robert F. Trent, "A New Model Army of Cromwellian Chairs," *Maine Antique Digest* 14 (September 1986): 10c–16c; Benno M. Forman, "Furniture for Dressing in Early America, 1650–1730: Forms, Nomenclature, and Use," *Winterthur Portfolio* 22 (Summer/Autumn 1987): 149–64.

21. Forman, "The Seventeenth Century Case Furniture of Essex County," p. 49.

22. Benno M. Forman, "Mill Sawing in 17th-Century Massachusetts," *Old-Time New England* 60 (April/June 1970): 110–30.

23. Ibid.

24. Perley, *History of Salem*, vol. 1, pp. 320–23, 394.

Catalogue Objects

1. Chest with one drawer

This impressive architectonic object, known as the "R. L." chest after the initials carved on its frieze, typifies a fairly large group of chests with one drawer that are attributed to the second generation of Symonds workmen, particularly to James Symonds (1633–1714) of Salem and Samuel Symonds (1638–1722) of Rowley Village, a town some ten miles north of Salem. The most significant documented chests in the group include the Conant family chest (Winterthur Museum, Winterthur, Delaware), the Trask family chest (New England Historic Genealogy Society, Boston), the Endicott family chest (Museum of Fine Arts, Boston), the Osborne family chest (New Hampshire Historical Society, Concord), and the "M. T. 1700/1701" chest (Concord Antiquarian Museum, Concord, Massachusetts). The origin and ownership of these objects all center on Salem and the immediate vicinity, and all suggest a date of 1670 to 1700.[1]

While all the chests follow the same general arrangement, two significant features vary in their overall composition. Three of the chests have applied columns of the multiple urn-and-reel type associated with the founder of the shop tradition, while three have Tuscan Doric applied columns that probably reflect Boston influence. Similarly, three of the chests have drawers divided into three great panels, while three have drawers with two panels, the latter again representing a Boston format.[2] Thus, the chests with Salem-type applied columns generally have tripartite drawers, and those with Boston-type applied columns have bipartite drawers. The "R. L." chest, with Salem-type applied columns and a bipartite drawer, represents the only exception to this schema. Of the two groups, the one with Salem-type applied columns and tripartite drawers seems to be the original pattern, because the drawer divisions correspond to divisions on the front of the chest and reinforce the idea of a self-contained architectural unit. When bipartite drawers were adopted from Boston usage, however, they blatantly disrupted the unity of the composition.

Like most joined furniture influenced by London practice, Symonds chests have strong, correctly drawn architectural base moldings, waist moldings, and frieze moldings that correspond to the surbase, shaft and capi-

1. *Chest with one drawer*
American, Salem or Rowley Village, Mass., 1670–1700
Attributed to the Symonds shop tradition
Red oak; walnut, maple, and white pine
H. 28¾ in (73 cm), W. 45⅞ in (116.2 cm), D. 20¾ in (52.7 cm)
The Henry Francis du Pont Winterthur Museum, Winterthur, Del., 58.688

tal, and entablature of classical antiquity. These horizontal elements are balanced by the vertical applied columns and glyphs. Many of the chests also have an octagonal sunburst design formed by a plaque, mitered moldings, and points or rays. This sunburst motif, as well as the complex mitered work in other panels, probably had no direct iconographical significance other than its obvious derivation from European pattern books.

Another urban trait seen in Symonds chests is the use of various hardwoods for subdued coloristic effects. The "R. L." chest has walnut plaques and moldings, but many of the related pieces have moldings and glyphs of cedar, as well as the standard applied columns, bosses, drawer knobs, and turned feet of ebonized maple. It is difficult to gauge how vivid these colored woods were originally, because they all have faded with exposure to sunlight, and many of the chests themselves have been painted or varnished over the years.

1. Benno M. Forman, "The Seventeenth Century Case Furniture of Essex County, Massachusetts and Its Makers," (M.A. thesis, University of Delaware, 1968), pp. 108–10.
2. Peter Arkell and Robert F. Trent, "The Lawton Cupboard: A Unique Masterpiece of Early Boston Joinery and Turning," *Maine Antique Digest* 16 (March 1988): 1c.

2. *Chest with one drawer*
English, probably London, 1640–70
Oak; various exotic woods, bone, and mother-of-pearl
H. 35 in (88.9 cm), W. 53 in (134.6 cm), D. 25½ in (64.8 cm)
The J. B. Speed Art Museum, Louisville, Ky., bequest of Preston
Pope Satterwhite, 49.30.298

2. Chest with one drawer

Both in its design and high-quality joinery, this beautifully preserved chest epitomizes the best London work of the mid-seventeenth century. The Italianate academic proportions, well-drawn moldings, and sophisticated mitered moldings, as well as the use of exotic woods, bone, and mother-of-pearl for turnings, plaques, veneers, and inlays, are outstanding even by English standards, and such chests, while quite expensive, were undoubtedly popular in prosperous ports like East Anglia and were a reasonable investment for the customer who could not afford a full-blown chest of drawers with doors in this style.

Nevertheless, the frieze and storage compartment of this chest are identical in size and layout to the upper case of the typical two-part chest of drawers made in London during this time. The drawer and light base molding differ slightly from those seen in the lower cases of such chests, while the feet have lost the upper sections of their necks and the flanges they originally had. In many respects, the piece also resembles a late seventeenth-century Boston chest with two drawers beneath the storage compartment.[1]

The great raised fields on the left and right panels of this storage compartment, however, may have been derived from sophisticated European designs but became simplified and standardized in London production. The turned round molding punctuated with four voussoirs and inscribed in an octagon is somewhat rarer but not

The Symonds Shops of Essex County

uncommon in London examples. And the bone inlay with engraving is virtually identical to that produced by gunsmiths, as are the mother-of-pearl blossoms.

The most significant structural feature of London chests, however, was the use of dovetails to attach the drawer sides to the fronts. With a shallow drawer like this, each side usually has two dovetails. Apparently, the drawer of this chest also once had applied colonnettes and smaller wooden knobs where the present brass pulls are located.

1. Benno M. Forman, "The Chest of Drawers in America, 1635–1730—The Origins of the Joined Chest of Drawers," *Winterthur Portfolio* 20 (Spring 1985): 1–30; see especially figs. 1, 10, and 11.

3. Cabinet

Three elaborate small cabinets attributed to the Symonds shop tradition survive. Each consists of a box on feet with a single large door, behind which are ten small sliding boxes or drawers of different sizes. Such cabinets were used for a variety of purposes by both sexes: women kept jewelry or sewing materials in them, while men, money, documents, or writing utensils. Large cabinets also housed collections of medals, antiquities, gems, or natural history specimens. Nomenclature for these cabinets was not uniform, and often they were simply called cases of boxes. The small versions, derived from larger cabinets on stands, were prominently displayed in aristocratic studies or counting-houses, and their ownership was considered a mark of gentility. Of the three Symonds cabinets, the Thomas and Sarah Buffington cabinet seen here (cat. no. 3) is dated 1676, the Ephraim and Mary Herrick cabinet (Metropolitan Museum of Art, New York) is dated 1679, and the Thomas Hart cabinet (Winterthur Museum, Winterthur, Delaware), also dated 1679, bears Hart's initials. All the original owners lived in the immediate vicinity of Salem.[1]

The Buffington cabinet is unique in having carved strapwork on the sides that directly relates to carved friezes on the Star Hotel paneling. The strapwork is quite elaborate and consists of quatrefoils, rosettes, and scrolled borders. (The Herrick and Hart cabinets have S scrolls in the same location.) The Buffington cabinet is also unusual in its use of Boston-style applied columns with softly modeled, multiple bead-and-reel motifs at the tops and bottoms. (The other two cabinets have far more standard Boston-style applied columns.) An explanation for the bead-and-reels of the Buffington cabinet is found in the horizontal turning seen between the corbels or consoles at the bottom of the doors

3. *Cabinet*
American, Salem, Mass., dated 1676
Attributed to the Symonds shop tradition
Red oak; red cedar, black walnut, and a soft maple
H. 17¼ in (43.8 cm), W. 17 in (43.2 cm), D. 9⅞ in (25.1 cm)
The Henry Francis du Pont Winterthur Museum, Winterthur, Del., 58.526

of the Buffington and Herrick examples; this horizontal turning represents a heavy gadroon molding seen on the Star Hotel paneling, and the maker of the Buffington cabinet extended the multiple turnings used on the horizontal gadroon turning to the columns.

The over-scaled architectural detailing of the cabinets is characteristic of all Symonds production, and each has consoles, voussoirs, or corbels at the corners of the door, a diagonally sawn dentil across the top, and mitered work in the center panel. The Hart cabinet has bosses and glyphs in place of the gadroon turning, a delightful inversion of classical architectural rules. All the cabinets have ebonized maple, walnut, and cedar elements on the façades and oak cases. The drawers inside are merely nailed oak boxes that slide on their bottoms. Two important Boston cabinets (Museum of Fine Arts, Boston; private collection) with paneled sides and walnut cases have the same general features, but are far more accurate architecturally and are not carved with the same prominent relief.[2]

1. Forman, "The Seventeenth Century Case Furniture of Essex County," pp. 111–13.
2. Jonathan L. Fairbanks and Robert F. Trent, eds., vol. 2 of *New England Begins—The Seventeenth Century* (Boston: Museum of Fine Arts, 1982), pp. 293–94.

4. Cupboard

Cupboards attributed to the Symonds shop are surprisingly rare. Only three are known, and two of these (Nelson-Atkins Museum of Art, Kansas City, Missouri; Metropolitan Museum of Art, New York) are so heavily restored that their original appearance is difficult to ascertain. The decorative elements on the well-preserved Essex Institute cupboard, however, can be compared with the other two to develop a model for how an original Symonds cupboard looked. All three cupboards have trapezoidal storage areas in the upper case, vase-shaped pillars with a deeply incised band near the top, three drawers with decorative mitered moldings, and applied columns of the sort associated with the work of John Symonds (as opposed to the Tuscan Doric columns made by the second generation of the shop). In many respects, the cupboards strongly resemble the only known Boston cupboard (collection of Eddy and Linda Nicholson) from the late 1670s, which has many of the same features. In view of the role Boston's London-inspired joinery had in spreading the use of drawers in case pieces made in eastern Massachusetts after 1670, the similarity between the Boston cupboard and the three Salem examples does not seem coincidental.[1] Equally striking is the degree to which Salem's joiners retained their own decorative traditions despite Boston influence.

The Essex Institute cupboard almost certainly belonged to Benjamin Putnam (1664–1715) of Salem Village (now Danvers), whose family helped to instigate the witch-hunts of 1692 to 1693. According to the family, the cupboard was saved from a fire that destroyed the Putnam's house in 1714, and extensive scorching appears on the rear of the cupboard, as if it had been standing against a hot wall. The 1772 inventory of Putnam's son Stephen Putnam (1694–1772) lists "one old Fashion cubburd" valued at eighteen shillings.[2] Family records also mention a restoration of the cupboard in 1869. But old photographs of it show large wooden urns attached to the upper shelf similar to neoclassical gateposts that were popular in Salem early in the nineteenth century, suggesting that the cupboard was repaired and modestly updated more than once in its history.

A motif found on all three Salem cupboards that is not seen elsewhere in surviving Symonds work is the double arch, located on the side panels of the trapezoidal storage areas. These arches are outlined with moldings that are interrupted by voussoirs at the bases, the springing of the arches, and at the apexes of the arches. The curved sections of these moldings were made on a lathe, a typical practice at the time. The use of the arch motif, in fact, may have been adopted from cupboards made by joiners in Ipswich and Newbury in northern Essex County, which survive in great numbers and obviously were popular among the Essex County elite.

Of all three Salem cupboards, the Putnam cupboard displays the finest and most imaginative mitered work on its three drawer fronts. The other two cupboards have three drawers with restrained bipartite paneling, of the type seen on the top drawer of the Putnam cupboard. By contrast, the middle and bottom drawers of the Putnam cupboard are tripartite, with richer geometric arrangements of mitered work. Possibly, the present drawer locations may not be as originally intended. Perhaps the bipartite drawer front was meant to be between the two tripartite ones, especially because the current second drawer (which might have been the original top drawer) is embellished with a sunburst motif at the center. However, as currently arranged, the separations between the drawer panels, which are emphasized by the applied columns, form a pyramidal composition rising toward the door of the upper storage compartment. Such compositional movement is rare in provincial Mannerist furniture, where a static equipoise is more usual. Whatever the original drawer arrangement, however, the individual compartments bear a striking resemblance to those seen on many Symonds chests and the Star Hotel paneling, some of which have mitered work possibly derived from pattern books of geometric designs that were commonly used in laying out coffered ceilings, inlaid floors, and joinery.[3]

1. Arkell and Trent, "The Lawton Cupboard: A Unique Masterpiece of Early Boston Joinery and Turning," pp. 1c–4c.
2. Irving P. Lyon, "The Oak Furniture of Ipswich, Massachusetts. Part VI. Other Affiliates: A Group Characterized by Geometrical Panels," *Antiques* 34 (August 1938): 81.
3. Anthony Wells-Cole, "An Oak Bed at Montecute: A Study in Mannerist Decoration," *Furniture History* 17 (1981): 1–19.

4. *Cupboard*
American, Salem, Mass., 1685–1700
Attributed to James Symonds (1633–1714)
Oak; maple, walnut, and pine
H. 58¾ in (149.2 cm), W. 45 in (114.3 cm), D. 21 in (53.3 cm)
Essex Institute, Salem, Mass., 108.889

5. *Chest of drawers*
American, Salem, Mass., 1675–1700
Attributed to the Symonds shop tradition
Oak; pine, walnut, cedar, and maple
H. 44¾ in (113.7 cm), W. 44¼ in (112.4 cm), D. 22³⁄₁₆ in (56.4 cm)
Society for the Preservation of New England Antiquities, Boston, Mass., museum purchase, 1944.22

5. Chest of drawers

Despite its restored feet and some replaced moldings, this previously unpublished Symonds chest of drawers is probably one of the finest to survive. It differs from all the others in having squared panels on the drawer fronts with no other angled projections. The moldings are skewed in section, with fillets and cyma moldings on the inner edges. They are executed in cedar and surround inset panels of figured walnut. Pairs of ebonized maple columns with sharp reels, pendant drops, and urn finials separate the panels and like the moldings were probably influenced by Boston prototypes. The drawer construction and other structural details are typical of Symonds pieces as are the base moldings, bed moldings between drawers, and tripartite corbels in the frieze.

Of all the Symonds chests of drawers, this one replicates most closely the heavy, modular proportions of Boston examples. The height and width are nearly identical and the depth half of that. It departs from the usual Boston formula in having drawers that become progressively deeper from top to bottom, a somewhat provincial variation of more subtle Boston designs, which organized the case into two sections. The arrangement of the paneled drawer fronts displays the same triangular formula seen on the Putnam cupboard (cat. no. 4).

6. *Chest of drawers*
American, Boston, Mass., 1675–1715
Joinery attributed to the Ralph Mason and Henry Messinger shop traditions
Turned ornament attributed to the Thomas Edsall shop tradition
Walnut; chestnut and pine
H. 36 in (91.4 cm), W. 37¾ in (95.9 cm), D. 21⅞ in (55.6 cm)
Private collection

6. Chest of drawers

This Boston walnut chest of drawers epitomizes the second- and third-generation works of a joinery and turning tradition transmitted to Boston in the 1630s by three London-trained craftsmen. Most such cases are made in two sections that divide above the waist molding and are distinguished by a deep drawer in the upper case, strong horizontal and vertical architectural elements, blocky proportions, and fine workmanship. Generally, chests of drawers with all-walnut façades usually date to later in the tradition, as evidenced by the use of fielded side panels in this example. The long-lived and prestigious Boston shop traditions that produced such chests were influential throughout eastern Massachusetts and significantly altered the practice of second-generation joiners in major provincial centers like Salem, Ipswich, Newbury, Cambridge, and Duxbury.

However, local joiners who adopted some fashionable details of Boston work rarely copied the dovetailed drawer construction that is its most important feature. Rather, joiners like the Symonds workmen concentrated on such obvious elements as applied columns and drawer moldings, as well as the very *idea* of making a chest of drawers to begin with.

Provincial joiners also invariably missed the point of organizing a chest of drawers into two cases. Moreover, the proportional consistency of the front and side façades seen here was often discarded in favor of panels that bear no relationship to the façade. The paneled stiles of the façade of this chest are an alternative to the use of applied columns, which were typical of Boston work. The stiles may also have been employed in London in order to make columns unnecessary, since obtaining them meant buying them from a turner. It was possible, in fact, to avoid turned ornament altogether by simply making the front feet extensions of the front posts. This chest, however, which has restored front feet, did have turned feet originally. The urbane form of the feet, with distinctly flattened spheres and narrow necks, contrasts sharply with the bulbous, inaccurately restored feet of the Salem example (cat. no. 5).

7. Serge chair

The upholstery trade, like silversmithing, was considered a luxury business and largely confined in New England to Boston until late in the seventeenth century. It is surprising, then, that three upholstered chair frames with turned ornament provided by the Symonds shops have been identified. One (present location unknown) has proportions and joinery that appear to be characteristic of Boston chairs and is thought to have been made entirely in one of the Symonds shops. Two others, this serge chair and a partially restored and nearly identical one (Museum of Fine Arts, Boston), have leaner, larger frames with pronounced spaces between the seats and the back panels. They are also carelessly constructed with mistakes in layout marks and poorly cut joints that are not consistent with the fine work of the Symonds shop. In fact, they appear to have been made by another Salem joiner altogether and merely provided with ornament by the Symonds workman who executed the turnings on the "SAH" chamber table, probably James Symonds.[1]

One explanation for the appearance of upholstered chairs in Salem is the arrival there of the upholsterer George Herrick in 1685. Herrick lived for ten years after that date, and he may have been financed by one of Salem's merchants who wanted to break into the lucrative upholstery market and compete with the established upholsterers in Boston. This effort seems to have

7. *Serge chair*
American, Salem, Mass., 1685–95
Turned ornament attributed to the Symonds shop tradition
Maple and oak; modern upholstery
H. 39¼ in (99.7 cm), W. 19¼ in (48.9 cm), D. 17¼ in (43.8 cm)
The Carnegie Museum of Art, Pittsburgh, Penn., Berdan Memorial Fund, 85.7

been largely a failure, and after Herrick's death no upholsterers worked in Salem for several decades.

This chair frame, which has been provided with historically accurate upholstery foundations and serge covers trimmed with silk fringe, was undoubtedly covered with a textile originally. Such chairs were always referred to by material, and since serge was a popular wool upholstery and has been used in this reconstruction, the chair has been called a "serge chair," although the original fabric used on it is not known.

The frame is somewhat eccentric by either English or Boston standards. Some English upholstered chairs have intermediate stretchers between the two lower side stretchers, but the practice was seldom used in Boston. The inclusion of a second intermediate stretcher between the higher front and rear stretchers is unheard-of in English or American chairs, and its presence here seems to indicate that the joiner who constructed the frame (presumably one of a set of six or twelve) was either unfamiliar with making upholstered chair frames or was instructed to add the extra intermediate stretcher by a patron who was not particularly knowledgeable about the furniture form. This frame and the Museum of Fine Arts example also have plain posts between the seat and the back panel, where ordinarily the posts were turned or chamfered and covered with the same material as the seat and back.

1. Robert F. Trent, "Two Seventeenth-Century Salem Upholstered Chairs," *Essex Institute Historical Collections* 116 (January 1980): 34–40.

8. Leather chair

This simplified version of a metropolitan upholstered chair frame could have been made in any one of two dozen provincial centers in England during the last half of the seventeenth century. The format, with a front stretcher set at the level of the lower side stretchers, is a typical Dutch one that was occasionally employed in London work, which characteristically favored the front stretcher being set opposite the upper side stretchers and provided with turned decoration. Other salient features include the great heels at the bottom of the rear posts and the partially upholstered rear posts between the seat and the back panel. The conjoined turnings, neither reel nor urn, are also commonly seen on provincial chairs and may have been executed in a joiner's shop.

While portions of the leather covers and upholstery foundations have been renewed, the treatment seen here is typical of most leather chairs. The front or show surfaces were embellished with brass nails, while the edges were turned over the frame and secured on the backside by iron tacks. The border or trim around the seat, however, is inaccurately restored; it should extend

8. Leather chair
English, 1660–1700
White oak; modern leather upholstery
H. 33 in (83.8 cm), W. 20¼ in (51.4 cm), D. 15¾ in (40 cm)
The Minneapolis Institute of Arts, gift of Mrs. John Washburn and daughters for the John Washburn Memorial Collection, 23.76

to the bottom of the rail in order to mask the roughly finished edges of the seat cover. However, the lack of tacking or nailing along the lower edges of the seat rails is standard, for generally a fringe with a decorative heading and loops or loose strands finished the border.

The overall design of this chair was extremely versatile. It could be adapted to any number of sizes by raising or lowering the seat and back rails to give the desired height for a particular use or to customize the frame for textile covers. The Salem chair (cat. no. 7), by contrast, is unusually eccentric in its lightweight, large size, and somewhat ungainly proportions, as well as in its use of intermediate crossed stretchers.

Wallace B. Gusler

The Anthony Hay Shop and the English Tradition

For more than twenty-five years (1751–76), the Anthony Hay shop in Williamsburg, Virginia, produced some of the finest furniture of the colonial period. In some forms—ceremonial chairs, china tables, and candlestands—the products of this small shop remain unparalleled in style and detail in the history of American furniture. In addition, the shop practiced the most advanced techniques of the time—methods developed in London's best shops and used by few other American cabinetmakers.

Eighteenth-century London is often cited today, as it was then, as the leading center of style and technology in the English-speaking world. It is important to understand, however, that the London cabinet industry was stratified into several levels of production, and consequently, an understanding of this stratification is helpful in discussing London influence on the Hay shop and its products.[1]

For the purposes of this study, London production will be designated by three levels. During the time of the Hay shop, such cabinetmakers as William Vile (c. 1700–1767), Thomas Chippendale (1718–79), and John Linnel (died 1796) represented the top level of the English hierarchy, and the nobility, their principal clientele. In fact, the majority of technological advances occurred in their shops, probably the result of expensive and complex commissions that required innovative skills and novel uses of materials.

The second level of furniture production was patronized by a wealthy middle class and is best documented in the works of Giles Grendey (1693–1780), who also had a flourishing export business. Often, Grendey's pieces show excellent technology, but are more conservative in style than the rococo furnishings of Chippendale or Linnel.

The third level was characterized by large-scale production and represented by such furniture makers as Phillip Bell (active 1758–74). Bell, like others in this category, made primarily for the export trade, and George Washington numbered among his many American patrons. But furniture in this third tier, while still of good quality, utilizes construction shortcuts not usual in the upper levels, and Bell's furniture, in particular, also contrasts with the higher levels in its stark simplicity and plainness of style.

Finally, it should be pointed out that many London shops participated in several levels of production. Since workers in the crafts were very mobile during the eighteenth century, the secrets of the trade traveled rapidly through the urban hierarchy as well as into the provinces.

The major factor governing the spread of these technologies, however, appears to have been economic. Economic pressures were so powerful, in fact, that ample evidence exists to show that even cabinetmakers with high levels of training and knowledge were forced to use cheaper, poorer, and quicker methods. In addition, several levels were often practiced simultaneously within the same shop, each aimed at a specific market and price tag. Moreover, these less expensive methods should not be confused with the production of high-quality "plain" style furniture at the top level. For frequently, only a careful analysis of technology separates pieces that otherwise appear the same externally.

The trade limitations found in any provincial American city were also many. Because there were fewer craftsmen in the colonies and less specialization of labor, each worker performed most aspects of carving and construction himself. More importantly, available tradesmen generally were less skilled than their London counterparts and more firmly rooted in regional practices.

Fierce competition between the workshops also made the time-consuming process of retraining unfeasible. Additional factors, too, especially the unavailability of certain materials, rendered the institution of all London practices here almost impossible.

This dependence of the trade on supplies may be illustrated by discussing drawer construction. Regardless of what level a London-trained cabinetmaker came from, he would have been accustomed to constructing drawers of quarter-sawn oak. He understood that such boards had superior qualities of stability and could be cut very thin to produce drawers that were extremely strong, but also delicate and lightweight. But obtaining such oak in colonial Philadelphia, for example, required making special arrangements since the timber business supplying cabinetmakers there was based on different woods. Instead, Philadelphia craftsmen usually used poplar for drawer sides and white cedar for the bottoms, and the cedar was usually riven or split rather than sawn. Likewise, Boston cabinetmakers relied principally on white pine, while those of Williamsburg utilized yellow pine for this purpose.

Although mature oak forests covered much of the East Coast, milled oak was not readily available to the cabinet trades. Softer woods were preferred and used as a provincial shortcut to avoid excessive work and higher costs. It should also be realized that by the mid-eighteenth century, such woods were becoming harder to find and were often imported from great distances. Agriculture, building, cooking, and heating had long since cleared the forests surrounding the principal towns and cities along the East Coast. In fact, the intense demand for fuel and tillable land stripped the terrain to a much greater extent than seen presently. In 1777, for example, on a visit to Williamsburg, Ebenezer Hazzard remarked that from the cupola of the College of William and Mary he could see the York and James rivers—a feat impossible today because of the trees.[2]

The small city in which Hay established his business differed significantly from larger American urban centers. With a population of only two thousand and lacking a port, it could support neither the commerce nor the hundreds of tradesmen found in Boston, Philadelphia, Charleston, or even nearby Norfolk. Notwithstanding, Hay and his competitors established one of the most technologically advanced cabinetmaking schools in colonial America and one closely aligned with the first level of London work.

The origin of Anthony Hay's training remains unknown, but the earliest products attributed to his shop indicate a strong reliance on Williamsburg furniture of a decade or more earlier.[3] This suggests that he learned his trade locally or was strongly influenced by Williamsburg-trained cabinetmakers. Regardless, Hay operated a very successful business that combined local traditions with aggressively fashionable English styles, an approach taken in most centers of American cabinetmaking.

In 1748 when Hay was first mentioned in a Williamsburg document, the city had been growing for over forty years.[4] By midcentury, an especially active building period, many of the most important town houses were constructed or expanded and a new capitol building and a major addition to the governor's palace were in progress. Major plantation houses also were rising along Virginia's rivers and the Chesapeake Bay, a building boom principally mounted by the third to fifth generations of upper-class Virginians.

But how could Williamsburg become an island of such extraordinary furniture development in the face of much larger colonial cities? While the answer to this question may never be fully addressed, three major conditions existed there that were not paralleled elsewhere.

The first and probably the most important cause was the existence of an upper class with extreme wealth. Virginia was the largest and richest of the thirteen colonies, and its plantation owners were building immense houses that needed fashionable furniture. Secondly, inherited tobacco fortunes also allowed the sons of the elite to be highly educated. They were taught to be English gentlemen—scholars and connoisseurs as well as planters. In that Age of Reason, they studied natural and political sciences, learned Greek and Latin, and were thoroughly acquainted with the principles of classical architecture and proportion. Some were even schooled in England or had visited London. As a result, Virginia's upper class—roughly 10 percent of the population—was well acquainted with London products, and their knowledge of art and architecture must have been a major contribution to the awareness of London aesthetics in Williamsburg cabinet shops.

The third major element to affect Williamsburg's uniqueness was the small scale of its furniture production. As discussed earlier, available materials and services in provincial cities were a controlling factor in each cabinetmaking school. In Williamsburg, the existence of a small number of cabinetmakers allowed each more freedom to adopt new styles and techniques more rapidly.

In most similar situations, extremely provincial products resulted from insufficient wealth and knowledge to support very high levels of quality or style. Williamsburg, being the capital and the only common meeting place for the area's wealthy and influential, provided an ideal location for the highly skilled cabinetmaker, especially one who practiced advanced styles and technologies.

But while Williamsburg was a center for avant-garde English design, a more provincial joiners' class of furniture was also produced there. This duality of the trade was especially pronounced during the second quarter of the century, when one group practiced a formal, advanced style and the other an imitative, misunderstood version of the formal. This dualism may have resulted from Peter Scott's arrival in Williamsburg in 1722. Scott (1694–1775), who was Hay's biggest competitor, was a craftsman of the first level, and his presence in Williamsburg seems to mark the city's transition from a provincial outpost for the cabinetmaking trade to one of extremely high standards and quality.[5]

In addition to Scott and the joiners' group, Hay also encountered a strong cabinetmaking business owned by James Spiers (active 1745–55). Spiers's shop was located next to Scott's, and ample documents survive to indicate he had a thriving business; however, at present, it is not possible to attribute exact pieces to his hand. Spiers disappears from the records in the mid-1750s, at a time when Hay's shop was expanding architecturally, and his business was gaining prominence.[6]

As stated earlier, Hay's early products were influenced by early Williamsburg practices, making it difficult to determine if he arrived in Williamsburg already trained or received his instruction there. But regardless, three factors distinguish his shop within the city: the use of first-level London construction techniques, the employment of London-trained cabinetmakers and carvers, and the use of London pattern books for some of his furniture designs.

For example, Hay shop case furniture (under all masters) utilized full-bottom dust boards (full thickness of the drawer blades or rails) that extend the entire depth of the case. These are a completely different type than those by Scott, who installed dust boards that had full-case depth but were thinner than the drawer blades and held in place by "kicker" strips that served as upper drawer guides. Both types of dust boards came from the first level of London production but indicate that Hay and Scott were trained in different, but parallel traditions. Moreover, craftsmen in Williamsburg adopted a combination of their two methods, most likely the result of journeymen moving from one shop to another.

Anthony Hay also employed at least two London-trained craftsmen: James Wilson (active 1755), a professional carver, and Benjamin Bucktrout (active 1764, died 1813), a cabinetmaker who later became master of the shop. The introduction of these tradesmen into Hay's business contributed to the shop's awareness of the latest English styles and techniques. The receptiveness of the Hay shop and its patrons to the latest fashions is well documented, and their adaptability is especially evident in the shop's last period (1770–76) under Edmund Dickinson (active 1764–76).

Always in pursuit of the "fashionable and neat" product, the Hay shop's earliest pieces are in a late baroque manner. They consist of tables with straight turned legs ending in turned pad feet and case furniture in a restrained style. These cases (figs. 1, 5) are dovetailed at the corners with full-bottom dust boards that extend the entire depth of the case and wooden strips (applied to the sides and front of the bottom) that form the foundation for the base molding, feet, and foot-support blocking. These strips are usually cut through with a saw every few inches. These kerfs (fig. 2) produce gaps that allow the bottom to expand and contract in response to humidity changes without being impeded by the strips. Similar kerfing of the bottom "frame" can also been seen on the products of Giles Grendey (1693–1780) of London.[7]

Also characteristic of Hay shop designs are bracket feet that are glued to the base molding. The foot support (fig. 3) is formed by a series of horizontally grained pine blocks set at right angles to one another, like modern plywood. This composite foot,[8] another technological development of London's first-level cabinetmakers, can also be seen in works by Chippendale, Linnel, William Ince (active 1758–1802), and John Mayhew (died 1811).[9]

This foot construction technique, however, was not normally used by the major schools of American furniture. Instead, they utilized a cheaper one that parallels lower levels of London and provincial English practice: a single vertical block placed inside brackets. The axial

Fig. 1. *Clothespress*. American, Williamsburg, Va., about 1770. Attributed to the Anthony Hay shop. Walnut; yellow pine. H. 56⅝ in (143.8 cm), W. 49½ in (125.7 cm), D. 23 in (58.4 cm). The Colonial Williamsburg Foundation, 1950-350.

Fig. 2. *Detail of clothespress* (expansion joints)

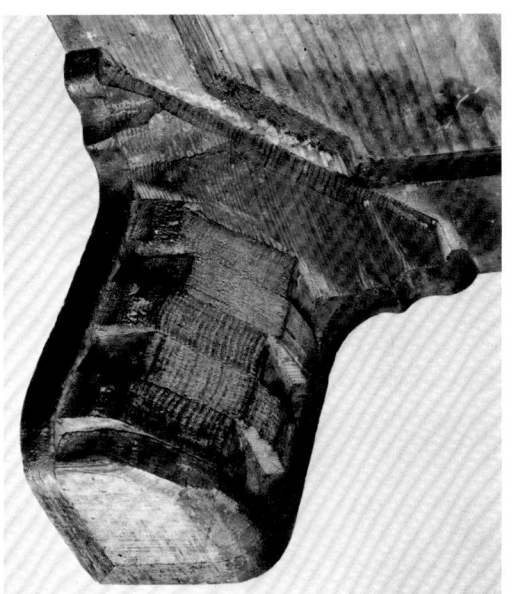

Fig. 3. *Detail of clothespress* (composite foot)

Fig. 4. *Detail of clothespress* (back)

grain of the brackets is horizontal, while that of the vertical block runs perpendicular to it. Humidity causes the greatest dimensional changes to occur tangentially, while the vertical axis remains relatively stable. Thus, the vertical block becomes a deterrent to the brackets' expansion and contraction. This often causes the brackets to split or their glue joints to break. The vertical block is also vulnerable to damage when the case was slid across floors. While much more time-consuming to make, the composite foot has its axial grain aligned parallel to that of the brackets, giving them a much more compatible ratio of expansion and contraction. The composite blocking is also much tougher in withstanding shocks and sliding movements. Additionally, the loss of the lower laminate (or even several) from the composite foot would not weaken it as drastically as it would the vertical block of the bracket foot.

Likewise, the full dust boards of Hay shop products align more compatibly with the graining of the tops, sides, and bottoms of the cases. This advantage is extremely important when compared with the more provincial nailed-in drawer supports, which often cause the sides of the case to split or push the drawer blades forward out of their dovetails or force the back boards out of the case. Found in provincial English furniture, such nailed-in systems were made throughout America in rural Pennsylvania, New England, New York, Virginia, Georgia, and North and South Carolina, and are also characteristic of such cities as Boston and Newport.

In addition, Hay shop cases frequently have paneled backs (figs. 4, 6). These, too, are the marks of high-quality London cabinetwork from the second quarter to the end of the eighteenth century. In Hay shop furniture, paneled backs are usually found in cases that open for use, like clothespresses or bookcases. The paneled back adds considerable strength to the case and provides a tighter seal against dust since its panels can expand and contract without gaping as is common with nailed backboards. Within the context of formal furniture, the use of paneled backs does not appear in other American schools until well into the federal period.

"Fashionable, Neat, and Good" was a phrase George Washington used when describing furniture from England, and the same could be said of Hay shop products. (Washington, incidentally, was also a patron of the Hay shop.) The clothespress illustrated (fig. 1), for example, shows the reserved style popular in eastern Virginia, but it also compares closely to an illustration in Chippendale's *Director*. Its features and execution align it with London's first level, and it gives strong evidence that "high style" furniture not necessarily be defined by opulence and lavish decoration. In the Age of Reason, in fact, the measure for first-level English cabinetry encompassed advanced technology, classical proportion, and high-quality workmanship. Objects could be "plain" and "neat" or highly decorative, but they had to incorporate these qualities of refinement and construction to be considered of the first rank.

While this press and desk and bookcase, along with others from Williamsburg, constitute the highest technical level achieved in colonial American cabinetmaking, they are provincial compared with the top London trade. Their composite feet, for instance, do not show the extraordinary attention to finish detail seen in London, and their drawers, backs, and other components are not made of quarter-sawn oak, which was standard in London, but of yellow pine, usually plane sawn (with the exception of the drawer sides that are often quarter sawn).

The Hay shop development of chairs and tables, however, was aggressive in style and reflected the rococo fashions then in vogue in Europe. The first Hay shop

Fig. 5. *Desk and bookcase*. American, Williamsburg, Va., about 1770. Attributed to the Anthony Hay shop. Walnut; yellow pine. H. 95½ in (242.6 cm), W. 38⅛ in (96.8 cm), D. 21⅜ in (54.3 cm) The Colonial Williamsburg Foundation, 1978-9.

Fig. 6. *Detail of desk and bookcase* (back of bookcase)

pieces in this new style, in fact, have rococo ornamentation applied to late baroque George II forms. The premier example of this period, and also the first in a series of four, is an elegantly carved armchair (cat. no. 9) that was made for the Williamsburg capitol building, probably for the royal governor in the General Court or Council Chamber.

James Wilson, a carver from London, is credited with its execution, which consists of lion's-paw feet, lion's-head arms, and rococo and acanthus foliage on the legs and arm supports. The superb carving of the lions' heads and the delicacy of the acanthus leaves attest to Wilson's London training, as does the ad he placed in the *Virginia Gazette* in 1755, which reads:

JAMES WILSON, Carver, from LONDON, MAKES all kinds of Ornaments in Stuco, human Figures and Flowers, &c. &c. Stuco Cornishes in Plaster, carved or plain, after the best Manner; likewise Stone finishing on Walls; he likewise carves in Wood, cuts Seals in Gold or Silver; and is to be spoke with at Mr. Anthony Hay's, Cabinet-Maker, in Williamsburg.[10]

Fig. 7. *Masonic master's chair.* American, Williamsburg, Va., about 1760. Attributed to the Anthony Hay shop. Mahogany. H. 52¼ in (132.7 cm), W. 29½ in (74.9 cm), D. 26¼ in (66.7 cm). Williamsburg Masonic Lodge Six.

Fig. 8. *Detail of chair* (back)

Equally imposing but of a quality well below that of Wilson's chair is the Masonic chair from Williamsburg's Lodge Six (fig. 7). Its carving closely relates to that of the capitol chair in the design of its arm supports, arms, and legs. Its smooth paw feet, however, a popular London alternative to hairy paws, represent the lone example of this type known in colonial American cabinetmaking.

The carving of the chair back (fig. 8), too, is exceptional. Usually, such a complex structure would have been built up in height with glued-on sections, but here the back was cut from a single piece of solid mahogany. Considering the importance that craft played in Masonic iconography and beliefs, the outstanding workmanship of this chair is in harmony and must have brought the maker great attention.

Related to these two chairs stylistically is a mahogany card table (cat. no. 15) whose construction is almost identical to earlier Hay shop examples.[11] Its knee carving (fig. 9), while much simplified, is a variation of the same formula used on the chair, including the asymmetrical fronds and tilted C scrolls. The entire leg design, in fact, resembles that on a London chair of the same period (cat. no. 16) and might provide clues to Hay's, or even Wilson's, training. The somewhat naïve knee carving on all three pieces, however, appears to be intentional since the card table and chairs all have finely carved volutes and feet, illustrating skill and design levels beyond that of the knee execution.

But the most expensive and complex chair produced in colonial America is the Masonic master's chair (cat. no. 10) signed by Benjamin Bucktrout, who arrived at the Hay shop in the early 1760s.[12] A journeyman from London, Bucktrout became master of the Hay shop in 1767, when Hay left the business after purchasing the Raleigh Tavern. Apparently, Hay leased the operation to Bucktrout and placed an ad in the *Virginia Gazette* turning over all his old customers and unfinished orders to Bucktrout. Hay's departure from cabinetmaking also illustrates the upward mobility of successful tradesmen; however, Hay was suffering from cancer of the lip and face, another strong reason for leaving the dusty atmosphere of the shop, and died two years later of this affliction.[13]

The Masonic master's chair was probably made shortly after Bucktrout assumed mastery of the shop, sometime between 1767 and 1770. Numerous details relate it to the capitol and Lodge Six chairs, most notably the carving of its arm supports. The Bucktrout chair, however, surpasses the others in its overall design. Typically, Masonic chairs followed standard armchair patterns but had lengthened stiles and legs. But here, Bucktrout scaled all of the elements of his design to match the chair's abnormally large size. The architectonic qualities of the back, including a bust of the English poet Matthew Prior, add to the chair's uniqueness, as does the incorporation of the dolphin legs (fig. 10). While the exact source for the bust remains unknown, the dolphin legs derive from plate XXI of Chippendale's *Director*. (For the English, the dolphin leg constituted the ultimate treatment, but no colonial American chairs—except Bucktrout's—are known.) Bucktrout's approach to using Chippendale's designs is especially worth noting. The dolphin and upper part of the leg

Fig. 9. *Detail of cat. no. 15* (knee of card table)

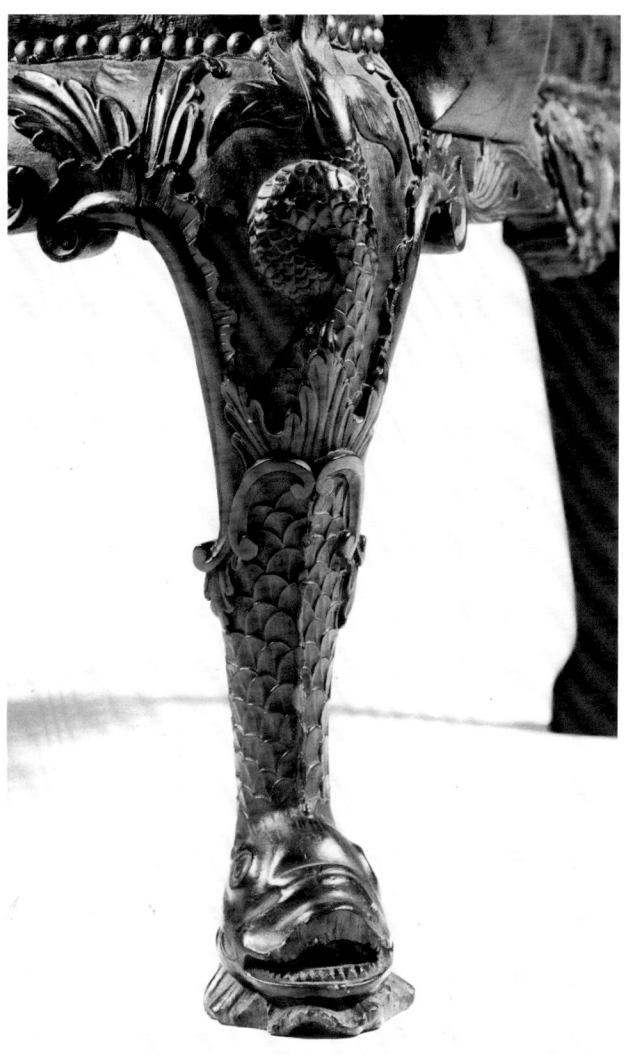

Fig. 10. *Detail of cat. no. 10* (leg of chair)

Fig. 11. *Masonic chair.* American, Williamsburg, Va., about 1775. Attributed to Edmund Dickinson and George Hamilton. Mahogany. H. 42½ in (108 cm), W. 27½ in (69.9 cm), D. 18⅞ in (47.9 cm). Fredericksburg Masonic Lodge Four.

were executed with a fidelity to Chippendale's illustration, but the flanged skirt with its acanthus carving is of Hay shop design. The hefty baroque quality of the skirt, however, also recalls the work of London's Giles Grendey and may be a clue to Bucktrout's background.[14] Bucktrout, for example, signed the chair in roman letters with individual hand stamps—a practice Grendey's apprentices used to mark their own works.

A fourth ceremonial chair (figs. 11, 12), also from the Hay shop and made with animal feet, has rich carving equal to that of Wilson's capitol chair, which was executed twenty years earlier. Commissioned by or for the Masonic Lodge Four in Fredericksburg, it and two other chairs in the lodge are attributed to Edmund Dickinson and George Hamilton (born 1749). In 1770, Dickinson took over the Hay shop as master, and Bucktrout left to establish his own business. Dickinson had been working in the Hay shop since the early 1760s; Hamilton, a Scottish carver and gilder, arrived in America in 1774 and became associated with the shop soon thereafter.[15]

Stylistically related to these ceremonial chairs are two elegant china tables (figs. 13, 14, cat. no. 17) that attest to the Hay shop's high level of stylistic awareness and excellent workmanship. The one dating to about 1760 and once owned by George Washington (figs. 13, 14) has carving that is closely related to that on the back of the Lodge Six Masonic chair. The second table (cat. no.

Fig. 12. *Detail of chair* (seat rail)

50 Wallace B. Gusler

Fig. 13. *China table*. American, Williamsburg, Va., about 1765. Attributed to the Anthony Hay shop. Mahogany; oak. H. 27 in (68.58 cm), W. 33 in (83.82 cm), D. 21¾ in (55.25 cm). Smithsonian Institution.

Fig. 14. *Detail of leg of china table* (fig. 13)

Fig. 15. *China table*. American, Williamsburg, Va., about 1765. Attributed to the Anthony Hay shop. Mahogany. H. 30⅛ in (76.5 cm), W. 36⅜ in (92.4 cm), D. 23¼ in (59.1 cm). The Colonial Williamsburg Foundation, G1980-95.

17), attributed to Edmund Dickinson, master, and George Hamilton, carver, was made around 1775 and shows an innovative use of the same set of designs utilized for the Washington table over a decade earlier.

Tables like these were sometimes made in pairs. The Dickinson example (cat. no. 17) has assembly marks indicating that it was one of two, and the probable mate to the Washington table—with a hexagonal fret gallery along the top—was illustrated in *Antiques* magazine in May 1932. This gallery has the same design as part of the skirt fret and suggests that the plain gallery on the Smithsonian example is an old replacement.

The Washington table's skirt, however, reverses the sequence of the fret seen on catalogue number 17, alternating bands of geometric patterns with foliate designs, and has closely related tapering legs with rococo carvings and *guttae* feet. In fact, the rosette, guilloche, and foliate designs of the Washington table's skirt resemble carvings at the bottom of the back of the Lodge Six chair. While the Washington skirt has an applied fret, that of catalogue number 17 was carved from a solid piece of mahogany, a technique seen in the front rail of the Lodge Four Masonic chair (fig. 12) where the carving was executed in solid wood. Likewise, the chair's gadroon and acanthus molding, like the rope and foliate molding of the table, was nailed and glued to the front of the rail. The attachment of such moldings to the face of the rail, rather than to its bottom as was more usual in American and English pieces, was a feature also used by the Peter Scott group that can be traced back to the 1730s in Williamsburg.

In addition, the tapered legs and *guttae* feet of the Hay shop tables are closely related to designs in Chippendale's *Director*. Numerous tapered legs in his book are shown ending in molded block feet or carved scroll block feet. Several *guttae* feet are shown as well, but terminate a straight rather than a tapered leg.

Such straight or marlborough legs, for example, can be found in a third china table (fig. 15) that probably dates closely to the Washington table. It is exceptional in having fretwork legs cut from solid mahogany rather than being formed by gluing separate pieces together. Descended in the family of William Byrd III of Westover Plantation in Virginia, it features a bird motif in the skirt (carved only on one side) that may well be an allusion to the family crest.

In addition to furniture making, a major part of the Hay shop's business was undertaking, which was a normal component of any cabinetmaking trade throughout Europe and America. All the masters of the shop made modest coffins as well as expensive ones, and the shop even participated in at least two state funerals for governors. Bucktrout and William Kennedy, for instance, made a very expensive coffin for Governor Fauquier that cost £32 in 1767 and was the single most expensive piece of documented furniture from the shop. (Regrettably, the price of the great chairs has not survived.) Bucktrout was also paid for the rental of his hearse and four days' attendance at the funeral of Lord Botetourt in 1770. While the details of the Bucktrout-Kennedy coffin are unknown, a description of Lord Botetourt's does exist. Made by Joshua Kendall, a carpenter brought to Williamsburg by the royal governor, it had two outer coffins made of black walnut and an inner lining of lead, covered with fine cloth and a mattress and pillow. The outer case, decorated with brass nails, was fitted with silver handles and escutcheons and a silver coffin plate all made by Williamsburg silversmith William Waddill.

Such a state funeral, in fact, involved the entire city in the procession, all arranged by rank. The coffin was carried by members of the governor's council, followed by the gentlemen of the town, professors of the college, tradesmen, and so on. Even the streets themselves were lined by the militia from James City and York counties. And while Bucktrout's and Hay's cabinet businesses have long since disappeared, Bucktrout's funeral service still survives by that name today and is the oldest in continuous operation in the country.

In addition to undertaking and cabinetmaking, the Hay shop provided many other services, several of which were essentially those of an upholsterer—setting up and taking down beds for seasonal changes, doing minor repairs to furniture, and repairing and making riding chairs, chariots, and coaches.

To carry out these numerous operations required a relatively large and skilled labor force. Information about workers in such a shop, however, is extremely sparse and often fragmentary. During the 1760s—the period with the most substantial documentation about the Hay shop—ten men are known to have worked there, including Hay; Bucktrout; Dickinson; a journeyman or apprentice named George Donald; another apprentice, David Davis; Wiltshire, a black cabinetmaker; and Anthony Hay's sons Thomas and Joe. Part or all of this decade Wilson may have been working in the shop as was William Kennedy, Bucktrout's partner after Hay's retirement. But these documented workers probably represent only a small percentage of those employed during the shop's quarter century of operation.[16]

Requests for journeymen, in fact, not solicitations for customers, dominate the extant *Virginia Gazette* ads written by Williamsburg cabinetmakers. Hay placed only a few notices, his earliest in 1751:

WANTED

A cabinet or Chair-maker, who understands his Business. May such man hear of Employment on applying to the printer.[17]

Bucktrout, Kennedy, and Dickinson also wrote ads appealing for journeymen as did a host of local cabinetmakers, including Matthew Moody, Richard Booker, James Honey, Richard Harrocks, James Spiers, and John Crump as well as the firm of Widdatch and Drummond. Only two masters in Williamsburg—John Ormeston and Peter Scott—did not advertise for journeymen, and Scott did not advertise at all, neither for workers nor for clients.

Apprentices, too, provided needed man power in Williamsburg and helped to disseminate information about style and technology. Unlike journeymen, apprentices were not usually documented in advertisements, making their whereabouts and duties very difficult to ascertain. In 1771, however, Bucktrout placed a newspaper ad for the return of his apprentice David Davis, who had run away.[18] He also took out another in 1775, seeking "one or two apprentices of bright Genius, and of good Dispositions."[19]

Black slaves were also important to Williamsburg's furniture industry. And like apprentices, black cabinetmakers are seldom mentioned in colonial records. Wiltshire, who was listed in Hay's shop during the 1750s and 1760s, was probably only one of several who worked there, and it is also known that Peter Scott owned at least two black cabinetmakers as well.[20]

Hay, freelance carvers, journeymen, apprentices, and slaves made their furniture, upholstery, riding chairs, and coffins in a two-room shop (measuring 24 × 32 ft and 12 × 24 ft) on Nicholson Street. The establishment also included a timber yard and another long, narrow building (6 × 20 ft), possibly a drying shed. (Hay's home stood adjacent to the shop.) By colonial standards when most cabinetmakers practiced their trade in the same house in which they lived, Hay's shop was big and even described, at the time of his estate sale in 1771, as "a large Cabinet Maker's Shop and Timber Yard."[21]

Also unusual in colonial America was the timber yard. Hay's would have most certainly had a pit saw, mahogany logs, and stacks of mahogany, walnut, cherry, yellow pine, cedar, ash, and oak timber. Moreover, taking into account the known production of the shop, the different sizes of lumber needed for each project, and the fact that five to seven years were required to dry the wood used for furniture, the yard must have contained several thousand board feet of timber.[22] In fact, Hay had such large quantities of fine lumber that he even laid mahogany boards as footings for the brick foundation of one of his buildings—wood that was still in almost pristine condition when the Hay shop and house were excavated in the 1960s!

Hay's business was highly successful, both for him and his successors. When he purchased the Raleigh Tavern for £4,000, he had no significant assets other than those he had gained through his twenty years as a Williamsburg cabinetmaker. And his reputation as a skilled craftsman continued long after he left the Nicholson Street address, since successive masters of the shop referred to it as having been "formerly kept by Mr. Hay."[23]

Hay's ownership of a major shop in the capital certainly brought him into contact with important political figures, and his purchase of the most elegant and popular tavern in the city continued these connections. His marriages are also indicators of his upward social mobility. His first wife was the daughter of a tanner, illustrating the frequent practice in colonial America of marriages within the craftsman community. However, his second wife, Elizabeth, was the daughter of William Davenport, Williamsburg's first town clerk. This appears to have been a step up socially and probably contributed to the success of his children.[24]

George and Charles, sons of this second marriage, studied law under Edmund Randolph and did well professionally. Charles Hay was admitted to the bar in 1786 and served as clerk of the House of Delegates until his death in 1795. George Hay gained national prominence as a United States attorney for Virginia and was appointed prosecutor of the Aaron Burr treason trial by President Thomas Jefferson. He also served as a representative from Henrico County in the House of Delegates (1816–17) and in 1825 was appointed a United States judge for eastern Virginia. In 1808 he married James Monroe's daughter Eliza.[25]

Hay's successor, Benjamin Bucktrout, also prospered. In addition to his cabinetwork, he made spinets and harpsichords, and repaired umbrellas, a specialty that required great dexterity and skill with a variety of materials. In the 1770s, he also operated a store and during the Revolution served as purveyor to Virginia's public hospitals[26] and invented a type of mill for the manufacture of gunpowder. In 1804, he was appointed town surveyor and, by the time of his death in 1813, personally owned eight and one-half lots in Williamsburg.[27] But sixty-four years later, it was for his accomplishments as a master craftsman that he was still known, when, in 1877, the Raleigh *Observer* hailed him as "an immemorial patronymic of cabinetmakers."[28]

The last master of the Hay shop was Edmund Dickinson, who ran it from 1770 until 1776. But with the outbreak of the American Revolution, he left Williamsburg as a captain in the Virginia regiment and later was promoted to major. While serving in that capacity, he was killed in the Battle of Monmouth on 28 June 1778.[29]

Ironically, Peter Scott's old shop (Scott died in 1775) was accidentally burned in 1775 by Virginia troops quartered there. And the remaining few years of the Hay shop's existence also supported the war effort, since it was utilized as an armory for the repair of muskets.[30] Thus, directly or indirectly, the American Revolution terminated the two Williamsburg cabinetshops that had been leaders in the colonial era.

By 1782 the Hay shop, which had produced some of the finest furniture in colonial America, lay in ruins, so deteriorated that it was not even included on a detailed map of the city. A victim of the damp climate and wet ravine in which it was constructed, the shop had crumbled into decay. But this same ravine, filled in by successive layers of silt, eventually became a time capsule —holding and preserving certain artifacts that became clues to the shop's activity when it was excavated.

But the Hay shop products that survived, especially the ceremonial chairs, help to form a picture of a cabinetmaking business that employed first-level London technology and excelled in the rococo style. In its use of lion's-head arm terminals, dolphin feet, and smooth-paw animal feet, the Hay shop distinguished itself from other schools of American cabinetmaking. For both the Virginia patron and the Williamsburg tradesman eschewed the provincial styles that flourished in Philadelphia, Boston, Newport, and Charleston, and instead looked directly toward London for their labor force and artistic and technological inspiration.

NOTES

1. Such a discussion is handicapped by the lack of published studies on English developments in style and technology during the first half of the eighteenth century. Therefore, I have pieced together this hierarchy from an examination of labeled or documented pieces of furniture that I have personally examined over the past fifteen years. Undoubtedly, many levels of production existed, but for this study a simple three-level approach is used. This is a general overview and a considerable overlapping of patronage at the various levels is evident.

2. Jane Carson, *We Were There: Descriptions of Williamsburg, 1699–1859* (Williamsburg and Charlottesville: The Colonial Williamsburg Foundation and The University Press of Virginia, 1965), p. 35.

3. Wallace B. Gusler, *Furniture of Williamsburg and Eastern Virginia, 1710–1790* (Richmond: Virginia Museum of Fine Arts, 1979), pp. 14–23, 68, 69.

4. York County Judgment Orders 1, 132, September 19, 1748, furnished by Harold B. Gill, Colonial Williamsburg Foundation, Department of Historic Trades.

5. Gusler, *Furniture of Williamsburg and Eastern Virginia*, p. 25.

6. Information about Spiers can be found in *Cabinetmaking in the Eighteenth Century*, an unpublished work by Mills Brown, Colonial Williamsburg Foundation, pp. 129–31.

7. A clothespress attributed to Grendey and on a frame with cabriole legs and paw feet is in the Colonial Williamsburg Foundation collection (acc. no. 1956-298). Another clothespress, structurally identical to the Colonial Williamsburg example and also on a frame, is in my personal collection. Both are stylistically and technically related to a labeled Grendey press at the Colonial Williamsburg Foundation (acc. no. 1935–344).

8. The term "composite foot" is one that I coined in my book *Furniture of Williamsburg and Eastern Virginia, 1710–1790*, p. 42.

9. A 1771 Chippendale clothespress made for Nostell Priory that I personally examined in 1982 also has composite feet. This press is illustrated in Christopher Gilbert, *The Life and Work of Thomas Chippendale* (London: Christie's, 1978), p. 134, fig. 239. Another composite foot by Ince and Mayhew is reproduced in Gusler, *Furniture of Williamsburg and Eastern Virginia*, p. 51, figs. 41, 41a.

10. *Virginia Gazette*, June 20, 1755, p. 3.

11. Gusler, *Furniture of Williamsburg and Eastern Virginia*, pp. 68–69.

12. Ibid., p. 63.

13. Ibid., pp. 61–62.

14. See, for example, the skirt of a labeled Grendey press in the Colonial Williamsburg Foundation collection (acc. no. 1935-344).

15. Gusler, *Furniture of Williamsburg and Eastern Virginia*, pp. 66–67.

16. Ibid., pp. 59–113.

17. *Virginia Gazette*, November 7, 1751, p. 2.

18. Ibid., April 4, 1771, p. 3.

19. Ibid., February 3, 1775, p. 4.

20. Ibid., January 17, 1771, p. 30. Apparently, when Hay rented his shop and timber yard to Bucktrout, Wiltshire was part of the lease. After Hay's death, his estate was offered for sale and listed first among the many slaves at the Raleigh Tavern was "a very good Cabinet Maker," undoubtedly Wiltshire.

21. Ibid.

22. Ibid., August 28, 1779, p. 3. Bucktrout documents the drying time when he makes reference to "a quantity of very fine board, one, two, and three inch mahogany plank, which has been cut this five years." John Scott, a cabinetmaker in Portsmouth, Virginia, also wrote, "I have . . . a quantity of good JAMAICA mahogany, fit for tables and desks, which has been by me 7 years."

23. Gusler, *Furniture of Williamsburg and Eastern Virginia*, p. 59.

24. Brown, *Cabinetmaking in the Eighteenth Century*, pp. 122–23.

25. William T. Hutchinson and William M. E. Rachal, eds., vol. 5 of *The Papers of James Madison* (Chicago: University of Chicago Press, 1967), pp. 73–75, 340.

26. Brown, *Cabinetmaking in the Eighteenth Century*, p. 143.

27. Ibid., p. 148.

28. Gusler, *Furniture of Williamsburg and Eastern Virginia*, p. 75.

29. Dickinson's death was reported in the London *Gentleman's Magazine*. See Gusler, *Furniture of Williamsburg and Eastern Virginia*, p. 67.

30. Ibid., p. 26.

Catalogue Objects

9. Armchair with reproduction footstool

Made for the capitol building in Williamsburg, this chair probably was used by the royal governor in the General Court or Council Chamber. The height of its seat and other proportions closely resemble the throne of England's King George III. Likewise, a speaker's chair dating to around 1730, also from the capitol but not illustrated here, is very similar in its architectural form to an eighteenth-century example used in the English House of Commons. Together, these Virginia ceremonial chairs closely parallel English prototypes and are extremely important in the study of early Williamsburg and American furniture.

But while the authorship of the speaker's chair remains unknown, the Hay shop armchair carving is attributed to James Wilson based on its design and detail. Two Hay shop Masonic chairs and a card table share related carving with the capitol chair. Wilson advertised from the Hay shop in 1755 that he was a carver from London, and his arrival in Williamsburg coincides with the rebuilding and subsequent refurnishing of the capitol building after its partial destruction by fire in 1747. This circumstance further strengthens the chair's attribution to Wilson, as does the extraordinary carving of the piece itself. The lion's-paw feet, rococo foliage of the knees, and lion's-head arm supports represent some of the best carving of their type in colonial America, and their exceptional quality attests to Wilson's London training.

9. *Armchair with reproduction footstool*
American, Williamsburg, Va., about 1755
Attributed to the Anthony Hay shop
Mahogany; beech and yellow pine repairs
H. 49 in (124.5 cm), W. 21½ in (54.6 cm), D. 24½ in (62.2 cm)
The Colonial Williamsburg Foundation, Williamsburg, Va., 1930-215

10. *Masonic master's chair*
American, Williamsburg, Va., about 1767
Stamped signature of Benjamin Bucktrout, Anthony Hay shop
Mahogany; black walnut
H. 65½ in (166.4 cm), W. 31¼ in (79.4 cm), D. 29½ in (74.9 cm)
The Colonial Williamsburg Foundation, Williamsburg, Va., 1983-317

11. *Masonic chair*
English, about 1730
Walnut
H. 67 in (170.2 cm), W. 26 in (66 cm), D. 21 in (53.3 cm)
Victoria and Albert Museum, London, W218-1923

10. Masonic master's chair
11. Masonic chair
12. Chair design

Exceptional design, condition, and the stamped signature of Benjamin Bucktrout place this chair in the highest ranks of eighteenth-century American furniture. While other colonial Masonic examples were made by "stretching" or lengthening domestic armchair forms (as can be seen in the English chair, cat. no. 11), Bucktrout developed the architectural back of this chair on a larger and more dynamic scale. Departing from the usual practice of modifying an existing set of patterns, he also enlarged his seat frame to match the back and incorporated dolphin legs from Thomas Chippendale's *Director* (cat. no. 12) into his design. The dolphin leg was the most advanced form in London, and this

58 Wallace B. Gusler

12. *Chair design*
Thomas Chippendale, *The Gentleman and Cabinet-Maker's Director* (London, 1762), plate XXI
Photograph courtesy of The Winterthur Library: Printed Book and Periodical Collection
Engraving on exhibit from the collection of John Hardy

example is the only known use of it in eighteenth-century America.

Bucktrout apprenticed in London (master unknown) and arrived at the Hay shop as a journeyman in the mid-1760s. In 1767, he took over Hay's business, leasing the shop and Wiltshire, Hay's black cabinetmaker. Apparently, Edmund Dickinson and George Donald (apprentices or journeymen) also came with the shop and timber yard. In 1768, Bucktrout entered into partnership with William Kennedy. The partnership, however, was short-lived and little is known about Kennedy, but their most expensive documented commission was a coffin for Governor Fauquier that cost £32. The price of Bucktrout's chair remains unknown, but it probably exceeded that of the coffin and was undoubtedly the most expensive ceremonial chair produced in colonial America.

13. *Clothespress*
American, Williamsburg, Va., about 1770
Attributed to the Anthony Hay shop
Walnut; yellow pine
H. 56⅝ in (143.8 cm), W. 49½ in (125.7 cm), D. 23 in (58.4 cm)
The Colonial Williamsburg Foundation, Williamsburg, Va., 1950-351

13. Clothespress
14. Clothespress design

Representative of a large percentage of eighteenth-century Virginia case furniture, this clothespress combines a restrained style with high-quality construction. "Neat and plain" is a phrase often encountered in Virginian orders for English furniture, and this piece undoubtedly represents that prevailing fashion. But while third- to fifth-generation wealthy Virginians preferred conservative styles, they spared no expense for public ceremony, as can be seen in the Bucktrout Masonic master's chair (cat. no. 10). And they also outfitted some of their plantation houses with such elaborate furnishings as the china table shown here (cat. no. 17).

Often, the plain and neat style Chippendale illustrated and made is overlooked in favor of his more well-known and elaborate designs. The press here, however, which is extremely close to plate CXXVI in his *Director* (cat. no. 14), exemplifies the plain style that dominated Williamsburg cabinet production during the 1760s and 1770s. Also characteristic of Hay shop pieces is its excellent workmanship. The press's interior base is constructed with saw cuts that allow the case to expand and contract in response to the relative humidity. Likewise, the feet are blocked in plywood fashion, and the back is paneled—both features found in Chippendale's documented works. The use of this first-level technology in Williamsburg is all the more important when compared with the cheaper and more provincial techniques found in Philadelphia, Boston, Newport, and Charleston. Thus, unlike Williamsburg, these major urban centers of American furniture are more closely allied with the lower levels of English production.

14. *Clothespress design*
Thomas Chippendale, *The Gentleman and Cabinet-Maker's Director* (London, 1762), plate CXXVI
Photograph courtesy of The Winterthur Library: Printed Book and Periodical Collection
Engraving on exhibit from the collection of John Hardy

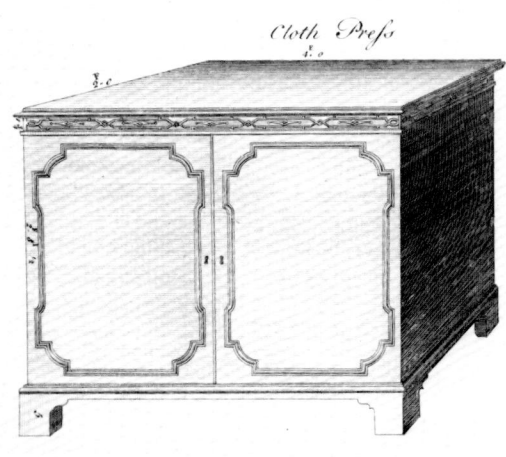

15. *Card table*
American, Williamsburg, Va., about 1760
Attributed to the Anthony Hay shop
Mahogany; yellow pine
H. 27⅝ in (70.2 cm), W. 33⅜ in (84.8 cm), D. (closed) 16½ in (41.9 cm), D. (open) 33 in (83.8 cm)
The Colonial Williamsburg Foundation, Williamsburg, Va., 1932-12

15. Card table

The dynamic quality of the cabriole legs, which appear to explode from the knee volutes downward to the large ball-and-claw feet, distinguishes this piece as the finest card table from the Hay shop. The sensuous curve of its leg is also seen in the capitol armchair (cat. no. 9) and an earlier tea table (not illustrated) from Williamsburg. The structure of its skirt, too, embodies a characteristic Hay shop feature: the horizontal grain of the mahogany continues to both back corners, allowing the swing leg to be constructed with an offset that enables it to neatly slide behind the skirt, thereby concealing the vertical joint. Earlier card tables with pad feet and straight legs also utilize this feature, which relates to "Chinese" joinery practices seen in Williamsburg tables of the 1720s and 1730s. The legs of this table, however, closely resemble those of a London chair (cat. no. 16) with similar knee volutes and stylized foliage. These design elements may have been introduced to Williamsburg by the London carver James Wilson (who arrived there in 1755), a supposition borne out by the likeness of the table's carving to that of the capitol chair (cat. no. 9). But regardless of who originated such London practices in Williamsburg, the card table is another important example of a shop tradition established early and ultimately transformed by a series of English influences over a prolonged period of time.

Wallace B. Gusler

16. *Armchair*
English, London, about 1730
Walnut and walnut veneer; beech
H. 39½ in (100.3 cm), W. 27 in (68.6 cm), D. 22¾ in (57.8 cm)
The Colonial Williamsburg Foundation, Williamsburg, Va., 1963-187

16. Armchair

Representative of a large number of English chairs and tables, the legs of this armchair possess a remarkable similarity to an Anthony Hay card table made around 1760 (cat. no. 15). The chair's strongly designed knee volutes frame naïve foliage that compares well with those of the Hay shop table. The flat and simplistic carving of the knees contrasts dramatically with the highly developed carving of the ball-and-claw feet and knee volutes, leaving the conclusion that the naïve knee foliage was deliberate.

As suggested in the essay, a possible source for this hybridized style in Williamsburg was the arrival there of James Wilson, a London-trained carver, in 1755. As of this writing, no Williamsburg examples utilizing the exceptionally beautiful arms seen on the London chair have been found. In consideration of this fact, we may conclude that a carver and not a chairmaker was responsible for introducing this style in Williamsburg. It is also extremely important to remember the wide specialization within London cabinetmaking when studying the dissemination of style and technology via tradesmen. Rather than expecting dramatic holistic transfers from England to America, bits and pieces from all levels of the English trade arrived here over extended periods of time. Thus, if examined on their own merits, American cabinetmaking schools both north and south are not English transplants but are distinct unto themselves—unique regional amalgams formed by various tradesmen, patrons, and local economies, both European and American.

17. *China table*
American, Williamsburg, Va., about 1775
Attributed to the Anthony Hay shop
Edmund Dickinson, master; George Hamilton, carver
Mahogany
H. 31½ in (80 cm), W. 36 in (91.4 cm), D. 22¼ in (56.5 cm)
Private collection

17. China table

China tables with pierced galleries around the tops became popular in the mid-eighteenth century and were used both for tea services and to display sets of fine china. They appear to have been the rococo version of an earlier rectangular tea table with applied moldings that had been common since the beginning of the century. Few true china tables, however, were produced in America, and the only fully developed pierced examples known are from the Hay shop.

This elegant china table, probably one of a pair, represents the high point of American rococo furniture. Its excellent overall design unites a serpentine top and frame with tapered square legs. This combination of the serpentine with the geometric, in fact, echoes throughout the piece: the undulating skirt is checked at the corners by square geometric blocks, while its surface is covered with highly controlled hexagonal frets (in the concave sections) and swirling foliate designs in the convex center. Likewise, the geometric legs end with architectonic *guttae* feet, but are energetically embellished with asymmetrical rococo foliage. The result is a skillful blending of two opposing forces: the exuberance of the late French rococo and the more classical restraint of eighteenth-century English traditions.

Such a command of style and technique is attributed to Edmund Dickinson, master, and George Hamilton,

64 Wallace B. Gusler

carver, the latter a Scotsman who arrived in Williamsburg in July 1774. The origin of their basic design, however, can be traced back to the 1760s, if not earlier, in the Hay shop's history. The small carved molding at the division between the solid skirt and the cut-through carving were nailed and glued to the flat face of the skirt. This structure closely parallels the Lodge Four Masonic chair (fig. 12, p. 50), which has a solid front rail and carved gadroon molding applied to its front. This technique of attaching moldings to the face of the rail, rather than to its bottom, was also unusual at the time but is a strong Williamsburg school feature that originated in the shop of Peter Scott and dates to the early 1730s.

The closest relative to the Dickinson-Hamilton china table, in fact, is one in the Smithsonian Institution that dates to the 1760s and was once owned by George Washington (fig. 13, p. 51). But the Washington table, in contrast, has a straight-sided rectangular skirt with applied carved fretwork. Like the Dickinson-Hamilton table, it also features *guttae* feet and square tapered legs with carved rococo details. Its carving, however, is more crudely executed than the Dickinson-Hamilton table and more closely related to earlier Hay shop examples from the 1750s and 1760s.

A third china table (fig. 15, p. 51), the only Hay shop example with a known provenance, was made around 1770 and descended through the Lewis-Byrd families of eastern Virginia. Its fretwork and legs were cut from solid pieces of mahogany, an unusual practice at the time. However, this solid-cut mahogany approach is seen in other Hay shop products: in the skirt of the Dickinson-Hamilton table, for instance, or in certain chairs from the shop (fig. 12).

Barbara McLean Ward

The Edwards Family and the Silversmithing Trade in Boston, 1692–1762

During the first years of the eighteenth century, the city of Boston was the largest and most important of New England's ports. The main port of entry for immigrants to the region, its life was invigorated by a constant influx of newly arrived settlers. Its merchants were the driving force behind New England's economy, trading its natural resources of lumber and fish for the riches of England and Europe. Hundreds of craftsmen, with occupations nearly as specialized and varied as could be found in the city of London, produced objects of all descriptions. The cosmopolitan flavor of the port, and the vast array of goods from throughout the world that could be purchased in its shops, amazed visitors.[1]

This Boston was a city caught between two worlds: between the mother country and the emerging colonial culture, between traditional economic relationships and the new relationships that would characterize the development of capitalism in the modern world. The lives of three artisans—John Edwards (1671–1746) and his sons Thomas (1702–55) and Samuel (1705–62)—exemplify the effect of these forces on the American craftsman. The response of the Edwardses to the market pressures within their environment provides evidence of how the traditional artisan came to think and act like an entrepreneur. The objects they made demonstrate the influence of foreign design ideas and the way in which these were manipulated and transformed into distinctively colonial material expressions.

The first English settlers to arrive in Boston came with an extensive array of household goods. Warned of the scarcity of certain commodities, they brought along useful tools such as steel-headed axes for felling trees and iron farm implements for working their newly cleared lands. Textiles, too, would be unavailable in the new land, and fine linens as well as utilitarian stuff for everyday use formed a large portion of their baggage. Evidence suggests that, in addition to necessities, the settlers brought with them some of the most precious reminders of their lives in England. Silver cups and finely embroidered bed hangings would have little utilitarian significance, but they formed the fabric of a social order that the settlers sought to transport to the New World. Historians have discussed the extent to which English village customs and institutions formed the basis for the government of New England towns.[2] The social order of established hierarchy and family interdependence had material manifestations as well. While the political and legal institutions of the mother country formed the intellectual baggage of the colonists, the objects they transported with them were, in a very tangible way, the baggage of a life-style they had left behind.

Puritan settlers wanted to purify rather than entirely reject the way of life they had previously known. They hoped to re-create all the advantages of their former lives, and they were acutely aware of the need to establish stable social relationships. The treasured family heirlooms and fashionable silver and textiles that the wealthiest settlers brought with them marked their status as leaders of the new society. Many of their silver objects would be among the most elaborate ones owned in America throughout the colonial period. A few, such as the extensive array of wares brought to the colony by Elizabeth Glover and her husband the Reverend Jose Glover in 1638 or Governor Winthrop's well-known silver steeple cup, are known either because they are still extant or from documentary evidence. Elizabeth Glover had "a faire and full cubbard of plate . . . as might ordinarily be seen in most Gentlemens houses in England."³ The collection, which had a value in excess of £200, included a ewer and basin, spoons, dishes, cups, "bere boules," tankards, porringers, plates, a "great siluer trunke with 4 knop to sta[n]d on the table and with suger," and a chafing dish. Elizabeth Glover displayed her silver as a public expression of the high social status of the clergy; Winthrop presented his cup to the First Church in Boston as a public gesture of his magnanimity. These items were monumental even by English standards; colonists would find it difficult to obtain anything like them in silver again until the end of the seventeenth century. Even then, the lack of specie (gold or silver coin) that characterized colonial economics would effectively limit the size of collections until after the attainment of independence.

Probate records indicate that most settlers owned no silver (or plate, as silver objects were known) at all. Among the 5 to 10 percent who did, the most common items owned during the early years of settlement were spoons, small pieces of jewelry such as rings, and tankards, beakers, dram cups, and porringers.⁴ These forms, introduced early in the history of colonial settlement, were the ones emigrants chose to bring with them from the vast array of objects available. In this way, the individuals who established the colonial culture also determined, to a significant degree, the decorative art forms that this culture would borrow from the parent culture. As has been observed in work on other colonial cultures, the first forms to take root do so firmly, and then undergo stylistic transformations that remain independent from stylistic developments in the parent culture.⁵ Throughout most of the seventeenth century, the inhabitants of the Bay Colony were content to exist independently and to create their own vision of a godly commonwealth. The objects they made continued to be based on the few forms they had brought with them and showed little influence from new stylistic trends in the mother country.

With the restoration of Charles II to the monarchy in 1660, the Puritan experiment in the Bay Colony came under new scrutiny. It was attacked for its persecution of non-Puritans and its blatant disregard for British sovereignty. In 1684 Charles's brother and successor, James II, responded to these criticisms by revoking the charter. Shortly thereafter (1686) he established the Dominion of New England, a consolidation of the New England colonies and New York, under a royal governor,

Sir Edmund Andros. Andros, whose policies infuriated Boston's leading citizens, was deposed in 1689 after rumors of the overthrow of James II and installation of William and Mary as the new monarchs reached Boston.

William and Mary, however, did not find the independent spirit of Massachusetts any more attractive than had Charles II or James II. Although they abolished the Dominion, they refused to reinstate the old charter, replacing it with a new royal charter in 1692. The Bay Colony no longer enjoyed the virtual autonomy that had marked the old charter government, but the royal governor, Sir William Phips, was a native New Englander, and many of the old guard maintained their positions of influence.⁶

Nonetheless, attitudes began to change as Puritan leaders looked for recognition from a new political elite. Even descendants of old Puritan families now sought to own stylish objects that would establish their affinity with the social and cultural institutions of the mother country. Anxious to prove their sophistication and erudition in matters of science and philosophy as well as matters of taste, Americans like Cotton Mather and his father Increase, ministers of the Puritan Old North Church in Boston, corresponded with the best scientific minds in England, and Cotton was elected a fellow of the Royal Society.⁷ The old Puritan elite was forced to compete with the new royal officials, men and women with sophisticated tastes and a desire to replicate an English style of life in their new setting, who had come to the colony to enforce the new royal charter. Artisans in the luxury trades benefited from the influence of this new clientele. The names of immigrant wigmakers, goldsmiths, clockmakers, and cabinetmakers began to appear in official records, indicating that the new political climate in Massachusetts made it a desirable destination for men in these trades.

When John Edwards set up shop with his partner John Allen in a tenement near Boston's town dock about 1695, the influence of this new clientele was just beginning to be felt, and Boston was enjoying a period of prosperity. Two of the twenty-seven men who worked as goldsmiths in Boston between 1680 and 1700, Edwards and Allen had the advantage of close ties to the community and good training with one of the town's leading practitioners of the craft.

John Allen, son of the Reverend James Allen, teacher of Boston's First Church, was a wealthy young man with ample funds to finance a large-scale goldsmithing operation. No doubt Edwards benefited from this relationship and from the local connections it established for him. Allen soon became Edwards's brother-in-law, marrying his sister Elizabeth in 1697. The two remained partners until at least 1700. Allen, a man of landed wealth, never diligently pursued his craft.[8]

Edwards, on the other hand, exemplified the ambitious artisan. One of the thousands of immigrants who swelled Boston's population in the final years of the seventeenth century, John arrived with his father, John, a surgeon, of Lymehouse, Stepney, Middlesex, England; his mother, Elizabeth (Walker) Edwards; and his two sisters Elizabeth and Anne, sometime between 1679 and 1685. All available evidence suggests that he was apprenticed to Jeremiah Dummer about 1685. His father went to sea as a ship's surgeon in 1689 and died shortly thereafter, probably in England. John was lucky to have secured a favorable apprenticeship. Perhaps his uncle, Benjamin Walker, a pewterer by trade, had helped in the selection of a trade for John. Young Edwards would have achieved his freedom about 1692, after which he probably worked as a journeyman for two or three years. In 1694 he married Sybil Newman, daughter of the Wenham minister Antipas Newman. Soon afterward he began practicing his trade in partnership with John Allen.[9]

Edwards differed significantly from his fellow silversmiths, including his early partner, in that he never invested heavily in land but plowed his resources back into his business. His contemporaries admired his diligence: he was elected to the most prestigious town offices —selectman and tax assessor. We have only the slightest hint that, in retirement, he began investing in shipping.[10] His trade was the focus of his life, and he was successful at it. He attracted clients from all over New England, and although his work attests to his awareness of new fashions as well as to his own creativity as an artisan, his silver objects are generally plain and often exceedingly traditional. They thus accurately reflect the work that dominated the craft in Boston between 1690 and 1740.

At the turn of the century, silversmiths in Boston's most productive shops were making every effort to add information on the latest London fashions to their repertoire of traditional forms. They received information about new styles in the same way that other artisans did—through immigrant artisans, design books, and imported objects. The question of design influence on American craftsmen is complex. The resolution of design problems involved a subtle interaction between artisans and between artisans and clients, and the constant challenge afforded by the confrontation of both groups with new objects.

Immigrant journeymen were perhaps the most important source of information on new styles for these leading firms. Although it is seldom possible to assess their impact from objects they themselves marked, material evidence does remain of their intimate knowledge of the latest styles, latest techniques, and newest design vocabulary of the British Isles. Their influence resulted in constant stylistic innovation and the use of a wide variety of designs in small ornamental parts, such as the castings used for thumbpieces and handle tips of tankards. The products of the largest shops display a diversity that suggests native masters and immigrant journeymen learned from each other as they worked side by side.

The earliest Boston goldsmith known to have been trained on the Continent was William Rouse, who was described as "a Dutchman" from Wesel in Germany.[11] Of all the objects made by immigrant goldsmiths in Boston between 1690 and 1730, Rouse's silver is the most distinctive and shows Continental influence in its engraved decoration. Unfortunately, only about a dozen objects by Rouse are known, and only four have the exquisite floral engraving that appears to have been Rouse's trademark.[12]

An immigrant who may have been responsible for introducing Germanic elements into Boston silverwork was Henry Hurst, a Swede who came to Boston after serving for a time as a journeyman in London. Hurst's ability as an embosser may account for the unexpected sugar boxes that emerged from the shop of Edward Winslow at this time. One of Hurst's two surviving tankards shows him to have been an innovator in the development of handle-tip designs in the Scandinavian fashion for use on traditional New England tankards.[13]

Among the goldsmiths trained in England whose work can be identified, few produced objects that can be called outstanding or even distinctively English. David Jesse and Richard Conyers, both of whom were trained in London and came to Boston about 1698, made objects that conformed to the work of native silversmiths of the same period. None of their work is characterized by elaborate chasing or engraving, although both made objects with uncomplicated cut-card ornament and simple gadrooning. They may have been responsible for introducing the fashion for these ornaments to Boston.[14]

Edward Webb (if attribution to him of the mark EW in a rectangle is correct) was the most prolific of the immigrant goldsmiths to enter Boston in the late seventeenth and early eighteenth centuries. He had served his apprenticeship with William Denny of London and had become a freeman of the Goldsmiths' Company in 1697. Royal commissions were often filled in Denny's prominent workshop, and Webb thus would have been familiar with the most sophisticated English silverwork of his day when he arrived in Boston about 1706. Denny, who fashioned a number of monteiths, made at least one with cast ornament similar to that found on the monteith made in the Boston shop of John Coney.[15] In spite of Webb's training, however, most of the surviving objects made by him are plain, with no engraving other than block initials or simple script and no embossing or elaborate cast and applied ornament.

Most of the goldsmiths who immigrated to America, whatever their country of birth, are known to have resided in England for at least a brief period prior to embarking for the colonies.[16] Several other English, Irish, and Huguenot goldsmiths came to Boston after 1700, but little is known about most of them. A few with French names, among them Francis Légaré, René Grignon, Moses Prevereau, Peter Boutet, and James Boyer, appear in the records, but none left any silver from which we can judge the nature of their work.[17] Abraham Barnes, Daniel Gibbs, and William Caddow from Ireland, and Thomas MacCollough from Ireland or Scotland, may have introduced additional design ideas from their native lands to the shops in which they worked as journeymen.[18] The presence of these immigrant craftsmen in Boston meant that there was direct interaction between native-born and native-trained craftsmen and men who had received their training abroad.

John Edwards's work reveals little in the way of influence from these and other foreign craftsmen. Most of the objects he produced were traditional in their form and ornament. He continued to make plain church beakers and standing cups, as well as caudle cups in the manner of John Hull and Robert Sanderson, Jeremiah Dummer, and John Coney until his death in 1746. Only a few of his works, such as a standing salt of about 1700 (cat. no. 21), indicate an awareness of the early baroque

Fig. 1. *Two-handled covered cup*. American, Boston, Mass., about 1701. John Coney, born Boston (1656–1722). Silver. H. 10 in (25.4 cm), Diam. (lip) 7 in (17.8 cm). Courtesy of the President and Fellows of Harvard College, Cambridge, Mass., gift of the Honorable William Stoughton, 1701.

style. Similar in form to English salts of a decade earlier (cat. no. 22), it is ornamented with spiral gadrooning at the foot and below the bowl in the latest fashion. The Allen and Edwards salt is very close in design to salts by fellow Bostonians Jeremiah Dummer and Edward Winslow, all of which may have been inspired by the same imported example.[19]

Evidence of artistic interchanges is often subtle. It is reflected more in the variety of objects produced by one shop than in single masterpieces. Objects bearing John Coney's mark, for instance, are uneven in technical proficiency and quality of design. The most skillfully wrought objects, such as the chocolate pot of about 1702 (cat. no. 19), are often those that are nearly exact copies of English prototypes and therefore were most likely influenced by the work of immigrant journeymen or imported examples (cat. no. 20). Other objects, like the two-handled covered cup of the previous year (fig. 1), show Coney's full assimilation of the details of the prevailing style and his recombination of these elements into a distinctively colonial expression.

These new design ideas were assimilated into the overall decorative vocabulary of other goldsmiths such as John Edwards, with influences sometimes being filtered through the work of other local artisans. The small spout cup made by John Edwards (cat. no. 18) shows a strong influence from the Coney chocolate pot (cat. no. 19). Although Edwards's inversion of the traditional spout cup form, in which the body of the pot is pear shaped and only slightly tapered, undoubtedly owes much to Coney's chocolate pot, Edwards's example retains the bulk of the colonial spout cup form rather than giving itself over to the strongly tapered grace of an English chocolate pot (see cat. no. 20).

In spite of this renewed openness to English designs, the majority of silver objects followed seventeenth-century precepts in their form. Most were unadorned. Silver metal was less available than in England, and the variety of forms adopted and replicated by colonial silversmiths was necessarily circumscribed. Although we find a small number of exceptional objects that reflect the latest English trends, the forms that found the most favor and that were made consistently from the early years of American production through the early years of the nineteenth century were among those that had been introduced in the seventeenth century—tankards, beakers, and porringers. These three forms show minimal response to English and Continental stylistic changes, but rather follow an independent pattern of formal and decorative development. They played a key role in the development of a conscious material identity and a local community aesthetic. Through these artifacts, colonists developed their own material traditions, which set them apart from the parent culture.

The brief period of prosperity and creative competition in Boston at the beginning of the eighteenth century was followed by fifty years of conservatism in design. One explanation for the New Englander's appreciation of traditional forms may be that the economic stagnation of the 1730s and 1740s increasingly isolated the port from information about new modes and styles. Inflation and recession following the resolution of Queen Anne's War in 1714 slowed economic growth in Boston, and by the 1730s and 1740s many artisans were unable to make more than a subsistence wage. As opportunities for immigrant craftsmen dwindled, the transmission of new styles from England to Boston slowed. Fewer craftsmen emigrated from the British Isles, and fewer of the stylish English gentlemen who demanded their services were present in Boston. Inflation made plate prohibitively expensive for all but the wealthiest members of the community, and so most people could not afford to replace their old plate with objects in the latest fashion. Furniture styles became static as well; there was little innovation in design and ornamentation from the late 1730s to the 1780s.[20] Twenty years of economic stagnation firmly entrenched familiar forms in the popular consciousness, and surviving objects indicate that most patrons preferred to own traditional objects that would not look outdated within a few years and that had certain shared connotations of social standing and cultural continuity.

The silver objects most representative of this increasing conservatism are tankards and porringers, for they clearly reveal the shift from an emphasis on style consciousness to an emphasis on traditional, and locally valued, forms. Tankards and porringers went out of favor in England in the early eighteenth century, and although early Boston examples of these forms show reliance on British models, tankards and porringers continued to be popular in New England long after English artisans had abandoned them. Boston designs developed beyond English precedents between 1710 and 1740, but then remained static until the 1790s.

Tankards are particularly illustrative of this point. The typical tankard of the late seventeenth and early eighteenth centuries, with its broad proportions and flat cover (fig. 2), was superseded by two competing forms during the first two decades of the eighteenth century: (1) the straight-sided tankard with domed cover (cat. no. 23) and (2) the tapered tankard divided by a molded midband and with a high-domed cover and finial. The second variation, the tapered body with midband, completely eclipsed the straight-sided form by the late 1730s, becoming the standard for the rest of the century. Cast ornaments for tankards and porringers exhibit a large number of variations before 1720, but after that date only a very limited number of designs persisted.

The quality of Edwards's silver shows that he had an ability to expand on the design ideas to which he was exposed. Although his work was essentially conservative, he developed his own sources for inspiration rather than relying solely on European stylistic innovations. Hence, although his mugs and tankards were exceedingly traditional in form, Edwards would make his mark in the trade as perhaps the most talented of Boston's

Fig. 2. *Tankard*. American, Boston, Mass., about 1695. Edward Winslow (1669–1753). Silver. H. 7⅜ in (18.54 cm). Essex Institute, Salem, Mass., 133.988.

mold designers in the second and third decades of the eighteenth century.

Close examination of two objects made by Edwards demonstrates this point. The first object, a tankard made for a member of the Clark family (cat. no. 23) about 1720, is straight sided and has a slightly domed top, scroll thumbpiece, and cast lion's-head terminal. The domed cover probably first appeared in the work of John Coney, who fashioned a tankard with a lavishly gadrooned and nearly domed cover for John Foster about 1705, not unlike an English tankard by Charles Overing of London dated 1697–98 (cat no. 24).[21] The fashion for a fully rounded cover was established in England by this time, but only Edwards, John Dixwell, Moody Russell, and Samuel Vernon have left behind American examples of the form.[22] Although related examples by John Coney and Edward Winslow are also known, and Edwards fashioned a number of domestic and church tankards with domed covers, such tankards are unusual in early American silver. Even when others of his generation began to produce taller tankards with midbands and stepped-dome covers, Edwards continued to favor this more traditional form. Instead of altering the form significantly, he chose instead to make minor additions to it. For this tankard he produced a fine casting of a lion's head to decorate the handle tip. The second object is a small mug with a similar cast terminal made for a member of the Russell family.[23] The mug itself is a purely traditional form, low and wide, with a midband of complex profile. The cast terminal, however, demonstrates Edwards's desire to create distinctive decorations for the objects he produced, without interfering with the generally accepted forms. Although it is not known who owned this mug, "S Russell," the name inscribed on the handle, may well refer to the young woman whose visage adorns the handle tip as a casting of a woman's head. No other Boston silversmith used either a lion's head or a woman's head as terminal designs, and it therefore appears that these castings were a hallmark of Edwards's work. Edwards and Allen may have made the earliest datable tankard with a cherub's-head handle tip, and Edwards may also have been the silversmith who introduced the satyr's-head ornament that became so popular in Boston.[24]

Both the tankard and the mug demonstrate the extent to which Boston craftsmen manipulated traditional forms to produce distinctively local expressions. As the new designs in turn became traditional rather than reflective of popular stylistic trends, goldsmiths responded to the shift in the status of these forms by making patterns for the cast ornaments, so that they could be produced in quantity. Standardized cast parts, such as handles and thumbpieces, could be readily fitted to objects made by jobbers working outside the master's shop and producing "tankard bodies" or "can bodies" to the exact specifications of the master artisan.[25] When cast parts were especially important, as in the making of porringers, casting patterns for handles could remain useful for twenty or thirty years. Initially inspired by familiar English geometric porringer-handle designs (cat. no. 30), American silversmiths began to manipulate the porringer form at the same time that the tankard form was changing: the first two decades of the eighteenth century. A distinctive handle shape, now referred to as the "keyhole" handle, was introduced before 1725 and rapidly replaced all other designs. This new handle form became so popular that it persisted until the eve of the American Revolution. John Edwards and both of his sons, Samuel and Thomas, produced examples (see cat. no. 29), as did his grandson Joseph (1737–83).

The work of Thomas and Samuel Edwards is, like the work of their father, essentially conservative in its design but sometimes, particularly toward the end of their careers, shows a renewal of interest in London styles among Boston's elite. In 1750, the Crown repaid the Massachusetts government for its contribution to the war effort against the French. This influx of specie made it possible for the colony to revalue its currency and put an end to spiraling inflation.[26] Imported silver objects became more affordable, and we begin to see a gradual accumulation of large collections of plate by the wealthiest merchants. Forms such as coffeepots and salvers were made in direct response to stylistic developments in England and demonstrate that Americans, while developing their own formal and ornamental traditions, were still interested in selectively adopting stylistic trends from the mother country.

From documentary evidence, we know that a few objects appeared in Boston that would have influenced local taste. In 1747, a brief note in the diary of Benjamin Walker, a Boston shopkeeper, hints at the impact a rare display of imported plate may have had on the most fashion-conscious inhabitants:

Att mr. Hurds Gold Smith in Cornhill Street in Boston I see ye finest Sight of Silver plate belonging To Gouernour Charles Knowles of Lewisburg on Cape Briton some part of his Sideboard, such fine Crafte work & Variety I can't Enumerate & Its's sd he has much more.[27]

Walker lived next door to the shop of Thomas Edwards at this time and was therefore no stranger to the variety of the goldsmith's art as practiced in Boston. Yet he was dazzled by the display of imported wares that he saw at Hurd's shop. Governor Knowles had been involved in impressing Boston seamen into the royal navy for several years and was, in October of 1747, on the verge of touching off a major riot.[28] Knowing that he was far from popular with the local citizenry, he may have felt it best to keep his silver under the watchful eye of a respected silversmith. Perhaps it was from Knowles's silver that Hurd first learned of the rococo forms and engraving style that he used on some of the objects he made during the 1750s. Samuel and Thomas Edwards, too, would have been influenced by this unprecedented public display of gold and silver.

Several extant objects give us more definite clues as to the impact of new design ideas on Boston craftsmen at midcentury. About 1740, Thomas Hancock, a prominent Boston merchant, imported a large two-handled covered cup by George Wickes of London. This cup was to provide the model for significant presentation pieces, such as the two-handled covered cup made by Jacob Hurd for presentation to Commodore Edward Tyng (fig. 3) in 1744. This same cup provided silversmiths and engravers with new information on the latest engraving styles. Printed bookplates and books such as John Guillim's *Display of Heraldry* also continued to be sources of inspiration for colonial artisans.[29] Other significant forms introduced to Boston at this time were salvers with rococo borders, sauceboats with shell feet, and coffeepots with fluted spouts. A coffeepot made by William Shaw and William Priest of London, dated 1751–52 and owned by Peter Faneuil (cat. no. 28), may have inspired Edwards's example of a few years later (cat. no. 27). Edwards's coffeepot is shorter and less assured in its design, but Edwards adapted the rococo spout well while choosing a lower-domed cover more in keeping with the squat form of the pot. Thomas and Samuel Edwards also made other objects that show rococo influence. Both made rococo-style teapots of the inverted pear shape, and some of their objects bear rococo-style engraving.[30]

Samuel and Thomas Edwards were among the fifty-five goldsmiths who began working in Boston between the years 1700 and 1730. As in the seventeenth century, the craft was dominated by a small number of artisans who operated large retail shops in addition to their production workshops. Six men—Jacob Hurd, John Burt, William Cowell, John Dixwell, Thomas Edwards, and Samuel Edwards—were responsible for more than 60 percent of the objects that survive. Approximately 20 percent of these second-generation goldsmiths were dependent journeymen during their careers in Boston.[31]

The work of Thomas and Samuel Edwards demonstrates that both brothers used the skills of these dependent artisans regularly and that some of the silver they sold may have been made outside of their own shops. The quality of the engraving on objects made by the Edwardses varies greatly, suggesting that they did not receive substantial training in this branch of their craft and that they employed specialists to do most of the engraving for them. In fact, the engraving on the ob-

Fig. 3. *Two-handled covered cup.* American, Boston, Mass., about 1744. Jacob Hurd, born Boston (1703–58). H. 15 1/16 in (38.3 cm), Diam. (lip) 7 3/4 in (19.7 cm). Yale University Art Gallery, New Haven, Conn., The Mabel Brady Garvan Collection, 1932.48.

jects owned by the Storer family is so similar as to suggest that the arms were all engraved by the same hand and at the same time.[32]

A study of Boston silversmiths at midcentury indicates that there was a steadily declining emphasis on production and an increased emphasis on merchandising and distribution activities throughout the craft. The three leading merchant-artisans in Boston during the 1740s were Jacob Hurd (1703–58) and Thomas and Samuel Edwards. Although Hurd was bankrupt by 1755 and died an insolvent debtor, his shop produced more than 50 percent of the surviving objects made by men who came of age and began working independently between 1720 and 1730. He made no significant investments that were not directly related to his goldsmithing shop. He had very little excess capital and was constantly in debt because of the substantial amounts of money he had to advance for raw materials.[33]

In spite of the several suits against Hurd by creditors, he was never sued by journeymen or jobbers for payment for labor or goods. He must have employed a large number of laboring artisans in his shop, and he ap-

The Edwards Family and the Silversmithing Trade   73

pears to have considered payment of their wages a high priority. The son of a joiner, he married the daughter of a mariner and maintained the outlook of an artisan in his business dealings. His goldsmithing shop differed from those of laboring artisans in its size but not in its general organization or its disposition of resources.

By contrast, the Edwards brothers, who were the two most financially successful goldsmiths working at midcentury, chose to concentrate on retail sales, and Thomas, at least, subcontracted most production work to jobbing goldsmiths like Thomas Townsend (1704–c. 1752).[34] Their father, John, established them both in his business and settled house lots and houses on them at the time of his death. After serving their apprenticeships, probably under their father, Thomas and Samuel married and opened separate independent shops. By the time he was twenty-two, Thomas's business was substantial enough to require the services of a journeyman, and in 1724–25 he employed John LeRoux, son of Bartholomew LeRoux of New York, for a daily wage of between three shillings and four shillings two pence.[35] In this way Thomas may have learned of techniques and design ideas current in New York. Little record survives of the early career of Samuel Edwards. He married the daughter of a wealthy Boston merchant and had accumulated a very large estate by the time of his death in 1762.[36]

The shop practices of both brothers suggest that they increasingly emphasized selling ready-made objects over production of bespoke work. Samuel's shop inventory lists so many pieces of plate in stock that he must have imported large numbers of objects from abroad in addition to running a large production workshop.[37] Samuel's production, however, was not nearly as extensive as that of Jacob Hurd. Only sixty-one surviving objects bear his mark, accounting for only 15 percent of the objects produced during his generation. Samuel was, nonetheless, the third largest producer of silver objects in Boston in the 1740s, exceeded only by John Burt and Jacob Hurd. His relationship with laboring artisans appears to have been a good one, although his extensive stock of tools provides evidence that he could have paid his debts to other artisans in tools and supplies rather than in cash. In spite of his alliance with a major merchant family, he displayed "1 Goldsmiths Arms" in his "lower room," which would have been the most public room in his home. The contents of his desk and bookcase further demonstrate that he had not completely assumed the outlook of a merchant, for it was filled with sleeve buttons, flukes and tongues for buckles, weights, tobacco boxes, and tools rather than with journals, books, or business papers. However, he had an extensive library of more than two hundred books, only three of which—*Artists Vade Mecum*, *New Touchstone for Silv^r*, and *Quarles's Emblems*—could have been directly related to his trade.[38] Samuel Edwards represents the merchant-artisan who valued his artisan identity and yet recognized that production was no longer as lucrative as merchandising and distribution. Like many of his generation, he called himself an artisan, but acted as a merchant.

Thomas Edwards, in contrast, took full advantage of his position as a large-scale merchant-artisan to utilize the labor of pieceworkers and journeymen. His accounts with two journeymen, John LeRoux and Thomas Townsend, demonstrate that he paid low wages and that as much as 40 percent was paid in goods rather than in cash. Furthermore, the wages paid in goods were paid in items such as drawing irons, wires, shears, crucibles, and allum, which were useful only in the practice of goldsmithing, rather than in food or items that could be used by journeymen to pay their own debts. Thomas was sued many times by other goldsmiths, and he may have been notorious for paying a high percentage of wages in goods. When he was sued by Townsend in 1751, three other goldsmiths were called in to act as referees to offer their opinions on the value of goods and services listed in the accounts between Townsend and Edwards.[39] Thomas, like his brother Samuel, called himself a goldsmith throughout his life. Thomas, however, was a capitalizing artisan who introduced new relationships between men like himself, who controlled the labor of others, and men like Townsend, who lived by selling their labor to others.

The careers of Jacob Hurd and of Samuel and Thomas Edwards demonstrate the extent to which artisans in Boston became polarized as a result of sudden inflation in a money-based urban economy. Artisans became divided in two significant ways: economically, between laboring artisans, who relied on their own skills for their subsistence, and merchant-artisans, who relied on the labor of others; and conceptually, between those who regarded themselves primarily as producers of consumer goods and those who thought of production as only one aspect of their business.

Boston was thus a city in which traditional assumptions about economic relationships came into conflict with an emerging capitalist ethic. The objects made by the city's goldsmiths demonstrate that in the eighteenth century Boston was a town caught between two worlds. After midcentury a few clients still looked back to England, as had been the practice at the turn of the century, to seek material affirmation of their status in the New World. For most Bostonians, however, the independent development of well-known object forms helped tie the mercantile elite and the artisan class together in a widely perceived community ideal. Although we often point to the sophistication of the forms which American artisans directly copied from English and European models, it is in the continued manipulation of traditional forms and the establishment of local design traditions that we see the beginnings of a distinctive American art.

NOTES

1. Carl Bridenbaugh, *Cities in the Wilderness: The First Century of Urban Life in America, 1625–1742* (New York: Alfred A. Knopf, 1955), pp. 411–13.

2. David Grayson Allen, *In English Ways: The Movement of Societies and the Transferal of English Local Law and Custom to the Massachusetts Bay in the Seventeenth Century* (New York: W. W. Norton, 1982).

3. Samuel Eliot Morison, "Mistress Glover's Household Furnishings at Cambridge, Massachusetts, 1638–1641," *Old-Time New England* 25, no. 1 (July 1934): 29–32; Robert W. Lovett, ed., *Documents from the Harvard University Archives, 1638–1750*, Publications of the Colonial Society of Massachusetts, vol. 49, *Collections* (Boston: Colonial Society of Massachusetts, 1975), pp. 70–77; Albert S. Roe and Robert F. Trent, "Robert Sanderson and the Founding of the Boston Goldsmithing Trade," in *New England Begins: The Seventeenth Century*, ed. Jonathan L. Fairbanks and Robert F. Trent (Boston: Museum of Fine Arts, 1982), pp. 480–81, 489–91.

4. Gerald W. R. Ward, "Silver and Society in Salem, Massachusetts, 1630–1820: A Case Study of the Consumer and the Craft" (Ph.D. diss., Boston University, 1984), pp. 19–22, outlines the pattern of silver ownership in Salem between 1641 and 1669. Ward found that the forms most often mentioned were spoons, wine cups, dram cups, and beer bowls, but many inventories did not specify forms.

5. Thomas S. Reese, "Colonial Transformations of Spanish Art: Sixteenth Century Mexico" (Unpublished paper, June 1978), pp. 6–8.

6. See G. B. Warden, *Boston, 1689–1776* (Boston: Little, Brown, and Company, 1970), pp. 3–14, 34–59; and Bernard Bailyn, *The New England Merchants in the Seventeenth Century* (1955; reprint, New York: Harper and Row, 1964), pp. 168–97.

7. Richard S. Dunn, *Puritans and Yankees: The Winthrop Dynasty of New England, 1630–1717* (1962; reprint, New York: W. W. Norton, 1971); and Kenneth Silverman, *The Life and Times of Cotton Mather* (New York: Harper and Row, 1984), pp. 227–60.

8. Although Allen seems to have retired from goldsmithing following his father's death in 1710 (he listed himself as a grazier in a deed of 1710, Suffolk Deeds 25:135–36, Suffolk County Courthouse, Boston; hereafter cited as S.D.), he later resumed his trade. His business does not appear ever to have been large during these years; he sold off most of the enormous wealth in land that his father had accumulated (John Allen inherited the largest single piece of Boston real estate ever owned by a single individual) and lived from the income derived from renting the remainder. With his wealth and the prestige it brought he could easily have been a leading figure in government and commerce. His position was one that every craftsman of the first generations must have envied. But his ability to manage that wealth was evidently limited, and so he lived a quiet life and sold his land to fulfill his needs.

9. For the facts of John Edwards's life, see Kathryn C. Buhler, "John Edwards, Goldsmith, and His Progeny," *Antiques* 59, no. 5 (April 1951). See also Francis J. Puig, "A Study of John Edwards, 1671–1746, Including a Partial Catalogue of His Silver . . ." (Unpublished seminar paper, Yale University, 1977), and S.D. 17:313–15.

10. Smith-Carter Family Manuscripts, Massachusetts Historical Society, Boston.

11. Jaspar Danckaerts, *Journal of Jaspar Danckaerts, 1679–1680*, ed. Bartlett Burleigh James and J. Franklin Jameson (New York: Charles Scribner's Sons, 1913).

12. The four objects are a covered skillet now in the Yale University Art Gallery, illustrated in Graham Hood, "A New Form in American Seventeenth-Century Silver," *Antiques* 94, no. 6 (December 1968): 879–81; a patch box and a tankard in the Garvan Collection, Yale University Art Gallery; and a tankard on loan to the Los Angeles County Museum of Art.

13. Barbara McLean Ward, "Boston Goldsmiths, 1690–1730," in *The Craftsman in Early America*, ed. Ian M. G. Quimby (New York: W. W. Norton, 1984), pp. 142–45.

14. Most sources say that Jesse was born in Hartford, Connecticut. However, there is no evidence of his birth there, nor is there any record of a man named David Jesse in the Barbour Abstracts, Connecticut State Library, Hartford. It is likely that the David Jesse who practiced the trade of goldsmithing in Boston was "David Jesse, son of John Jesse, citizen and Joiner of London," who was apprenticed to Alexander Roode, goldsmith of London, on March 7, 1682 (extract from the records of Goldsmiths' Hall, London, in a letter from G. R. Hughes of Goldsmiths' Hall to John Marshall Phillips, April 29, 1935, Correspondence files of John Marshall Phillips, Yale University Art Gallery, New Haven, Conn.). Conyers was bound apprentice to Roger Graing, citizen and goldsmith of London, from 1682 to 1689. He became a freeman of the Goldsmiths' Company in 1689, and was elected to the livery in 1694 (extract from the records of Goldsmiths' Hall, London, taken by E. Alfred Jones, Correspondence files of John Marshall Phillips). According to Ambrose Heal, *The London Goldsmiths, 1700–1800* (1935; reprint, Newton Abbott, England: David & Charles, 1972), p. 129, Conyers had a shop in the parish of St. Mary Woolnoth, London, during 1695–96. The Winterthur Museum owns tankards by both Jesse and Conyers that are decorated with cut-card ornament. See Martha Gandy Fales, *American Silver in the Henry Francis du Pont Winterthur Museum* (Winterthur, Del.: Henry Francis du Pont Winterthur Museum, 1958), cat. nos. 9, 11.

15. Extract from the records at Goldsmiths' Hall, London, in a letter of Walter Prideaux of Goldsmiths' Hall to Francis Bradbury, January 27, 1923. Correspondence files of John Marshall Phillips; Georgina E. Lee, *British Silver Monteith Bowls Including American and European Examples* (Byfleet, Surrey, England: Manor House Press, 1978).

16. For biographical details on these individuals see Barbara McLean Ward, "The Craftsman in a Changing Society: Boston Goldsmiths, 1690–1730" (Ph.D. diss., Boston University, 1983), pp. 349–71.

17. One object that survives, a small porringer, may bear the mark of René Grignon. It also has an erased mark of Jeremiah Dummer

on the bowl to the left of the handle. See Kathryn C. Buhler and Graham Hood, *American Silver: Garvan and Other Collections in the Yale University Art Gallery* (New Haven, Conn.: Yale University Press, 1970), pp. 26–28.

18. Their most important contribution may have been the introduction of the Irish or Scottish tankard form with high-domed cover, finial, and a midband around the body. See National Museum of Ireland, *Irish Silver from the Seventeenth to the Nineteenth Century* (Washington, D.C.: Smithsonian Institution Traveling Exhibition Service, 1982), p. 12.

19. Kathryn C. Buhler, *American Silver, 1655–1825, in the Museum of Fine Arts, Boston* (Greenwich, Conn.: New York Graphic Society for the Museum of Fine Arts, Boston, 1972), pp. 23–24, 81–82.

20. See Gary B. Nash, *The Urban Crucible* (Cambridge, Mass.: Harvard University Press, 1979), pp. 102–19, on the economic situation in Boston. For further analysis of traditional styles in Boston silver and furniture see Barbara McLean Ward, "Stylistic Change and the Development of a Conscious Material Identity in Colonial Boston and Philadelphia" (Paper presented at the annual meeting of the East Central Society for Eighteenth Century Studies, October 1984).

21. Michael K. Brown, "A Tankard by John Coney," *Bulletin of the Museum of Fine Arts, Houston*, n.s. 8, no. 2 (Winter 1983): 2–10.

22. See Buhler and Hood, *American Silver*, Yale, 1:71–73, 78–80, 105–6, 273–75. There is another example of the form by Edwards in the Cleveland Museum of Art (40.192).

23. Buhler, *American Silver, MFA*, p. 98. The lion's-head terminal also appears on tankards by Edwards in the Virginia Museum of Fine Arts (74-40), and the Cleveland Museum of Art (40.188).

24. A tankard marked by Edwards and Allen with a cherub's-head terminal decoration was advertised by Doyle's Antiques several years ago. I have not examined the object, however, and am not aware of its present location. A tankard by Edwards with an early example of the satyr's-head terminal was formerly in the Cornelius C. Moore collection. See Anne E. Spokas et al., *American Silver, 1670–1830: The Cornelius C. Moore Collection at Providence College* (Providence, R.I.: Rhode Island Bicentennial Foundation and Providence College, 1980), pp. 92–93.

25. An account between Thomas Edwards and Thomas Townsend, dated October 22, 1748–August 8, 1749, indicates that Townsend was making tankard and cann bodies for Edwards. Suffolk File Papers, Suffolk County Court of Common Pleas, January 1750/51 Session, no. 128. Social Law Library, Suffolk County Courthouse, Boston.

26. Nash, *Urban Crucible*, pp. 225–26.

27. Benjamin Walker, Diary, vol. 1743–49, October 7, 1747.

28. Nash, *Urban Crucible*, pp. 221–23.

29. *Paul Revere's Boston, 1735–1818* (Boston: Museum of Fine Arts, 1975), pp. 52–53; Barbara McLean Ward and Gerald W. R. Ward, eds., *Silver in American Life: Selections from the Mabel Brady Garvan and Other Collections at Yale University* (New York: American Federation of Arts; Boston: David R. Godine, 1979), p. 76.

30. Teapots by Edwards are pictured in Fales, *Winterthur Silver*, no. 27, and Buhler, *American Silver, MFA*, p. 641.

31. Ward, "The Craftsman in a Changing Society"; see appendixes, pp. 348–71 for estate values and rankings of individual goldsmiths. These and other productivity figures are based on a survey of objects in the Art Institute of Chicago; the Museum of Fine Arts, Houston; Bowdoin College Museum of Art, Brunswick, Me.; the Clark Art Institute, Williamstown, Mass.; the Cleveland Museum of Art; Colonial Williamsburg; the Detroit Institute of Arts; the Essex Institute, Salem, Mass.; the Fogg Museum of Art, Cambridge, Mass.; the Henry Ford Museum, Dearborn, Mich.; Historic Deerfield, Deerfield, Mass.; the Metropolitan Museum of Art, New York; the Cornelius Moore Collection formerly at Providence College, Providence, R.I.; the Munson Williams Proctor Institute, Utica, N.Y.; the Museum of Fine Arts, Boston; the St. Louis Art Museum; the Society for the Preservation of New England Antiquities, Boston; the Virginia Museum of Fine Arts, Richmond; the Wadsworth Atheneum, Hartford, Conn.; the Henry Francis du Pont Winterthur Museum, Winterthur, Del.; the Worcester Art Museum, Worcester, Mass.; Yale University Art Gallery, New Haven, Conn.; numerous private collections; and the Decorative Arts Photographic Collection, Winterthur Museum. Objects published in the following catalogues were also included: Kathryn C. Buhler, *Massachusetts Silver in the Frank L. and Louise. C. Harrington Collection* (Worcester, Mass.: Privately printed, 1965); Kathryn C. Buhler and Mark A. Clark, *Silver Supplement to the Guidebook to the Diplomatic Reception Rooms* (Washington, D.C.: U.S. Department of State, 1973); Carl Christian Dauterman et al., *Checklist of American Silversmiths' Work, 1650–1850, in Museums in the New York Metropolitan Area* (New York: Metropolitan Museum of Art, 1968); and Philip Hammerslough, *American Silver Collected by Philip H. Hammerslough*, 4 vols. (Hartford, Conn.: Privately printed, 1958–73). E. Alfred Jones, *The Old Silver of American Churches* (Letchworth, England: Privately printed for the National Society of Colonial Dames of America, Arden Press, 1913), provided the bulk of the information on church silver. I referred to Kathryn C. Buhler, *Colonial Silversmiths, Masters and Apprentices* (Boston: Museum of Fine Arts, 1956), for key objects in small museums or private collections.

32. Buhler, *American Silver, MFA*, pp. 172, 173, 175, 246.

33. Suffolk Court Files, no. 62302, Office of the Clerk of the Supreme Judicial Court of Suffolk County, Suffolk County Courthouse, Boston (hereafter cited as Suffolk Court Files). Hurd died approximately three years after he went bankrupt. The inventory of his estate totaled £58, and he was declared insolvent (Suffolk Probate 54:58). For information on his various land transactions, see Hollis French, *Jacob Hurd and His Sons, Nathaniel and Benjamin, Silversmiths, 1702–1781* (Cambridge, Mass.: Walpole Society, 1939).

34. Suffolk File Papers, January 1750/51 Session, no. 128.

35. Suffolk Court Files, no. 185000.

36. For general biographical information on the Edwardses, see Kathryn C. Buhler, "John Edwards, Goldsmith, and His Progeny."

37. Smith-Carter Family Manuscripts, Massachusetts Historical Society, Notebook kept by Isaac Smith as one of the executors of the estate of Samuel Edwards. This detailed inventory was abbreviated and summarized for a submission to the probate court. It lists £775 worth of ready-made plate in the shop and enough tools to supply six workbenches.

38. Smith-Carter Family Manuscripts, Notebook kept by Isaac Smith.

39. Suffolk File Papers, January 1750/51 Session, no. 128.

Catalogue Objects

18. *Spout cup*
American, Boston, Mass., about 1706
John Edwards, born England (1671–1746)
Silver
H. 5½ in (14 cm), Diam. (base) 3 1/16 in (7.8 cm)
Worcester Art Museum, Worcester, Mass., bequest of Stephen Salisbury III, 1907.118

18. Spout cup / 19. Chocolate pot / 20. Chocolate pot

John Coney's chocolate pot (cat. no. 19) is one of the earliest examples of this form made in the colonies. Its plain surfaces and cut-card ornament were the height of fashion in England in 1701, when it was made to fulfill a bequest from Lieutenant Governor William Stoughton of Massachusetts to his niece Sarah Byfield Tailer, wife of William Tailer of Boston.[1]

This form, similar in appearance to a Chinese vase, was one of the two most common forms for chocolate pots in contemporary England. It is known by surviving pots from London, as in the example shown here by Isaac Dighton (cat. no. 20) and in simpler examples made in provincial goldsmithing centers. The Chinese vase form was also used for silver and ceramic tea caddies. The influence of Chinese decorative arts was especially strong during the last decades of the seventeenth century, and porcelain vases played an important part

The Edwards Family and the Silversmithing Trade   77

19. *Chocolate pot*
American, Boston, Mass., 1702
John Coney, born Boston (1656–1722)
Silver
H. 8 1/16 in (20.5 cm), Diam. (base) 3 5/8 in (9.2 cm)
Museum of Fine Arts, Boston, gift of Edward Jackson Holmes, 29.1091

in baroque room decoration.[2] Although we commonly associate these forms with the drinking of tea, because tea came from China, it seems evident that Chinese forms were considered appropriate for any type of exotic food or drink, including chocolate, which originated in the West Indies.

Edwards borrowed the form of the chocolate pot for his small spout cup (cat. no. 18), after seeing this or similar examples in the shop of John Coney, which was situated only three or four blocks from his own, near the town dock.[3] This pot shows the way in which a silversmith like Edwards adopted and absorbed the design ideas imported by his contemporaries. Spout cups were used primarily for feeding children and invalids, and therefore the placement of the handle at a right angle to the spout was particularly convenient. Perhaps to facilitate the stirring of chocolate with a long stick, known as a molinet, inserted through the aperture created when the finial was removed, the earliest chocolate pots were all made with the handle at a right angle to the spout. Edwards thus saw, in Coney's chocolate pot, a form very similar to that which he was making in this spout cup.

Knowing that his spout cup was destined for one of Boston's most prominent citizens and the minister of Edwards's own Brattle Street Church, the Reverend Benjamin Colman, Edwards was doubtless eager to impress. This may explain why he appropriated an inno-

78 BARBARA McLEAN WARD

20. *Chocolate pot*
English, London, 1697
Isaac Dighton (active 1697–99)
Silver
H. 7¾ in (19.7 cm)
The Metropolitan Museum of Art, New York, gift of George O. May, 1943, 43.108

vative form rather than relying on the traditional globular shape for an object usually not used for ostentatious display. Particularly significant here is Edwards's use of fashionable cut-card ornament for the cover of his spout cup. By lavishing extra attention on such a small object, Edwards endowed it with a sophistication worthy of a presentation piece. John George gave the cup to Colman in 1706, perhaps on the occasion of his daughter's entrance into the membership of the church.[4]

1. Kathryn C. Buhler, *American Silver, 1655–1825, in the Museum of Fine Arts, Boston* (Boston: Museum of Fine Arts, 1972), pp. 59–61.
2. Michael Clayton, *The Collector's Dictionary of the Silver and Gold of Great Britain and North America* (New York: World Publishing Company, 1971), pp. 63, 66–67, 296, 299. Jessie McNab Dennis, *English Silver* (New York: Walker and Company, 1970), pp. 55, 58–59. Reinier Baarsen, Gervase Jackson-Stops, Phillip M. Johnston, and Elaine Evans Dee, *Courts and Colonies: The William and Mary Style in Holland, England, and America* (New York and Pittsburgh: Cooper-Hewitt Museum and the Carnegie Museum of Art, 1988), pp. 18, 128–29, 225, 228–29.
3. Buhler, *American Silver, MFA*, p. 39.
4. Kathryn C. Buhler, *American Silver from the Colonial Period through the Early Republic in the Worcester Art Museum* (Worcester, Mass.: Worcester Art Museum, 1979), pp. 18–19). On the major categories and significance of presentation silver, see Gerald W. R. Ward, Introduction to *Marks of Achievement: Four Centuries of American Presentation Silver*, ed. David B. Warren, Katherine S. Howe, and Michael K. Brown (New York: Museum of Fine Arts, Houston, in association with Harry N. Abrams, Publishers, 1987), pp. 15–21.

21. *Standing salt*
American, Boston, Mass., about 1696
John Allen, born Boston (1672–1760), and John Edwards, born England (1671–1746)
Silver
H. 5⅞ in (14.9 cm), W. (base) 5 3/16 in (13.2 cm)
The Metropolitan Museum of Art, New York, gift of Sarah Hayward Draper, 1972, 1972.204

21. Standing salt / 22. Standing salt

Salts like the English one shown here (cat. no. 22) were among the earliest silver objects brought to the colonies. Unlike some other forms introduced soon after colonization, however, the standing salt was not extensively replicated in America; in fact, only three by American artisans are known, all made in Boston.

The Allen and Edwards salt (cat. no. 21) serves to demonstrate how quickly new design ideas reached the colonies during the last years of the seventeenth century. It is one of the earliest datable examples of gadrooned ornament on an American object. Decoration of this type became popular in England during the reign of William and Mary; Allen and Edwards were using it for this salt as early as 1696, when they are first recorded as partners renting a shop near the town dock. This salt is similar in form to the other two American examples: Jeremiah Dummer's, with two bands of straight gadrooning, and Edward Winslow's, with one band of spiral gadrooning. All three were made at approximately the same time.[1]

The overall stylistic similarity of the three salts, including the almost identical profiles of their projecting knops, argues against any influence from possible master to possible apprentices, even though Allen, Edwards, and Winslow are thought to have served their apprenticeships under Jeremiah Dummer.[2] Rather, it suggests that three silversmiths serving a wealthy and fashionable clientele produced slightly varied responses to an imported design idea. It is even possible that all three men had seen the same object and had had an opportunity to study it, replicate its moldings, and design similar knops.

The Allen and Edwards and Dummer salts are particularly alike in their form and overall disposition of ornament. The main difference is that the Dummer salt, like the English example shown here, has a broad

22. *Standing salt*
English, London, 1686/87
Silver
H. 5 5/16 in (13.5 cm), W. (base) 5 1/2 in (14 cm)
The Colonial Williamsburg Foundation, Williamsburg, Va., 1965-132

stem that gradually widens into an octagonal base. The Allen and Edwards salt, in contrast, has a very straight shaft that joins both bowl and base at a rather abrupt angle. The partners further modified the familiar design by creating a gadrooned border that dominates the base molding, whereas Dummer's gadrooned band is no greater in depth than the last step of the molded base. In the Dummer and the Allen and Edwards examples, the bowl of the salt occupies nearly the entire area between the projecting knops, whereas on the English example, and also on the salt made by Bostonian Edward Winslow, the bowl is smaller in comparison with the overall width of the upper section. All three American examples have knops nearly identical to those on the English salt, although those on the Dummer salt have by far the most pronounced collar below the scroll. The others, although possibly made from the same mold, are not as well finished as Dummer's.

Because the salt was not a popular form in America, we find no significant development of it at the hands of American craftsmen. Most likely the clients who ordered these salts wanted silver in traditional English forms to display as evidence of their close connections with the traditions of the mother country and with the first families of the colony, rather than as evidence of fashionable taste.[3] The fact that the American silversmiths used variations of the newly fashionable gadrooned ornament suggests that they had seen an example that was similarly decorated.

1. Buhler, *American Silver, MFA*, pp. 23–24, 81–82.
2. Kathryn C. Buhler, *Colonial Silversmiths, Masters and Apprentices* (Boston: Museum of Fine Arts, 1956), pp. 27–29.
3. For further information on the owner of the Allen and Edwards salt, the Reverend Solomon Stoddard, and his probable reasons for acquiring it, see *The Great River: Art and Society of the Connecticut Valley, 1635–1820* (Hartford, Conn.: Wadsworth Atheneum, 1985), p. 279. See also Frances Gruber Safford, "Colonial Silver in the American Wing," *The Metropolitan Museum of Art Bulletin* 41, no. 1 (Summer 1983): 23.

23. *Tankard*
American, Boston, Mass., 1715–20
John Edwards, born England (1671–1746)
Silver
H. 6⅞ in (17.5 cm), Diam. (lip) 4¼ in (10.8 cm), Diam. (base) 4¾ in (12.1 cm)
Yale University Art Gallery, New Haven, Conn., The Mabel Brady Garvan Collection, 1930.1167

23. Tankard / 24. Tankard

The tankard was one of the earliest forms introduced to the colonies from England, and it shows the most important independent development of any form in American silver. Its popularity was tenacious, persisting until after the American Revolution. Boston silversmiths made tankards and other objects in the latest London fashions up to about 1720, but after that, the continuation of certain traditional forms became increasingly important and took precedence over the adoption of stylistic innovations from England. This change in attitude is best exemplified by the tankard.

After evolving to a certain point in the early 1720s, tankards became fixed in design and craftsmanship until the end of the century.[1] Both examples shown here have domed covers of the type popular during the first years of the eighteenth century. In England this design phase marked the final development of the tankard form, and catalogue number 24 shows its full elaboration, with repoussé and gadrooning on the cover and body and an elaborate cast finial.[2] In America, however, the tankard form continued to develop, becoming taller and more slender, with a stepped domed cover and central flame finial. Most tankards made in Boston after 1720 also have midbands segmenting the body. John Edwards made tankards without midbands throughout his career, and his son Samuel followed this preference.[3]

Although the form developed at first along English lines, Americans adopted distinctive types of ornament,

82 Barbara McLean Ward

24. *Tankard*
English, London, 1697/98
Charles Overing (active 1692–1718)
Silver
H. 7⅝ in (19.4 cm), Diam. (lip) 4⅝ in (11.7 cm), Diam. (base) 5⅝ in (14.3 cm)
Wadsworth Atheneum, Hartford, Conn., The Elizabeth B. Miles Collection of English Silver, 1979.27

such as decorative handle tips, not found on English examples. These innovations occurred in both Boston and New York and may have been introduced by Dutch and Scandinavian immigrant craftsmen.

John Edwards used a number of different designs for the small castings that decorate the handle tips of his tankards, and also made distinctive designs for thumbpieces. This tankard (cat. no. 23) bears one of Edwards's most attractive handle-tip designs, the lion's head. There is reason to believe that these handle-tip designs had iconographic significance. A tankard made for Colonel Jeremiah Moulton to commemorate his role in the 1745 capture of Louisburg, for instance, has a handle tip engraved with a map of the siege.[4]

The earliest American tankards had only plain or shield-shaped handle tips. The use of cast cherubs' heads began during the first decade of the eighteenth century. The cherub may have been used because cherubs ranked second in the hierarchy of angels and their special attribute was the knowledge and contemplation of divine things. Tankards adorned with cherubs' heads may have symbolized divine election and acceptance into the full communion of the church. There is evidence that tankards were given as gifts to mark the beginning of manhood or womanhood, an event associated with formal entrance into church membership. Tankards were also used in the communion service in some churches, and although the handle tips of most church tankards are plain, a significant number are decorated with cherubs.[5]

By the 1720s the handle tip most frequently found on Boston tankards was the satyr's head, a design that may have originated with Edwards. An obvious bacchanalian symbol, the satyr was connected with the use of tankards for the imbibing of beer and wine; it indicates the increasingly secular connotations of tankards as gifts. The warriorlike figure that appeared on many tankards by midcentury may hark back to the idea of the tankard as a symbol of maturity.

After 1750, most tankards lacked such obvious symbolic devices. Although the form persisted, the need for it may have changed. As carriers of tradition and as symbols of family and position, tankards remained nearly identical in form from 1740 until well after the Revolution. They filled the need among Americans to develop and nurture a tradition of their own.[6] The persistence of an old form that had evolved to a distinctive American design unknown in England is physical evidence of the growing independence of the colonies and the development of an American symbolic tradition.

1. Barbara McLean Ward and Gerald W. R. Ward, eds., *Silver in American Life: Selections from the Mabel Brady Garvan and Other Collections at Yale University* (New York: American Federation of Arts; Boston: David R. Godine, 1979), pp. 124–27.

2. Elizabeth B. Miles, *The Elizabeth B. Miles Collection: English Silver* (Hartford, Conn.: Wadsworth Atheneum, 1976), p. 43. English tankards with finials are relatively rare. Irish and Scottish tankards, however, often display characteristics very close to those that we associate with American tankards, although the form was never as popular in those two countries as in the North American colonies. See National Museum of Ireland, *Irish Silver from the Seventeenth to the Nineteenth Century* (Washington, D.C.: Smithsonian Institution Traveling Exhibition Service, 1982), p. 12. Several journeymen silversmiths working in Boston during the 1710s had names that suggest they were Irish or Scottish. Two, Peter Denman and William Caddow, can definitely be identified as Irish.

3. For examples of tankards by Samuel Edwards, see E. Alfred Jones, *The Old Silver of American Churches* (Letchworth, England: Privately printed for the National Society of the Colonial Dames at Arden Press, 1913), pp. 137, 489.

4. Kathryn C. Buhler and Graham Hood, *American Silver: Garvan and Other Collections in the Yale University Art Gallery* (New Haven, Conn.: Yale University Press, 1970), pp. 100–102.

5. For further information on the use of tankards in the communion ritual, see Barbara McLean Ward, "'In a Feasting Posture': Communion Vessels and Community Values in Seventeenth- and Eighteenth-Century New England," *Winterthur Portfolio* 28, no. 1 (Spring 1988): 1–24.

6. For further information on the cultural meaning of tankards to New Englanders, see Gerald W. R. Ward, "Silver and Society in Salem, Massachusetts, 1630–1820: A Case Study of the Consumer and the Craft" (Ph.D. diss., Boston University, 1984), pp. 124–39.

25. Salver / 26. Salver

In England, monumental salvers were often showpieces of the engraver's art. The heraldic devices and symbols of office with which they were embellished further served to communicate the importance of the owner.[1] Smaller salvers, like the one shown here by William Peaston (cat. no. 26), were not intended solely for display but were used at the dining table during lavish entertainments.

This English salver (and its mate) originally belonged to Peyton Randolph and his wife, Betty Harrison, of Williamsburg, Virginia.[2] The family's crest is engraved at the center. Imported salvers like this provided American silversmiths with information about new stylistic developments and engraving fashions. Thomas Edwards may well have learned of fashions in salvers from an example like this one; certainly the Edwards salver shown here (cat. no. 25) has a border design directly inspired by an English example like Peaston's. The engraving on imported monumental plate such as the two-handled covered cup made by George Wickes of London, which was owned by Thomas Hancock, would have enhanced Edwards's knowledge of that art.[3]

The engraved coat of arms on this Edwards salver closely resembles the engraving on two salvers and a two-handled covered cup made by Jacob Hurd and was probably the work of a specialist engraver.[4] The most likely candidate is Thomas Johnston (1708–67), japanner, painter, and engraver, of Boston. Johnston is well known as a japanner and pictorial engraver, but he was also an engraver and painter of heraldic devices. A bookplate he made for William P. Smith in 1745 bears a coat of arms engraved in the same style as the arms on this salver and on objects made by Jacob Hurd.[5] This suggests that Edwards and Hurd sent objects to Johnston for engraving or that their clients bought blank salvers and took them to Johnston's shop for engraving.

Further comparison of salvers by both Edwards and Hurd provides additional evidence that some salvers were purchased without heraldic engraving. A Hurd salver with central engraving at the Museum of Fine Arts, Boston, and an Edwards salver with no central engraving in the Henry Francis du Pont Winterthur Museum have identical engraved border designs that are almost surely the work of the same engraver.[6] The bold, deep engraving of these borders is quite unlike the small, intricate designs of the lightly engraved coat

25. *Salver*
American, Boston, Mass., about 1750
Thomas Edwards, born Boston (1702–55)
Silver
H. 1⅞ in (4.8 cm), Diam. 11½ in (29.2 cm)
The Henry Francis du Pont Winterthur Museum, Winterthur, Del., 61.938

26. *Salver*
English, London, 1753/54
William Peaston (active 1746–63)
Silver
H. 1⅛ in (2.9 cm), Diam. 8½ in (21.6 cm)
The Colonial Williamsburg Foundation, Williamsburg, Va., 1945-16.1

of arms at the center of the Hurd salver (and of the Edwards salver shown here). The borders clearly were engraved before the salvers were sold, and some clients, such as the purchaser of the plain Edwards salver, chose to leave the center of the plate blank. Much of the silver produced in the shop of Thomas Edwards is not engraved; that which is varies greatly in style and technical competence, suggesting that Edwards relied on specialists and did little engraving himself. Hurd's shop, on the other hand, was known for the talents of its engravers, and Edwards may well have sent his salvers to Hurd for finishing.[7] As an important display object directly inspired by new fashions in English silver, the salver exhibited the talents of the finest Boston craftsmen. A seemingly simple object like this might therefore be the work of two or more artisans.

1. Charles Oman, *English Engraved Silver, 1150–1900*, (London: Faber and Faber, 1978), pp. 72–107.

2. John D. Davis, *English Silver at Williamsburg* (Williamsburg, Va.: Colonial Williamsburg Foundation, 1976), pp. 133–34.

3. *Paul Revere's Boston, 1735–1818* (Boston: Museum of Fine Arts, 1975), pp. 52–53; Martha Gandy Fales, *American Silver in the Henry Francis du Pont Winterthur Museum* (Winterthur, Del.: Henry Francis du Pont Winterthur Museum, 1958), figs. 30, 49.

4. Two of the objects by Jacob Hurd are in the Museum of Fine Arts, Boston (Buhler, *American Silver, MFA*, pp. 223–24, 226–27). The other is in the Yale University Art Gallery (Buhler and Hood, *American Silver: Yale*, pp. 130–31).

5. Sinclair Hitchings, "Thomas Johnston," and Martha Gandy Fales, "Heraldic and Emblematic Engravers of Colonial Boston," in *Boston Prints and Printmakers, 1670–1775*, ed. Walter Muir Whitehill (Boston: Colonial Society of Massachusetts, 1973), pp. 83–131, 205. Hitchings includes documentary evidence that Johnston's apprentices were given the task of engraving bookplates. As master of the shop, Johnston provided the apprentices with designs from which they worked.

6. The plain Edwards salver is illustrated in Fales, *American Silver, Winterthur*, fig. 114.

7. Fales, "Heraldic Engravers," pp. 202–4, 210–12.

27. Coffeepot / 28. Coffeepot

The coffeepot with the Faneuil family coat of arms (cat. no. 28) was ordered from England by Benjamin Faneuil in 1751. It was similar to a pot ordered by Benjamin's brother Peter in 1745–46. These two coffeepots evidently impressed Boston silversmiths, for a number of similar pots by American makers exist, including one made for the Symmes family of Boston by John Coburn and this example by Samuel Edwards (cat. no. 27), made for his niece Elizabeth Storer Smith. The coat of arms on the Faneuil pot shown here would have been among the earliest examples of rococo engraving to appear in Boston.[1]

These stylish coffeepots, owned by members of Boston's mercantile elite, illustrate the renewal of fashion consciousness that occurred around midcentury. The much-inflated colonial currency was revalued in 1750, bringing a return of economic stability that enhanced the ability of Boston merchants to trade abroad. With the balance of payments restored to a level more favorable to the colony, Bostonians found themselves with a supply of specie (silver coin) that could be converted into silver objects as well as used to buy goods from England and Europe.

The Edwards coffeepot shows an attempt on the part of the colonial silversmith to replicate the new design. Edwards appears to have been somewhat uneasy with the shape of the pot; like other American examples of this date, his pot is squatter than its London counterpart.[2] He also chose a lower domed cover and settled on plain handle junctures, rather than creating new patterns for fancy rococo mounts like those on the Shaw and Priest pot.

Forms like the coffeepot, introduced long after the settlement of the colony, never underwent extensive modification at the hands of American craftsmen, but rather artisans responded directly to design innovations from the mother country. Intended for elite patrons and lacking any connection to the early families and traditions of the colony, the coffeepot never achieved the status of a public presentation object, as did the tankard and the porringer.

1. *Paul Revere's Boston*, pp. 53–57. The pot by Coburn has the same squat proportions as the Edwards example but bears rococo engraving and has a bell finial similar to the one on the Shaw and Priest coffeepot. See Buhler, *American Silver, MFA*, pp. 308–9.

2. In addition to the coffeepot made by John Coburn for the Symmes family, see also two pots by Paul Revere (Buhler, *American Silver, MFA*, pp. 389–92) and the pot made by Samuel Buell for the Putnam family of Hartford (*The Great River*, p. 285).

27. *Coffeepot*
American, Boston, Mass., about 1755
Samuel Edwards, born Boston (1705–62)
Silver
H. 9¾ in (24.7 cm)
The Metropolitan Museum of Art, New York, Rogers Fund, 1941, 41.70.1

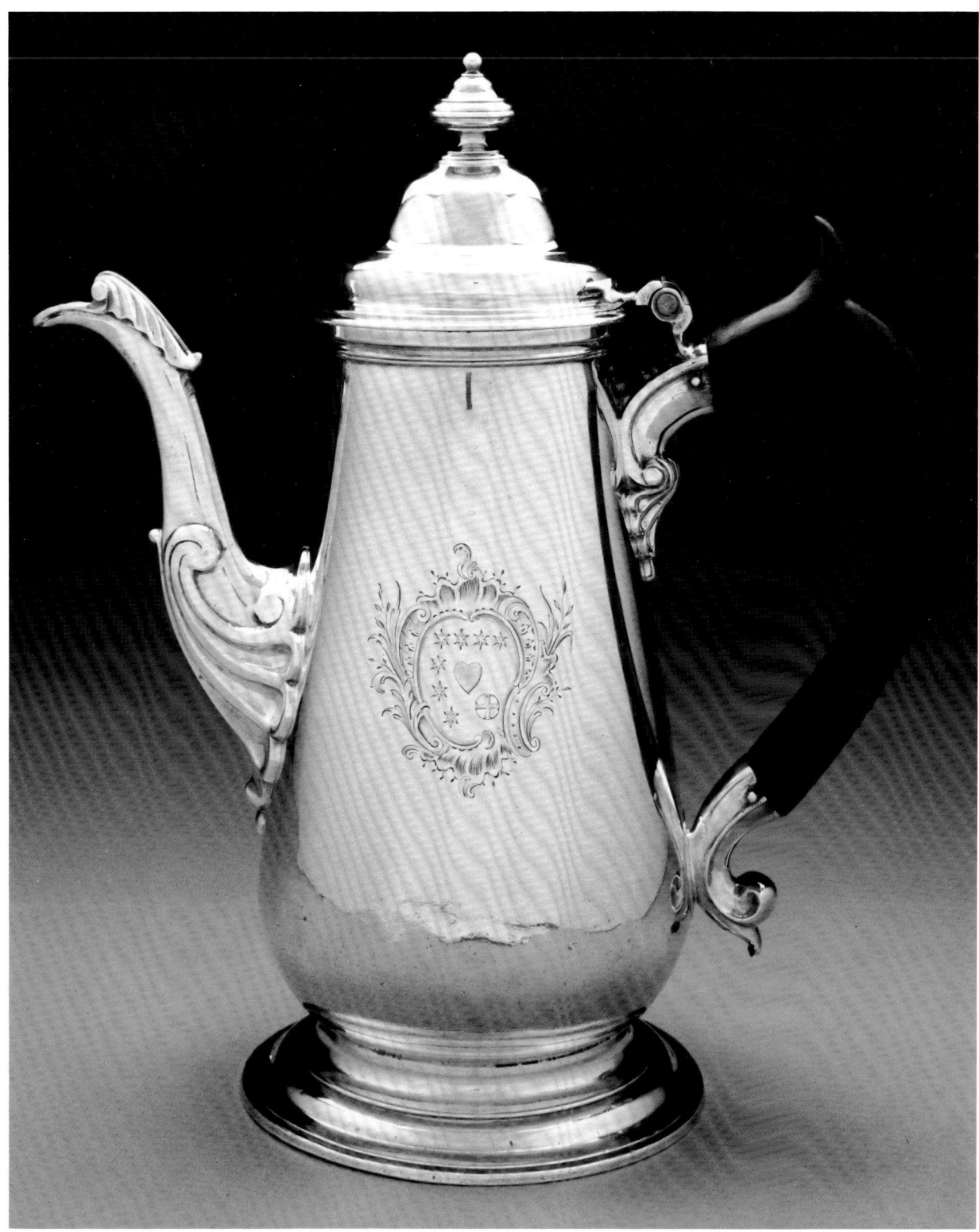

28. *Coffeepot*
English, London, 1751/52
William Shaw and William Priest (active in partnership 1749–58)
Silver
H. 10⅝ in (27 cm), Diam. (base) 4⅞ in (12.4 cm)
Museum of Fine Arts, Boston, gift in the name of Jane Bethune
Craig Hawkins, wife of General John P. Hawkins, 13.2857

29. *Porringer*
American, Boston, Mass., about 1762
Samuel Edwards, born Boston (1705–62)
Silver
H. 1⅞ in (4.8 cm), Diam. (lip) 4⅞ in (12.4 cm), W. 7½ in (19.1 cm)
Museum of Fine Arts, Boston, bequest of Dr. Samuel A. Green, 19.1388

29. Porringer / 30. Porringer

Like tankards, porringers were introduced to the colonies during the early years of settlement and enjoyed more than 150 years of popularity. Porringers made in New England during the seventeenth century and the early years of the eighteenth century closely followed prevailing English models. The earliest American porringers have either trefoil or relief cast handles.[1] These were soon superseded by porringers with geometrically pierced handles like the English example shown here (cat. no. 30).

Porringers were made by soldering a cast handle to a raised bowl. Handle designs could be readily duplicated through the use of molds made from metal patterns. The goldsmith made an impression of the metal pattern in wet sand and then poured molten silver into the sand mold. When the silver was cool, the casting was removed from the mold. Although the mold itself did not last for more than one casting, the goldsmith could use the same metal pattern to replicate a particular design over and over.

Two American porringers of the geometrically pierced type suggest that colonial silversmiths either imported patterns from England or used actual handles from English porringers in making their molds. These porringers, made by Isaac Anthony (trained in Boston, later worked in Newport, Rhode Island) and Edward Winslow of Boston, have the impression, in the casting itself, of an English mark registered at Goldsmiths' Hall, London, in 1674–75, a WR crowned. The casting sand was so fine that every detail of the English handle was duplicated, including the maker's mark on its underside.[2]

American porringers continued to follow English styles and to exhibit a wide variety of handle designs

30. *Porringer*
English, London, 1692/93
Silver
H. 2 in (5.1 cm), Diam. (lip) 5 in (12.7 cm), W. 7⅛ in (18.1 cm)
The Minneapolis Institute of Arts, gift of the Charles Bolles Rogers family:
Frederick Van Dusen Rogers, Nancy Rogers Pierson, Mary Rogers Savage, 59.11.19

until the early 1720s. After that, the porringer became less popular in England, so there were fewer models for colonial silversmiths to copy. About 1725 the design seen here on the Edwards porringer (cat. no. 29), known as a keyhole handle, was introduced. It quickly became the dominant handle design on New England porringers and after 1750 was used almost exclusively. Probably the wide distribution of handle patterns, specialization in the production of cast parts, and association of the keyhole design with local traditions all contributed to its popularity.

The use of patterns significantly affected the look of porringers in another way. The size of the patterns dictated standardization in the size of porringer bowls. Bowls became so uniform that a porringer handle produced in 1750 could easily be used twenty or thirty years later. One surviving porringer attests to the continued use of the same patterns and actual cast parts through successive generations of the Edwards family. Joseph Edwards (1737–83), grandson of John and nephew of Thomas and Samuel, overstruck his own mark on the back of a porringer handle originally marked by his uncle Thomas.[3] Samuel too, as the example illustrated here shows, used the keyhole handle.

1. Jonathan L. Fairbanks and Robert F. Trent, *New England Begins: The Seventeenth Century*, 3 vols. (Boston: Museum of Fine Arts, 1983), 2:246.
2. Wendy A. Cooper, "New Findings on Colonial New England Goldsmiths and English Sources," *The American Art Journal* 10, no. 2 (November 1978): 107–9.
3. Barbara McLean Ward, "The Craftsman in a Changing Society: Boston Goldsmiths, 1690–1730" (Ph.D. diss., Boston University, 1983), pp. 263–66, 335; idem., "Boston Goldsmiths, 1690–1730," in *The Craftsman in Early America*, ed. Ian M. G. Quimby (New York: W. W. Norton, 1984), pp. 147–49.

Morrison H. Heckscher

Philadelphia Furniture, 1760–90
Native-Born and London-Trained Craftsmen

The furniture made in Philadelphia in the third quarter of the eighteenth century comprises the largest and finest body of rococo furniture produced in colonial America. These pieces have a distinctive "Philadelphia Chippendale" style. To understand how this furniture came to be designed and made, we must examine it in relation to the physical, social, economic, and political terrain of the city at that time.

Visiting Philadelphia in 1765, Lord Adam Gordon, a colonel in the British army, called it "a great and noble city" and "one of the wonders of the world."[1] This enthusiastic praise reflected Philadelphia's position as the leading urban center in America. In 1765 the city is estimated to have had upwards of five thousand dwellings and a population of twenty-five thousand. This was a three-fold increase in twenty years, and rapid growth continued through the mid-1770s. In contrast, Boston's population remained at about fifteen thousand throughout the third quarter of the century, and New York's lagged until the federal period. In the English-speaking world, Philadelphia was probably the fourth largest city, after London, Edinburgh, and Dublin.[2]

But it was more than size alone that impressed Gordon. Philadelphia's physical presence was commanding, its society cosmopolitan. The grid plan of streets and public squares laid out by William Penn's surveyor in 1683 was now well developed in the areas abutting the Delaware River. There were rows of brick houses, large and small, and there were handsome public buildings — the skyline was punctuated with church steeples and the great State House tower. Philadelphia also had notable public amenities — paved sidewalks, street lights, municipal water supply, and a charity hospital — most of which had been instituted in the early 1750s. Benjamin Franklin, the city's preeminent citizen, was active in many of these efforts, and Franklin was but the brightest in a galaxy of local intellectuals, including the scientists David Rittenhouse and John Bartram, who corresponded frequently with their peers at the Royal Society in London. Many other prominent Philadelphians, such as Samuel Powel, who had lived some years in London and taken the Grand Tour, were comfortably conversant with European culture.

Upper-class Philadelphians divided time between their city houses and their retreats in the countryside. Two of the grandest examples, under construction or recently completed at the time of Gordon's visit, were the Third Street house of Charles Stedman (begun 1765, completed 1766; sold to Samuel Powel 1769), and Cliveden, in nearby Germantown, begun in 1763 for Attorney General Samuel Chew. Both were accomplished exercises in English Georgian design, with pedimented front door surrounds and paneled and carved interiors. They typify the settings in which urbane and wealthy Philadelphians lived in the sixties and seventies. A measure of that opulence survives in these two houses, which now are open to the public. Indeed, today only at Cliveden is it possible to see much of one family's elaborate rococo furniture in what may be its original setting.[3]

Commerce and trade were the basis of the city's growth and wealth. Philadelphia was the port from which the produce of the vast hinterlands of the middle colonies was shipped. The largest trade was coastal, to the West Indies (flour, foodstuffs, lumber) and to the other American colonies (flour and foodstuffs to the South; wheat and iron to New England). The New England trade was particularly lucrative. And with these profits Philadelphia was able to import, mostly from England, all manner of dry goods and luxuries. Business was basically good from the 1750s through the 1770s, except between 1764 and 1768, when consumption slowed abruptly as the troops who had prosecuted the French and Indian War departed.

The merchants who masterminded Philadelphia's economic expansion after midcentury were, for the most part, new faces in town. Predominantly Anglican, they gradually assumed the power that a Quaker oligarchy had wielded since first settlement. In addition, forward-looking members of the old order saw fit to convert from Quakerism to the Church of England. John Penn, grandson of William, did so in 1751; Samuel Powel, heir to the greatest Quaker fortune in Pennsylvania, in 1767.

Philadelphia also had its share of domestic manufactures. Numerous trades were plied, but the largest group of artisans must have been those who worked with wood. Philadelphia was the largest shipbuilding center in America, though no physical remnants survive. From 1750 to 1775 as many as three thousand houses were built, a goodly number of which still stand.[4] Masses of furniture were required for these houses, and great quantities survive, probably constituting the largest body of artifacts from eighteenth-century Philadelphia. This furniture can be identified by its distinctive Philadelphia style. How that style developed is our present concern.

The names of a large number of Philadelphia furniture craftsmen are known.[5] Many of these men were native-born and locally trained; others were immigrants, trained abroad. Since it was not customary for them to sign or label their work, few pieces of furniture can be identified by maker. However, a survey of such documented examples as exist indicates that the two groups produced consistently different kinds of furniture. There is plain, generally uncarved furniture in traditional Philadelphia patterns that is the product of native-born craftsmen; and there is costly, high-style furniture commissioned to order that is the work of immigrant makers. The latter pieces frequently show ornament from fashionable 1760s London pattern books applied to traditional Philadelphia forms. This distinction between the work of native-born makers and that of immigrants will help explain how the furniture styles of Thomas Chippendale's London were transmitted to Philadelphia and ultimately transformed into a unique Philadelphia style.

It might seem reasonable to assume that the grand pieces were for the great houses of the wealthy, the plain ones for the modest houses of the middle class. Alternatively, it has often been suggested that Quaker clients ordered furniture "of the best sort but plain," Anglicans furniture of the best sort but richly carved.[6] However, bills from two of Philadelphia's most famous cabinetmakers, documenting the refurnishing in the early seventies of two of the city's finest houses (neither surviving), tell another story. Both richly carved pieces and plain furniture were purchased simultaneously for each house, the former for the parlors and other reception rooms, the latter for subsidiary rooms.

One of the houses was that of John Cadwalader (1742–86), a wealthy and widely traveled Anglican merchant. In 1768 Cadwalader married an heiress, Elizabeth Lloyd of Maryland, and the following year he bought a large house on Second Street. In 1771–72, after having gutted and refitted the house, he furnished it with the most elaborate of all the suites of Philadelphia furniture known.[7] James Pemberton (1723–1809), a merchant and prominent Quaker, undertook a similarly ambitious refurnishing project shortly after his third marriage in July 1775. Both men employed Thomas Affleck for the great things (at a cost to Cadwalader of £119.8.0 and to Pemberton of £117) and William Savery for the lesser pieces and repairs (at a cost of £10.2.7 and £6.5.6).[8] Among Affleck's pieces for Cadwalader was a set of four fire screens, the carving subcontracted to the firm of Bernard and Jugiez (fig. 1); among Savery's pieces, "a walnut Chamber table fluted corners / Swell'd brackets," similar, except for possibly having a recessed "knee-hole" center, to a chest of drawers bearing Savery's label (fig. 2).[9] Both artisans were Quakers, but that had nothing to do with the type and style of their work. Rather, it appears that where they were trained determined what they could do. Affleck was London trained, Savery locally trained.

To test the validity of this distinction between the work of native-born and that of London-trained craftsmen, let us survey those Philadelphia makers whose place of origin is known and for whom securely documented pieces exist (labeled, signed, or unequivocally tied to bills or receipts).[10]

Fig. 2. *Chest of drawers*. American, Philadelphia, Pa., 1760–80. Labeled William Savery. Walnut. Private collection.

Fig. 1. *Firescreen*. American, Philadelphia, Pa., 1771. Documented to Thomas Affleck, carving attributed to Bernard & Jugiez. Mahogany. H. 62⅞ in (159.7 cm), W. 21 in (53.3 cm), D. 17¾ in (45 cm). The Metropolitan Museum of Art, New York, gifts and funds from various donors, by exchange, 49.51.

The Native-Born Craftsmen

The native-born makers were firmly in the majority. Best known is William Savery (1721/22–87), the only Philadelphia maker of the period to have left a documented oeuvre large enough for us to identify his own style. Savery's precise place of birth is not known. He was apprenticed to the Philadelphia chairmaker Solomon Fussell (died 1762) between about 1735 and 1742, married in 1746, and is first recorded in business for himself, as a chairmaker in Second Street, in 1750. Later advertisements and labels record his transition from a maker of rush-seated chairs (about 1742–50) to a chairmaker and joiner (about 1750–87). His various printed labels have been found pasted on more than twenty pieces of Philadelphia furniture. The works of his hand are generally plain, with little or no ornamental carving.[11]

Savery's oeuvre consists of a variety of chair types, one of the most ambitious being a cabriole-leg armchair with pierced splat (cat. no. 31); a plain round tea table (cat. no. 35); four plain slant-top desks; two chests of drawers with quarter columns (fig. 2); a tall clock; a dressing table; and a high chest (cat. no. 38). Except for the carving on the high chest, not one of these objects has even the suggestion of rococo ornament.

Samuel Mickle was another locally trained craftsman. No actual furniture by him is known, but a series of

94 Morrison H. Heckscher

dimensioned drawings, executed by him in 1766, possibly when he was apprenticed to Jonathan Shoemaker (1726–93), illustrates some of the furniture forms produced in that shop. All are solid, unexceptional examples readily recognizable as Philadelphia furniture. Only one drawing, showing details of a fretwork frieze and pitch pediment, is more ambitious. Mickle moved from Philadelphia to Haddonfield, New Jersey, in 1770; by 1779 he had left his craft and become a merchant.[12]

David Evans (1748–1820), son of Philadelphia ship joiner Edward Evans, is known primarily from three volumes of his business accounts, covering the years 1774 to 1811, now at the Historical Society of Pennsylvania. They show that this cabinetmaker's work was of two types. He did repairs and odd jobs and made vast numbers of venetian blinds and coffins; and, with a total of seventeen journeymen and four apprentices, he made more than nine hundred pieces of furniture (unfortunately their style is not described in the accounts). With one exception, the pieces that bear his brand are modest and uncarved.[13]

Jonathan Gostelowe (1744–95; born in Passayunk, Philadelphia County) was apprenticed to the cabinetmaker George Claypoole (1730–93) in the early sixties. In 1788 he was chairman of the Cabinet and Chair-Makers in the Federal Procession. The few pieces bearing his label are of two kinds—simple, straight-leg pieces, and serpentine chests with canted corners.[14]

Several other makers who appear to have been native-born—William Connell, Nathaniel Dowdney, Jonathan Shoemaker, Daniel Trotter, and Adam Hains—are known only by one or two labeled or signed pieces, all of which are plain, with almost no carving.[15]

There were a handful of other craftsmen, also thought to have been native-born and locally trained, some of whose known work differs from the foregoing in having carved ornamentation that obviously aspires to the manner of the London rococo. As we shall see later, native-born craftsmen sometimes employed immigrant carvers to embellish their work, and this may explain the rococo carving on a card table by Benjamin Randolph (son of Isaac Fitz-Randolph of Monmouth County, New Jersey), on a chair by James Gillingham (1736–81; born in Bucks County, Pennsylvania), and on work by Thomas Tufft (died 1788) and Edward James.[16] These four men were also the only Philadelphia woodworkers to have engraved cards or labels in the rococo taste.[17]

The London-Trained Craftsmen

The immigrant makers, except for carvers, are notably few. One of the first cabinetmakers to arrive after midcentury was John Elliott (1713–91), born in Bolton, Lancashire. He apparently served an apprenticeship in London and then was indentured as a journeyman in Leicester until 1740. When he sailed for Philadelphia in 1753 it was as an experienced craftsman. For about five years, from his arrival until about 1758, when he left off cabinetmaking to set up as a looking glass importer, Elliott made furniture for leading Philadelphians: for the jurist Edward Shippen, Jr., in 1754 and for the merchant Charles Norris from 1755 to 1758. That furniture has not been identified with any certainty, but the descriptive account entries indicate that it was in a style then new to Philadelphia. For example, in March 1754 he billed Shippen for "Eight Walnut Chairs Carved Claw, and Knees. open back." Carved knees and open backs—that is, pierced splats—are features of a proto-rococo style that Elliott evidently played a role in introducing.[18]

The principal figure among the immigrant cabinetmakers was undoubtedly Thomas Affleck (1740–95). Born in Aberdeen, he was apprenticed to Alex Rose of Ellen, Scotland, beginning in 1754, and moved to London in 1760. He arrived in Philadelphia in 1763, probably in the company of John Penn, lieutenant governor of the colony from 1763 to 1771 and again from 1773 to 1776.[19] Affleck was prominent in the furniture trades in Philadelphia for more than thirty years. He paid the highest occupational tax of all local furniture craftsmen in 1783; he was also the only Philadelphia maker to own a copy of Thomas Chippendale's *Gentleman and Cabinet-Maker's Director*. Affleck's work for a large and wealthy clientele is documented in surviving bills and account books.[20] But other than a chest-on-chest with a superbly carved scroll pediment made for David Deshler in 1775 and the elaborate Cadwalader tables and fire screens, few of those pieces can be convincingly identified.[21] William Macpherson Hornor's claim that a number of the most elaborately carved of all Philadelphia rococo pieces are the work of Affleck for Governor Penn has not been substantiated. Though much remains to be done to sort out the authorship of high-style carved Philadelphia furniture, there is no question about Affleck's importance as a maker of such furniture.

We know more about the immigrant carvers. Of twenty-one carvers known to have been working in Philadelphia between 1750 and 1793, at least nine were immigrants. One, Gabriel Valois, was from Paris by way of London; another, James Connell, was Irish; all the others appear to have been from England. Carvers did not have occasion to sign their work, but serious efforts have recently been made to identify the individual achievements of four of these men who, to judge from their clientele, were among the most prominent. They are Hercules Courtenay, James Reynolds, Nicholas Bernard, and Martin Jugiez, all of whom arrived in Philadelphia between 1762 and 1766 and did architectural and furniture carving.[22]

In architectural matters the four carvers were employed simultaneously, about 1770, in the embellishment of interior fittings for two of the grandest of townhouses in the city, those of Samuel Powel (the former Stedman house) and John Cadwalader. In addition, the firm of Bernard and Jugiez worked at Cliveden in about 1766, and Courtenay did carving for the splendid John Dickinson townhouse in 1772. The Cliveden and Powel house interiors, with carved chimney pieces and door pediments, are very much in the English rococo style of Abraham Swan's *British Architect*, first published in London in 1745 and reissued in Philadelphia in 1775.

In furniture work, the carvers were also brought together on major commissions. Most notably, Reynolds and Bernard and Jugiez were employed by Affleck, their fellow immigrant, to carve the furniture he was supplying to Cadwalader. The fire screens in figure 1 (attributed to Bernard and Jugiez) and the commode card tables and en suite side chairs, with carved backs and skirts and hairy-paw feet (attributed to Reynolds), represent about the fullest development of the rococo style in American furniture.

Bills and receipts show that the immigrant carvers also decorated furniture made by native-born cabinetmakers. Bernard and Jugiez did work for James Gillingham in 1767 and for Benjamin Randolph in 1771. Courtenay worked for Randolph, probably under an indenture, between 1766 and 1769 and for William Wayne in 1773.[23] None of the work of these collaborative ventures has yet been identified.

From this brief survey a pretty consistent pattern emerges: Highly skilled immigrants, especially carvers, received the major commissions in the rococo style. On their own, native makers made fine, serviceable furniture of standard Philadelphia patterns and also did repairs, set up bedsteads, and performed other odd jobs. In concert with English carvers, the native makers produced rococo furniture; but not one richly carved high-style piece can be ascribed solely to native talent. Now, let us see how this information about native-born and immigrant furniture makers in Philadelphia helps elucidate the sources and evolution of Philadelphia cabinet and chair styles.

The Sources of the Philadelphia Chippendale Style

The 1750s saw the introduction of what may be called a proto-rococo style in Philadelphia. Traditional Queen Anne forms were now made in mahogany and highlighted with naturalistic carving: cabriole legs with acanthus leafage on the knees and claw feet; chairs with pierced and carved "strapwork-style" splats (fig. 3); high chests with enclosed bonnet tops, asymmetrical cartouches, central drawers with shells and streamers (fig. 4). We have seen that John Elliott must have been instrumental in introducing this style, but the best example of it is a high chest signed by Henry Clifton and dated 1753 (fig. 4). (Clifton, or Cliffton, worked with Gillingham in the late 1760s, but we do not know where he was born or trained.)

The high chest—a chest of drawers on a high-legged stand—and its companion dressing table (popularly called highboy and lowboy) came to preeminence in Philadelphia at this time. The form originated in England and attained its greatest popularity there in the William and Mary style (c. 1690–1715), characterized by tall turned legs (four in front, two in back) and a flat top. This type was widely copied in Boston from 1700 to 1730. The Boston examples of this period are nearly identical to the English, though the English ones tend to be squatter. Both have either burl-figured veneers or painted decoration. The only clear difference is in the secondary woods—oak and deal were used in England, maple and eastern white pine in Boston. Then, in the 1730s, when the high chest was being superseded in England by the chest-on-chest, Boston cabinetmakers transformed it into a grand, and uniquely American, furniture form. They replaced the four outer turned legs with cabriole legs, the two center ones with pendants; they replaced the flat top with a bonnet top (an

Fig. 3. *Armchair.* American, Philadelphia, Pa., 1750–60. Mahogany. H. 44 in (111.8 cm), W. 33¼ in (84.5 cm), D. 21½ in (54.6 cm). The Metropolitan Museum of Art, New York, Rogers Fund, 25.115.18.

Fig. 4. *High chest of drawers.* American, Philadelphia, Pa., 1753. Signed by Henry Clifton. Mahogany. H. 95½ in (242.6 cm), W. 44¼ in (112.4 cm), D. 22½ in (57.2 cm). The Colonial Williamsburg Foundation, 1975-154.

Philadelphia Furniture   97

Fig. 5. *High chest of drawers*. American, Boston, Mass., 1730–40. Walnut and walnut veneer; eastern white pine. H. 90 in (228.6 cm), W. 44 in (111.8 cm), D. 22¼ in (56.5 cm). The Metropolitan Museum of Art, New York, gift of Mrs. Russell Sage, 10.125.62.

enclosed broken scroll pediment); and they inserted large drawers with recessed carved shells in the tympanum of the bonnet and in the skirt (fig. 5). Lightly constructed of walnut and walnut veneers over an eastern white pine frame (or, alternatively, japanned in imitation of oriental lacquerwork), this form was for thirty years the standard for cabinetmakers throughout New England. By contrast, on the few high chests made in England after 1730, almost the only concession to modernity was the cabriole leg.

The extensive coastal trade between New England and Philadelphia guaranteed that what was fashionable in Boston would be known in Pennsylvania. And it was the Boston high chest that inspired Henry Clifton and other Philadelphia makers in the 1750s. Clifton adopted the bonnet top, the cabriole legs, and the shell drawers. But he used them on a wider, more massive form, constructed of solid mahogany and local secondary woods (poplar and yellow pine). Unfettered by remembrances of the turned-leg form from which the New England model had evolved, he did away with the two awkward pendants in the skirt. The naturalistic carved ornament —leafage on the knees, streamers on the shell drawers, and the asymmetrical cartouche—has no New England precedent and must have been derived from imported English furniture of the 1730s and 1740s.

A dramatic shift in the sources of Philadelphia furniture design occurred in the 1760s. Top-of-the-line bespoke furniture now clearly emulated London work, frequently employing motifs copied directly from designs in the revised and enlarged third edition of Chippendale's *Director* (1762).[24] Designs for chair splats were borrowed in toto: for example, the pattern for a set of chairs for the Fisher family (cat. no. 33) was copied in detail from plate IX (cat. no. 34). Cornice and scroll-pediment elements from desk-and-bookcase designs were used as tops for high chests, the most famous instance being the so-called Pompadour high chest (cat. no. 39), with carved scrolls taken from plate CVIII (cat. no. 41), and a modillion cornice copied precisely from plate CVII (cat. no. 40). The carving on the central drawer is taken from a chimney tablet design in a 1762 carver's booklet by Thomas Johnson (cat. no. 42).

These motifs were almost always applied to established Philadelphia furniture forms. The Chippendale splat (cat. no. 33) replaced the strapwork splat on a typical slip-seated chair with claw-and-ball-footed cabriole legs (fig. 3). The scroll pediment and the chimney tablet carving (cat. no. 39) supplanted the enclosed bonnet top and the shell and streamer drawer on a standard high chest form (fig. 4). The maker of the Pompadour high chest resolved a design problem that had engaged American cabinetmakers ever since the bonnet-top high chest was first introduced in Boston: how to treat the juncture of the tympanum of the scroll pediment with the façade of drawer fronts below. The answer, inspired by Chippendale, was to separate them with a full cornice.

A combination of events resulted in the third edition of Chippendale's *Director* greatly influencing the stylistic evolution of Philadelphia furniture in the 1760s, though the first edition had gone virtually unnoticed in the previous decade. We have seen that in the 1760s Philadelphia became the largest and wealthiest of American colonial cities. The city had strong economic and cultural ties with London, and thus it is not surprising that prosperous Philadelphians wanted the latest London styles. Their aspirations, however, coincided with a general deterioration in political relations between mother country and colonies. Several colonial nonimportation agreements were in effect during this decade, and in Philadelphia it was imprudent to import London manufactures, especially if local substitutes were available.[25] Ambitious London woodworkers saw an opportunity here: by immigrating to Pennsylvania they would have a ready market for their wares, which would be locally made but in the London manner.

The leader among these immigrants was Thomas Affleck. We know that he had his own copy of the *Director*. Very likely he brought it with him, hot off the press, when he arrived in 1763. What better way to promulgate the latest style than with the updated and greatly enlarged third edition of Chippendale's *Director*, published in 1762? The book was soon readily available to other cabinetmakers as well. Sometime between 1764 and 1769 the Library Company of Philadelphia acquired a copy, by which time its subscribers included no fewer than nine prominent furniture makers. Among them were Benjamin Randolph, James Gillingham, and William Savery. We know Randolph and Gillingham hired English carvers to embellish their work, and for both of them we have labeled pieces with modest, but nonetheless London-style, rococo carving. William Savery was not a carver either. His oeuvre includes no rococo carved work, with the magnificent exception of a high chest of drawers (cat. no. 38). We do not know who carved the scroll terminals of the pediment and the rococo C- and S-scroll ornaments on the skirt and knees.[26] Hesitant in handling, this carving does not look like London work. But clearly, with this piece Savery was emulating the overall design of a *Director*-inspired high chest like catalogue number 39. The style brought to Philadelphia by the London immigrants had been taken up by the local makers.

On stylistic evidence, Savery's high chest is later than most of his other, uncarved furniture and must postdate the 1762 edition of the *Director*. It also bears the latest of the several types of labels Savery used, the one that refers to his shop as "At the Sign of the Chest of Drawers, Coffin, and Chair" rather than just "At the Sign of the Chair."[27] Indeed, this is the label found on all the Savery pieces that, though uncarved, show the influence of the Chippendale style.[28]

Savery's earlier furniture, and, we may assume, that of his contemporaries, was inspired by other sources. Benno Forman has shown that during the late thirties Savery learned from his master, Solomon Fussell, to make slat-back chairs with rush seats and "crookt feet," or cabriole legs. The form was Germanic in origin. Forman also demonstrated that during the 1740s Fussell and Savery made square-seated chairs with solid baluster splats, cabriole legs, and turned front stretchers. Stylistically, these chairs relied heavily on the "Boston chairs" then being exported from New England to Philadelphia in great numbers.[29]

In the 1750s Savery must have been influenced by an altogether different source: imported English furniture made during the preceding quarter century. Though we know it must have been there—the importation of English furniture in the eighteenth century is amply documented—today there is not one piece of English-made furniture whose presence in eighteenth-century Philadelphia can be proved. The only evidence is stylistic. A labeled Savery armchair (cat. no. 31) has the traditional Philadelphia square seat frame and cabriole legs, but now the cabriole legs terminate in trifid feet and the splat is pierced in a tripartite pattern. The source of the trifid feet is English or Irish chairs,[30] and the splat pattern is clearly based upon a plain and not uncommon English model (cat. no. 32).

The only table bearing a Savery label is that ubiquitous Philadelphia form the circular tilt-top tea table (cat. no. 35). It has the raised-edge dish top common to uncarved Philadelphia examples. On the other hand, the turnings, particularly the pillars of the bird-cage box (which allows the top to rotate), have straight shafts in the English manner. Here again, Savery apparently was inspired directly by an English model.

The tilt-top tea table does not feature in the *Director*, but it was extremely popular in Philadelphia throughout the third quarter of the eighteenth century. In keeping with the prevailing taste for the rococo, the dish top was transformed by scalloping the raised edge into a "piecrust," the top of the shaft was fluted, the bulbous lower section of the pillar and the knees were leaf-carved, and the feet were rendered with the claw and ball. Catalogue number 36 is a classic example; Bernard and Jugiez, to whom its carving has been attributed, would have known such work in England.[31] An English teakettle stand (cat. no. 37), for instance, has decoration markedly similar to that of the American table.

When all is said and done, the distinctive school of cabinet- and chairmakers that flowered in Philadelphia in the 1760s and 1770s was the result of a unique combination of circumstances. This was a period of great economic growth. A boom in house building created a large demand for new furnishings, and newly wealthy colonists wanted to be up-to-date with the latest London fashions. Locally made furniture already had an individual style and design vocabulary—a style that, as a result of extensive New England trade, showed the influence of Boston furniture. But prominent Philadelphians were cosmopolitan in outlook. The Samuel Powels of the time had taken the Grand Tour; they knew London and had friends and business contacts there.

Political tensions between the mother country and the colony led to curtailment of the market for imported English furniture. In consequence, a number of highly skilled English craftsmen, primarily carvers, immigrated to Philadelphia to take advantage of the demand for high-quality locally made furniture in the latest London fashion—that of the third edition of Chippendale's *Director*. It was these immigrants, above all, who developed the Philadelphia Chippendale style, applying London ornamentation to locally popular furniture forms made in the traditional Philadelphia manner.

The native-born makers were mostly obliged to do the less glamorous part of the trade—repair work and utilitarian furniture. They also made "plain" furniture, with minimal carving, such as clients like John Cadwalader would have wanted for their lesser rooms. Some of these pieces were based upon Philadelphia furniture designs of the 1750s, updated with motifs taken from middle-class English furniture imported before the non-importation agreements of the 1760s (cat. nos. 31, 35). But some plain furniture was influenced by the immigrants' work. William Savery's famous high chest (cat. no. 38) is a modest rendition of the "Pompadour" (cat. no. 39): the American craftsman's transformation of the European tradition.

NOTES

1. As quoted in Newton D. Mereness, ed., *Travels in the American Colonies* (New York: Macmillan, 1916), p. 410.

2. For recent accounts of Philadelphia in the second half of the eighteenth century, see "Town into City, 1746–1765," by Theodore Thayer, and "The Revolutionary City, 1765–1783," by Harry M. Tinkom, in *Philadelphia: A 300-Year History*, ed. Russell F. Weigley (New York: W. W. Norton, 1982), pp. 68–154; Thomas M. Doerflinger, *A Vigorous Spirit of Enterprise: Merchants and Economic Development in Revolutionary Philadelphia* (Chapel Hill: University of North Carolina Press, 1986).

3. For the Powel house see George B. Tatum, *Philadelphia Georgian: The City House of Samuel Powel and Some of Its Eighteenth-Century Neighbors* (Middletown, Conn.: Wesleyan University Press, 1976); for Cliveden see Raymond V. Shepherd, Jr., "Cliveden and Its Philadelphia-Chippendale Furniture: A Documented History," *The American Art Journal* 8 (November 1976): 2–16.

4. In 1746 there were about 1,500 dwellings for a population of about 10,000; in 1765 there were nearly 5,000 houses for some 25,000 people; see Thayer, "Town into City," p. 79. From 1760 to 1774 the number of houses increased by 80 percent; see Doerflinger, *Spirit of Enterprise*, p. 178.

5. The principal lists of Philadelphia furniture makers including the period 1750 to 1800 are (1) names culled from the Occupational Tax lists of 1783 and 1786, in William Macpherson Hornor, Jr., *Blue Book: Philadelphia Furniture, William Penn to George Washington* (1935; reprint, Washington, D.C.: Highland House, 1977), pp. 317–26; (2) Dard Hunter, Jr., "A Directory of the Cabinet Makers and Allied Trades in Philadelphia to 1820," 1954, MS on deposit in the Winterthur Library; (3) Arthur Leibundguth, Index of Names of Furniture-Making Craftsmen Active in Philadelphia, c. 1730–c. 1760, in "The Furniture-Making Crafts in Philadelphia, c. 1730–c. 1760" (M.A. thesis, University of Delaware, 1964), pp. 132–36.

6. For example, Carl and Jessica Bridenbaugh, *Rebels and Gentlemen: Philadelphia in the Age of Franklin* (1942; reprint, New York: Oxford University Press, 1962), p. 206, claimed that "wealthy Quakers admired fine workmanship, but demanded simplicity of design."

7. For a complete history of the Cadwalader house and furnishings, see Nicholas B. Wainwright, *Colonial Grandeur in Philadelphia: The House and Furniture of General John Cadwalader* (Philadelphia: Historical Society of Pennsylvania, 1964).

8. The Affleck bills are reproduced in Wainwright, *Colonial Grandeur*, p. 44, and Hornor, *Blue Book*, p. 113. The Savery bills are reproduced in Wainwright, *Colonial Grandeur*, p. 62, and W. M. Hornor, Jr., "William Savery: Chairmaker and Joiner," *The Antiquarian*, July 1930, p. 32.

9. The *Prices of Cabinet and Chair Work*, published in Philadelphia by James Humphreys in 1772, lists, under "High Chest of Drawers," the following: "Chest on Chest & Sweld Braqet" with "Table to Suit Ditto" in walnut for £3.5.0. See Martin Eli Weil, "A Cabinetmaker's Price Book," *Winterthur Portfolio* 13 (1979): 181.

10. The Decorative Arts Photographic Collection at the Winterthur Museum has photographs of most of the documented pieces discussed in this essay.

11. For a biographical sketch of Savery, see *Philadelphia: Three Centuries of American Art* (Philadelphia: Philadelphia Museum of Art, 1976), pp. 50–51.

12. The Mickle drawings are in the Philadelphia Museum of Art. For biographical information on Mickle see *Philadelphia: Three Centuries*, p. 87.

13. See Dard Hunter, Jr., "David Evans, Cabinet Maker: His Life and Work," 1954, MS on deposit in the Winterthur Library. The Marlborough-leg serving table that Hunter illustrates (pls. 14–18) has elaborate fretwork and richly carved moldings and brackets which are unlike any other known Philadelphia work.

14. See Raymond B. Clarke, Jr., "Jonathan Gostelowe (1744–95), Philadelphia Cabinetmaker" (M.A. thesis, University of Delaware, 1956).

15. A labeled Connell clock case is illustrated in Joseph Downs, *American Furniture in the Henry Francis du Pont Winterthur Museum* (New York: Macmillan, 1952), no. 207; a Dowdney clock case in *Antiques*, March 1955, p. 236; a Shoemaker chest in *Antiques*, May 1985, p. 1172; Trotter chairs in Robert D. Schwarz, *The Stephen Girard Collection: A Selective Catalog* (Philadelphia: Girard College, 1980), nos. 12–14; a Trotter chest in *Antiques*, October 1937, inside back cover; a Hains table in Downs, *American Furniture*, no. 314.

16. A labeled Randolph card table is illustrated in Charles F. Hummel, *A Winterthur Guide to American Chippendale Furniture: Middle Atlantic and Southern Colonies* (New York: Crown, 1976), fig. 101; a Tufft dressing table in *Antiques*, October 1927, pp. 292–93; a Tufft chair in Downs, *American Furniture*, no. 134; a James clock case in *Philadelphia: Three Centuries*, p. 94; a Gillingham chair in Luke Vincent Lockwood, *Colonial Furniture in America*, 3d ed. (New York: Charles Scribner's Sons, 1926), vol. 2, fig. 558.

17. The Randolph trade card is illustrated in Marshall B. Davidson, *The American Heritage History of Colonial Antiques* (New York: American Heritage Publishing Company, 1967), p. 201; the Tufft label in *Antiques*, August 1940, p. 75; the James label in *American Antiques from Israel Sack Collection*, vol. 1 (Washington, D.C.: Highland House, 1981), p. 200; the Gillingham label in Lockwood, *Colonial Furniture*, vol. 2, fig. 559.

18. Mary Ellen Hayward, "The Elliotts of Philadelphia: Emphasis on the Looking Glass Trade, 1755–1810" (M.A. thesis, University of Delaware, 1971), pp. 17–21.

19. For a biographical sketch of Affleck, see *Philadelphia: Three Centuries*, pp. 98–99.

20. Hornor, *Blue Book*, pp. 73–74; 184–85.

21. For the Deshler chest-on-chest see Hornor, *Blue Book*, pl. 123; for the Cadwalader pieces see the Affleck bill in Wainwright, *Colonial Grandeur*, p. 44.

22. Luke Beckerdite, "Philadelphia Carving Shops," part 1, "James Reynolds," *Antiques*, May 1984, pp. 1120–33; part 2, "Bernard and Jugiez," September 1985, pp. 498–513; part 3, "Hercules Courtenay and His School," May 1987, pp. 1044–63.

23. Beckerdite, "Bernard and Jugiez," p. 503, and "Hercules Courtenay," pp. 1045–46.

24. For a detailed survey of the *Director*'s influence on furniture design in Philadelphia, see Morrison Heckscher, "Philadelphia Chippendale: The Influence of the *Director* in America," *Furniture History* 21 (1985): 283–95.

25. Some three hundred Philadelphia merchants agreed to a policy of nonimportation of most British goods in response to the Stamp Act (1765) and to the Townshend Revenue Act (1767). See Tinkom, "The Revolutionary City," pp. 112, 115.

26. As illustrated here in cat. no. 38, the central finial is a conjectural modern restoration.

27. Actually, the latest type of label is pasted on the top of the lower section; fragments of an earlier label are in a drawer of the upper section. The various Savery labels are illustrated in Hornor, *Blue Book*, pls. 89–93.

28. Savery's Chippendale-style pieces include a chest of drawers (fig. 2); a Gothic-splat armchair at the Winterthur Museum (illus. Hummel, *Winterthur Guide*, fig. 44); and a tall clock that descended in Savery's family (illus. *Antiques*, November 1928, p. 310).

29. Benno M. Forman, "Delaware Valley 'Crookt Foot' and Slat-Back Chairs: The Fussell-Savery Connection," *Winterthur Portfolio* 15 (Spring 1980): 41–64.

30. For example, John T. Kirk, *American Furniture and the British Tradition to 1830* (New York: Alfred A. Knopf, 1982), fig. 800.

31. Beckerdite, "Bernard and Jugiez," pp. 505–6.

Catalogue Objects

31. *Armchair*
American, Philadelphia, Pa., 1750–60
Labeled William Savery (1721/22–87)
Walnut; yellow pine
H. 40 in (101.6 cm), W. 29¼ in (74.3 cm), D. 22½ in (57.2 cm)
The Henry Francis du Pont Winterthur Museum, Winterthur, Del., 58.2680

32. *Side chair*
English, 1740–70
Mahogany
H. 36³⁄₁₆ in (91.9 cm), W. 20¾ in (52.7 cm), D. 20¼ in (51.4 cm)
The Colonial Williamsburg Foundation, Williamsburg, Va., 1975-195

31. Armchair / 32. Side chair

The armchair (cat. no. 31) has a printed paper label glued to the inside of the back seat rail, which reads: "All Sorts of Chairs and Joiners Work Made and Sold by *William Savery*, At the Sign of the Chair a little below the Market, in Second Street, PHILADELPHIA." William Savery was apprenticed to Philadelphia chairmaker Solomon Fussell between about 1735 and 1742. During his career he used labels with three different messages on them. This one is of the second type, probably used between 1750 (when he first advertised as being in business on Second Street) and about 1765.

The chair frame is entirely of black walnut, the separate seat frame of yellow pine, both woods indigenous to eastern Pennsylvania. With its trapezoidal seat frame, rectangular eared back, and pierced splat, the chair appears to be a plain "Chippendale" chair. Actually, it is made in large part like a Philadelphia Queen Anne chair of the 1740s, with curvilinear arms and arm supports, cabriole front legs, trifid pad feet, and stump rear legs with beveled edges, octagonal in section. Savery must have learned this method of design and construction in Fussell's shop.

The pierced splat—the visual focus of the chair—has a different source. It is of a pattern seen fairly often

102 Morrison H. Heckscher

33. *Side chair*
American, Philadelphia, Pa. 1762–75
Possibly by Thomas Affleck, born Aberdeen, Scotland (1740–95)
Mahogany; tulip poplar and yellow pine
H. 39¼ in (99.7 cm), W. 24¼ in (61.6 cm), D. 22 in (55.9 cm)
The Philadelphia Museum of Art, given by Mrs. William Macpherson Hornor, 46-87-1

33. Side chair / 34. Side chair design

The side chair (cat. no. 33) is one of a set of six thought to have been made for Sarah Logan Fisher of Philadelphia. For her marriage in 1772, her father, William Logan, ordered furniture from Thomas Affleck, the London-trained cabinetmaker who came to Philadelphia in 1763. Affleck's bill totaled £72.15.00, of which £50 was owed to the carver James Reynolds, who arrived from London in 1766. There is no proof that these chairs were a part of that transaction, but the high quality of their carving is consonant with the work of such a highly skilled immigrant.

The chair has a most graceful back, the crest rail and

in plain English chairs of the third quarter of the century. Since Savery was untraveled and since this splat design does not appear in furniture pattern books of the time, it is safe to conclude that Savery's inspiration was an imported chair. No example with a Philadelphia history is known, but catalogue number 32 is representative of the type. We don't know where in England it was made. The straight front legs and stretchers are standard features of inexpensive English chairs but were never popular in Philadelphia. The local chairmakers' preference for cabriole legs, established back in the 1740s, prevailed.

Philadelphia Furniture 103

34. *Side chair design*
Thomas Chippendale, *The Gentleman and Cabinet-Maker's Director* (London, 1762), plate IX (detail)
Photograph, The Metropolitan Museum of Art, New York, The Elisha Whittelsey Collection, The Elisha Whittelsey Fund, 1982, 1982.1133
Engraving on exhibit from the collection of John Hardy

35. Tea table
36. Tea table
37. Teakettle stand

The round tea table pictured as catalogue number 35 has the printed paper label of William Savery, native Philadelphia furniture maker, pasted on the underside of the top. This is the label Savery used between about 1750 and 1765. The only such table known by him, it has the neatness and simplicity characteristic of his work. The raised rim of the circular top, a bead and narrow cavetto molding, is typical of Philadelphia practice, as is the treatment of the legs. The profiles of the turnings, however, are not. The straight-sided columnar shape of the four small pillars of the bird-cage box beneath the top and the tapered column and fillet forming the main pillar are in the English manner.

The other round tea table (cat. no. 36) is enriched with all the varieties of carving that money could buy, with "claw feet," "Leaves on the knees," and "Scollop'd Top & Carv'd Pillar." The Philadelphia price book for 1786 valued such a table at £5.15, and at £6 with "Fluting the pillar." (A plain table sold for as little as £1.15.) The turnings here have profiles characteristic of Philadelphia work, the main pillar being of the vase-and-column type, and the four small pillars of the box having a bold baluster shape. The carving has been attributed to Bernard and Jugiez, a partnership of two London carvers who had set up shop in Philadelphia by 1762.

The round tea table was immensely popular in Philadelphia, almost to the exclusion of other tea table types. It is a versatile form. When the table is placed in the center of the room, its top can be rotated like a lazy susan to distribute tea and cookies. With its top tilted to the vertical, the table can be pushed into a corner. The tipping and rotating are made possible by the box, or "bird cage," that is hinged to the top and rests upon the main pillar.

Although barely noted in the engraved furniture pattern books of Chippendale and others, this form was widely made in England as full-size tea tables and also as diminutive kettle stands. These English pieces were, perforce, the inspiration for their Philadelphia counterparts. The English kettle stand shown here (cat. no. 37), though it has no Philadelphia history, is representative of the stylish carved prototype. The "pie-crust" rim of its top and the vase-and-column pillar have obvious

splat joined by unbroken strapwork scrolls. This back design is very closely modeled on that of a pattern (cat. no. 34) in plate IX of Chippendale's *Director* of 1762, a copy of which Affleck owned. It is only on custom-designed and richly carved furniture that this kind of direct copying of pattern-book motifs was practiced in Philadelphia.

The back design may have been cribbed from Chippendale, but the rest of the chair is pure Philadelphia. The seat rails are uncarved and have a flat-arched bottom edge. The front legs have claw-and-ball feet. The rear legs are of the simple "stump" type, a rounded oval in section. The secondary woods, tulip poplar and yellow pine, are native to Pennsylvania. In sum, this bespeaks local craft practices to which even the leading immigrant masters of the 1760s had to adapt.

35. *Tea table*
American, Philadelphia, Pa., 1750–60
Labeled William Savery (1721/22–87)
Mahogany
H. 29½ in (74.9 cm), Diam. 34¹⁵⁄₁₆ in (88.7 cm)
The Philadelphia Museum of Art, Haas Community Funds and J. Stogdell Stokes Fund, 68-174-1

36. *Tea table*
American, Philadelphia, Pa., 1765–75
Carving attributed to Nicholas Bernard and Martin Jugiez (in partnership c. 1762–83)
Mahogany
H. 28¼ in (71.8 cm), Diam. 35 in (88.9 cm)
The Philadelphia Museum of Art, bequest of R. Wistar Harvey, 40-16-2

37. *Teakettle stand*
English, 1740–60
Mahogany
H. 21¼ in (54 cm), Diam. 13¾ in (34.9 cm)
Museum of Art, Rhode Island School of Design, Providence, bequest of Charles L. Pendleton, 04.043

Philadelphia Furniture 105

affinities with the carved Philadelphia table, even if the handling is subtly different. The "English" profiles of the turnings on the documented Savery table prove that such turnings were to be found in Philadelphia, but they were the exception rather than the rule.

38. High chest of drawers

In overall design this high chest is identical to catalogue number 39 (the Pompadour), with a continuous cornice surmounted by a scroll pediment and a large drawer centered in the skirt. Its decoration, however, is much plainer. There is less carving and what there is, is less good—particularly that on the knees and skirt.

This high chest is clearly a native maker's production ultimately inspired by the Pompadour. It bears the label of William Savery, a native-born and -trained maker. In all respects but one, the construction of the two chests is similar, and typical of Philadelphia cabinetwork. The one difference is that Savery's pediment is a separate, removable unit, whereas the Pompadour's is not. The laborious manner in which the maker of the Pompadour fashioned the top suggests that it was his first essay in that design. Most Philadelphia case pieces with this type of continuous cornice and scroll pediment have the much more simply made (and less expensive) removable top with pierced latticework. Such a piece must have been the immediate source for the Savery high chest.

38. High chest of drawers
American, Philadelphia, Pa., 1762–75
Labeled William Savery (1721/22–87)
Mahogany; yellow pine, tulip poplar, and Atlantic white cedar
H. 94 in (238.8 cm), W. 45 in (114.3 cm), D. 24 in (61 cm)
Collection of H. Richard Dietrich, Jr.

39. High chest of drawers
40. Desk and bookcase design
41. Desk and bookcase design
42. Chimney tablet design

This high chest of drawers (cat. no. 39), called the Pompadour because of an erroneous association of its portrait bust with Madame Pompadour, combines native Philadelphia construction with overall design features from Boston and ornamentation from English pattern books. The construction is in the traditional Philadelphia manner, with solid primary woods, yellow pine top and bottom boards, and finely dovetailed drawer linings of poplar and cedar. The mahogany veneer on the drawer fronts is an English element, but an English cabinetmaker would not have veneered over a solid mahogany core.

39. *High chest of drawers*
American, Philadelphia, Pa., 1762–75
Mahogany, mahogany veneer; yellow pine, tulip poplar, and northern white cedar
H. 91¾ in (233 cm), W. 44⅝ in (113.3 cm), D. 24⅝ in (62.5 cm)
The Metropolitan Museum of Art, New York, John Stewart Kennedy Fund, 1918, 18.110.4

Philadelphia Furniture 109

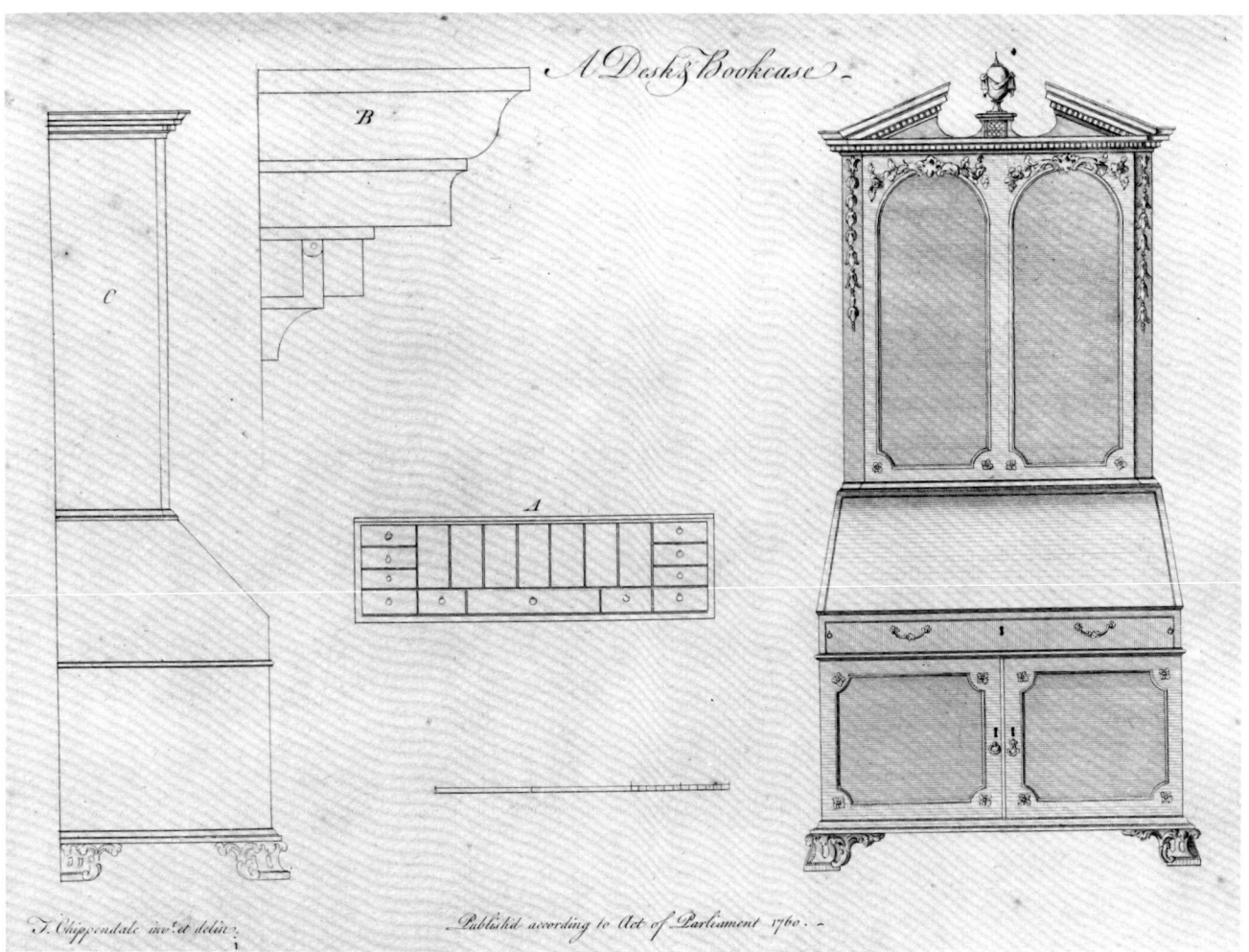

40. *Desk and bookcase design*
Thomas Chippendale, *The Gentleman and Cabinet-Maker's Director* (London, 1762), plate CVII
Photograph, The Metropolitan Museum of Art, New York, The Elisha Whittelsey Collection, The Elisha Whittelsey Fund, 1982, 1982.1133
Engraving on exhibit from the collection of John Hardy

Two important design features of the high chest derive from Boston: the scroll pediment and the large carved central skirt drawer (see fig. 5, p. 98). But the ornamentation of these elements is taken from English pattern-book designs. The broken pediment with foliate scrolls and portrait bust above a continuous cornice shows a general debt to plate CVIII in Chippendale's *Director* (cat. no. 41). The cornice moldings are copied directly from cornice detail B in plate CVII (cat. no. 40), conclusively demonstrating the direct influence of the Chippendale designs. The draped-urn finials, not found on other Philadelphia work, can also be traced to plate CVII. The high chest's central lower drawer is carved with a swans-and-serpent image designed for a tablet in a chimneypiece and borrowed in toto from Thomas Johnson's *A New Book of Ornament* (cat. no. 42). The dimensions of the drawer front ($8\frac{1}{4} \times 15$ in) are nearly identical to those specified in the engraving for the chimney tablet ($8 \times 13\frac{1}{16}$ in). Johnson was a leading London woodcarver. One of his apprentices, Hercules Courtenay, moved to Philadelphia about 1763; he may well have carved this piece.

110 Morrison H. Heckscher

41. *Desk and bookcase design*
Thomas Chippendale, *The Gentleman and Cabinet Maker's Director* (London, 1762), plate CVIII
The Metropolitan Museum of Art, New York, The Elisha Whittelsey Collection, The Elisha Whittelsey Fund, 1982, 1982.1133
Exhibited in Minneapolis only

42. *Chimney tablet design*
Thomas Johnson, *A New Book of Ornament* (London, 1762), plate 5
The Metropolitan Museum of Art, New York, gift of Harvey Smith, 1985, 1985.1099

Philadelphia Furniture   111

Robert F. Trent

The Colchester School of Cabinetmaking, 1750–1800

Despite an upsurge of interest in American regional furniture made during the last half of the eighteenth century, those with a vested interest in studying the material life and design trends of the time still have no adequate interpretive framework for furniture makers working outside urban stylistic centers. The polarity "urban/rural" (or "city/country") still persists, as does use of the terms "high style" (or "elite"), "popular," "provincial," and "folk" to denote supposedly recognizable and mutually exclusive sets of formal attributes, which in practice are hard to define. High style refers to the most expensive and up-to-date urban production. Popular is generally understood to mean stylish but inexpensive urban production. Provincial, even more problematic, is usually taken to mean ambitious work produced near major urban centers that fails to achieve the effects it aspires to. And folk means conservative, ethnic, or idiosyncratic furniture made in rural areas by artisans isolated from fashionable trends. To this inadequate, often confusing classification dealers and collectors have added "high country," meaning furniture that is nonurban yet stylish.

To escape the quandary of distinguishing among these overlapping categories, sensitive commentators on architecture have employed the terms "metropolitan" and "vernacular" to describe historical building traditions. Many of these architectural historians choose to stress the process by which traditions are disseminated or conserved, without making judgments about quality that have no historical justification.[1] Another approach is to consider the terms high style, popular, provincial, and folk as representing mental attitudes that all members of a given society share to some degree. Thus, any building or piece of furniture can have high-style, popular, provincial, and folk aspects. A Philadelphia Chippendale high chest, for instance, can be regarded as embodying high-style rococo ornament, a popular furniture form, a provincial heaviness and overabundance of ornament, and Germanic folk construction techniques.[2]

There is much to commend the latter approach. The obvious truth is that almost every stylistic expression of one culture can be viewed as in some way inferior to or dependent on a style or styles of another contemporary culture. The ambivalent reaction of English artists and designers to the French rococo style is a classic example of how transmission of formal attributes was hindered by moral and religious strictures, national chauvinism, and jealousy.[3] The highly selective way in which prosperous Americans adopted the successive styles fashionable in London mercantile and courtly society throughout the eighteenth century is another example. Acceptance of London styles was conditioned by colonial (or colonialist) sympathies, religious convictions, and political jealousies. The same ambivalence persists in the value judgments made by modern architectural and furniture historians. Few English scholars would be willing to state that Philadelphia Chippendale high chests are as good as the best works of Thomas Chippendale. They classify them as "provincial," which to them means influenced by a metropolitan stylistic impulse but made outside of London and therefore inherently inferior.

Furniture scholars in America tend to treat furniture production from the maker's point of view. The ingrained tradition of connoisseurship (here defined as the study of workmanship and style, not the making of judgments about quality) has been sustained by studies of the account books of cabinetmakers, joiners, and turners and of listings in probate inventories. Emphasis on connoisseurship at least prompts scholars to assess objects in terms that are historically accurate and explicitly descriptive. The paucity of well-documented furniture for which the original maker, owner, price, and primary setting or use are known forces a continuing search for labeled or otherwise documented examples by various makers as an aid in organizing the great body of surviving undocumented objects. In a broader context, this approach leads to the formulation of "regional attributes," stylistic and structural traits that can, with reasonable accuracy, place an object within the orbit of a major stylistic center.[4] This kind of investigation has proven very successful in the study of eighteenth-century furniture production in major American urban centers, where quantity production, long-standing shop traditions, and division of the trade into specialties like joinery, cabinetmaking, turning, carving, and gilding resulted in a certain uniformity in practice. It has also led to the recognition of related schools of production in ancillary centers, which still, to some degree, constitute urban phenomena.[5]

Where this approach has failed is in identifying and interpreting schools of production well outside urban centers. In nonurban areas wealth was significantly less than in cities, communication with cultural and economic centers was uncertain, production was sporadic and quality less consistent, and ethnic and social differences interfered with the transmission and adoption of metropolitan styles. Certainly scholars have documented schools that can be variously described as provincial, vernacular, or folk, but they have not explained how local schools of furniture evolved or how they reflected local identities. The successful and pervasive traditions of workmanship in nonurban areas have been explained away as expressions of the "individuality" of the artisans or the "naïveté" of their patrons.

This kind of thinking has influenced attitudes toward furniture made in Connecticut between 1750 and 1800. As early twentieth-century collectors, dealers, and curators repeatedly discovered either severely plain or fantastically ornamented case pieces with strong histories of ownership in Connecticut families, they developed explanations for how the makers of this furniture thought and worked. Plain furniture was said to reflect lingering Puritan objections to waste and ostentation. Furniture heavily decorated in a manner not obviously derived from that of a major urban center was thought to testify to the individuality, or worse, the ingenuity of the maker. Connecticut furniture makers were never credited with either the ability or the desire to consciously *select* from a wide range of stylistic sources.

Of all the types of eighteenth-century Connecticut furniture recognized by the 1930s, the one that has most interested collectors and dealers is the block-fronted case piece with carved shells made in the manner of the Goddard-Townsend shops of Newport, Rhode Island. Early in this century Newport case pieces assumed the status of masterpieces of American design and workmanship, challenging even Philadelphia Chippendale high chests. That a school of Connecticut cabinetmakers should have emulated Newport work lent the Connecticut case pieces a certain cachet.[6] Theories about how the block-and-shell tradition was transmitted to Connecticut included the (now known to be mistaken) idea that John Townsend (1732–1809), one of the most famous of the Newport workmen, resided in Middletown on the Connecticut River during the Revolution, when Newport was sporadically attacked or occupied by the British.[7]

The key work of the Connecticut block-and-shell tradition is a desk at the Metropolitan Museum of Art with a blocked front and an elaborate interior (cat. no. 43), first published in 1891.[8] This desk bears the ink inscription "This desk was maid in the year of 1769 Buy Benjn Burnam that sarvfed his time in felledlfay" (that is, the maker, Benjamin Burnham, served his apprenticeship in Philadelphia). One might think it easy to discover exactly who Benjamin Burnham was and where he lived. However, the best efforts of Connecticut's genealogists have not established his identity with certainty. Of five possible candidates found in the records, the most likely was the husband of Catherine Trumbull Burnham (1731–1803) of Colchester, Connecticut. According to family tradition, her husband was a skilled cabinetmaker who left on a voyage for England in 1773 and was never heard from again. Their son Joseph Trumbull Burnham (1771?–1852) trained with the Colchester cabinetmaker Amos Wells (1735–1802) and later moved to the nearby town of Hebron, where he worked until his death. Joseph's son Griswold Burnham (1813–1904) recorded the family traditions about his mysterious grandfather, and the Metropolitan's desk was said to have been found in Hebron, so this desk may indeed have been one owned and used by the Colchester Benjamin Burnham's descendants.[9]

A nearly identical desk originally owned by Eliphalet Bulkeley (born 1746) of Colchester, who was Catherine Trumbull Burnham's cousin, is considered an equally important piece related to Burnham's work. The desk has the name "Loomis" inscribed on the interior center drawer. This signature has been associated by Minor Myers, Jr., and Edgar deN. Mayhew with the Colchester cabinetmaker Samuel Loomis (1748–1814); they speculated that Loomis was Burnham's apprentice and that he made the desk in 1769 as his proof piece when concluding his apprenticeship, for he would have been nearly twenty-one years old at that time. Myers and Mayhew substantiated this theory by noting that the construction of the Loomis desk is much like that of the Burnham one.[10]

A number of minor problems interfere with this hypothesis. Although both desks were obviously made with the same patterns and are remarkably similar in detail, the Loomis desk was originally the bottom half of a desk and bookcase—the nail holes from a retaining molding are visible on the top, and the top is made up of a narrow front strip of mahogany and a wider back strip of cherry, a sure indication that the top was meant to be covered by an upper case. On the lid, a later addition of thick, book-sawn mahogany panels surrounded by a molding may conceal inlaid compass stars like those on the lid of the Burnham desk. One might conclude, therefore, that Loomis made the desk using Burnham's patterns but that this desk and its lost bookcase may not be Loomis's "masterpiece" of 1769—it could conceivably date as much as ten or fifteen years later.

In 1963, Houghton Bulkeley noted the discovery of an entry in the probate docket of the wealthy Colchester merchant Jonathan Deming (died 1788) wherein certain furniture listed in the inventory was attributed to Samuel Loomis (numbers on right are pounds sterling):[11]

1 case drawers	16	00	00
1 desk	14	00	00
1 mahogany stand table	4	00	00
1 do fall do	4	00	00
2 cherry stand tables @ 53/4	5	06	00
1 do fall do	2	06	00
1 do bureau	4	13	04
6 framed chairs [@] 20/	6	00	00
1 mahogany bureau table	6	13	04
1 do dressing do	6	13	04
12 mahogany chairs	13	09	04
6 framed cherry chairs @ 24/	7	04	00
1 cherry bureau table	5	06	00
1 server		03	04
	95	16	00

This furniture was expensive and pretentious by Connecticut standards of the 1780s, and the cabinetmaker appears to have enjoyed a considerable regional reputation. Undoubtedly the estate appraisers, two of whom were Deming's cousins Henry Champion, Jr. (1751–1836), and Epaphroditus Champion (1756–1834), were less concerned with bolstering Loomis's reputation than with justifying the high values they placed on the furniture. The case of drawers (a chest-on-chest), the bureau tables, and the joined chairs with upholstered seats that they recorded were among the most elaborate furniture forms produced in Connecticut, forms that only a small percentage of the population could aspire to own.

One of the two major case pieces on the list, the case of drawers valued at £16, has been securely identified (cat. no. 44); the desk valued at £14 has been tentatively identified with a desk in the Henry Ford Museum.[12] These pieces by Samuel Loomis firmly link the Benjamin Burnham and Samuel Loomis desks discussed above to the large group of extant Connecticut block-fronted case pieces with carved shells. Now we must ask why major case pieces made in the tradition of a shop whose master trained in Philadelphia should have been modeled on Rhode Island work and also why Burnham and Loomis augmented the rather austere design of the Rhode Island case pieces with twisted columns, pagodalike finials, and less-than-accomplished incised carving (like that on the knees of the Burnham desk and the tympanum of the Loomis case of drawers). The problem is further complicated by examples of other furniture forms obviously related to the Burnham-Loomis shop tradition.

High chests like that owned by the well-to-do land speculator Epaphras Lord (1709–99) of Colchester survive in great numbers, and all are heavily ornamented. The Lord high chest (cat. no. 49) has typical Burnham-Loomis incised work on the knees, but it also has a pediment outline that is one of the most consistent features of Colchester case pieces and one that is not seen on the Loomis chest-on-chest, perhaps because of that object's great height and width. The pediment is composed of two arcs of different radii, separated by a short section of straight molding. The foot of the larger, outside arc is set inside the baselines of the sides of the case, and the outer ends of the scrolls therefore kick up at the ends instead of terminating in straight sections suitable for lying atop implied pilasters. In other Colchester high chests, even those with pilasters, the same violation of strict classical rules occurs. The general effect suggests a pair of rearing caterpillars. This pediment design further muddies the origins of the Connecticut block-and-shell style, because Rhode Island scroll pediments have a far lower outline, being composed of two arcs of equal radius without any section of straight molding intervening. The basic form of Colchester high chests, however, is derived from the Boston high chests that had been in fashion in eastern Connecticut since the 1740s.

Another furniture form characteristic of the Burnham-Loomis school is the chest of three drawers on high cabriole legs. These chests, which survive in some numbers, are consistently executed. From the base molding up, they follow Rhode Island precedents closely, with blocked drawer fronts surmounted by carved shells and a deep cove molding immediately under the top. But the high cabriole front legs, which are offset by immense ogee bracket feet at the rear, are never seen on Rhode Island examples, or, for that matter, on any other type of Connecticut chest of drawers.

In view of the various motifs and proportional systems that Burnham and Loomis employed in their case pieces, one must conclude that they *consciously* borrowed from many sources and combined their borrowings in ways that are not immediately evident. As already noted, some of these sources are known. The rearing scroll pediment almost certainly can be attributed to a reinterpretation by Benjamin Burnham of high pediments he had seen while working in Philadelphia, where cabinetmakers had a specific reason for employing the high-pitched pediment (cat. no. 50). The pediment was designed to provide a large scroll board or tympanum on which to mount rococo carving. Occasionally the large area created is occupied by a drawer with a carved front. That rococo carving was the express intention of those Philadelphia cabinetmakers who specialized in highly ornamented case pieces for wealthy clients is demonstrated by Philadelphia pieces that were not designed for extensive ornamentation; those high chests, chests-on-chests, and bookcase tops have far lower scroll pediments, often springing from a frieze.

Much the same explanation holds for the high cabriole front legs on Colchester chests with three drawers. The form of the legs and of the carved claw feet is derived from Philadelphia prototypes, although the particular context in which they are used forced their makers to elide the upper portions of the cabriole leg. The incised carving on the knees of some of the case pieces represents a simplified version of carved leafage on the legs of Philadelphia pieces, although the peculiar, fine work on the tympanum of the Loomis chest-on-chest is entirely unacademic in character and must be seen as an attempt to supply rococo scrollwork and leafage where the training to execute it was wanting.

The full-round twist columns and complementary twist carving on pagodalike finials seen on Colchester case pieces appear similar to a genre of twist-turned stair banisters that were a specialty of Boston turners. The Boston versions are exceedingly fine and elaborate; they were fashioned on special lathes with attachments of a type that had evolved in Germany in the sixteenth century but was not adopted by English workmen until the late seventeenth century. The taste for such twist ornamentation may have been transmitted to eastern Connecticut by actual banisters ordered from Boston or by workmen who had seen such work in Boston and sought to incorporate it in their own designs. The Connecticut versions are laboriously plotted and carved by hand. The exact precedents for the pagoda finials may have appeared in English design books illustrating ornaments in the Chinese taste. Some versions of these finials on case pieces from the Connecticut River valley are unambiguously orientalizing; those on Colchester examples could be inventive variations on the urn-and-flame familiar from Boston work.

It is extremely frustrating that the bulk of the furniture listed in the Jonathan Deming inventory has not been identified. In particular, the form of the expensive sets of mahogany and cherry joined chairs would be of the greatest interest. Despite the abundance of case pieces in the Colchester style that survive, none of the numerous joined chairs that descended in eastern Connecticut families can be said to resemble them in either composition or ornamentation. In part this can be attributed to an enduring and apparently nearly universal preference in outlying New England towns: people were willing to buy elaborate case pieces but not elaborate seating furniture. In view of the regiments of heavily ornamented seating furniture from Boston, New York, and Philadelphia that today form a prominent feature of museum installations, it may be hard to believe that wealthy families in Connecticut and western Massachusetts uniformly owned plain, sturdy joined chairs with only the most perfunctory carving. A chair from eastern Connecticut (cat. no. 52) exemplifies this genre. The back is based on a recognized English type, but it is fused to a generic Connecticut base with plain Marlborough legs and stretchers. This chair has tentatively been attributed to the shop of Felix Huntington (1749–1822) of Norwich, and a similar type of chair (Colonel Daniel Putnam Association) is thought to have originated in an unidentified shop in Windham. No eastern Connecticut chair with cabriole legs and carved feet is known.

The cabinetmakers working in Colchester between 1770 and 1795 that have been identified are far too few to account for the astoundingly large number of case pieces in the Colchester style that survive, not to mention the equally large number that must have been lost due to fire, changing fashion, and neglect. Perhaps other artisans remain to be documented. Currently only two other than Burnham and Loomis are known: Pierpoint Bacon (1724–1800) and Amos Wells (1735–1802).[13] Both began working too early to have been influenced significantly by the style Burnham practiced. About the only other cabinetmaker who can conclusively be proven to have worked in the Burnham-Loomis style is Abishai Woodward (1752–1809) of New London. He made what is acknowledged to be the finest Connecticut tall clock case for works provided by the famous Norwich clockmaker Thomas Harland (1735–1807). Woodward's father was a prominent joiner, but he died when Abishai was eight years old. Abishai's master may have been his father-in-law, the successful Groton cabinetmaker Oliver Spicer (1726–1804). But the style of his clock case strongly suggests that he may have apprenticed in Benjamin Burnham's shop in Colchester. His apprenticeship would have overlapped with Samuel Loomis's term, and he would have finished the year that Benjamin Burnham is said to have left for England, 1773.[14]

Although relationships between Burnham and Loomis and other cabinetmakers cannot be documented, variants of the Colchester style were undoubtedly made in Norwich and New London, the other two regional centers. Most of these elaborate and expensive case pieces were made after 1780 and before about 1800. (Their style probably was rendered old-fashioned by 1810, when the neoclassical style came into vogue.) The quantity produced could only have been possible if a great many eastern Connecticut people enjoyed fairly high incomes, and this was a time when much of the rest of the new nation was caught in a postwar depression.

New London County and Windham County today are depressed areas. The prosperity they experienced between 1820 and 1945 was built on textile mills and tool-and-die factories that have declined and disappeared since the Second World War. It is difficult to visualize this area in its preindustrial heyday, between the last French and Indian War (1754–63) and the early federal period. The rocky hills and low meadows around the major river systems were devoted to intensive cultivation or to livestock grazing. The population was high by eighteenth-century standards. Norwich and New London were among the most densely populated towns in the colony, and many of the towns immediately around them, like Colchester, were almost as populous. The resultant strain on land resources was a source of intense anxiety.

The combination of agriculture and livestock droving on which the region depended was fraught with difficulties. The primary markets for agricultural commodities were the West Indies and armies recruited to fight the successive French and Indian wars. The economy underwent extremes of expansion and contraction, and local merchants regularly incurred massive debts to Boston and London merchants that they barely could repay. Their ability to secure payments for commodities they had sold on credit was hobbled by a lack of hard currency, an undependable paper currency issued by the colony, and a slow-moving barter economy.

The problems of eastern Connecticut were part of the difficult economy of all New England. There was no profitable staple crop like tobacco or indigo. Produce and livestock were bulky, low-return commodities to process and market. In times of recession, the economy collapsed in pyramids of indebtedness that extended from the great English and Scottish merchant factors to major importers in Boston, Newport, and New York to local merchants who were chronically overextended to many petty debtors—skilled artisans and dirt farmers alike.

Eastern Connecticut never really emerged from this economic rollercoaster until well into the industrial era. From the 1690s on, the regional leaders, who were mostly small-time import-exporters, relied on the high taxation and demand for foodstuffs generated by the successive colonial wars to pull themselves out of economic stagnation. After each war the region slipped inexorably back into debt, for the immense profits the wars generated were never adequate to cancel accumulated debt, and the better-established mercantile factions in eastern Massachusetts and western Connecticut opposed issuing paper money to relieve debtors.

This situation became acute just before the Revolution. In an outburst of enthusiasm at the end of the French and Indian War, local merchants such as Jonathan Trumbull of Lebanon (later governor of the colony) had imported large consignments of English goods—textiles, hardware, and consumer products like ceramics, glass, and other "notions" and become seriously overextended. A desperate attempt by local leaders to press a claim to the Susquehanna Territory in western Pennsylvania came to nothing. The coming of the Revolution was looked on by these merchants as a solution to indebtedness and land starvation, and Jonathan Trumbull and his cronies used their favorable position with the Continental Congress to secure extremely lucrative commissary offices to supply the Revolutionary armies. Privateering on Long Island Sound was also a profitable venture, while the armies siphoned off young men who otherwise would have faced grim career prospects.[15]

The result was that these local merchants emerged from the Revolution with a great deal of cash to invest in new houses and furnishings, and the farmers who had supplied grain and livestock to the armies also were in a favorable financial position. The eastern Connecticut merchants who belonged to the intermarried Deming and Champion families, all of whom had served in the commissary during the Revolution, built new houses in the 1780s and 1790s. These were designed and constructed by two master joiners, Isaac Fitch (1734–91) of Lebanon and William Sprats (1747–1810) of Litchfield (cat. no. 51). Certainly these merchants were typical of a large group who sought to use their wartime profits to establish their social, political, and economic positions after the war. This, then, is the explanation for the large number of surviving case pieces in the Colchester and related styles.[16]

The pretensions and demands of these nouveaux-riches clients certainly affected the direction of the eastern Connecticut cabinetmaking tradition during the last twenty years of the eighteenth century. Not only did these patrons want large, expensive furniture, they wanted the most elaborate versions of the various furniture forms that the cabinetmakers could produce. Furthermore, the cabinetmakers received many such orders at the same time. Because their clients were related through family and business ties and were likely to visit each others' homes, the cabinetmakers had to develop variations of ornamental schemes. The Jonathan Deming chest-on-chest represented the limits of Samuel Loomis's ability to supply ornament, and the strain it placed on his skills is evident. He multiplied moldings, added extra shells, and even resorted to the strange engraved style of incised leafage in the tympanum alluded to above. The pressure to quickly produce many variations undoubtedly explains the free combination of Boston, Newport, and Philadelphia compositional strategies that characterizes much eastern Connecticut work. It also explains why the Burnham-Loomis shop tradition (if Burnham and Loomis were indeed the first to use the block-and-shell formula) was copied so swiftly over the entire region, for other cabinetmakers were under the same pressure.

This places the entire group of shop traditions in a new light. Rather than being an outburst of willful or naïve enthusiasm, the creativity involved can be seen as a response to a specific and short-lived patronage situation. The compositional formulas and heavy ornamentation—which seem ungainly and even crude by urban American standards, never mind London ones—can be placed in a context of economic opportunity, patronage demands, and limited design vocabulary. Finally, these artisans can be viewed as part of the eastern Connecticut cultural mindset. Caught in the conflicting economic and cultural influences emanating from England, Boston, Newport, and Philadelphia, they synthesized these influences as successfully as they could. In their society, as in most others, accommodating the interests and inspirations of their patrons was the measure of their success.

Future investigations of the various eastern Connecticut schools can address other questions. For example, if Samuel Loomis and his competitors suddenly were faced with unprecedented demands that sorely taxed their resources, how did they cope with this? Did they bring extra apprentices and journeymen into their shops to step up production? Could such journeymen have introduced more structural, compositional, and decorative features into the tradition as it rapidly progressed?[17]

As these questions suggest, the new perspectives on the lives and work of provincial artisans that the

Burnham-Loomis shop tradition offers reflect a desire to view these artisans in context. The extremely complicated patterns of stylistic diffusion from London to major colonial centers and on into the hinterlands cannot be reduced simply to categories applied uncritically. Whether Burnham and Loomis are regarded as provincial, vernacular, or folk is irrelevant if an understanding of their exact place in furniture-making history is lacking, for the context in which they worked explains to a great degree how they worked and why they chose certain forms and decoration over others.

NOTES

1. R. W. Brunskill, *Illustrated Handbook of Vernacular Architecture* (New York: Universe Books, 1970).
2. Robert F. Trent, *Hearts and Crowns* (New Haven, Conn.: New Haven Colony Historical Society, 1977), pp. 12–13.
3. *Rococo—Art and Design in Hogarth's England* (London: Victoria and Albert Museum, 1984).
4. Charles F. Montgomery, "Regional Preferences and Characteristics in American Decorative Arts, 1750–1800," in *American Art: 1750–1800 Towards Independence*, ed. Charles F. Montgomery and Patricia E. Kane (New Haven, Conn.: Yale University Art Gallery, 1976), pp. 50–67.
5. Brock Jobe, "Urban Craftsmen and Design," in Brock Jobe and Myrna Kaye, *New England Furniture—The Colonial Era* (Boston: Houghton Mifflin Company, 1984), pp. 3–46.
6. *Three Centuries of Connecticut Furniture—1635–1935* (Hartford, Conn.: Tercentenary Commission, 1935).
7. Houghton Bulkeley, "John Townsend and Connecticut," *The Connecticut Historical Society Bulletin* 25, no. 3 (July 1963): 65–79.
8. Irving W. Lyon, *The Colonial Furniture of New England* (Boston: Houghton Mifflin, 1891), p. 121, fig. 50.
9. Minor Myers, Jr., and Edgar DeN. Mayhew, *New London County Furniture, 1640–1840* (New London, Conn.: Lyman Allyn Museum, 1974), pp. 111–13.
10. Ibid., pp. 32–35.
11. Houghton Bulkeley, "The 'Aaron Roberts' Attributions," *The Connecticut Historical Society Bulletin* 28, no. 3 (July 1963): 65–79.
12. Myers and Mayhew, *County Furniture*, pp. 38–39.
13. Robert F. Trent with Nancy Lee Nelson, "New London County Joined Chairs: Legacy of a Provincial Elite," *The Connecticut Historical Society Bulletin* 50, no. 4 (Fall 1985): 15–195.
14. Ada R. Chase and Houghton Bulkeley, "Thomas Harland's Clock—Whose Case?" *Antiques* 87, no. 6 (June 1965): 700–701.
15. Richard L. Bushman, *From Puritan to Yankee—Character and the Social Order in Connecticut, 1690–1765* (Cambridge, Mass.: Harvard University Press, 1967); Bruce C. Daniels, *The Connecticut Town—Growth and Development, 1635–1790* (Middletown, Conn.: Wesleyan University Press, 1979).
16. William L. Warren, "William Sprats and His Civil and Ecclesiastical Architecture in New England—Part I," *Old-Time New England* 44, no. 3 (January/March 1954): 65–78; idem., "William Sprats and His Civil and Ecclesiastical Architecture in New England—Part II," *Old-Time New England* 44, no. 4 (April/June 1954): 93–99; idem., "The Domestic Architecture of William Sprats and Other Litchfield Joiners," *Old-Time New England* 46, no. 2 (October/December 1955): 36–51; idem., "William Sprats, Master Joiner—Connecticut's Federalist Architect," *The Connecticut Antiquarian* 9, no. 2 (December 1957): 11–21; idem., *Isaac Fitch of Lebanon, Connecticut, Master Joiner, 1734–1791* (Hartford, Conn.: Antiquarian and Landmarks Society, 1978).
17. Myers and Mayhew, *County Furniture*, pp. 94–102.

Catalogue Objects

43. *Desk*
American, Colchester, Conn., dated 1769
Benjamin Burnham (1737?–alive 1773)
Cherry; white pine and tulip poplar
Signed on bottom board *This Desk was maid in the / year of 1769 Buy Benjn Burnam, / that sarvfed his time in felledlfay*
H. 49¾ in (126.4 cm), W. 44½ in (113 cm), D. 24½ in (62.2 cm)
The Metropolitan Museum of Art, New York, John Stewart Kennedy Fund, 1918, 18.110.58

43. Desk

As noted by Morrison Heckscher, this desk is a combination of Boston, Newport, Philadelphia, and perhaps New York traits. Overall it follows Boston prototypes, including the use of a giant dovetail joining the front base molding and the bottom board of the case. The spectacular interior with three tiers of drawers, shell-carved drawers over pigeonholes, central amphitheater niche, blocked prospect without door, and distinctive, softly modeled horizontal fluting, is an elaboration on Boston and Salem formats. Heckscher identified the stop-fluted pilasters as a Newport motif. The legs and feet are unambiguously modeled on Philadelphia patterns, right down to the peculiar incised carving of the knees and the form of the carved feet.[1]

The close similarities between this desk and a desk signed "Loomis," which was originally owned by Eliphalet Bulkeley (born 1746) of Colchester, provide grounds for compositional analysis and speculation. The theory that the Bulkeley desk was made in Benjamin Burnham's shop in 1769 by Samuel Loomis upon completion of his apprenticeship, advanced by Myers and Mayhew,[2] is here rejected because the Bulkeley desk

The Colchester School of Cabinetmaking   119

once had a bookcase. The desk and its lost bookcase conceivably could date from 1769 to 1800. In 1800 Samuel Loomis moved from Colchester to Essex on the Connecticut River, and Eliphalet Bulkeley moved from Colchester to Wilkes-Barre, Pennsylvania. The most plausible date for the desk would be the early 1780s. However, the conclusion is inescapable that the Burnham desk and the Bulkeley desk were made from nearly identical patterns, the second set presumably drawn by Loomis from Burnham's original set. Another important detail is the similarity of the rounded tops of the blocking on the Burnham desk to the blocking on the façade of a desk at the Henry Ford Museum, thought by Myers and Mayhew to be the desk attributed to Samuel Loomis in the inventory of Jonathan Deming, a Colchester merchant.[3] This further ties Loomis's work to Burnham's. A final telling feature is that the lid of the Burnham desk is notched to fit over the projecting drawers of the interior, whereas the Bulkeley desk betrays no such signs of layout problems.

A troublesome aspect of the Burnham and Bulkeley desks is the exact source for their elaborate knee brackets, which are decorated by three pierced scrolls or volutes facing outward. This feature was much elaborated on by other cabinetmakers working in the Colchester style. Among the small group of desks that are closely related, that in the Henry Ford Museum and one at the Connecticut Historical Society have the same form of bracket foot with single great unpierced volute as is seen on a case of drawers owned by Jonathan Deming. The lower case of a desk and bookcase at the Connecticut Historical Society that dates well into the federal period also has this foot. A desk at the Yale University Art Gallery has two spurs and continuous volutes along the entire base molding. The Ebenezer Huntington desk at the Art Institute of Chicago has two inwardly facing volutes that are not pierced and that are outlined by a heavy bead; similar, grotesquely heavy bracket feet with one inwardly facing volute outlined by a heavy bead are seen in a group of Newport-inspired chests of drawers made in Colchester or New London. Other shops not directly related to the Burnham-Loomis tradition but heavily influenced by it seem to have favored a formula of many elaborate volutes along the base, suggestive of a Chinese cloud motif.

1. Morrison Heckscher, *American Furniture in the Metropolitan Museum of Art* (New York: Random House, 1985), pp. 270–72.
2. Minor Myers, Jr., and Edgar DeN. Mayhew, *New London County Furniture, 1640–1840* (New London, Conn.: Lyman Allyn Museum, 1974), pp. 32–35.   3. Ibid., p. 39.

44. Chest-on-chest
45. Chest-on-chest

Since 1928 the large and pretentious case piece shown as catalogue number 44 has been recognized as a major monument of Connecticut blockfront furniture, but its history and maker were not fully investigated. In the 1960s William L. Warren and Houghton Bulkeley correctly identified it as the "1 case drawers" valued at £16 listed in Jonathan Deming's 1788 probate inventory, where it is noted as the work of Samuel Loomis. This documentation establishes the case of drawers as a landmark amid the sea of attributions to the post-Revolutionary cabinetmaking schools of Colchester, Norwich, and New London, Connecticut. It also points up the nouveau-riche context in which most of these elaborate case pieces were made.

The merits of the Deming case of drawers can be assessed by comparison with the lamentably unprovenanced example known as the Ingersol case of drawers after its last private owner, now in the collections of the Connecticut Historical Society (cat. no. 45). The Ingersol case of drawers is slightly smaller, lacks the incised vine tracery on the tympanum and the multiple dentil courses on the scrolls of the pediment, and has slightly different carved shells, but otherwise is virtually identical to the Deming case of drawers. In the 1935 Connecticut Tercentenary exhibition at the Wadsworth Atheneum, the two were displayed side by side and were assumed to be the work of the same maker. Minor Myers, Jr., and Edgar DeN. Mayhew shied away from such an attribution in their 1974 exhibition and catalogue *New London County Furniture, 1640–1840* and did not even include the Ingersol piece in the show, perhaps because at that time it was disfigured by an unpleasant oil finish, Victorian brasses, and replaced finials. In 1987 these minor drawbacks were rectified in a restoration undertaken by Robert F. Trent and Peter Arkell, who decided to make replacement finials based on those of the Deming case of drawers. The rationale for this was the restorers' conviction that the two case pieces were indeed made under the direct supervision of Samuel Loomis.

This conviction was arrived at through a detailed examination of the layout and structure of both objects. Myers and Mayhew placed great emphasis on drawer construction, particularly dovetail configurations, in developing their attributions of case pieces associated with Benjamin Burnham and Samuel Loomis. Although re-

44. *Chest-on-chest*
American, Colchester, Conn., about 1771–88
Attributed to Samuel Loomis (1748–1814)
Mahogany; tulip poplar and pine
H. 88 in (223.5 cm), W. 45 in (114.3 cm), D. 26 in (66 cm)
Wadsworth Atheneum, Hartford, Conn., gift of Mr. and Mrs. Arthur L. Shipman, Jr., 1967.140
Exhibited in Minneapolis only

The Colchester School of Cabinetmaking 121

45. *Chest-on-chest*
American, Colchester, Conn., 1780–1805
Attributed to Aaron Roberts
Cherry; tulip poplar and pine
H. 90 in (228.6 cm), W. 40¼ in (102.2 cm),
D. 23¾ in (60.3 cm)
The Connecticut Historical Society,
Hartford, 1965-10-1
Exhibited in Pittsburgh only

cent, more detailed modes of analysis have cast some doubts on their analysis, their work nevertheless strongly buttresses an attribution of the Ingersol case of drawers to Loomis: the paradigms for drawer construction are the same as those displayed by the Deming case of drawers and by the desk signed "Loomis" that originally belonged to Eliphalet Bulkeley of Colchester. Other index features of both cases of drawers appear to support a Loomis attribution for the Ingersol example but in fact may not. The blocking of the drawers, the carved shells, and the twist columns are virtually identical, but these are all decorative features that could have been farmed out among a group of journeymen or independent artisans working under contract. If Loomis had distributed the construction and embellishment of a large group of case pieces among a small group of allied artisans, as he certainly might have in the case of the order by Jonathan Deming for a houseful of elaborate and expensive furniture, he would have ensured consistency of the results by supplying patterns.

Far more reliable as evidences of one mind and hand at work are the construction of the bases and the layout of the scroll pediments. The large size of both case pieces and their multiplication of base moldings necessitated unusual construction in the bases. In the Deming example, the triple base molding posed immediate structural problems because it projects so far beyond the case it supports. Rather than attach the base to the lower case with a horizontal platform and horizontal and vertical glue blocks, Loomis made a separate base frame in which the lower case rests. He began by laying out and running the triple moldings on a stout piece of squared timber. The extension of the inward diminution of the moldings to correspond with the center negative blocking of the drawer fronts resulted in a compressed, alcovelike area that Loomis may have decided to fill with a pendant shell after the fact. Because the pieces of timber needed for the triple molding were so thick, Loomis violated the usual practice of working the base moldings and bracket feet in one piece of wood and pieced the feet, the volutes, and the lower section of the shell. All of this suggests a design problem that was out of the ordinary. In the Ingersol case of drawers, a similar approach augments the base molding, but this molding consists of two stages rather than three. The base molding does not project far out from the lower case and thus could be supported by a double platform and blocking. The overall approach, however, obviously is related to that displayed by the Deming example.

The layout of the scroll pediments constitutes another telling similarity between the two case pieces. The layout differs in one particular, the positioning of the baseline of the outer arcs of the scrolls relative to the outsides of the upper case. The baselines of the Deming outer scrolls are located well inside the outsides of the case, and the arcs are extended by a substantial run of straight molding that never achieves a level line over the twisted columns. Loomis was probably stretching the pediment to extend across the great width of the case, which is four to five inches wider than was usual. On the Ingersol example, the baselines of the outer arcs are set slightly within the outsides of the case, and the arcs begin a decidedly unacademic upward sweep at their outer limits, a feature also seen on the Lord high chest of drawers (cat. no. 49). Otherwise, the two pediments are identical in the size and positioning of the upper arcs and the positioning of the two round apertures underneath them.

46. *Chest-on-chest*
English, 1780–1800
Mahogany, (oak?)
H. 83½ in (212.1 cm), W. 47 in (119.4 cm), D. 26½ in (67.3 cm)
Collection of Anthony Scornovacco

46. Chest-on-chest

Case furniture of a rather plain style became almost standard among the middle classes and provincial gentry of England, especially after the popularity of neoclassicism made a studied simplicity fashionable around 1760. Such objects, which survive in great numbers, were often executed with the highest-quality workmanship. Frequently the cases are of oak, with mahogany veneers. The uniform excellence of these pieces is probably due to the spread of London standards of workmanship to provincial centers. But alongside this tradition of fine workmanship there existed a tradition of cheaper furniture, with cases made of conifers and covered with walnut veneer. These objects are of slipshod construction and have a generally lower tolerance for finish. They, too, were based upon London practice, for a tradition of flashy, cheap case furniture flourished in the capital.

In this fine example of an English case of drawers, conservative and fashionable elements are mixed. The case of drawers itself was a conservative furniture form at a time when design books and the London trade were emphasizing the one-case bureau, often with a bowed or elliptic front and outwardly curving French feet. The veneered drawer fronts with cockbeading attached to the edges were also somewhat conservative, for many new-fashioned bureaus lacked protective cockbeading altogether. The fashionable elements include the cove molding with a Greek profile and dentil course and the post-and-bail brasses without backplates, a type which slowly supplanted complex brasses during the 1770s and 1780s. (Even more fashionable would have been stamped oval or octagonal brasses with bails that conformed to the backplates.)

Although this is a solid, conservative object by English standards, it is far more up-to-date than the American high chest (cat. nos. 49, 50). Massive case pieces raised on "crook'd," or cabriole, legs had passed from fashion in most parts of England by the 1750s, and their survival as high-style case pieces in the colonies is regarded by modern English furniture historians as remarkable. However, certain of the former colonies like New York and South Carolina had followed English practice and abandoned the high chest of drawers by the 1760s.

Without question, English designers and cabinetmakers of the 1760s and 1770s would have found the heavily blocked façades of case pieces from Rhode Island and Connecticut hopelessly outdated, for both Palladianism and neoclassicism had condemned such baroque massing and movement by the 1750s. The twisted columns and other idiosyncratic detailing of Colchester case pieces would have received extremely harsh criticism as well. Because most American stylistic centers had been cut off from English developments during the Revolution, American artisans had persisted in baroque massing, and in Connecticut significant neoclassical influence did not filter down to regional centers like New Haven and Hartford until the mid-1790s.

47. Chest of drawers

Among the more delightful design variants associated with the Burnham-Loomis shop tradition is a group of five chests of drawers with three drawers, blocked façades surmounted by three shells, and cabriole legs with carved feet and pierced volutes on the knee brackets. The most elaborate of the group (Webb-Deane-Stevens Museum, Wethersfield, Conn., Connecticut Society of the Colonial Dames of America) has stop-fluted pilasters topped by miniature shells (a motif also seen on other case pieces). It differs from the other four (this example; Winterthur Museum; two in private collections) in having low cabriole legs, a nearly square façade, and incised carving on the knees. The others have taller legs and are 1½ to 2 inches taller. Another related piece is a cellarette atop two drawers (Winterthur Museum), which is built in two cases and is considerably taller in relation to its width (39⅝ inches high by 31⅛ inches wide); the cellarette also lacks carving on the knees and is a good deal smaller in scale. One of the taller of the five chests of drawers was owned by the Norwich clockmaker Thomas Harland (1735–1807), who came to Connecticut in 1773 from England. This suggests that his chest was not made by Benjamin Burnham, who is said to have sailed for England that year, never to be heard from again.

Of all the Burnham-Loomis designs, these chests of drawers follow most faithfully a recognized Newport format for a chest with three drawers; none of the Newport examples, however, have cabriole legs. Among the index features of the Newport prototypes are the cove

47. *Chest of drawers*
American, probably Colchester, Conn., 1770–95
Possibly the Burnham-Loomis shop tradition
Cherry; white pine
H. 37½ in (95.2 cm), W. 38¾ in (98.4 cm), D. 19 in (48.2 cm)
Museum of Fine Arts, Houston, The Bayou Bend Collection, gift of Miss Ima Hogg, B. 69.26

moldings under the top, the blocked façades with shells, and the fine cove base moldings. The somewhat idiosyncratic combination of cabriole front legs and bracket rear legs on the Connecticut chests is difficult to explain; it is also seen on Burnham-Loomis desks.

48. Chest of drawers

Chests of drawers and bureau-tables in the Goddard-Townsend shop tradition of Newport were produced in great numbers in the years immediately before the Revolution. These highly organized shops produced plain furniture for export to the southern colonies and the Caribbean, but they are remembered today for their custom furniture with elaborate carved shells on the façades. This particular example has not been attributed to any particular Newport cabinetmaker.

Newport chests of drawers were made in a four-drawer version like the present example and also a three-drawer pattern, both of which were highly influential in Connecticut. Like most Newport furniture, they are somewhat severe in aspect. Aside from the blocked façade and carved shells, the case has little

48. *Chest of drawers*
American, Newport, R.I., 1760–75
Mahogany; yellow pine and chestnut
H. 34¾ in (88.3 cm), W. 35 in (88.9 cm), D. 19¼ in (48.9 cm)
Museum of Fine Arts, Boston, The M. and M. Karolik Collection of
18th-Century American Arts, 39.140

ornamentation. Connecticut makers picked up on many salient features of the Newport pieces, notably the cove base molding, the edge molding of the top, and the cove molding between the top and the uppermost drawer. Benjamin Burnham and Samuel Loomis, however, altered this format in significant ways. They dispensed with the absolutely square proportions of the façade in order to insert cabriole front legs, and they tightened the composition by flanking the drawers with pilasters. This was a major innovation: not a single Newport chest of drawers or bureau-table with both carved shells and cabriole legs is known.

The more linear appearance of Colchester case pieces is partly due to the simpler shells and leafage on the knees. Most modern furniture historians merely say that Newport carving is "better," an explanation which has some validity but which does not tell the whole story. The Newport shops that produced shell-carved façades specialized in that kind of ornament, and the layout and execution of the shells was taught to a select group of close relatives. The Goddard-Townsend workmen rarely attempted carved ornament for which they had no established pattern. However, the group of artisans associated with the Colchester style, though not highly skilled carvers, often experimented with leafage, vine tracery, and twist columns and finials—with mixed results.

49. High chest of drawers

This high chest, which epitomizes the main features of the better high chests of the Colchester school, is an exception to the idea that such case pieces were owned by nouveau-riche members of the post-Revolutionary elite. It first belonged to Epaphras Lord (1709–99) of Colchester and Marlborough, a landowner who inherited a great deal of land and money from his father, Richard Lord (1669–1712), the wealthiest merchant in Hartford.

In 1742 Lord married his second wife, Lucy Bulkeley (1720–1800), daughter of the Reverend John Bulkeley of Colchester. This marriage linked Epaphras Lord to the Burnham-Loomis shop tradition in several ways. For example, Benjamin Burnham married Lucy Bulkeley Lord's niece, Catherine Trumbull (1731–1803). In addition, the desk signed "Loomis" that is directly related to the signed Benjamin Burnham desk (cat. no. 43) belonged to Lucy Bulkeley Lord's nephew, Eliphalet Bulkeley. Finally, Samuel Loomis married one of Lucy Bulkeley Lord's great-nieces. These intimate genealogical ties do not prove that either Benjamin Burnham or Samuel Loomis was the maker of the Lord high chest, but they strongly suggest this.

Save for its pediment, the Lord high chest follows Boston precedents for high chest designs. These designs had been in circulation in eastern Connecticut for a generation. The Boston influence is particularly striking in the profile of the skirt of the lower case and the overall drawer arrangement. The legs and carved feet are reminiscent of Philadelphia modeling, especially the stringy incised leafage on the knees. The pediment is an amalgam of a Philadelphia scroll contour and the pediment panels and carved shell of a Newport high chest; here the Newport panels are evoked by the upper contours of the side drawers, which conform to the line of the scrolls. This fusion of elements from many traditions is the key to understanding the design of the Colchester high chests, which in the past have been dismissed as eccentric rural fantasies.

The principal forms of ornament not seen on the Lord high chest are flat pilasters and full-round twist columns. Either of these features adds almost two inches to the width of the cases and necessitates junctions with the pediment moldings (for pilasters) or a complex blocking out of the façades of the cases to form corner niches (for twist columns). The incised carving on the knees of the lower Lord case is rare on Colchester high chests and may indicate the hand of either Burnham or Loomis. A final treatment that appears consistently in Colchester work is the use of two differing shells in the upper and lower cases; the contrast seen here between a naturalistic upper shell and a geometric lower shell or fan is quite common. The wide horizontal fluting beneath the shell in the lower case, which is echoed in the interior of the Burnham desk (see cat. no. 43), is found on a number of other high chests.

49. *High chest of drawers*
American, probably Colchester, Conn., about 1770–95
Possibly the Burnham-Loomis shop tradition
Cherry; pine
H. 84¾ in (215.3 cm), W. 38¼ in (97.2 cm), D. 19¼ in (48.9 cm)
The Connecticut Historical Society, Hartford, gift of Frederick K. and Margaret R. Barbour, 1964-33-1

The Colchester School of Cabinetmaking 129

50. High chest of drawers

Philadelphia high chests with rococo carved ornament began to be made in the early 1750s and probably continued to be made until the late 1780s. Some examples show evidence of German construction techniques like wedged dovetailing and the use of pegs to attach drawer bottoms, and a certain heaviness of proportion in many of them may also be the result of German influence. Another possibly German characteristic is the high-pitched scroll pediment on chests that have carved ornamentation on the typanum or scroll board. This type of pediment may well have been modeled on the similar high-pitched scroll pediments of the traditional German schranks made in outlying settlements, for the restricted area under the scrolls could accommodate a significant amount of carving. The carving itself is entirely in the English manner, although high chests from Lancaster do feature flattened German-style carving with fine veining that is alien to the English rococo style.

Most Pennsylvania high chests are large by New England standards. Some are as tall as 105 inches (266.7 cm), and generally speaking they are 6 inches (15.24 cm) broader than most New England examples. Benjamin Burnham and Samuel Loomis, and their apprentices and emulators, saw that such heaviness was incompatible with New England taste, and they immediately scaled down their patterns when formulating standard high-chest dimensions. Only the Deming case of drawers (cat. no. 44) approaches the absolute dimensions of a Philadelphia case piece; the dimensions of the Lord high chest (cat. no. 49) are far more typical. This change in format is especially apparent in the variable and sometimes clumsy integration of the high-pitched scroll pediments of Colchester high chests and in their lack of extensive carving on the typanum, which is instead filled with drawers, in the Newport manner.

50. *High chest of drawers*
American, Philadelphia, Pa., 1760–90
Mahogany; yellow pine, tulip poplar, and northern white cedar
H. 86 in (218.4 cm), W. 44 in (111.8 cm), D. 21½ in (54.6 cm)
The Minneapolis Institute of Arts, gift of James F. and Louise H. Bell in memory of James S. and Sallie M. Bell, 31.23

The Colchester School of Cabinetmaking

51. Stand

This stand is one of two catalogued as a pair. Though obviously by the same hand, the stands differ slightly in their dimensions and in the detail of the carved ornament. On the base of this one is a nineteenth-century label reading "This stand was made about the year / 1778, for Samuel Hunt of Charlestown / No. 4, by an [English] soldier taken / prisoner at [the *Battle of*] *Bennington* / [on] Aug 16, 1777 [by the N] H and Vt / militia under Gen John Stark / [a sentence effaced] the / old Secretary is also his make." In the past this inscription has been misinterpreted; "Charlestown No. 4" has been thought to mean Charlestown, Massachusetts, but in fact means Charlestown, New Hampshire, originally known as Fort No. 4 of the Massachusetts defenses during the French and Indian War. Samuel Hunt (1734–99) was a prominent landholder and political figure in Charlestown and was married to a sister of Massachusetts governor Caleb Strong of Northampton.

It is curious that a slab table and a case of drawers, with carving identical to that on the stand, descended in the Trumbull family of Lebanon, Connecticut, probably from David Trumbull (1751–1822), son of Connecticut's Revolutionary War governor and an officer in the commissary.[1] Some furniture owned by members of the Trumbull family was made by Isaac Fitch (1734–81), a joiner and master carpenter who oversaw many construction jobs for the Trumbulls. However, the strong prisoner-of-war tradition recorded on the label may point in the direction of William Sprats (1747–1810), a Scots joiner who was made prisoner by General Stark's troops at the capture of Fort Edward and who later worked for the Cowles, Deming, and Champion families in Connecticut. In 1779 and 1781 Sprats was listed as a prisoner of war in Connecticut, but his place of confinement is not known. William L. Warren speculated that Sprats may have been boarded in either Farmington or Litchfield,[2] but in view of the history cited on the Samuel Hunt stand and the Trumbull histories of related objects, it seems likely that Governor Trumbull and his sons brought Sprats to Lebanon between 1779 and 1781 to fashion furniture for them. The only piece of furniture attributed to Isaac Fitch is a desk with later bookcase (Garvan Collection, Yale University Art Gallery) with a traditional history of having belonged to Governor Jonathan Trumbull (1740–1809). From Trumbull's account books it is known that Fitch made a desk for Trumbull in 1769. The desk is a slightly de-

51. *Stand*
American, Charlestown, N.H., or Lebanon, Conn., 1778–81
Cherry
H. 28 in (71.1 cm), Diam. (top) 9¼ in (23.5 cm)
The Henry Francis du Pont Winterthur Museum, Winterthur, Del., 59.1874.1

based version of Colchester-style desks and bears no relationship to the Trumbull slab table and case of drawers.[3]

The two Samuel Hunt stands at Winterthur are nearly identical to a stand at the Metropolitan Museum of Art with no dependable history of ownership. All three stands have tops that were turned on a lathe, separate turned supports held under the top by screws, posts that are fitted to the turned supports and turned base blocks by die-cut wooden screws worked on both ends of the posts, and three legs dovetailed to the base blocks. All have highly detailed but somewhat crude carving. The top surface of the tops has fluted moldings, the outer edges of the tops have waterleaves and stippling, the shafts are carved with dentil collarinos and fully articulated Corinthian columns and swirl-carved urns, and the legs have leaves on the knees that end in two volutes and pointed claw-and-ball feet with three claws.

While the attribution of the Trumbull furniture to Sprats may never be substantiated, the group represents a distinctive subset of New London County furniture. At the same time, the case of drawers in the group incorporates a wavy base molding and Newport-style carved shells on blocked drawers of the sort found on many other New London County case pieces. The possible contribution of Sprats adds yet another factor to the evolution of the Colchester school and of furniture from surrounding towns—direct English provincial influence.

1. William Voss Elder III and Jayne E. Stokes, *American Furniture, 1680–1880, from the Collection of the Baltimore Museum of Art* (Baltimore: Baltimore Museum of Art, 1987), pp. 80–81.
2. William L. Warren, "The Domestic Architecture of William Sprats and Other Litchfield Joiners," *Old-Time New England* 46, no. 2 (October/December 1955): 36–51.
3. Gerald W. R. Ward, *American Case Furniture in the Mabel Brady Garvan and Other Collections at Yale University* (New Haven, Conn.: Yale University Art Gallery, 1988), pp. 348–50.

The Colchester School of Cabinetmaking

52. *Side chair*
American, Norwich, Conn., 1770–85
Possibly by Felix Huntington (1749–1822)
Santo Domingo mahogany; hard maple
H. 37⅝ in (95.6 cm), W. 21¼ in (54 cm), D. 17⅝ in (44.8 cm)
The Minneapolis Institute of Arts, gift of the Decorative Arts Council, 87.31.2

52. Side chair

This is one of two chairs surviving from a set owned by Nathaniel Hebard (1741–1803) of Lebanon, Connecticut. They are the most elaborate version of a joined chair type that has descended in many families in the immediate Norwich area. Many antique dealers in Connecticut have long attributed chairs of this type to Samuel Loomis, but circumstantial and documentary evidence points to the Norwich cabinetmaker Felix Huntington as at least one of the principal makers of this pattern. Loomis certainly made joined chairs with upholstered seats, but no examples by his hand have been identified through documents or histories of ownership. Lamentably, the expensive sets of joined chairs by Loomis listed in Jonathan Deming's estate inventory have not been traced. None of the traits of the Hebard chair or the many related examples that are known can be seen in Loomis's case pieces.

The banister of the Hebard chair, with two round apertures drawn up immediately under the crest rail, is the most common pattern. Other banister patterns seen on Norwich chairs include a scroll, a somewhat weak Gothic interlace, and a vase with six piercings. All of these banister types are fused with the same softly modeled crest rail terminating in vertical volutes that appear to be part of the rear stiles. The only options for carved ornament appear to be carved ears on the crest and carved volutes on the banisters. Somewhat plainer banister patterns are known, especially a vase pattern, and the same chair type was also available in a plain but moderately stylish cross-slat pattern with two horizontal slats set between the rear stiles. The slats are never pierced or carved, but are chamfered with more or less elaboration, principally for comfort.

These chairs in all their variations exist in great numbers and are undoubtedly the most common of the better-quality seating furniture available in New London County between 1770 and 1800.

53. *Side chair*
American, eastern Massachusetts, 1760–80
Mahogany
H. 38¾ in (98.4 cm), W. 21½ in (54.6 cm), D. 18 in (45.7 cm)
The Minneapolis Institute of Arts, bequest of Emma C. Tate, 49.12

53. Side chair

This chair represents the most common Boston chair pattern of the Chippendale period. Similar chairs were exported throughout New England, thereby influencing many local cabinetmakers. More expensive chairs had extensive carving on the crest rail and banister, cabriole legs, and turned stretchers. In view of the strong Massachusetts influence seen in eastern Connecticut, it is curious that this pattern was not adopted there. The execution is no more complex than that of the best Norwich patterns.

The sharpest contrast between this Massachusetts chair and the chair attributed to Felix Huntington of Norwich (cat. no. 52) is in the banister pattern. Here the two great scrolls of the back, which lend this pattern its modern popular name "owl's eyes," are set in the upper central portion of the back panel; on Norwich chairs, the scrolls are drawn up to immediately under the crest rail, and the banister and crest are joined by an elaborate rabbeted joint so that the upper volute piercings are partially in the crest. The Norwich chair pattern is derived from English prototypes that undoubtedly were imported directly from England; the pattern was made in many American colonial centers.

The adoption of English chair types and the rejection of Boston prototypes is one of the strongest regional traits of the eastern Connecticut cabinetmaking schools. The choice probably resulted from the desire of local joiners to compete with Boston makers by offering plain patterns that were distinctly different but somewhat less expensive; shipping and handling undoubtedly contributed greatly to the cost of a set of Boston chairs.

54. *Side chair*
English, 1765–75
Mahogany
H. 38¼ in (97.2 cm), W. 21¾ in (55.2 cm), D. 21¼ in (54 cm)
The St. Louis Art Museum, purchase, 220:16

54. Side chair

The high-style back of this otherwise plain chair is a conflation of two chair backs shown in plates X and XI of the 1762 edition of Thomas Chippendale's *Director*. The design of overlapping Gothic ribs with touches of rococo leafage is fairly elevated in concept but is not carried through into the base, with its Marlborough legs and sturdy stretchers. Similar disjunctions appear in many provincial English joined chairs of 1755 to 1780, and such chairs are to be distinguished from those in which the overall design was simplified from the beginning. Connecticut chairs were based on English designs that required little or no carving.

The Colchester School of Cabinetmaking

Gerald W. R. Ward

The Dutch and English Traditions in American Silver

Cornelius Kierstede

In 1932 the legendary curator John Marshall Phillips organized a special loan exhibition of the work of Cornelius Kierstede (1674–1757) at the Yale University Art Gallery in New Haven, Connecticut. Containing twelve objects (more than a third of the extant silver by Kierstede), that exhibition gave Phillips the opportunity to explore the career of "one of the most colorful of Colonial smiths" and to examine the same issue that confronts us in this exhibition—the relationship of American silver to its English, Dutch, and other European counterparts.[1]

Kierstede's work, Phillips noted, represents the "two great traditions of American silver, the rich ornamented Dutch tradition of New York and the chaste simplicity of the English tradition of New England." This reification of the two principal design traditions of early colonial America in the work of one man presents an excellent opportunity for study in this volume. Moreover, as Phillips also noted, Kierstede's work retains an individuality that results from the intermingling of the two traditions and shows Kierstede's obvious personal concern for the design and craftsmanship of objects leaving his shop and bearing his mark. Unlike the strong Anglo-American tradition exemplified by the Edwards family of silversmiths in Massachusetts, Kierstede's work draws on numerous sources.[2]

As is the case with so many American craftsmen, we know relatively little about Kierstede's life. We do know that he lived in at least three locations—New York City; Albany, New York; and New Haven, Connecticut; his moves supply what little documentation of his career exists. His travels also forced him to deal with three groups of patrons, and it was the influence of these patrons that proved to be decisive in the look of his silver.

For Kierstede's work is almost a textbook example of how greatly patronage affected the look of objects in the preindustrial era. Kierstede was clearly a man of talent, as revealed by the design and craftsmanship of his surviving objects, a craftsman capable of creating whatever objects he chose. He produced work in both the Dutch and English traditions, and the variations in his work can best be explained by the hypothesis that he responded primarily to the wishes of his patrons when fashioning his silver. Most of the factors that influenced every craftsman undoubtedly came into play with Kierstede. His work may reflect the use of printed pattern and design sources, he was no doubt aware of individual imported objects, he was molded by the craft tradition imparted to him by his master, and he undoubtedly responded to the work of other craftsmen who came to America during his working career. But of all these forces shaping his work, the ethnic preferences and social standards of his patrons seems to have been the strongest and most decisive.

The kind of work Kierstede was called on to produce reflected the nature of silversmith patronage in eighteenth-century America. In England and in continental Europe, a tripartite hierarchy of patronage had sustained goldsmiths for many centuries. At the top stood royalty and the court, the hereditary aristocracy and nobility, and the church, all responsible for commissions on the most lavish and expensive scale. In the second rank were the smaller town governments and organizations such as guildhalls, commissioning at a less ostentatious level, but nevertheless important patrons. At the bottom, and most numerous, were private individuals, acquiring objects for their own daily use or as gifts. Although Kierstede produced a few objects for churches, his primary source of commissions—perhaps as much as 90 percent of his work, judging from surviving examples—was this lower tier of the hierarchy. The limitations of this local, individual patronage determined the types of objects he produced.

Kierstede began his career in the midst of the flourishing silversmithing tradition in New York City. Boston and New York were the two centers of the craft in early colonial America, and Kierstede had the good fortune of entering a market rich in patrons and suffused with a variety of strong stylistic influences. Born in 1674 and baptized early the next year, Kierstede came of age just before the turn of the century and was admitted as a freeman of New York in 1698. From the birth records of his children, Kierstede appears to have lived in Albany for about two years; he was there in late 1704 but had returned to New York by late 1706. He then spent about fifteen more years in New York before becoming involved in a copper-mining venture just north of New Haven, Connecticut, in the early 1720s. By 1724 he had moved to New Haven, where he remained for the next three decades. His working career was probably over before 1753; in that year, he was judged to be old and infirm, and was placed in the care of a guardian. He apparently died several years later.[3]

Kierstede's working career thus began in the midst of one of the most culturally and ethnically diverse towns in early America. Unlike cities and towns in the more homogeneous New England area, New York City at the beginning of the eighteenth century contained populations with Dutch, English, and French backgrounds. It was, in the words of the historian Michael Kammen, "a social hodgepodge." The Dutch were the most significant ethnic group in early colonial America, and their presence was particularly strong in the greater New York area. Although New Netherlands came under English rule in 1664, Dutch values and traditions remained strong in New York City, the Hudson valley, and northern New Jersey well into the eighteenth and even into the nineteenth century, and were reflected in language, social customs, architecture, furniture, and a wide variety of behaviors and objects, including silver. Among the values usually ascribed to the Dutch in early New York are a high regard for domesticity and the family; an emphasis on religion (particularly the Dutch Reformed church) accompanied, however, by a tolerance for others; and an esteem for materialism and economic gain.[4]

Kierstede made silver in both the Anglo-American and Dutch-American styles during his New York and Albany years. Some of these objects stand as tangible symbols of the high value placed on the maintenance of an ethnic identity by at least some of his patrons, whether of Dutch or English background. In those cases, ethnic background and style meshed, and there was what we might call a high level of ethnic correlation. In other instances, when there was a lack of correlation between background and style (as when, for example, an individual of Dutch descent acquired an object in the English tradition), the object may have represented an effort by an individual of one heritage to adapt to (or, to phrase it more coarsely, to buy into) the dominant culture, or it may simply indicate that a specific individual had already undergone a significant degree of acculturation and that questions of ethnic identity held little significance in his or her life.[5]

During the first two decades of the eighteenth century, the silversmithing community in New York was still predominantly Dutch in character. Even as late as 1750 more than half of the silversmiths in New York were of Dutch background. Kierstede's master, possibly Jesse Kip (1660–1722), undoubtedly belonged to this group, and moreover was part of Kierstede's extended family network. His peers in terms of age and Dutch heritage included Everardus Bogardus, Benjamin Kip, Gerrit Onckelbag, Bartholomew Skaats, Koenraet Ten Eyck, Jacob Van der Spiegel, Benjamin Wynkoop, and others.[6]

These Dutch-American craftsmen produced a diverse range of forms for different clients. Before 1720, according to the scholar Kristan McKinsey, "Dutch silversmiths produced basically Dutch forms for Dutch patrons and English styles for the English," while "French silversmiths fashioned French forms for French patrons." Dutch middle-class clients, in particular, seem to have placed a high value on retaining their ethnic identity through the purchase of objects that clearly spoke of their Dutch heritage. Wealthier Dutch citizens were more likely to cross cultural boundaries and purchase objects in an English style. Patrons in both groups often acquired silver, reflecting the strong Dutch tradition of presenting silver gifts.[7]

In Dutch silver of the early eighteenth century, it is not uncommon to find American-made objects that are almost identical to their counterparts from the Netherlands; the American object is distinguished primarily by its marks. The same observation can be made concerning English-style silver. However, pinpointing exact prototypes and specific design sources for these visual intersections and relationships is a slippery business, for American silver was fashioned in an international context. It is often difficult to determine, for example, if an American silversmith was responding directly to a Dutch tradition or to an English tradition that in turn had been affected by a Dutch tradition. Dutch influence in England, and on English silver in particular, had been strong for centuries in East Anglia, where Dutch immigration and trading connections had been significant for centuries. Dutch influence on high-style English silver was strong after the restoration of Charles II in 1660; the deposed king had spent much of his exile in Holland. Although French influence became more pervasive toward the end of the century, when many Huguenot craftsman arrived in England after the revocation of the Edict of Nantes in 1685, relations between England and the Netherlands remained close during the reign of William and Mary (1689–1702).[8]

Thus Kierstede's work needs to be understood in the context of these complex international design sources. Helping us sort out this often confusing picture is the objective characteristic of function; a patron's preference for an object designed to fulfill a specific function is often an excellent indication of that person's cultural attitudes and values. Kierstede's most directly Dutch-inspired object is the large bowl (cat. no. 57) in the Metropolitan Museum of Art that he made, according to tradition, for a prosperous Dutch-American baker named Theunis Jacobsen Quick and his wife, Vroutje. As several scholars have noted, its lobate form and ornament probably derive from northern European, specifically German and Dutch, prototypes. The Kierstede bowl, for example, is closely related to a bowl made by Arent Hamminck of Groningen in 1681/82, which shares the same general form of cast handles and the same general pattern of lobes decorated with flowers and engraving (cat. no. 59). The Kierstede bowl is generous in size and rich in decoration, surpassing the common expression of the form in Dutch silver, such as a much smaller example made in 1696 by Bastiaan Denting in Groningen, where the form was popular. But the size was probably simply a function of the depth of the patron's purse, since Kierstede also made two smaller bowls: a handleless one in the Yale University Art Gallery that is seven and one-half inches in diameter, and an even smaller version, only four and one-half inches in diameter, now in the Bayou Bend Collection at the Museum of Fine Arts, Houston (cat. no. 58).[9]

The Metropolitan Museum's bowl also reveals its ties to Dutch tradition through its function. A *brandewijnskom*, or brandy bowl, was filled with brandy and raisins and passed from hand to hand by its cast handles on festive occasions and feast days, each person being supplied with a silver spoon. This Dutch custom was much favored by those of Dutch heritage in New York, judging by the relatively large number of surviving examples. One might therefore argue that the Quicks' bowl is an instance of high ethnic correlation: Dutch patron acquires Dutch object. After nearly a century of settlement and a half century after the end of Dutch rule, of course, intermarriage and other factors make it difficult and perhaps misleading to label a specific individual in 1700 as Dutch or English, or, for that matter, even to give a precise meaning to the term *Dutch*. Despite the inherent dangers of reductionism, however, it seems useful to consider questions of ethnic correlation when assessing Kierstede's production, as one means of trying to understand the appearance of his work.[10]

Kierstede's Dutch-inspired work also includes a teakettle of about 1715 in the Metropolitan Museum of Art (cat. no. 60); only a handful of American examples of the form are known. It relates closely to a Dutch water kettle of 1729 made by Hendrik van Beest, now in the Historisch Museum, Rotterdam (cat. no. 61). The two share the same ovoid form and domed cover, and rely for their visual success primarily on smooth, flowing curves. Kierstede has embellished his kettle with a birdlike or grotesque spout, a feature also found on Dutch and Swedish examples. Like the Dutch example, Kierstede's kettle was probably made to rest on a supporting stand, but the stand has been lost. Kierstede's teakettle has a history of ownership in a family of Dutch descent, and thus represents another instance of high ethnic correlation.[11]

Kierstede's New York work also reflected Anglo-American tradition. His two-handled covered cup, now in the Art Institute of Chicago, closely resembles other examples made by Gerrit Onckelbag and Jurian Blanck, Jr., after an English form of the 1670s and 1680s. Probably made for a member of the Van Cortlandt family, for whom Kierstede also made a large tankard now at the Museum of the City of New York, this cup may reflect the desire of an upwardly mobile New York family of Dutch descent to acquire objects in the more fashionable and increasingly dominant Anglo-American mode. The cup thus represents an instance of reverse ethnic correlation, an instance where a taste for fashion may have outweighed older bonds of heritage.[12]

The most common form made by Kierstede, judging from surviving examples, was the tankard. Of the approximately thirty-two objects in silver and gold marked by or, in one case, attributed to Kierstede today, more than half are tankards. Perhaps his finest surviving tankard is the one now in the Yale collection (cat. no. 62). When contrasted with a London tankard of 1694/95 by Samuel Dell in the Minneapolis Institute of Arts (cat. no. 63), the Kierstede example reveals the source of its straight-sided, barrel-shaped body, flat lid, and large, scrolled handle. The New York silversmiths grafted Dutch (and perhaps some French and Scandinavian) ornament onto this primarily Anglo form. The applied foliate bands on the Kierstede tankard, for instance, are a decorative feature often seen on Dutch beakers of the same period. The handle ornament, in its richness, might well derive from Scandinavian prototypes. Tankards made in Stockholm by Henrik Moller the Elder about 1670–75 and by Ferdinand Sehl the Elder in 1691, both in the Victoria and Albert Museum, are Scandinavian examples of the same type as the Kierstede tankards, as is a magnificent tankard made in Boston about 1710 by Henry Hurst, a Swedish immigrant.[13]

The Kierstede tankards, like other New York examples of this form, are hybrids. They show a moderate level of ethnic correlation, and their ownership must have sent mixed signals. Of the seventeen Kierstede tankards extant, the original owners of only a few are known. Most of these owners appear to have been Dutch, but the evidence is too scarce to draw any firm conclusions about the stylistic orientation of the owners as a group.

These New York tankards suggest that form was considered more important than ornament. Patrons felt obliged to order an English form, but allowed it to be decorated with details drawn from the Dutch tradition. The visual success of this combination should not obscure the fact that these objects represent the mingling and perhaps even clashing of two variant traditions, and may well be nonverbal evidence of the tensions between people of differing backgrounds.

Another tankard, now in the Winterthur Museum, illustrates Kierstede's use of English printed pattern and design books for heraldic and ornamental devices, a practice also followed by many other American silversmiths. This tankard bears initials derived from a plate in Joseph Sympson's *Book of Cyphers* (London, 1726) and an engraved coat of arms derived from John Guillim's *Display of Heraldry* (London, 1724, 6th ed.). Both initials and arms are associated with the Sill family of Connecticut. Some New York silversmiths are known to have made use of Dutch printed sources. The monumental beaker by Cornelius van der Burch in the Yale collection, for example, is engraved with numerous scenes taken directly from a Dutch emblem book published in the 1650s by Jacobus Cats (1577–1660).[14]

Kierstede's monumental candlesticks (cat. no. 55) and snuffer stand, made en suite, represent another instance of a Dutch patron ordering a fashionable Anglo-American form. They were probably fashioned for Johannes and Elizabeth (Staats) Schuyler, members of a prominent Dutch family. Schuyler was mayor of Albany from 1703 to 1706, roughly the same time that Kierstede is thought to have been in that town, and was active in Indian and commercial affairs. Schuyler may have ordered these candlesticks, which stand nearly a foot tall, as a badge of office. (Many Albany citizens ordered their silver from New York City makers, so Schuyler need not have commissioned them while Kierstede was in Albany; the candlesticks may date a few years before or after Kierstede's Albany interlude.)[15]

The sticks represent a blending of an English form with some Dutch-inspired and English-inspired decoration. The form is similar to that of candlesticks made in 1681/82 by Richard Morrell of London, now at the Wadsworth Atheneum (cat. no. 56), and to sticks made by another London smith with the mark WE between two mullets, of 1685 and 1692. The fanciful flat-chased chinoiserie decoration on the Kierstede sticks is a decorative device also drawn from the English tradition; such ornament was popular in England during the last half of the seventeenth century. Its precise source, however, remains unknown.[16]

The snuffer stand, with its bulbous knop and double-headed eagle, follows Dutch precedents more closely. The double-headed eagle, for example, is the town seal of Groningen and appears on medals from that area, and the knop is reminiscent of forms found on Dutch mannerist silver.[17]

Another characteristic of Dutch New York silver is the use of coins as decorative devices, often on tankards.

One of Kierstede's tankards now in the Museum of the City of New York has a medal of 1654 in its lid with the arms of the Province of Hanover and the monogram of Christian Louis. He also employed this device on his smallest two-handled bowl, which incorporates a French coin of 1693 bearing the likeness of Louis XIV.[18]

Kierstede's tankards reflect still another instance of cross-cultural adaptation. One example, now in a private collection, is a peg tankard, a rare form in American silver. Such tankards are fitted with a vertical row of small pegs soldered to the inside of the barrel, usually below the handle. They were a popular form in Scandinavia, and were also made in the English provincial towns of York, Newcastle, and Hull.[19]

After Kierstede moved to Connecticut about 1724, his work (with some major exceptions) began to take on a decidedly Anglo-American character, no doubt in response to the tastes of his patrons along the central Connecticut shore. New Haven was Connecticut's wealthiest town when Kierstede arrived, and the community was without a goldsmith, perhaps one reason why Kierstede was attracted there. Among the objects dating to his New Haven years are a baptismal basin made about 1731 for the Milford Congregational church and a caudle cup dating from the 1730s, both made to standard English forms. Kierstede was also called upon to fashion a gold mourning ring for a New Haven client, probably about 1731; it descended in the Trowbridge family and has recently been acquired by the New Haven Colony Historical Society. This object, one of two works in gold known by his hand, represents his adaptation to a custom that was a strong Anglo-American tradition; Dutch silversmiths were more often asked to make funeral spoons. This may explain the simplicity of the Kierstede ring, an unadorned band bearing only an inscription; Kierstede probably did not own a death's-head swage (a specialized tool), and he may not have been familiar with the practice of enameling.[20]

During his Connecticut years Kierstede also fashioned a tankard in the English form, the only tankard in his oeuvre that stands clearly outside the New York style. Its domed lid with a bell-shaped finial (the only instance of this decorative device in Kierstede's tankards), its double-scroll thumbpiece (many of Kierstede's other tankards have the common corkscrew thumbpiece), and its tapered barrel mark it as an Anglo form. Conversely, it lacks features found on tankards in the New York style, including an applied foliate band, meander wire, and elaborate engraving. Made in the 1730s for an unknown couple with the initials AC/M, this tankard was later owned by Mary Hillhouse, who bequeathed it to Trinity Church in New Haven in 1822.[21]

Yet some of Kierstede's Connecticut work retains a Dutch air. One example is the simple two-handled cup he fashioned for the Congregational church in Milford about 1729. This object, essentially a beaker with thin, flat handles, retains the band of applied ornament at its base that distinguishes it from the common Anglo version of the form. The band is, however, a restrained series of semicircles or flat scalloping, unlike the bolder and better-articulated bands found on his tankards in the New York style. This element of restraint may reflect the wishes of the cup's donor, Abigail Beach, who later married the church's minister, the Reverend Samuel Andrews.[22]

Kierstede's last major object was a punch bowl made in 1745 for Thomas Darling, a tutor at Yale University. It is in his New York style and harks back to the bowl he made for the Quicks several decades earlier. The Darling bowl rests on a simpler molded foot ring without the applied stamped band in the Dutch style, and the floral decoration in its six lobes has lost much of its vitality of line and precision of definition. The Darling bowl's tulips, for example, are sketchier, weaker, and more stylized.[23]

It is significant that the Darling bowl, made at this late date and in this location, was fashioned in the New York style. There was not a strong local tradition for Kierstede to work from, for in Connecticut during the first half of the eighteenth century silversmithing was not a major craft. Although Kierstede retained the general form and ornament of the Quick bowl in the Darling bowl, he did make a significant change: he omitted the cast caryatid handles. This suggests that it was made to be used as a punch bowl, from which beverages were ladled, rather than being passed from hand to hand, as were *brandewijn* bowls. This may indicate a change in manners from 1710 to 1745, but it may also indicate that the Darling bowl, despite its decoration, was in an Anglo tradition. Its ambiguity still reflects Connecticut's, and especially New Haven's, intermediary position between the strong influences of Boston and New York.[24]

Kierstede's career, spanning nearly half a century, thus exemplifies the various forces at work on the design of early American silver. The atmosphere was not one in which design innovation was highly prized. Fine craftsmanship—and nearly all of Kierstede's work is exceedingly well wrought—was undoubtedly valued, but it was clearly important that the patrons immediately understand the form and ornament of their objects. They had to be recognizable and intelligible symbols, ones that a patron, and the people the patron was trying to influence or impress or simply please, could grasp. The career of Kierstede's fellow silversmith of Dutch heritage, William Rouse, bears this out. Rouse spent his working career in Boston and married a woman of English descent. Although he was capable of exquisite workmanship, the dozen or so objects known by him are all strongly in the Anglo style. His Dutch background is discernible only in such details as the superb engraving found on some of his objects, such as the sunflower that embellishes a patch box in the Yale collection.[25]

In the final analysis, perhaps the most interesting aspect of Kierstede's work and that of most of his New York City contemporaries is its reflection of the confrontation between the fading Dutch tradition and the soon-to-be-dominant Anglo tradition in New York as the eighteenth century began. Only about 10 percent of Kierstede's surviving work is in an exclusively Dutch mode; the remainder is a mixture of Anglo forms with or without Dutch-inspired elements. As nonverbal documents, Kierstede's silver thus gives evidence of the process of assimilation while simultaneously revealing the survival of rich elements of Dutch culture and, in turn, their influence on the culture that was coming to be known as American.

NOTES

1. John Marshall Phillips, "Cornelius Kierstede," *Bulletin of the Associates in Fine Arts at Yale University* 4, no. 3 (October 1932): 149–51; quotation p. 149.
2. Ibid., p. 150. The diverse nature of Kierstede's work has attracted the attention of many silver scholars over the years, including C. Louise Avery, V. Isabelle Miller, Graham Hood, and Frances Gruber Safford.
3. Biographical information on Kierstede is found in a number of sources. There is some disagreement in the literature concerning the dates of certain events in Kierstede's life; fortunately, these do not concern points central to this essay. Among the most useful secondary sources are Henry N. Flynt and Martha Gandy Fales, *The Heritage Foundation Collection of Silver, with Biographical Sketches of New England Silversmiths* (Old Deerfield, Mass.: Heritage Foundation, 1968), p. 262; Milo M. Naeve, "Dutch Colonists and English Style in New York City: Silver Syllabub Cups by Cornelius Kierstede, Gerrit Onckelbag, and Jurian Blanck, Jr.," *American Art Journal* 19, no. 3 (Fall 1987): 41–43; see also notes 7 and 8 for references to genealogical articles; and Richmond Huntley, "The Artistic Cornelius Kierstede," *American Collector* 7, no. 11 (December 1938): 5.

4. Michael Kammen, *Colonial New York: A History* (New York: Charles Scribner's Sons, 1975), p. 151. Dutch American culture is covered thoroughly in Roderic H. Blackburn and Ruth Piwonka, *Remembrance of Patria: Dutch Arts and Culture in Colonial America, 1609–1776* (Albany, N.Y.: Publishing Center for Cultural Resources for the Albany Institute of History and Art, 1988); see especially pp. 35–41 for an overview. Past research and present opportunities for study are summarized in several essays published in Eric Nooter and Patricia U. Bonomi, eds., *Colonial Dutch Studies: An Interdisciplinary Study* (New York: New York University Press, 1988). See also Esther Singleton, *Dutch New York* (New York: Dodd, Mead and Co., 1909); Thomas J. Archdeacon, *New York City, 1664–1710: Conquest and Change* (Ithaca, N.Y.: Cornell University Press, 1975); and Oliver A. Rink, *Holland on the Hudson: An Economic and Social History of Dutch New York* (Ithaca, N.Y.: Cornell University Press; Cooperstown, N.Y.: New York State Historical Association, 1986). For an engaging look at life in the Netherlands during this period, see Simon Schama, *The Embarrassment of Riches: An Interpretation of Dutch Culture in the Golden Age* (New York: Alfred A. Knopf, 1987).

5. The literature on questions of assimilation and acculturation in early Dutch America is summarized in Joyce D. Goodfriend, "The Historiography of the Dutch in Colonial America," in Nooter and Bonomi, *Colonial Dutch Studies*, pp. 11–32, especially pp. 14–16 and the accompanying notes.

6. Kristan Helen McKinsey, "New York City Silversmiths and Their Patrons, 1687–1750" (M.A. thesis, University of Delaware, Newark, 1984), chap. 1. John Marshall Phillips, "Identifying the Mysterious IK: Jesse Kipp, New York Goldsmith," *Antiques* 44, no. 1 (July 1943): 19–21. Graham Hood, in conversation, suggested that Kierstede may have left New York due to increasing competition from Huguenot silversmiths. Although no modern comprehensive work on early New York silver has been published, each generation of scholars has contributed to the literature on the subject. Among studies that have been most useful for this essay are *Catalogue of an Exhibition of Silver Used in New York, New Jersey, and the South* (New York: Metropolitan Museum of Art, 1911; reprint, New York: Arno Press, 1974), which contains a note on early New York silversmiths by R. T. Haines Halsey and includes works by Dutch, Swedish, and English, as well as American, silversmiths; C. Louise Avery, *American Silver of the XVII and XVIII Centuries: A Study Based on the Clearwater Collection* (New York: Metropolitan Museum of Art, 1920); C. Louise Avery, "Early New York Silver," *Antiques* 6, no. 5 (November 1924): 246–49; C. Louise Avery, *Early American Silver* (New York: Century Company, 1930; reprint, New York: Russell and Russell, 1968), chap. 5; C. Louise Avery, *An Exhibition of Early New York Silver* (New York: Metropolitan Museum of Art, 1931; reprint, New York: Arno Press, 1974); Harold Donaldson Eberlein and Cortlandt Van Dyke Hubbard, "Seventeenth Century New York Silver Was both Dutch and English," *American Collector* 5, no. 6 (July 1936): 4–5, 9; V. Isabelle Miller, *Silver by New York Makers, Late 17th Century to 1900* (New York: Museum of the City of New York, 1937); V. Isabelle Miller, *New York Silversmiths of the Seventeenth Century* (New York: Museum of the City of New York, 1962); V. Isabelle Miller, "New York Silver of the Seventeenth Century," *Antiques* 82, no. 6 (December 1962): 636–38; Frances Gruber Safford, *Colonial Silver in the American Wing* (New York: Metropolitan Museum of Art, 1983). A useful and convenient listing of makers is given in Paul von Khrum, *Silversmiths of New York City, 1684–1850* (New York: Privately printed, 1978). Dutch influence on Long Island is discussed in Dean F. Failey, *Long Island Is My Nation: Decorative Arts and Craftsmen, 1640–1830* (Setauket, N.Y.: Society for the Preservation of Long Island Antiquities, 1976).

7. McKinsey, "New York City Silversmiths," pp. 8–9.
8. The origin of designs of American silver, particularly English

sources, has been of interest to nearly every scholar. One of the first attempts to place American work in an international context was E. Alfred Jones's *Old Silver of Europe and America from Early Times to the Nineteenth Century* (London: B. T. Batsford, 1928). Martha Gandy Fales has been particularly perceptive concerning design sources; see, for example, her article "English Design Sources of American Silver," *Antiques* 83, no. 1 (January 1963): 82–85. Dutch influence on English silver before and during Kierstede's life is discussed in Judith Banister, *Old English Silver* (New York: G. P. Putnam's Sons, 1965), chaps. 4–6. See also John J. Murray, "The Cultural Impact of the Flemish Low Countries on Sixteenth- and Seventeenth-Century England," *American Historical Review* 62 (1957): 854; and D. W. Davies, *Dutch Influence on English Culture, 1558–1680* (Ithaca, N.Y.: Cornell Unviersity Press, 1964).

9. Many authors have written about the Kierstede bowl and its antecedents. The form was discussed most thoroughly in two well-illustrated articles by John N. Pearce: "New York's Two-Handled Paneled Silver Bowls," *Antiques* 80, no. 4 (October 1961): 341–45, and "Further Comments on the Lobate Bowl Form," *Antiques* 90, no. 4 (October 1966): 524–25. The Dutch bowls are illustrated and discussed in A. L. den Blaauwen, *Dutch Silver, 1580–1830*, trans. Patricia Wardle (Amsterdam: Rijksmuseum, 1979), cat. no. 85, and M. H. Gans and Th. M. Duyvene de Wit-Klinkhamer, *Dutch Silver*, trans. Oliver van Oss (London: Faber and Faber, 1961), fig. 52. See also, for example, *Fries Zilver: Catalogus Fries Museum, Leeuwarden* (Leeuwarden, Netherlands: Fries Museum, 1968), cat. no. 106. The Darling bowl is discussed in Kathryn C. Buhler and Graham Hood, *American Silver, Garvan and Other Collections in the Yale University Art Gallery* (New Haven, Conn.: Yale University Press, 1970), cat. no. 329. For the Bayou Bend bowl, see David B. Warren, *Bayou Bend: American Furniture, Paintings, and Silver from the Bayou Bend Collection* (Houston: Museum of Fine Arts, 1975), cat. no. 302. I am grateful to Michael K. Brown for his generosity in making available additional information about the bowl.

10. Roderic H. Blackburn, "Transforming Old World Dutch Culture in a New World Environment: Processes of Material Adaptation," in *New World Dutch Studies: Dutch Arts and Culture in Colonial America, 1609–1776*, ed. Roderic H. Blackburn and Nancy A. Kelley, Proceedings of a symposium held August 2–3, 1986, in conjunction with the exhibition "Remembrance of Patria: Dutch Arts and Culture in Colonial America, 1609–1776" (Albany, N.Y.: Albany Institute of History and Art, 1987), p. 96. Dutch use of the brandy bowl is discussed in den Blaauwen, *Dutch Silver*, p. 370.

11. More elaborate Dutch examples are illustrated in J. W. Frederiks, *Dutch Silver*, vol. 4, *Embossed Ecclesiastical and Secular Plate from the Renaissance until the End of the Eighteenth Century* (The Hague: Martinus Nijhoff, 1961), figs. 334, 337. Swedish examples are illustrated in Erik Andren, *Swedish Silver*, trans. Lillian Ollen (New York: Gramercy Publishing Company, 1950), figs. 27, 28. I am grateful to Karel A. Citroen for assistance in locating parallel Dutch objects.

12. Naeve, "Dutch Colonists and English Style," pp. 50–52; the closest English prototype is illustrated in fig. 16. "The Van Cortlandt Tankard by Kierstede," Museum of the City of New York *Bulletin* 3, no. 3 (Spring 1973).

13. The distinctive characteristics of the New York tankard have been discussed by many authors. For the Yale tankard, see Buhler and Hood, *American Silver*, cat. no. 578, and Graham Hood, *American Silver: A History of Style, 1650–1900* (New York: Praeger, 1971), p. 55. For Dutch beakers with applied foliate bands and bands of stamped ornament, see J. W. Frederiks, *Dutch Silver*, vol. 3, *Wrought Plate of the Central, Northern, and Southern Provinces from the Renaissance until the End of the Eighteenth Century* (The Hague: Martinus Nijhoff, 1960), figs. 185, 186, 190, 192, 201, 203, 215, 217, 237, 240, 241, 292, 322–25, 327, 397; these are representative of many other examples found in the literature. The two Swedish tankards are discussd in R. W. Lightbown, *Catalogue of Scandinavian and Baltic Silver* (London: Victoria and Albert Museum, 1975), cat. nos. 79, 81. The Hurst tankard and Hurst's Swedish background are discussed in Barbara McLean Ward, "The Craftsman in a Changing Society: Boston Goldsmiths, 1690–1730" (Ph.D. diss., Boston University, 1983), pp. 161–62.

14. The Winterthur tankard is discussed in Donald L. Fennimore, "Cornelius Kierstede Tankard," *Silver* 16, no. 3 (May–June 1983): 30–32; Mrs. Russel Hastings, "The Sanders-Garvan Beaker by Cornelius Vanderburch," *Antiques* 27, no. 2 (February 1935): 52–55.

15. For Schuyler and Albany patrons, see Norman S. Rice, *Albany Silver, 1652–1825* (Albany, N.Y.: Albany Institute of History and Art, 1964), p. 16 and passim.

16. Kierstede's sticks and snuffer stand, like most of his major works, have been published many times; once again, a good visual analysis is presented in Hood, *American Silver*, pp. 69–72. The Morrell candlesticks are discussed in Elizabeth B. Miles, *English Silver: The Elizabeth B. Miles Collection* (Hartford, Conn.: Wadsworth Atheneum, 1976), cat. no. 150; see also Charles Oman, *English Silversmiths' Work, Civil and Domestic: An Introduction* (London: Her Majesty's Stationery Office, 1965), fig. 78. Those with the initial mark WE are pictured in Charles Oman, *Caroline Silver, 1625–1688* (London: Faber and Faber, 1970), fig. 60B, and in John F. Hayward, *Huguenot Silver in England, 1688–1727* (London: Faber and Faber, 1959), fig. 73A. English chinoiserie is discussed in Carl C. Dauterman, "Chinese Imagery on Restoration Silver," *Antiques* 88, no. 4 (October 1965): 511–15.

17. See Frederiks, *Dutch Silver*, vol. 3, figs. 382, 391, 392, 393.

18. Dutch, German, and Scandinavian objects incorporating coins and medals in their design are fairly common in the literature. See, for example, Lightbown, *Scandinavian and Baltic Silver*, cat. nos. 35, 84; and Raimo Fagerstrom, *Suomalaista hopeaa* (Helsinki: Werner Soderstrom Osakeyhtio, 1983), pp. 46, 51, 52. For the Kierstede objects, see Margaret Stearns, *Gold and Silver Treasures of New York: A Checklist* (New York: Museum of the City of New York, 1979), cat. no. 118; and Warren, *Bayou Bend*, cat. no. 302.

19. For Kierstede's peg tankard, see *Colonial Silversmiths, Masters and Apprentices* (Boston: Museum of Fine Arts, 1956), cat. no. 193. Scandinavian examples are given in Lightbown, *Scandinavian and Baltic Silver*, cat. nos. 4 (Denmark, c. 1670), 6 (Denmark, 1696), 32 (Norway, 1652), 34 (Norway, 1689), 35 (Norway, c. 1680). See Margaret Holland, *English Provincial Silver* (New York: Arco, 1971), pp. 62, 63, 76, 211, 217, for a discussion of the tradition of peg tankards in East Anglia.

20. For Kierstede's Connecticut work, see George Munson Curtis, *Early Silver of Connecticut and Its Makers* (Meriden, Conn.: International Silver Company, 1913); Peter Bohan and Philip Hammerslough, *Early Connecticut Silver, 1700–1840* (Middletown, Conn.: Wesleyan University Press, 1970); and *An Exhibition of Early Silver by New Haven Silversmiths* (New Haven, Conn.: New Haven Colony Historical Society, 1967). I am grateful to Robert Egleston, curator at the New Haven Colony Historical Society, for information on the Kierstede gold rings.

21. The Kierstede tankard is illustrated in Bohan and Hammerslough, *Early Connecticut Silver*, cat. no. 9. For a general discussion and comparison of Boston and New York tankards over time, see Barbara McLean Ward and Gerald W. R. Ward, eds., *Silver in American Life: Selections from the Mabel Brady Garvan and Other Collections at Yale University* (Boston: David R. Godine; New York: American Federation of Arts, 1979), cat. nos. 126–33.

22. Bohan and Hammerslough, *Early Connecticut Silver*, cat. no. 6.

23. For the Darling bowl, see Buhler and Hood, *American Silver*, cat. no. 329.

24. For silversmithing in Connecticut, see Bohan and Hammerslough, *Early Connecticut Silver*.

25. For Rouse, see Marc Simpson, "Tracing the Possibility of Dutch Influence in Boston Silver of the Seventeenth Century" (Seminar paper, Yale University, New Haven, Conn., 1978), and B. Ward, "Craftsman in a Changing Society," pp. 158–59.

Catalogue Objects

55. Candlestick / 56. Candlesticks

Cornelius Kierstede's monumental candlesticks (cat. no. 55) are generally considered the masterpieces of his work and the most ambitious early American examples of the form. They are based on an earlier English tradition represented here by the London examples of 1681/82 by Richard Morrell (cat. no. 56). A comparison of the two reveals that they share the same general form of stepped base and drip pan; the vertical thrust of each is carried out by a stop-fluted column, and each terminates in a similar type of socket. Relatively few Dutch examples of this specific form are known.[1]

The Kierstede candlesticks are embellished with fanciful chinoiserie figures and animals from an as yet unidentified source, but also clearly derived from an English tradition of the 1670s, 1680s, and early 1690s.[2] They also have the familiar meander wire in the Dutch-American manner, and their bold gadrooning and leafage are evocative, at least, of the richness of the Dutch tradition.

It is thought that the Kierstede candlesticks and their accompanying snuffer stand were made for Johannes and Elizabeth Schuyler of Albany. These same patrons had commissioned one of the earliest American silver teapots to survive, an example made by Killian Van Rensselaer, and they may have used these objects in the impressive Schuyler house, built in 1667, in Albany. Other silver owned by the couple is known, including a pair of mugs by Koenraet Ten Eyck, and portraits of the couple painted about 1735 are in the collection of the New-York Historical Society.[3]

The Kierstede candlesticks, according to tradition, are the only two to survive of four examples originally owned by the Schuylers. They may have been acquired by Johannes Schuyler at about the same time that he was mayor of Albany (1703–6). If such was the case, they would have been impressive badges of office and symbols of gentility in an era when artificial light was expensive, troublesome to maintain, and largely controlled by the well-to-do. A contemporary view of the banquet given at The Hague in honor of Charles II in 1660 illustrates how candlesticks like the Kierstede examples were used to enliven a festive occasion for upper-class members of society.[4]

55. *Candlestick*
American, New York City or Albany, N.Y., 1700–1710
Cornelius Kierstede, born New York City (1674–1757)
Silver
H. 11½ in (29.2 cm)
The Metropolitan Museum of Art, New York, gift of Robert L. Cammann, 1957, 57.153

144   Gerald W. R. Ward

56. *Candlesticks*
English, London, 1681/82
Richard Morrell (1641–1703)
Silver
H. 7 in (17.8 cm)
Wadsworth Atheneum, Hartford, Conn., The Elizabeth B. Miles
Collection of English Silver, 1979.122.1–2

Despite their high place in the context of early American silver, the Kierstede candlesticks do not compare in size and weight to the massive silver objects produced for the court and aristocracy in England and continental Europe at the opening of the eighteenth century, a reminder that court taste was absent in American society.

1. The Kierstede candlesticks have been published many times, most recently in an entry by Phillip M. Johnston in Reinier Baarsen et al., *Courts and Colonies: The William and Mary Style in Holland, England, and America* (New York: Cooper-Hewitt Museum; Pittsburgh: Carnegie Museum of Art, 1988), cat. no. 72. A series including examples from England, the Netherlands, and Boston precedes the Kierstede entry in this same volume (cat. nos. 69–71). For Dutch examples of varying form dating between 1670 and 1720, see A. L. den Blaauwen, *Dutch Silver, 1580–1830* (Amsterdam: Rijksmuseum, 1979), cat. nos. 80, 86, 87, 96, 102. An elaborate Dutch example of 1694, embellished with meander wire, is in the Victoria and Albert Museum. The Morrell candlesticks are shown in Elizabeth B. Miles, *English Silver: The Elizabeth B. Miles Collection* (Hartford, Conn.: Wadsworth Atheneum, 1976), cat. no. 150. A set of six tall English examples is in the Middle Temple, London.

2. For a discussion of English chinoiserie, see Charles Oman, *Caroline Silver, 1625–1688* (London: Faber and Faber, 1970), pp. 15–16.

3. For the Schuylers, see Roderic H. Blackburn and Ruth Piwonka, *Remembrance of Patria: Dutch Arts and Culture in Colonial America, 1609–1776* (Albany, N.Y.: Publishing Center for Cultural Resources for the Albany Institute of History and Art, 1988), pp. 76, 86, 289.

4. A good introduction to the social history of lighting is provided in Alastair Laing, *Lighting* (London: Her Majesty's Stationery Office, 1982), in the Victoria and Albert Museum's series The Arts and Living. See also Peter Thornton, *Seventeenth-Century Interior Decoration in England, France, and Holland* (New Haven, Conn.: Yale University Press, 1978), fig. 257.

57. *Two-handled bowl*
American, New York City, 1700–1710
Cornelius Kierstede, born New York City (1674–1757)
Silver
H. 5 3/8 in (13.7 cm), Diam. 10 in (25.4 cm)
The Metropolitan Museum of Art, New York, Samuel D. Lee Fund, 1938, 38.63
Exhibited in Minneapolis only

57. Two-handled bowl
58. Two-handled bowl
59. Two-handled bowl

Bowls like this one by Arent Hamminck (cat. no. 59) were popular in Groningen, Friesland, and elsewhere in the Netherlands for nearly a century and a half, from about 1650 through the eighteenth century. Although every lobe of the Hamminck bowl is decorated, half with floral ornaments, the panels on many other Dutch examples are undecorated. Although some Dutch bowls have cast handles in the horizontal plane, in a fashion akin to a porringer handle, American examples invariably are fitted with S-shaped handles in the vertical plane, like the cast handles on the Kierstede bowls illustrated here (cat. nos. 57, 58). Dutch examples are often supported on a high lobed foot, rather than by the simple ring foot found on the Kierstede bowls, a variation that accentuates the horizontal character of the American versions. Dutch bowls are more often divided into eight lobes or panels, as opposed to the six such divisions ordinarily found on American examples. Both the Dutch and the American bowls are of a type that was made in northern Europe from the mid-seventeenth century on, and that derives ultimately from Italian Renaissance sources.[1]

Of the several forms of silver produced by Kierstede, this type of bowl is most closely associated with Dutch customs. Such bowls, known as *brandewijnskom*, were used to hold a mixture of brandy and raisins that would be eaten with a ceremonial silver spoon as the bowl was passed from hand to hand at funerals, weddings, and other feast days, including the social event known as the *kindermaal*, marking an infant's birth. The bowls mark the retention of a tradition related to the Anglo custom of passing grace cups and tankards from hand to hand, another form of communal drinking that strengthens the bonds between the members of a group and emphasizes the group's cohesiveness and sense of identity.[2]

Kierstede produced at least three such bowls (the other example is in the Yale University Art Gallery). These objects represent that aspect of his work most closely attuned to his patrons' desire to maintain their Dutch identity. No other object in his oeuvre speaks as eloquently of the desire of his patrons to sustain and reaffirm the customs and traditions of their ancestral

58. Two-handled bowl
American, New York City, about 1704–6
Cornelius Kierstede, born New York City (1674–1757)
Silver
H. 2³⁄₁₆ in (5.6 cm), W. 6¼ in (15.9 cm)
The Museum of Fine Arts, Houston, The Bayou Bend Collection, gift of Miss Ima Hogg, B. 63.3
Exhibited in Pittsburgh only

59. Two-handled bowl
Dutch, Groningen, 1681/82
Arent Hamminck (active 1668–84)
Silver
H. 6 in (15.2 cm), W. 10⁷⁄₁₆ in (26.5 cm)
Groninger Museum, Groningen, Netherlands

homeland. Even the tulips chased on catalogue number 57 (and on the Yale example) are a reminder of the Netherlands, where the flowers had been introduced in the fifteenth century from Turkey and where tulipomania had been rampant in the early seventeenth century.

1. The best articles on the form remain those by John N. Pearce: "New York's Two-Handled Paneled Silver Bowls," *Antiques* 80, no. 4 (October 1961): 341–45, and "Further Comments on the Lobate Bowl Form," *Antiques* 90, no. 4 (October 1966): 524–25. These illustrate numerous related examples. Like many of the Kierstede objects, the Metropolitan Museum bowl has been published many times; commentary by C. Louise Avery, Graham Hood, Frances Gruber Safford, and Wendy A. Cooper is particularly helpful. It has appeared most recently in print in Baarsen et al., *Courts and Colonies*, p. 69, fig. 74. The Hamminck bowl is illustrated in den Blaauwen, *Dutch Silver*, cat. no. 85.
2. The use of the form is discussed in Blackburn and Piwonka, *Remembrance of Patria*, cat. no. 296.

Dutch and English Traditions in American Silver 147

60. *Teakettle*
American, New York City, 1710–20
Cornelius Kierstede, born New York City (1674–1757)
Silver
H. 10¼ in (26 cm), Diam. (base) 7⁵⁄₁₆ in (18.6 cm)
The Metropolitan Museum of Art, bequest of
James Stevenson Van Cortlandt, 1917, 40.145

60. Teakettle
61. Water kettle and brazier

Cornelius Kierstede's teakettle (cat. no. 60), one of the few early American examples of the form and perhaps the earliest, closely follows Dutch prototypes such as the example made in 1729 in Rotterdam by Hendrik van Beest (cat. no. 61).[1] Like his tankard (cat. no. 62), Kierstede's teakettle is decorated with a band of meander wire around the rim. The "duck-neck" spout is richly ornamented and also strongly associates Kierstede's work with the Dutch tradition, although Dutch and Scandinavian kettles often have elaborate embossed bodies rather than the smooth, gently curving body seen on the American object. The budlike finial on Kierstede's teakettle is paralleled by a similar device on an Amsterdam salt of 1646.[2]

Designs for a teakettle of this general form were published by the designer Daniel Marot about 1712, suggesting that Kierstede's design was not far behind European fashions. The earliest American teapots date from the first decade of the eighteenth century. Along with this teakettle, they may have been used on the equally rare tea tables that survive from this early period of tea drinking.[3]

The Kierstede kettle has a flat bottom without a foot rim, suggesting that, like its Dutch counterpart, it was designed to be supported on an accompanying stand that contained a warming device for keeping the beverage hot.

1. An unmarked American example is illustrated in Kathryn C. Buhler, *American Silver, 1655–1825, in the Museum of Fine Arts, Boston* (Greenwich, Conn.: Museum of Fine Arts, Boston, 1972), cat. no. 498. The Kierstede example has been published most recently in Blackburn and Piwonka, *Remembrance of Patria*, cat. no. 322. In this entry Blackburn suggests that the traditional history of ownership by Elizabeth de Peyster and her husband, John Hamilton, may be in error.
2. Dutch examples of teakettles and teapots with related spouts are illustrated in J. W. Frederiks, *Dutch Silver*, vol. 4, *Embossed Ecclesiastical and Secular Plate from the Renaissance until the End of the Eighteenth Century* (The Hague: Martinus Nijhoff, 1961), figs. 334, 337, and in den Blaauwen, *Dutch Silver*, cat. nos. 89, 98. For Swedish teapots with related spouts, see Erik Andren, *Swedish Silver* (New York: Gramercy, 1950), figs. 27, 28. The Dutch salt is illustrated in Alain Gruber, *Silverware* (New York: Rizzoli, 1982), fig. 220.
3. See the entries by Deborah Sampson Shinn in Baarsen et al., *Courts and Colonies*, cat. nos. 59, 62, in which this relationship is pointed out. See also cat. no. 63 for a discussion of William and Mary-style teapots, and cat. no. 175 for a discussion of early tea tables. A tea table attributed to New York is illustrated in Blackburn and Piwonka, *Remembrance of Patria*, cat. no. 45.

61. *Water kettle and brazier*
Dutch, Rotterdam, 1729
Hendrik van Beest
Silver
H. 15 15/16 in (40.5 cm), Diam. 7 7/8 in (20 cm)
Historisch Museum, Rotterdam

Dutch and English Traditions in American Silver

62. *Tankard*
American, New York City, 1695–1705
Cornelius Kierstede, born New York City (1674–1757)
Silver
H. 7¾ in (19.7 cm), Diam. (lip) 5⅛ in (13 cm), Diam. (base) 6⅛ in (15.6 cm)
Yale University Art Gallery, New Haven, Conn., The Mabel Brady Garvan Collection, 1934.356

62. Tankard / 63. Tankard

The form of the Kierstede tankard (cat. no. 62) is clearly derived from tankards in the Anglo tradition, including the representative example made in London by Samuel Dell and now in the Minneapolis collection (cat. no. 63).[1] The two tankards share the same basic form. Each body is a slightly tapering vertical cone, covered with a stepped lid with a flat top and crenellated lip, and each has a similar scrolled handle.

The hybrid character of the Kierstede example (and other Dutch-American tankards) is revealed by the presence of several discrete design elements grafted onto an essentially Anglo form. These include the band of meander wire encircling the base below an applied band of foliate decoration, and the lavishly engraved coat of arms (for an unidentified family) with its pendants of pomegranates and its surround of florid mantling. The rich handle decoration—here a lion couchant—is also derived from Dutch and perhaps Scandinavian examples. Of the approximately seventeen Kierstede tankards, all but one are in this hybrid form typical of New York silver.[2]

The engraved pomegranates on the Kierstede tankard, and on other tankards in the same tradition, perhaps carried a symbolic message of fertility. Similar decoration in painted form was also used on some case furniture in the Dutch and Dutch-American traditions, particularly on the doors of large cupboards known as kases. Perhaps the Yale tankard, which may have been displayed on the flat top of a kas, is similarly evocative of the Dutch tradition of domesticity.[3] Engraved pomegranates are also found on Kierstede tankards in the collections of the Museum of the City of

63. *Tankard*
English, London, 1694/95
Samuel Dell (active 1679–1703)
Silver
H. 7½ in (19 cm), Diam. (lip) 4¾ in (12 cm), Diam. (base) 5½ in (14 cm)
The Minneapolis Institute of Arts, gift of James F. and Louise H. Bell, 61.55.12

New York and the Art Institute of Chicago, and pomegranates appear as a cast element on the handle of the Museum of the City of New York tankard and another example in the Metropolitan Museum of Art. Pomegranate feet and other elements are not unusual in tankards in the Scandinavian tradition, including examples made in provincial England.[4]

Although far from unknown, Dutch silver tankards do not survive in as great a number as Dutch American examples, perhaps underlining the importance of the form in the New World.[5] The preference in America for specific forms such as the tankard and the high chest of drawers suggests that questions of function deserve serious consideration in any evaluation of Americans' dependence on or independence from English and continental European prototypes.

1. Kathryn C. Buhler and Graham Hood, *American Silver in the Mabel Brady Garvan and Other Collections at Yale University* (New Haven, Conn.: Yale University Press, 1970), cat. no. 578. Judith Banister and Francis J. Puig, *American and English Silver in the Minneapolis Institute of Arts* (Minneapolis: Minneapolis Institute of Arts, forthcoming), will discuss the Dell tankard.
2. For a recent summary of the characteristics of New York tankards, see the entry by Phillip M. Johnston in Baarsen et al., *Courts and Colonies*, cat. no. 57.
3. Blackburn and Piwonka, *Remembrance of Patria*, pp. 287–88. See also pp. 257–70 for a discussion of painted kases and the symbolism of their decoration.
4. See Alain Gruber, *Silverware* (New York: Rizzoli, 1982), fig. 74, for a representative Stockholm example.
5. For Dutch examples, see J. W. Frederiks, *Dutch Silver*, vol. 3, *Wrought Plate of the Central, Northern, and Southern Provinces from the Renaissance until the End of the Eighteenth Century* (The Hague: Martinus Nijhoff, 1960), figs. 194, 221, 238, 290, 332, 347, 426.

Francis J. Puig

The Early Furniture of the Mississippi River Valley, 1760–1820

Although several historians have researched the furniture of the Mississippi River valley, few general publications on the American decorative arts have dealt with the products of the region.1 The French who originally settled the area, however, enriched the architectural and artistic heritage of the American landscape. They also determined the geographic, political, and cultural boundaries of a vast section of the United States well into the late eighteenth century. Their influence can even be seen in the names of such cities as New Orleans, Baton Rouge, Mobile, St. Louis, Natchez, Vincennes, and Ste. Genevieve, some of which still bear strong evidence of French building practices, town planning, and land division systems. Of particular significance to this essay are the traditional French crafts of the region, especially the eighteenth-century furniture produced in the upper Mississippi River valley in settlements clustered around St. Louis, as well as that from the lower valley and particularly New Orleans, which was established in 1718.

While English settlers along the Atlantic seaboard made furniture during the latter part of the eighteenth century that was strongly influenced by French metropolitan styles, the furniture of the French settlements on the upper Mississippi River—like St. Louis, Ste. Genevieve, Cahokia, and Kaskaskia—reflected more conservative traditions. Furniture in the French taste from the East Coast used more up-to-date designs and was crafted by émigrés fleeing France's political turmoil. Surviving examples of such furniture dating to the late eighteenth century are common and include the various suites of seating furniture made by Adam Hains (born 1768) of Philadelphia or the large quantities of furniture fashioned by Charles-Honoré Lannuier (1779–1819) in New York.[2]

By contrast, the French settlements of the upper Mississippi River valley appear not to have been affected by metropolitan fashions current on the East Coast, France, or other French colonies. Instead, most of the furniture produced there was a continuation of French styles from the seventeenth and the first half of the eighteenth century, when most of the region was explored and settled. And although some furniture made late in the eighteenth century blended English and French traditions, it appears not to have been standard production there. The regional predilection for designs of an earlier period may have resulted from circumstances surrounding the region's settlement. From the 1670s to the late eighteenth century, much of the Mississippi River valley was geographically and culturally isolated. French interest in the area was directly related to the revenues it could obtain there, and consequently France made no serious effort to improve the lot of settlers in the territory. It merely protected its assets as cheaply as possible.[3] French settlers in the region, however, were frequently in danger of Indian attack or English infiltration and led frontier existences based on farming, fur trapping, and, to a lesser extent, on lead and salt mining.

Such conditions did not encourage the stylistic development of indigenous furniture forms. Few people could pay for the relatively elaborate furniture popular elsewhere after the middle of the eighteenth century, and as a result few local craftsmen appear to have specialized. Furniture makers, for example, apparently relied on house construction for their livelihood. The few instances where innovative furniture was created in the region during the late eighteenth century can be explained by outside influences: from émigrés originating in French Canada, the English colonies to the east, and such French and Spanish settlements in the Caribbean as Santo Domingo and Cuba.

Politics also affected immigration to the area as well

as economics and trade patterns, factors that are important to understanding the arts of the region. While the St. Lawrence River was explored in the 1530s and Quebec and Montreal founded in 1608 and 1640 respectively,[4] the entire middle of the continent was not officially claimed for the French crown until 1682, when the French explorer René-Robert Cavelier, sieur de LaSalle, discovered the mouth of the Mississippi River.[5] Then called Louisiana, this vast territory included not only all the land west of the Allegheny Mountains but much of Canada as well (fig. 1). Significantly, it was governed by Canada until 1718, at which time responsibility for the territory was shifted to the newly established city of New Orleans.

The earliest European occupants of the region were French fur trappers. Outfitted in Montreal or Quebec, these men ranged the area trapping beaver, hunting deer and other animals, or trading with the native Indian population for furs. By the end of the seventeenth century, French *coureurs de bois* (runners of the woods), as these trappers and traders were known, and French missionaries had established outposts at various locations between present-day Minneapolis in the north and Biloxi in the south. The wealth they generated was enormous. The fur-trapping region known in the eighteenth century as La Baye, for instance, which included land from Green Bay north to the Lake Superior watershed and south to a region below the Wisconsin River, is reputed to have generated an annual profit of 150,000 livres, which was shared by the commander of the region, the governor of Canada, and his quartermaster general.[6]

The first settlements in this vast region were established near trading posts or missions. For instance, Detroit (1699); Cahokia (1700) and Kaskaskia (1703), both in present-day Illinois; Natchez (1699) in present-day

Fig. 1. *Map of New France (Carte du Canada et de la Louisiane qui forment la Nouvelle France).* J. B. Nolin, 1756. Courtesy of the James Ford Bell Library, University of Minnesota.

Mississippi; and Mobile (1699), now in Alabama, were all settled during this early period.[7] Until 1718 when governance of the territory switched to New Orleans, these villages were closely tied to France, both politically and economically, through Canada. Moreover, the various waterways between the middle of the continent and the Atlantic—the Great Lakes and the St. Lawrence River—constituted the region's lifeline. In a very real sense, these waterways provided the only feasible way of transporting raw materials to the outside world. In fact, as late as the mid-1700s, furs trapped in the vast areas of the upper valley, called the Illinois Territory by the French, and lead mined in such cities as Kaskaskia and Cahokia found their way to Canada and France via these inland routes.[8] And open hostilities with the English over the possession of French-held territory precluded both the importation and exportation of goods to European markets through English colonies on the East Coast.

Not surprisingly, even after the founding of New Orleans in 1718, people in the Illinois Territory continued to look to France via Canada. Many of the settlers in the Mississippi River valley, in fact, had emigrated from Canada and retained ties with Canadian communities. An analysis of militia rolls dating to the late eighteenth century, which list not only a person's name but birthplace, corroborate this. For example, the 1779 roster for the town of Ste. Genevieve in Missouri (founded around 1750) included 175 names. Of these, 65 had moved there from the Illinois Territory, while 71 had come from Canada.[9] The St. Louis militia roles of 1780 also suggest a strong influence from Canada: of the 210 men listed, 97 had been born in the village or in the surrounding region (like Cahokia, Kaskaskia, or Vincennes) and had moved there when territories to the east were transferred to English control. The remaining 29 people cited had been born in Canada. In fact, Charles Peterson, who compiled these statistics for St. Louis (which was established in 1764), suspected that at least 50 percent of the population in 1780 had originated in Canada.[10]

Two major political upheavals in the 1760s caused a significant influx of French-Canadians and French settlers from the east bank of the Mississippi River into such newly established settlements west of the river as St. Louis and Ste. Genevieve. These refugees reinforced the influence of French craft traditions in the upper Mississippi River valley. Their aesthetics, however, were not metropolitan in flavor, but rather those found in the more rural regions of France, particularly from Burgundy, Brittany, and Picardy. Moreover, their furniture forms and craftsmanship reflected traditions typical in France during the seventeenth and early eighteenth centuries, when Canada was originally populated.

The first of these population shifts occurred between 1755 and 1764 as a result of the forced migration of the Acadians, French settlers who had occupied Nova Scotia and New Brunswick since the early seventeenth century.[11] Having come under British rule in 1713 when the territory was ceded to England under the Treaty of Utrecht, which ended the War of the Spanish Succession, Acadians never accepted being British subjects. Starting in 1755, the British, exasperated by Acadian refusals to pledge allegiance to the king of England and give up the Catholic faith, forcibly deported as many as fifteen thousand settlers. Many of them relocated to the upper Mississippi River valley in established French communities.[12] And much later in 1793, several thousand more Acadians who had been sent to France arrived in New Orleans and influenced the arts in rural Louisiana.[13]

The second population shift resulted when France ceded Canada and all of its territory east of the Mississippi River to England in 1763 at the end of the French and Indian War. The Treaty of Paris, in fact, virtually ended the French empire in North America. Not only was land lost to the English, but holdings west of the Mississippi went to Spain in the secret Treaty of Fontainebleau, signed in November 1762. (Although Spain returned Louisiana to France in 1802, the territory was sold the next year to the United States in a preemptive move by the French to keep it out of English hands. The sale was also a means of raising revenue to compensate Spain for its own loss of Florida to England during treaty negotiations.) More significantly, however, the Treaty of Paris resulted in an almost immediate exodus of Frenchmen from settlements east of the Mississippi as English military forces and settlers began to occupy the territory. Moreover, most of these French refugees and many Canadians moved to Spanish settlements on the west bank of the river, thereby swelling the populations of Ste. Genevieve and St. Louis.[14]

These migrations reinforced well-established French traditions in the upper Mississippi River valley. Surviving descriptions and documents suggest that the villages in this region looked like those of seventeenth- and early

Fig. 2. *Typical house of the Illinois country.* Charles Warin, dated 1796, published in Victor Collot, *A Journey in North America*, Paris, 1826. Courtesy of the State Historical Society of Wisconsin.

eighteenth-century France.[15] Town layouts were based on medieval prototypes with communally owned fields divided into strips ranging from one to three arpents wide (one arpent is equivalent to about 192 feet) and as much as 60 arpents long. Animals grazed freely in the surrounding countryside, and the villages themselves were laid out with house lots (at least in the St. Louis area) measuring 120 by 150 feet and enclosed by a stockade of posts set into the ground.

The architecture of these early houses, in fact, was a direct imitation of the predominant type found in central and southwestern France, as well as from the northern provinces of Normandy and Picardy.[16] In addition to having porches on at least one side (fig. 2), a feature that some scholars believe was of Caribbean origin,[17] these houses, with their steep hipped roofs, flared eaves, and casement windows, were primarily constructed of wood, which was found in great abundance in the New World. The technique used, probably original to settlements in North America, is called *poteaux en terre* (posts or stakes in the ground).[18] Contemporary accounts for such construction appear frequently in the notarial archives of St. Louis. One of the best, dated 1779, describes the house built for Pierre de Laclede in Grand Prairie:

A house of posts in the ground thirty feet long and twenty two feet wide, with a lean-to at one end of the said house and a double chimney of stone between the house and the lean-to; the whole to be roofed with shingles. The main posts—that is to say, those at the corners and openings in the wall—shall be of mulberry of suitable dimensions, as shall be the frames of the doors and windows in the said house. There shall be four windows so placed as to allow beds in the corners. The

Furniture of the Mississippi River Valley 155

Fig. 3. *Armoire*. American, Cahokia, Ill., or St. Louis, Mo., 1760–1800. Walnut. H. 95¾ in (243.2 cm), W. 59⅜ in (150.8 cm), D. 25⁵⁄₁₆ in (64.3 cm). Cahokia Courthouse Historical Site.

balance of the posts shall be of white oak, well seasoned and squared up. The said house shall be floored and ceiled with boards well planed and grooved, with a partition in which shall be placed one door at the end near the main room. The main room shall be sixteen feet long with two doors cut opposite each other and two windows. There shall be two similar windows in the bedroom. The lean-to shall have one door and one window and shall be floored and ceiled with grooved boards. In addition there shall be excavated under the said house a cellar twenty feet long, fourteen feet wide and six feet deep. The said house shall be well plastered and whitewashed inside and out and the lean-to as well. The said house shall have a ceiling height of eight feet, the floor raised one foot above ground level and the lining of the cellar well made. The lumber for construction shall be subject to examination by experts. All the lumber of said house shall be of white oak and walnut, the doors and the windows shall be well fitted with the necessary hardware.[19]

As in this house, the usual interior consisted of one large common or keeping room, at least two bedrooms, and a kitchen. Most also had a gallery or porch on at least one side, which shaded the house and provided additional living space in hot weather. Generally, however, even the largest of these buildings were relatively sparsely furnished. This was true even in the homes of the wealthy. The estate of Louis Bolduc, a rich cloth merchant in Ste. Genevieve who died in 1773, for example, included only the following pieces of furniture:

— a feather bed with an old cover and a small feather bolster
— an old feather bed and a small couch
— a small buffet with its vaisselier [a set of shelves for holding dishes]
— a huche [bread trough] without its cover
— twelve chairs as many good as bad
— two chairs
— an old sawyer's trestle and a little table
— one folding table
— one table with drawer
— two small armoires, one over another.[20]

Such inventories, when compared to similar ones from New Orleans, suggest that many pieces made in the upper Mississippi valley as late as the 1770s were stylistically conservative. The armoire (fig. 3) illustrated here, for example, probably dates to the 1760s or later and seems typical of furniture produced in the region. It is in a style popular in France from the mid-1600s well into the nineteenth century. Rectilinear in outline, armoires like this depended for their decorative effect on the elaborate patterns created by the structure of the object itself: the mortise-and-tenon framework built around small, often faceted or square panels.

The table in figure 4, also from the mid-seventeenth century, is probably not unlike the table with drawer

Fig. 4. *Table*. American, probably Vincennes, Ind., or St. Louis, Mo., 1750–1800. Pecan. H. 27⅛ in (68.9 cm), W. 42 1/16 in (106.8 cm), D. 25 1/16 in (63.7 cm). Courtesy of The Henry Francis du Pont Winterthur Museum, Winterthur, Del., 80.229.

Fig. 5. *Table.* Canadian or American, possibly Detroit, Mich., 1750–1800. Pine. H. 26¾ in (67.9 cm), W. 39¼ in (99.7 cm), D. 27¼ in (69.2 cm). The Detroit Institute of Arts, gift of Mrs. Edsel B. Ford, 46.97.

Fig. 6. *Table.* French, late 18th or early 19th century. Walnut. H. 21½ in (54.6 cm). Courtesy of Judith and Martin Miller, *Miller's International Antiques Price Guide*, 1987.

listed in the Bolduc inventory. In all probability a very common form, this table seems to be a unique survivor from the region, although similar pieces exist that were made in Canada and France during the eighteenth and early nineteenth centuries. Such examples of a Canadian and a prototypical French table are illustrated in figures 5 and 6. Each has trumpet-shaped turnings on the legs and a turned finial that is centrally placed on the medial stretcher, also frequently turned. The one from the Mississippi River valley, however, unlike most French and French-Canadian tables that are of walnut, painted pine, or yellow birch,[21] is made entirely of pecan, a wood that does not commonly grow north of Illinois and Indiana. Moreover, the history of the region's settlement suggests that it was fabricated between 1750 and 1800, when any number of joiners or carpenters with lathes could have turned the legs, stretchers, and finial.

But why were objects like these made in the Mississippi River valley as much as one hundred years after they were fashionable in France? Part of the answer lies in the fact that even in France furniture styles of the mid-1600s remained popular in rural areas long after they were first introduced. Also, Canada and, ultimately, the Mississippi River valley were populated by provincial Frenchmen who were cognizant of these earlier furniture styles.²² Having come from rural France to a distant and isolated colony, New France, and subsequently migrating to an even more remote wilderness, the craftsmen in the Mississippi River valley were simply making furniture in styles that were familiar to them and appear to have been unconcerned with more fashionable developments in metropolitan centers. Familiar, if conservative, furniture forms constituted part of a recreated, recognizable environment, including town layouts, architectural designs, social customs, and civil laws, that provided settlers with their identity as Frenchmen.

Trade schools established in Canada in the late seventeenth century also helped to reinforce early French design traditions.²³ The first of these was set up in 1675 by Bishop Laval of the Archdiocese of Canada and remained open until 1701. Its two branches, one at Cap Tourmente and another at the seminary in Quebec, employed a staff of instructors that included carpenters, woodworkers, wood carvers, masons, and stonecutters. Another school was founded in 1694, when Louis XIV approved François Charon de la Barre's plan to establish a charitable institution in Montreal that could provide "a refuge for poor children and orphans . . . instruct the said children in the crafts, and give them the best possible education, all for the greater glory of God and the well-being of the colony." Both schools trained generations of craftsmen who, in turn, working in small isolated communities throughout Canada, trained numerous apprentices who passed down and perpetuated traditional designs and forms of construction. Some of these undoubtedly immigrated to French settlements in the Illinois Territory. Unfortunately, the backgrounds of most craftsmen working in the Mississippi River valley through the early nineteenth century remain unknown, although the birthplaces of a few are recorded.²⁴

Nonetheless, a surprising similarity of construction exists between furniture made in the upper Mississippi River valley, Canada, and rural France. Like the case pieces already mentioned, most French provincial and Canadian furniture was very heavily framed with mortise-and-tenon joints, crude dovetails, and thick wooden planks created with pit saws, planes, and adzes. (The only documented use of a sawmill in the St. Louis region occurred in the early 1770s.²⁵) This sharply contrasts with furniture made in English settlements along the East Coast, where large, thinly cut boards and fine dovetails became standard after 1700.

Historical construction contracts describing building techniques used in the manufacture of these early pieces also suggest that the men who made furniture in the region were primarily housewrights. This is true of the only documented piece of furniture from the upper river valley: an armoire (fig. 7) from St. Louis that dates to the 1770s or 1780s and was fabricated by Jean-Baptiste Ortes, a native of Bearn, France, who earned his living building houses. In 1767, for instance, he and Jean-Baptiste Cambas were described as *menuisier associez* (furniture makers in partnership) and not only built a number of houses over the next few years but the first church in St. Louis.²⁶ Cambas, in fact, had a large collection of cabinetmaking tools among his possessions at the time of his death, including:

> Thirty-five carpenter's planes and jack planes
> Two large gimlets, a draw knife and a hammer
> A lot of old chisels of various kinds and sizes
> A large squaring axe
> A saw
> Two small saws
> Three small hand saws
> A small paper with a lot of screws
> A carpenter's large bench with a vise.²⁷

Others described as joiners or carpenters in contracts, both for house construction and interior carpentry work, included Jacques Denis, Pierre Lupien, and Antoine Hubert.²⁸ Each is also likely to have made furniture. Lupien's inventory, taken in October 1775, included a very large set of cabinetmaking tools and, more significantly, "four pieces of wood for the feet of an armoire."²⁹ Indeed, the simplicity and heaviness of most early furniture from the upper Mississippi River valley closely ties it to house construction and joinery rather than cabinetmaking. And given the predominant woodworking technique of the region—joinery, the practice of fitting together the parts of an object, usually small wooden panels, using mortise-and-tenon joints—it was not unusual that the same people building houses also built furniture. Clearly, the art of the joiner and builder remained part of provincial French life throughout much of the eighteenth century, and it can be assumed that a similar relationship existed concurrently in the Mississippi River valley.

This was certainly also true in England and the English colonies along coastal North America during the seventeenth century. By the end of the 1600s, however, most joiners in these areas primarily built houses. Due to a change of furniture styles in English-speaking com-

Fig. 7. *Armoire*. American, St. Louis, Mo., about 1780. Attributed to Jean Baptiste Ortes, born France, worked in St. Louis about 1765–1780s. Walnut. H. 92¾ in (235.6 cm), W. 56½ in (143.5 cm), D. 20½ in (52.1 cm). Missouri Historical Society, St. Louis.

Fig. 8. *Petite Commode*. American, St. Louis, Mo., 1770–1800. Cedar; white pine. H. 13¾ in (34.9 cm), W. 21⅜ in (54.31 cm), D. 12¾ in (32.4 cm). Missouri Historical Society, St. Louis.

munities during the early eighteenth century, furniture production became the responsibility of cabinetmakers. That joiners continued to make furniture in French settlements well into the 1770s and 1780s might seem unusual in a North American context. However, taking into account the small population size of these villages and their local economies and payment systems, which consisted largely of bartering furs rather than currency, great specialization in the crafts may not have been possible. Nor would their economies have supported full-time furniture makers. Nor, for that matter, would many settlers have been interested in or able to afford more up-to-date, more difficult to produce, and therefore more expensive furniture forms.

True cabinetmaking techniques—the joining of large, thinly cut boards, the use of dovetails, and the creation of standard drawers—as well as more innovative furniture designs reached the upper Mississippi River valley in the 1770s and 1780s, probably as a result of French-Canadian émigrés fleeing English rule in Montreal or Quebec. These newer furniture forms (cat. nos. 66, 67, and fig. 8), however, show a mingling of English and French designs: the French *arbalète* or crossbow shape for the furniture front was combined in numerous documented pieces from Quebec with English ball-and-claw feet, especially after the mid-eighteenth century. Yet, this combination of motifs did not gain general acceptance in the Mississippi River valley. Moreover, several of the more technically and stylistically innovative objects from the region—including an armoire (cat. no. 69) and a small table[30]—were made for the Chouteaus, who were probably the best educated and wealthiest family in the territory.[31] Well read and highly sophisticated, they were in the minority of regional settlers familiar with and appreciative of high-style French and European designs and culture. Their armoire and a closely related petite commode (fig. 8), in fact, are so similar in design and carving that they were undoubt-

Furniture of the Mississippi River Valley 161

edly made by the same person. But while the commode seems to be a close copy of pieces from the Quebec region after the 1760s, the armoire may be unique. Even though it uses the *arbalète* shape for the carcass with a cusped skirt, carved ball-and-claw feet, and a central shell pendant as was common in French-Canadian case pieces (cat. no. 66), no armoire of this exact form—with its bombé front and sides—is known to have been made in France (cat. no. 71) or French Canada.

A third piece (cat. no. 68) also using the ball-and-claw motif has no provenance and unlike the armoire and petite commode, which are made of walnut or red cedar, it is cherry with white pine as the secondary wood. Yet of the three, the full-scale commode is the most interesting stylistically, for the carved ball-and-claw feet might have been executed by someone trained in Providence or Newport, Rhode Island. The sophisticated construction of the piece—thinly cut drawer sides joined with finely cut dovetails—is also very unlike that of provincial French or French-Canadian commodes. This suggests that it may have been built by a cabinetmaker of English descent before the purchase of the territory west of the Mississippi River by the United States in 1803.

Thoroughly French in style are three armoires that are believed to have been made in the Vincennes area of Indiana.[32] These pieces, represented here by one in the Missouri Historical Society (fig. 9) that also belonged to the Chouteau family, are among the most sophisticated examples of French furniture from the entire river valley. Each is slightly different, although all are executed in the Louis XVI style, which reached its greatest popularity in court circles from about 1775 to 1800. Much taller, restrained, and more rectilinear than the styles preceding it, each armoire is also superbly crafted and carved, suggesting manufacture by one of the many highly trained craftsmen who left France for America after the beheading of Louis XVI in 1794.

In contrast to pieces from the upper Mississippi River valley, the majority of furniture from the New Orleans region has a much different flavor: it closely reflects stylistic developments in French metropolitan centers. Despite two disastrous fires (1788 and 1794) that destroyed the city and most of the furniture made there to that time, this characteristic is substantiated by eighteenth-century inventories.[33] The greater style consciousness of the lower valley is also understandable given its economic development. While St. Louis and other cities in the Illinois Territory developed largely as frontier communities (bartering with the native populations, trapping, farming, and mining lead), New Orleans emerged as a major trade center with connections throughout the world. The perspective of settlers in that region, their awareness of political and artistic shifts in Europe and also South America, led to much different attitudes about the arts in general. While the early architecture of the area, for instance, was the same as in settlements further north,[34] a wealthy merchant class quickly demanded different building materials and architectural styles. Although founded in 1718, New Orleans already had a number of buildings by the 1730s that reflected strong European influences and adaptations to their humid tropical environment.[35]

Although the surviving furniture from the region is generally later in date and style than that further north, eighteenth-century inventories give evidence that lifestyles in New Orleans were dramatically different from those in the Illinois Territory. New Orleans interiors were generously and frequently expensively furnished, and as the following excerpts make clear often included objects not found in the upper Mississippi River valley:

1763   Couch with its mattress and bolster of calamascio
1769   Large mirror measuring 40 × 30 inches in a gilt frame with a pair of enamelled sconces for flowers
       A large armchair with back upholstered in damask
       Walnut chest of four drawers ornamented with gilt brass
       A marble topped table on a gilt pedestal
       A cedar bureau containing three large drawers and two small ones, with a book case above it, furnished with glass doors, iron bound, closing with a lock with a poor brass decoration
       A marqueterie table
1773   One sofa on roebuck feet, upholstered in chintz
       A small day bed
       Two couches
       Walnut chest of drawers closing with a lock and key with silver ornaments.[36]

By the late eighteenth century, however, the region was changing dramatically as several population groups arrived and influenced the artistic heritage of the area. In 1769, shortly after the Spanish claimed the Mississippi River valley, the city of New Orleans had 3,190 residents, 1,225 of whom were slaves.[37] By 1795, eight years before the United States purchased Louisiana from France, the population had increased to 8,000 inhabitants, about half of whom were slaves.[38] During the intervening years, a large number of Spaniards had immigrated to the region as had Frenchmen, French

Fig. 9. *Armoire*. American, probably Vincennes, Ind., 1780–1800. Cherry; walnut and tulip poplar. H. 96 in (243.8 cm), W. 54 in (137.2 cm), D. 22 in (55.9 cm). Missouri Historical Society, St. Louis.

Fig. 10. *Armoire*. American, Philadelphia, Pa., 1796. Jean-Baptiste Laurent and Charles Comballe, born Santo Domingo, worked in Philadelphia about 1791–98. Mahogany; eastern white pine. H. 69½ in (176.5 cm), W. 51¾ in (131.4 cm), D. 19 in (48.3 cm). The Girard Collection, Philadelphia.

Canadians, and Acadians leaving English territories east of the river after 1764.[39] In addition, the population was swollen by refugees fleeing the French Revolution and the slave revolts in Santo Domingo in 1791.[40] Moreover, during the same years New Orleans developed as a major port city and had trade connections not only with Europe but with all of Spanish America—Central and South America as well as the Caribbean islands.

Such diverse cultural and economic influences resulted in a decorative arts tradition very different from that of settlements in the Illinois Territory. Certain furniture forms, like sofas, upholstered armchairs, and marble-topped tables, were imported or actually made in the New Orleans region and not in the upper Mississippi valley. On the other hand, some forms, like slat-back chairs, developed along parallel lines, while others, such as armoires, took totally different directions.

The furniture form to receive the most lavish attention in New Orleans was the armoire. Stylistically, these pieces copied aspects of armoires made in Santo Domingo (fig. 10), were short in height, and depended for their decorative effect on extremely high-quality mahoganies, flush panel construction, and elaborate undulating skirts.[41]

Surprisingly, despite large numbers of English-American merchants in New Orleans by 1769, this group did not affect the decorative arts there until the turn of the century. Indeed, East Coast interpretations of English traditions, primarily patterned inlays and stringing adapted from designs in Thomas Sheraton's or George Hepplewhite's pattern books, show up only after 1810. A lack of craftsmen experienced in making inlays and the lack of tools necessary for their manufacture undoubtedly resulted in a scarcity of English-inspired pieces. But it also seems clear that the predominant culture of the region was French, and that the adoption of English motifs was done selectively. English elements, for example, were often merely grafted onto familiar French forms, especially with armoires (cat. no. 70). And in some instances, the use of English inlays depended upon the development of strong trade links between New Orleans and such American cities as New York.[42]

Except for a small number of armchairs with upholstered backs and seats, the most common type of chair produced in the lower Mississippi River valley was like those from the St. Louis area (cat. no. 64). Similar chairs were also made in France (cat. no. 65) and throughout Europe for hundreds of years. The predominant characteristics of such chairs include two or three shaped slats; turned, often turnip-shaped, feet; and acorn- or ball-shaped finials capping the rear stiles.[43]

Tables made in eighteenth-century New Orleans, too, were French in character and executed in the Louis XV style, having cabriole legs and sometimes *pied-de-biche* (cloven feet). While the majority of such tables (cat. no. 72) are believed to have been from the lower Mississippi River valley, a relatively elaborate one from the upper valley is known and like the more sophisticated pieces from there has a Chouteau family provenance.[44] With curved legs and curvilinear skirts, the examples from New Orleans, however, were generally made of walnut or mahogany, while their French prototypes (cat. no. 73) were frequently constructed of pine or some other inexpensive wood.

Although the Spanish controlled the entire Mississippi River valley from 1764 to 1803, their influence on the territory outside New Orleans appears to have been nominal. Therefore, it is not surprising that the one identifiable Spanish influence in the decorative arts, the *butaca* (fig. 11), an armchair with a continuous back and

Fig. 11. *Butaca*. Probably Mexican, possibly Campeche, 1780–1800. Mahogany. H. 36 in (91.4 cm), W. 24 in (61 cm), D. 34 in (86.4 cm). Courtesy of the Neal Alford Auction Company, New Orleans.

a seat supported by curule-type legs, is believed to have been first made in America in the New Orleans area. Further north, even late into the eighteenth century, the culture remained almost entirely French, so much so in fact that most records in St. Louis during the Spanish era were kept in French.

The *butaca*, nonetheless, is an interesting object for the study of design transference, for, although introduced to the region by Spaniards, its origins are not European. Rather, they are South or Central American, where historians have identified ancient prototypes that were later modified by Spanish settlers in the area.[45] The pieces from New Orleans do not differ significantly in either structure or decoration from those made in Central or South America. Mahogany seems to have been the most common wood for all the chairs and leather the standard upholstery. (The Hispanic examples, however, frequently have tooled leather upholstery rather than the smooth surfaces found in Louisiana.) By the early nineteenth century, the form was also introduced to other parts of North America, and some examples were made as far away as New York City.[46]

By the 1820s, the production of traditional French forms in the lower Mississippi River valley began to end. By that time, cheaper imports had become standard in the region, and the French and Spanish cultures in the entire valley had been completely overrun by Anglo-American settlers and, in the St. Louis region, by German immigrants. As traditional forms were replaced by ones with Anglicized styles, they were relegated to outbuildings and servants' houses. Unfortunately, because these earlier pieces were never numerous to begin with, few of them have survived.

As more research is done on the furniture from the Mississippi River valley, more pieces are likely to be found that will add to our knowledge of the region and lead to a better understanding of all the American decorative arts, not just those of the English who dominated stylistic developments on the East Coast. The process of change in the valley—the influx of various immigrant groups, changing frontier life-styles, and the introduction of new technologies and materials—helped to create innovative forms that deserve to be seen as an integral part of our national heritage. And furniture like the commode (cat. no. 68) or the armoire (cat. no. 70), in their combination of ethnic styles and elements, must be seen as important and unique statements in the history of American decorative arts.

NOTES

1. Several regional historians have written on the arts of the Mississippi River valley, including Jessie Poesch, Jack Holden, Charles Peterson, Charles Van Ravenswaay, and H. Parrott Barot. Of these, the most prolific is Jessie J. Poesch. See her *Early Furniture of Louisiana* (New Orleans: Louisiana State University, 1972); "Early Louisiana Armoires," *Antiques* 94 (August 1968): 196–203; "Furniture of the River Road Plantations in Louisiana," *Antiques* 111 (June 1977): 1184–93; "Living with Antiques: The Poydras-Holden House in Louisiana," *Antiques* 127 (April 1985): 870–77. Also see Jack Holden, Robert E. Smith, and Frances Love, *Early French Louisiana Furnishings, 1700–1830: Bicentennial Exhibition at the Art Center for Southwestern Louisiana* (Lafayette, La.: The Art Center for Southwestern Louisiana, 1974); Charles Peterson, *Colonial St. Louis: Building a Creole Capital* (St. Louis, Mo.: Missouri Historical Society, 1949); Charles Van Ravenswaay, "The Forgotten Arts and Crafts of Colonial Louisiana," *Antiques* 64 (September 1953): 192–95 and "The Creole Arts and Crafts of Upper Louisiana," *Bulletin of the Missouri Historical Society* 12 (April 1956): 213–48. Also useful are Barot's articles; see his "The Henri Penne House Complex, Saint Martin Parish, Louisiana," *Antiques* 133 (April 1988): 906–13; "Kent Plantation House in Alexandria, Louisiana," *Antiques* 126 (July 1984): 134–41; "The Anglo-American Art Museum of Louisiana State University in Baton Rouge," *Antiques* 125 (March 1984): 637–45; and "History in Houses: Magnolia Mourd Plantation House in Baton Rouge, Louisiana," *Antiques* 123 (May 1983): 1054–61. Authors who discuss the arts of the Mississippi River valley as part of the national experience include Wendy Cooper and Jonathan Fairbanks. See Wendy A. Cooper, *In Praise of America: American Decorative Arts, 1650–1830* (New York: Alfred A. Knopf, 1980) and Jonathan Fairbanks and Elizabeth Bidwell Bates, *American Furniture: 1620 to the Present* (New York: Richard Marek Publishers, 1981).

2. Examples of furniture by Hains are illustrated in Cooper, *In Praise of America*, p. 77, nos. 93, 95; pieces by Launnier are also illustrated on p. 254, nos. 286, 288; p. 262, no. 304; p. 306, no. 305. Furniture only attributed to Launnier is illustrated on p. 244, pl. 48, p. 261, no. 302.

3. W. J. Eccles, *The Canadian Frontier: 1534–1760* (Albuquerque, N. Mex., 1969), pp. 110, 147. The author notes the French "were no more interested in occupying land than were New England seamen who voyaged to Africa for cargoes of slaves or tropical produce. Eventually they had to claim these lands and maintain military garrisons to protect their interests." He also states that "in the mid-eighteenth century the profits to be made at certain of the posts were reputed to be enormous." The territory of La Baye, for instance, gave an annual profit of 150,000 livres, split between the commander of the territory and the Canadian governor and his intendant.

4. Ibid., pp. 12, 23, 39.

5. Ibid., p. 109. For more information about the discovery of the mouth of the river and subsequent attempts to locate it from the gulf, see Richebourg Gaillard McWilliams, "Ibervilel at Birdfoot Subdelta: Final Discovery of the Mississippi River," in John Francis McDermott, ed., *Frenchmen and French Ways in the Mississippi Valley* (Chicago: University of Chicago Press, 1969), pp. 127–40.

6. Eccles, *The Canadian Frontier*, p. 147. Because the French crown was constantly devaluing the livre throughout the eighteenth century, its monetary value is difficult to establish. Some indication of its worth at midcentury, however, may be ascertained by noting the construction of Fort Massac, located on the Ohio River below the mouth of the Tennessee River. In 1745, the fort, which was to be of stone and measure 128 feet on each side with circular watchtowers on the corners, was estimated to cost 31,045 livres. The compound was also to include a commandant's quarters, barracks, guardhouse and prison, magazine, and storehouse, all of stone. See John B.

Fortier, "New Light on Fort Massac," in John Francis McDermott, ed., *Frenchmen and French Ways*, pp. 59–60.

7. Van Ravenswaay, "The Creole Arts and Crafts," pp. 213–14, notes the founding dates for a number of villages in the upper Mississippi River valley, including Cape Girardeau (1792) and New Madrid (1785), both in present-day Missouri.

8. Carl J. Eckberg, *Colonial Ste. Genevieve: An Adventure on the Mississippi Frontier* (Gerald, Mo.: The Patrice Press, 1985), p. 147.

9. Ibid., p. 46.

10. See Van Ravenswaay, "The Creole Arts and Crafts," p. 216 and Peterson, *Colonial St. Louis*, p. 41.

11. Carl A. Brasseaux, *The Founding of New Acadia: The Beginnings of Acadian Life in Louisiana, 1765–1803* (Baton Rouge: Louisiana State University Press, 1987). This is the best history of the Acadian population and its dispersal throughout America.

12. Ibid., pp. 20–34. Brasseaux discusses the dispersal of the Acadian population, noting that many avoided British efforts to resettle them in Maryland, Pennsylvania, and even Santo Domingo by immigrating to the Mississippi River valley. It remains unclear, however, how many ultimately settled in the upper Mississippi River settlements such as Cahokia, New Madrid, St. Louis, or Kaskaskia. Brasseaux (p. 33) quotes an English letter of November 1764 suggesting a population movement to the upper Mississippi River area: "I apprehend that all those people [Acadians] who live in and about this town [Halifax], have so peremptorily refused to take the Oath of Allegiance, by the best information I can obtain of their purposes, they intend going directly to Cape François [sic], from thence to the Mississippi and finally to the Country of the Illinois and there to make a settlement."

13. Ibid., p. 72. Holden et al. in *Early French Louisiana Furnishings* also discuss Acadian influences on the arts of the lower Mississippi River valley.

14. The English, upon occupying the east bank of the river after the treaty, also noted that many Frenchmen moved west. One of these was Captain Thomas Stirling, who wrote to his commanding officer, General Thomas Gage, in 1765: "The settlement [i.e., British Illinois] has been declining since the Commencement of the War [French and Indian War], and when it was Ceded to us many Families went for fear of the English, and want of Troops to protect them from the Indians; they have formed a Settlement Since the Peace [of Paris] Opposite to Caho [Cahokia] called St. Louis, where there is now [1765] about Fifty families, and they have another opposite to Caskaskias [Ste. Genevieve], which has . . . about the same number of Families, to these two Places they have retired." Quoted in Eckberg, *Colonial Ste. Genevieve*, p. 41.

15. The best analysis of settlement patterns in St. Louis and the surrounding communities appears in Peterson, *Colonial St. Louis*, pp. 5–24.

16. Peter N. Moogk, *Building a House in New France: An Account of the Perplexities of Client and Craftsmen in Early Canada* (Toronto: McClelland and Stewart, 1977), p. 22. Marcel Trudel in *Introduction to New France* (Toronto: Holt, Rinehart & Winston of Canada, 1968), pp. 132–34, notes that seventeenth-century settlers came primarily from Normandy; the Ile-de-France and Paris; Poitou; Aunis and the Iles de Ré and d'Oléron (the area around La Rochelle from which most ships departed to Canada); and Brittany. During the eighteenth century, settlers came from the Ile-de-France and Paris; Normandy; Brittany; Poitou; Guienne and Artois; Aunis and the Ile de Ré; Saintonge; and Languedoc. (These regions are arranged in the order of the largest number of settlers.)

17. Van Ravenswaay, "The Creole Arts and Crafts," pp. 218–19. Jessie J. Poesch in *The Art of the Old South: Painting, Sculpture, Architecture and the Products of Craftsmen, 1560–1860* (New York: Alfred A. Knopf, 1983), p. 136, quotes C. C. Robin regarding these porches: "The heat of the climate makes galleries around the houses a necessity. All of them have one, some around all four sides of the house, others on two sides only, and rarely, only on one side . . . . The galleries are usually eight or nine feet wide. These wide galleries have several advantages. First, they prevent the sun's rays from striking the walls of the house and thus keep them cool. Also, they form a convenient and pleasant spot upon which to promenade during the day . . . . one can eat or entertain there, and very often during the hot summer nights one sleeps there." On page 136, another traveler in 1806, Thomas Ashe, makes comments about the origin of the architecture: "The houses of a parish, which are built with all the embellishments of the French, in the West Indies style, are not crowded together, but are separated by groves and gardens, which give them a charming effect."

18. Moogk, *Building a House*, p. 32, notes that this technique was not commonly used for house building except in Canada among the Acadians: "Round posts or squared timbers planted in the ground (*pieux* or *poteaux en terre*) have been described as a common feature of house building in New France. While this may be true for Acadia and the settlements of the Upper Mississippi, it is not applicable to the area now known as the Province of Quebec. Barns and stables were built in this manner, but it was regarded as unsuitable for a permanent human shelter."

19. Peterson, *Colonial St. Louis*, pp. 35–37. Peterson also gives more specifics about this type of construction: "The poteaux in this type of construction were set in a trench some three feet deep and backfilled. The part buried in the earth was left in the round. Above grade the poteaux were left round or hewn about nine inches square, depending on the quality of the work, and spiked at the upper end to the plate or mortised into it. Between each was a space about equal to their diameter. This was channelled and filled in with stones and mortar or set with sticks and plastered with mud and grass or straw. The former is the Norman and Canadian method, the latter came up from the Louisiana Coast. Outside and inside the wall was plastered, using laths if necessary, making a neat and snug wall."

20. Colonial Archives Manuscript Collection, Missouri Historical Society, Estate Inventory, Mrs. Louis Bolduc, August 11, 1773, Ste. Genevieve Archives, estates no. 37.

21. Jean Palardy, *The Early Furniture of French Canada* (Toronto: MacMillan of Canada, 1963), pp. 369–70. Palardy notes that the woods most commonly used and mentioned in early inventories were white pine, yellow birch, and butternut. He says: "The friezes and legs of tables were usually of yellow birch, while the top was often of pine or butternut. Solid wood or rush seat chairs were usually made of yellow birch; sugar maple or red maple were also used but the seats were generally made of pine. Armoires and low buffets were made of pine or butternut, with the exeption of a few two-tiered buffets which date from the end of the seventeenth century and according to inventories were made of solid yellow birch. A few of these are still to be seen today."

22. See, for instance, Suzanne Tardieu-Dumont, *Le Mobilier regional français: Normandie* (Paris: Berger-Levrault, 1980); Paul Baneat, *Le Mobilier breton* (Paris: Charles Massin et Cie., 1935); Joseph-Stany Gauthier, *Le Mobilier bas-breton* (Paris: Charles Massin et Cie., 1927). Tardieu-Dumont's book dates many of the pieces illustrated in the catalogue to the nineteenth century.

23. Palardy, *The Early Furniture of French Canada*, pp. 376–78.

24. Van Ravenswaay, "The Creole Arts and Crafts," pp. 242–48, includes a checklist of carpenters and joiners working in the settlements of the upper Mississippi River valley. This helpful compilation was made from references found in regional records.

25. Peterson, *Colonial St. Louis*, p. 26.

26. Ibid., pp. 45–46.

27. Ibid., p. 46.

28. These men are frequently listed in documents found in the colonial archives of St. Louis, which are on deposit with the Recorder of Deeds for the city. The documents are written in both French and Spanish and are accompanied by English translations. References to Denis, for instance, appear in documents 2, 4, 80,

and 1538, dated March 15, 1765 (nos. 2 and 4); July 24, 1770; and April 1, 1775. References to Lupien are found in documents 1561 and 1566, dated February 21, 1771, and July 9, 1771. References to Hubert appear in documents 5, 6, 26, and 2840, dated July 31, 1765; January 31, 1765; May 14, 1768; and November 2, 1765, respectively. These documents range from disputes over boundaries, requests for overdue payments, and building contracts for houses to the buying of goods and, in one instance, the purchase of a slave woman (Lupien, no. 1556, July 9, 1771).

29. Peterson, *Colonial St. Louis*, p. 47.

30. This table is illustrated in Van Ravenswaay, "The Forgotten Arts and Crafts of Colonial Louisiana," p. 194.

31. For biographical information on Auguste Chouteau, see John Francis McDermott, "Auguste Chouteau: First Citizen of Upper Louisiana," in McDermott, ed., *Frenchmen and French Ways*, pp. 1–13.

32. These three armoires are owned by the Missouri Historical Society, the Pierre Menard House in Kaskaskia, Illinois, and a private collector in the Baton Rouge area. The armoire in Baton Rouge is illustrated in Poesch, "Living with Antiques," p. 873. This example bears close comparison with the French armoire from Bourguignon. See, for instance, Lucile Oliver, *Mobilier bourguignon* (Paris: Editions Charles Massin, n.d.), pp. 9, 31.

33. Poesch, "Early Louisiana Armoires," p. 197.

34. Peterson, *Colonial St. Louis*, p. 35, notes that palisaded construction was common during the early years of Detroit, Biloxi, and New Orleans.

35. See Samuel Wilson, Jr., "Ignace François Broutin," in McDermott, ed., *Frenchmen and French Ways*, pp. 213–94. Broutin was the first engineer in New Orleans and designed a number of government buildings there. The first brick building in the city, also by him, was the prison built in 1730. Although his earliest plans are French in every respect, one of his last commissions (1749), the Intendance, was significantly different and included "two story columned galleries across the entire front and rear facades of the main building, with the main roof extended over them at a lower pitch. Here for the first time a drawing appears for a great house with galleries in the form which was adopted for most of the major plantation houses of Louisiana of the subsequent French and Spanish colonial periods and which continued to be used well into the nineteenth century" (p. 289). Wilson also notes that this galleried design was well suited to the hot and humid climate of the region.

36. Holden et al., *Early French Louisiana Furnishings*, pp. 8–10.

37. Margaret Fisher Dalrymple, ed., *The Merchant of Manchac: The Letterbook of John Fitzpatrick, 1768–1790* (Baton Rouge: Louisiana State University, 1978), p. 4. These figures are taken from a 1769 census that records New Orleans as having 468 houses.

38. Van Ravenswaay, "The Creole Arts and Crafts," p. 220.

39. Fifteen hundred Acadians, expelled from their homelands in the 1750s, found their way to Louisiana in 1785. Brasseaux, *The Founding of New Acadia*, p. 72.

40. Samuel Eliot Morison, *The Oxford History of the American People* (New York: Oxford University Press, 1965), p. 353, notes that in 1798 the French consul estimated that there were 25,000 refugees in the United States. Included among these were Santo Domingans. Because New Orleans was French and close to Santo Domingo, many Frenchmen fled there. However, because this occurred before the land west of the Mississippi became part of the United States, census information is not available for those years. Howard Mumford Jones in *America and French Culture, 1750–1848* (Westport, Conn.: Greenwood Press, 1973), p. 134, notes that nine-tenths of the white population of Santo Domingo fled after the slave revolts of 1791 and an English attempt to occupy the island in 1793: "The number who came to the United States can not be exactly known; it was probably not lower than 10,000, and may have been as high as 70,000." Again, however, these are estimates of émigrés to the United States; New Orleans did not come under the American flag until 1803.

41. Perhaps the best-documented examples of such armoires have shown up in Philadelphia. One of these is in the collection of Girard College. See Robert D. Schwarz, *The Stephen Girard Collection: A Selective Catalog* (Philadelphia, 1980), no. 34. This piece, as well as a marble-topped buffet and a buffet with glass doors, was made in 1797 for Girard by two Santo Domingan refugees in Philadelphia named Jean-Baptiste Laurent and Charles Domballe. Two similar armoires also appeared on the market in 1978; one of them bears the inscription: "Made by slaves on the estate/of Etienne Bellumeaude la/Vincendiere in San Domingo/prior to 1770/Adelaide de la Vincendiere Lowe 1820/Enock Louis Lower 1861/Adelaide Lower Jenkins 1892/Mary Adelaide Jenkins 1918." See Frank S. Schwarz & Son, *Philadelphia Collection VI: American Painting & Decorative Arts, November, 1978* (Philadelphia, 1978), no. 46.

42. Such inlays could either have been imported from New York or made by New York-trained craftsmen. See, for instance, Charles Montgomery, *American Furniture: The Federal Period* (New York: Viking Press, 1966), p. 38, no. 115.

43. Slat-back armchairs from the lower valley also relate, though less directly, to armchairs made in France and French Canada. Designed to be used with large seat cushions, these chairs are exceptionally comfortable. Canadian examples are often described as "salamander" chairs because of their curvaceous form; their legs, stiles, and stretchers combine block elements with turned trumpet shapes, and they also have another distinctive feature: the arm support passes through the seat rail and the upper of the two side rails for added stability and strength. Despite these shared characteristics, however, the chairs from New Orleans and St. Louis are not nearly as elaborate as those from France or French Canada. The lone surviving St. Louis example, for instance, has vestigial trumpet turnings only on the arm supports and nearly straight slats in the back —either an indication of the prohibitive cost of turning a more elaborate chair or, more likely, the limited technical skill of the maker and his knowledge of the design. Similar factors may have also influenced the chairs from New Orleans. Examples of chairs made in New Orleans (or possibly in France) are illustrated in Poesch, *Early Furniture of Louisiana*, p. 45, no. 29. An example from the St. Louis area is in the collection of the Missouri Historical Society, no. 56.387.2. An exceptionally elaborate one from Canada is found in Jean Palardy, *The Early Furniture of French Canada*, no. 322. Somewhat simpler French examples without the turned trumpet elements are illustrated in Suzanne Tardieu-Dumont, *Le Mobilier regional français: Normandie* (Paris: Berger-Levrault, 1980), pp. 214–17.

44. This table is illustrated in Van Ravenswaay, "The Creole Arts and Crafts," p. 194. Made by an unknown craftsman, it probably dates to the late eighteenth century and incorporates several high-style elements into its design. Cock beading outlines the inside of the legs and continues onto the lower edge of the skirt and is reminiscent of gilt bronze beading found on very sophisticated tables from metropolitan centers. It also has carving on the center of the skirt, both on the front and the two sides, as well as carved ornament on the top of the front legs similar to gilt bronze mounts seen on much more expensive furniture of the period.

45. *El Mueble Mexicano: Historia, evolucion e influencias* (Mexico City: Fomento Cultural Banamex, A. C., 1985), p. 185. Among the traditional furnishings illustrated on this page is a *butaca*. It, like the other pieces in this section, is described as a twentieth-century form copying "pero de muy antigua tradicion" (very old traditions). See also Teresa Castello de Iturbide, "El Mueble Mexicano," *Artes de Mexico* 16 (1969): 88, no. 131, for an illustration of an indigenous Mexican *butaca* made in Tehuantepec. I am indebted to Donna Pierce for bringing this chair to my attention.

46. J. Michael Flanigan, *American Furniture from the Kaufman Collection* (Washington, D.C.: National Gallery of Art, 1986), pp. 144–45, cat. no. 53.

Catalogue Objects

64. Side chair / 65. Side chair

The most common form of side chair found in the Mississippi River valley throughout the eighteenth century was a version of the slat-back side chair illustrated as catalogue number 64, which was inspired by such French chairs as the one reproduced as catalogue number 65. As in the Mississippi River valley, chairs like this continued to be made in France into the twentieth century. But whereas French chairmakers frequently varied significant elements of the design—by fluting the front legs and stiles above the seats, carving the seat rails, or using more elaborate turnings—surviving chairs from the Mississippi River valley are remarkably consistent in style.[1] Virtually all of them are of unpainted mulberry or walnut and are characterized by turned legs and stiles highlighted with ring-and-sausage turnings, turnip-shaped front feet, acorn- or ball-

65. *Side chair*
French, late 18th century
Mixed hardwoods
H. 35½ in (90.2 cm), W. 18 in (45.7 cm), D. 14 in (35.6 cm)
Au Vieux Paris Antiques, Breaux Bridge, La.

shaped finials, and two or three curving arched slats. Generally only slight variations in the turnings are discernible, pinpointing certain minor details to specific shops or regions in the Mississippi River valley.

Surprisingly, while this basic side chair was only one of several designs available in France and Canada, it seems to have been the most common type throughout the Mississippi River valley during the eighteenth century. No good explanation for this exists, since the production of other chairs found in Canada and France required basically the same technology. It also remains unclear whether the design for these slat-back chairs reached the Mississippi River valley directly from France or through Canada. But because of the similarity of several dozen known examples, scholars speculate that they were derived from one chairmaking "school." In other words, one craftsman might have brought the tradition to the region and trained a number of others who then slightly varied the original design.

64. *Side chair*
American, St. Louis, Mo., or Cahokia, Ill., about 1800
Hickory; ash
H. 33 in (83.8 cm), W. 18 in (45.7 cm), D. 13½ in (34.3 cm)
Missouri Historical Society, St. Louis

1. Examples of French chairs of this type are numerous. Several are illustrated in Suzanne Tardieu-Dumont, *Le Mobilier regional français: Normandie* (Paris: Berger-Levrault, 1980), pp. 206–12.

Furniture of the Mississippi River Valley 169

66. Commode / 67. Chest of drawers / 68. Commode

The four commodes illustrated here (cat. nos. 66, 67, 68, and fig. 8, p. 161) represent the transmission of stylistic elements from Boston (and other New England urban centers) to Quebec province and from there to the developing French settlements of the upper Mississippi River valley. This transmission began with the introduction of English cabinetmaking practices into French Canada after 1763, when the region became governed by the English following the French and Indian Wars. The new English regime there brought with it furniture styles and craftsmen that dramatically influenced the products of the area. In metropolitan centers such as Quebec, where the curly maple commode (cat. no. 66) was made, English designs quickly spread through the furniture industry, resulting in hybrid styles combining English and French elements.

The Boston area chest of drawers (cat. no. 67) and the curly maple commode (cat. no. 66) from Quebec clearly show the influence of New England furniture designs on Canadian cabinetmaking. The Boston chest is English in its proportion and use of ball-and-claw feet, architectural moldings for the façade, bat-wing brasses, and even imported mahoganies, a rare wood in Canadian cabinetmaking. The construction of the piece is also typically English in its utilization of thinly cut boards and dovetail joints for the drawers and carcass.

These characteristics dramatically differ from those of the Quebec commode (cat. no. 66). In addition to exposing the wood grain as an integral element of the design (painted softwoods being more typical), this piece combines English ball-and-claw feet with such French elements as the *arbalète* (or crossbow-shaped) front, shaped side skirts, the pendant central shell, and the stump rear feet, which are formed by the continuation of the rear stiles. The thick wooden planks used throughout for its construction are also non-English by this late date. The shaped drawer fronts, for instance, are close to three inches thick in sections. Likewise, the commode makes less extensive use of dovetails than English case pieces. The drawer sides, for example, are joined with two large dovetails instead of the four or five commonly found on English works. Another typical feature of most nonurban French and French-Canadian case furniture is the paneled construction of the sides and back. While the backs of English pieces consist of boards nailed to the rabbeted (or grooved)

66. *Commode*
Canadian, Province of Quebec, late 18th century
Maple; pine
H. 35³⁄₁₆ in (89.4 cm), W. 45⅝ in (115.9 in), D. 24½ in (62.2 cm)
The Montreal Museum of Fine Arts, gift of Miss Mabel Molson, 1938.Df.8

67. *Chest of drawers*
American, eastern Mass., about 1780
Mahogany; white pine
H. 32½ in (82.6 cm), W. 40⅜ in (102.6 cm), D. 21¹³⁄₁₆ in (55.4 cm)
The Minneapolis Institute of Arts, gift of the Decorative Arts Council, 88.89

edges of the back, case furniture in the French tradition, like this commode, have backs composed of panels held in mortise-and-tenon frameworks.

As craftsmen and settlers from French Canada migrated to the Mississippi River valley late in the eighteenth century, they took a knowledge of French-Canadian furniture forms to that region. One early piece that documents this is the petite commode (fig. 8, p. 161) from the St. Louis area. While it appears unique for the region because of its size and use of cedar, it nonetheless seems to be an exact copy of such Quebec area commodes as catalogue number 66. This small piece retains all of the construction and design characteristics of the larger Quebec commode, including the detailing of the ball-and-claw feet.

All of these influences can be found in the cherry and walnut commode (cat. no. 68) from St. Louis or Vincennes. More so than the petite commode or the Quebec commode, it unites English and French designs and construction techniques. Deeper and higher in proportion to its width than English case pieces, it possesses a true French commode form. Its shape, swelled or bombé along the front and sides, is also common in French commodes of the period, as are its shaped front

172 Francis J. Puig

68. *Commode*
American, probably St. Louis, Mo., or Vincennes, Ind., about 1800
Cherry and walnut; cedar and white pine
H. 39 in (99.1 cm), W. 54 in (137.2 cm), D. 30¾ in (78.1 cm)
Collection of David A. Wojciechowski

and side skirts. The carved molding outlining the corners of the piece and the edges of the skirt, too, typify French designs. This carving, along with the carved leafage at the top front corners of the chest, imitates the gilt bronze mounts found on French case pieces. Despite these features, however, other elements strongly suggest that the commode was made by a cabinetmaker trained in one of the English colonies along the East Coast, probably Rhode Island. The most convincing evidence for this is the carving of both the front feet and the shells, which bears a clear resemblance to that found on many Newport and Providence objects. Moreover, the construction is of exceptional quality: fine dovetails are used throughout, the boards are thinly sawn, and the construction of the back, made of horizontal boards nailed to the rabbeted edges of the case sides, is as expected on an English case piece. Altogether, these characteristics suggest that the commode was made in the late eighteenth or early nineteenth century by a craftsman familiar with both English and French traditions. But in its interpretation of French, French-Canadian, and English designs and construction techniques, this piece must be seen as uniquely American.

69. *Armoire*
American, St. Louis, Mo., 1780–1800
Walnut; tulip poplar
H. 96 in (243.8 cm), W. 63 in (160 cm), D. 33½ in (85.1 cm)
Missouri Historical Society, St. Louis

Francis J. Puig

69. Armoire / 70. Armoire / 71. Armoire

French, French-Canadian, Caribbean, and English influences can be detected in a number of late eighteenth- and early nineteenth-century armoires produced by French settlers and their descendants in the Mississippi River valley. These armoires closely reflect immigration patterns into the area and differ substantially from contemporaneous French examples like that illustrated as catalogue number 71, which is in the Louis XV style and serves as an archetype of French construction and design. The piece is typically French in its joined carcass and doors. Framed asymmetrical panels compose the doors and sides, and form a major decorative element in the entire composition. The front and side skirts are shaped and flow into scroll feet. It is made of cherry, a frequently used wood, although oak, walnut, and pine are more often encountered. Regardless of the material, however, French armoires of the period are usually generously carved and rarely painted.

Surprisingly, relatively few French-Canadian armoires in the Louis XV style have survived. More common for the storage of clothing by the late eighteenth century in Canada were commodes (see cat. no. 66), a form more closely associated with the English, who governed Canada after 1763. It seems likely, however, that a French-Canadian made the walnut armoire (cat. no. 69) now in the Missouri Historical Society. Stylistically related to the petite commode (fig. 8, p. 161), which was probably made by the same person, it has a history of having belonged to Pierre Chouteau, one of the wealthiest and most urbane settlers of the territory. But the armoire is particularly intriguing because of its unique shaping. It has a French bombé front and sides, English ball-and-claw feet, and despite its reserved use of carving is the most complicated example of case furniture construction to have survived from Canada or the Mississippi River settlements.

The third armoire (cat. no. 70) shows the influence of Louis XVI and English designs. Louis XVI elements appear to have been introduced to the New Orleans area by Santo Domingan refugees fleeing slave revolts after 1791. The armoires they produced were streamlined with flush panels, curvilinear skirts, cabriole feet, and cove cornices, and relied on rich tropical woods for their primarily decorative effect (see fig. 10, p. 164). American craftsmen and merchants introduced English elements to these designs, especially the use of patterned inlays from such East Coast centers as New York.

The combination of these English and Santo Domingan influences led to the creation of armoires like catalogue number 70, which are unique to the lower Mississippi River valley. Taller in proportion than either Santo Domingan examples or most earlier regional armoires, these pieces combine patterned inlays with flush panels, curvilinear skirts, and cabriole legs and use richly grained tropical woods to great decorative effect. The most successful of these, like the example illustrated here, also include pictorial inlays.

70. *Armoire*
American, New Orleans, La., about 1815
Cherry; tulip poplar
H. 86¼ in (219.1 cm), W. 58¾ in (149.2 cm), D. 25½ in (64.8 cm)
Collection of the Jack Holden family

71. *Armoire*
French, 1780–1800
Cherry
H. 87 in (221 cm), W. 53½ in (135.9 cm), D. 23 in (58.4 cm)
David Lindquist and Associates, Whitehall Shop, Chapel Hill, N.C.

Furniture of the Mississippi River Valley

72. *Table*
American, New Orleans area, La., about 1800
Walnut
H. 26½ in (67.3 cm), W. 33⅜ in (84.8 cm), D. 25 in (63.5 cm)
Collection of the Jack Holden family

73. *Table*
French, late 18th or early 19th century
Walnut
H. 27 in (68.6 cm), W. 30 in (76.2 cm), D. 24 in (61 cm)
Collection of Dr. and Mrs. Richard Robichaux

72. Table / 73. Table

Tables with cabriole legs and curvilinear scalloped skirts were popular in France after the 1740s and continued to be made during much of the nineteenth century. Their design was relatively uniform, varying only in the type of materials used and the degree to which they were elaborated. Some consisted of wood or boulle marquetry with gilt bronze mounts; others were of solid wood, usually walnut or pine. A French table of this sort dating from the early nineteenth century is illustrated as catalogue number 73. Closely related tables were also found in French Canada after the 1750s, and a number of them are reproduced by Jean Palardy in *The Early Furniture of French Canada*.[1]

Surprisingly little stylistically was lost in the transfer of designs from France to the Mississippi River valley. Often, only the use of indigenous woods identify a table's origin: those made in the lower valley (cat. no. 72), for instance, were of mahogany or walnut, whereas French tables were typically of walnut, pine, or some other commonly available wood. Construction, simple to begin with, remained unchanged. While the shaping of the skirt or curve of the legs varied from table to table, they cannot be considered regional or national traits.

1. Jean Palardy, *The Early Furniture of French Canada* (Toronto: Macmillan of Canada, 1978), nos. 390–99.

Francis J. Puig

Donna L. Pierce

New Mexican Furniture and Its Spanish and Mexican Prototypes

Seven centuries of Moorish domination, from the eighth to the fifteenth century, set the art and culture of Spain apart from those of the rest of Europe. Islam prohibited the depiction of the human figure in art, resulting in a vocabulary of artistic motifs based on geometric patterns and stylized plant forms. The inevitable merging of Moorish and Christian artistic traditions in Spain created a distinctive style known as Mudejar. The Christian kingdoms of northern Spain gradually pushed the Moors southward. The marriage of Ferdinand and Isabella created an alliance that finally triumphed by expelling the last Moorish ruler from Granada in 1492. As Christianity again prevailed in Spain, the Gothic style of art and architecture replaced Moorish monuments as the official Christian art.

Furniture Development in Spain and Mexico

The Sixteenth Century

Large late Gothic churches were built in many cities of Spain as the Reconquest moved southward. The ecclesiastical furniture that outfitted these great cathedrals and churches was also Gothic in style.[1] It included sacristy chests, tables, benches, chairs, and writing desks. Similar pieces of furniture gradually came to be used in domestic settings. In a society that had been plagued with warfare for centuries, domestic furniture was generally simple and portable, even among the aristocracy. Boxes and chests were the most common items and served multiple purposes, such as the safeguarding of valuables, storage of food and clothing, seating, a surface for writing, and even support for boards used as beds or dining tables. The most lavishly decorated chests belonged to ladies of the court and to brides. During the late fifteenth and early sixteenth centuries, versatile chests in all sizes and shapes were decorated with either Gothic or Mudejar motifs in paint, ironwork, carving, or inlay. Other furniture that became popular during this period included stools and master's chairs, benches, and writing desks, all usually collapsible for portability, and built-in shelves.

During the fifteenth century, furniture makers in Spain belonged to the carpenters' guild, which included all artisans who worked with wood.[2] During the sixteenth century and later, some of these artisans, including turners, chairmakers, and cabinetmakers, broke away and formed guilds of their own. The guilds were under strict royal and municipal supervision and possessed charters and statutes. In addition to regulating the quality and sale of goods, the guilds cared for the artisans and their families in sickness and misfortune.

An artisan began his career by serving as an apprentice for four years in the workshop of a guild-certified master, in return for room and board. The apprenticeship was followed by three years of journeyman status, with a daily salary. A journeyman was required to pay an entrance fee to the guild and to pass an examination that included construction of a sample piece judged by officials of the guild. Only when a carpenter became a guild-certified master himself could he open a shop and sell his furniture, but he continued to be subject to inspection by guild officials. This ensured the quality of workmanship and the conformity of prices.

Renaissance motifs had begun to appear in furniture in Spain at the end of the fifteenth century. In the early sixteenth century, Charles I of Spain, grandson of Ferdinand and Isabella, became Charles V of the Holy Roman Empire. As a Hapsburg he ruled over Flanders and parts of Germany, Austria, and Italy, as well as over Spain. Artistic influences from these areas affected Spanish art at the same time that wealth from the New World made major royal art commissions possible. Concurrently, a strong middle class was rising in Spain and acquiring household goods, including furniture.

The new stylistic elements of the Renaissance were combined with Gothic and Moorish motifs to create a distinctly Hispanic style of decoration. Few changes occurred in structure, but surfaces were covered with an intricate combination of motifs in a patterning similar to that used in metalwork, inspiring the name "plateresque," meaning "like silverwork." In the second half of the sixteenth century, the austere Renaissance style of the Escorial monastery, designed by Juan de Herrera for Philip II, influenced furniture as well. Characterized by sober classicism and lack of decoration, this style is often known as *desornamentado* (unadorned) or Herreran. Also during the sixteenth century, several new forms evolved in Spain, including the trestle table, the chest of drawers, the cupboard, the armchair popularly known as a priest's or monk's chair (*sillón de frailero*), and a type of portable writing desk with numerous small drawers now known as a *vargueño*.

The highly portable furniture common in Spain at the time of the discovery and conquest of the New World in the late fifteenth and early sixteenth centuries was ideal for transporting to the Americas. Indeed, several types of chests and chairs popular in Spain at this time appear in illustrations by Indian artists of the conquest and early colonization of Mexico.[3] As in Spain, the chest was the most important item of furniture in the New World during the sixteenth century, and there were many variations.[4]

Guild ordinances similar to those of Spain were issued in Mexico in 1568 for carpenters, sculptors, joiners, and makers of stringed instruments and revised in 1589 for carvers and sculptors.[5] In Mexico, however, Indians were allowed to practice the craft of carpentry outside the guilds and were unrestricted by their ordinances. Beginning shortly after the conquest, Indians were trained in various crafts, including woodworking, in convent schools under the direction of Franciscan friars. Indians also trained with Spanish master carpenters.[6] Later in the colonial period, Indians were admitted to the guilds.

Furniture decoration in Mexico throughout most of the sixteenth century was based on Mudejar and plateresque prototypes from Spain. Motifs that had been used in pre-Hispanic Mexico were common; they included the sun and moon, birds, feathers, snakes, lions (jaguars), and foliage.[7] In preparation for the Third Provincial Council, held in 1585 to confirm the actions of the Council of Trent, most New World cathedrals were renovated. During renovation the Herreran style was introduced to New World architecture and eventually to the decorative arts.

In 1565 a trade route was established between the Orient and Spain via the Philippines and Mexico.[8] The galleons of the king of Spain sailed from Manila to Acapulco. From there goods were carried overland to Mexico City and eventually to Veracruz on the Gulf Coast, where they were loaded onto galleons for the trip to Spain. Many oriental products remained in Mexico and, along with oriental craftsmen who immigrated there, directly influenced the decorative arts of New Spain, particularly ceramics, furniture, and lacquerware.[9] As oriental motifs became popular in European furniture in the seventeenth century, imports of such furniture reinforced the oriental trend in Mexican furniture production.

The Seventeenth Century

Early seventeenth-century Spain saw the beginnings of a sober baroque style that soon gave way to an exuberant and unrestrained style characterized by elaborately carved surfaces often covered with gold and polychrome.[10] Salomonic (twisted) and turned columns, embossed leather, embroidered upholstery, ivory carvings, inlay, scrolls, and volutes all became part of the decorative vocabulary in art and architecture as well as in furniture. During this period, the bed became an important furniture item for the first time.

In Mexico, the Renaissance plateresque and Herreran styles, as well as Mudejar and even Gothic elements, persisted into the middle of the seventeenth century in all the decorative arts. Around 1650, ecclesiastical and luxury furniture imported from Spain began to reflect the European baroque style and to influence local production. Exquisite marquetry and inlay work were produced in certain areas of Mexico, including Puebla, Oaxaca, Campeche, Chiapas, San Luis Potosí, and Michoacán. From the late sixteenth century on, Michoacán became well known for its furniture, particularly chip-carved, brightly polychromed, and lacquered pieces. A pronounced oriental influence is evident in the lacquered pieces. Production of folding screens as a type of furniture to decorate the drawing room or to divide the bedroom was stimulated in Mexico when a Japanese shogun presented ten oriental screens to the viceroy of Mexico in the early seventeenth century.[11]

The Eighteenth Century

When Philip V, the Bourbon grandson of Louis XIV, assumed the throne of Spain at the beginning of the eighteenth century, he introduced French styles to the arts of Spain. French rococo elements, along with English Queen Anne, Georgian, and Chippendale motifs, became prevalent in Spanish furniture. Cabriole legs, serpentine and pleated contours, crested tops, and oriental motifs were popular during this era. New forms included console tables, commodes, settees, and mirrors, and coordinated suites of furniture became common.

In the second half of the eighteenth century, the neoclassical style was introduced to the Spanish court during the reign of Charles III, often with direct influence from Italy and France. Various English interpretations of the classical revival, by Adam, Hepplewhite, and Sheraton, became available through imports as well as through pattern books, resulting in precise reproductions in furniture.

Partially as a result of exploitation of rich silver mines, the eighteenth century in Mexico was a time of affluence, with a growing class of wealthy Mexican-born citizens. A distinctly Mexican style in art and architecture evolved, based on mannerist decorative motifs that had been revived during the rococo period. Furniture was often constructed along the traditional rectangular Spanish lines with the addition of elaborate rococo decoration. The influence of the many oriental artists who had immigrated to New Spain on the Manila galleons became even stronger in this century, when oriental motifs were being popularized in Europe as well. The various influences from the Orient and Europe and some indigenous motifs were freely combined and altered to create a lavish and exuberant late baroque style that was uniquely Mexican.

The neoclassical style was introduced to Mexico by the Spanish professors at the Royal Academy of San Carlos, founded in Mexico City in 1778. The town of Puebla had long been known for exquisite marquetry, and elegant examples of neoclassical furniture were produced there toward the end of the colonial period in the late eighteenth and early nineteenth centuries.

Furniture in New Mexico

In 1598, more than twenty years before the English settlers landed at Plymouth Rock, a small group of Spanish civilians, soldiers, and priests established a settlement on what is today United States soil. This group, led by Juan de Oñate, the son of one of the original conquerors of Mexico, founded a village near the Indian pueblo of San Juan (Ohke) in what is now northern New Mexico. Thus, while northern Europeans were developing New England and Virginia on the eastern shore of North America, the Spanish were actively colonizing Mexico's northern frontier.

Spanish conquest and colonization in the New World were stimulated by both religious evangelism and the search for mineral wealth. Franciscan missionaries undertook the task of converting the Pueblo Indians, and by 1630, fifty churches had been built by the Indians under the direction of approximately twenty friars.[12] In 1609, the capital of the small colony was moved a few miles south and named Santa Fe. The local economy was based on subsistence agriculture. This early period on the frontier was characterized by conflict between civil-military and religious factions in competition for Indian labor.[13] Finally, after nearly a century of subjugation, the Pueblo Indians united in 1680 to stage one of the most successful Indian rebellions in North American history. The surviving Spaniards fled south to El Paso del Norte, now in Texas, where they remained for thirteen years, until Don Diego de Vargas became governor of the Province of New Mexico and reconquered Santa Fe in 1692–93.

Many Spanish buildings and artifacts, particularly those of a religious nature, were destroyed during and after the Pueblo revolt. The only Spanish artifacts known to survive from prerevolt New Mexico are the walls and foundations of some buildings and a statue of the Virgin Mary that was rescued and carried south by the fleeing Spaniards.[14] Remnants of roof beams with carved rosette and diamond patterns have been found in the ruins of several seventeenth-century churches.[15] No extant furniture can be documented as from the prerevolt period, but the furniture of that time is assumed to have been similar to that made after the reconquest of New Mexico. During archaeological excavations at the prerevolt mission church of San Gregorio de Abó, fragments of carved and polychromed floral decorations were found.[16] These decorative fragments may have been part of an altar screen, a picture frame, or a piece of furniture. The burned remains of an armless bench were also encountered by archaeologists, but could not be preserved. This bench of mortise-and-tenon construction, though no longer extant, is the earliest documented piece of furniture from New Mexico.[17] Evidence of furniture in the seventeenth-century missions suggests the presence of skilled carpenters in New Mexico, but mission records also list some examples of furniture, and even entire altar screens, being imported from Mexico at that time.[18]

Trained carpenters undoubtedly moved to New Mexico during the colonial period. Indeed, at least one person listed himself as a carpenter by trade, and six others in the first group of settlers under Oñate in 1598 brought carpenter's tools.[19] According to Fray Alonso de Benavides, writing in 1630, Spanish master carpenters trained Indian craftsmen at Pecos pueblo in woodworking skills.[20] The Pecos carpenters became well known as craftsmen and were commissioned by Spaniards and Indians alike to make furniture and architectural details from the early seventeenth century through at least the end of the eighteenth century.[21] Unfortunately, no surviving furniture has been traced to Pecos carpenters.

The era of resettlement after the Pueblo revolt produced a different atmosphere from the earlier period. Santa Fe was rebuilt, and new Spanish settlements were founded along the river valleys with an economy based on agriculture and sheep raising. The threat of attack by Apaches, Comanches, Navajos, and Utes, together with economic interdependence, forced an alliance between the Spanish and Pueblo peoples in New Mexico. In general, an attitude of accommodation and a decrease in exploitation prevailed in the eighteenth century. Once the population increased and the fledgling towns began to prosper, the "golden age" (c. 1750–1850) of New Mexico folk art evolved, characterized by locally made objects that were used alongside some imported goods from Mexico, Europe, and the Orient.[22]

Throughout the colonial period, the Spanish Crown maintained a monopoly on many important goods and prohibited independent trade with foreign countries. As a result, New Mexico remained cut off from European settlements on the East Coast and in the Mississippi River valley. Some French traders dared to enter New Mexico from Canada and New Orleans, but several were imprisoned. Consequently, imported goods that reached New Mexico generally came from Europe or the Orient by ship and then were hauled overland to Mexico City, then north on the Camino Real to Chihuahua. New Mexican traders went south with blankets, prepared hides, wool stockings, and eventually sheep to trade for these goods at the fairs in Chihuahua and elsewhere in Mexico.[23] The journey was long and arduous, with the result that imported goods were expensive.

During the eighteenth century many necessities of everyday life were produced in New Mexico, including not only furniture but also religious objects such as sculpture, painting, and large altar screens for churches. E. Boyd has pointed out that carpenters in New Mexico continued to repeat the forms of sixteenth-century Spanish furniture, particularly those common to the poorer classes.[24] Lonn Taylor and Dessa Bokides, in their study of New Mexican furniture, noted that many pieces were constructed according to a formula based on multiples of the *vara* (33 inches), the colonial standard of measurement.[25]

Methods of construction in Spain changed little from early periods through the eighteenth century. According to Gertrude Burr, with the exception of those used in royal factories, the tools used by Spanish craftsmen were the same as those employed in prior centuries; consequently, Spanish furniture was less elegantly finished than that of other European countries.[26] These tools included planes, bucksaws, straight saws, axes, compasses, adzes, augers, pincers, mallets, claw hammers, and hatchets. New Mexican and Mexican craftsmen used the same tools. In Spain, good woods were available for furniture construction, walnut being the favorite followed by oak and chestnut. In Mexico, the sturdy hardwoods available included cedar and mahogany. In New Mexico, however, the only wood readily available for furniture making was local Ponderosa pine. Because of the softness and dryness of pine and the crude tools available, furniture in New Mexico had to follow sturdy designs that would have precluded elaborate baroque carving, even if it had been desired.

If formal guilds existed in New Mexico, their ordinances have not survived. In both Spain and Mexico, master craftsmen often accepted members of their own families into apprenticeship. This practice of keeping a craft within a family was probably continued in New Mexico in an informal manner. As in Mexico, master craftsmen in New Mexico, in at least one instance, trained Indian artisans at the request of the friars, as described by Benavides.[27] Benavides also mentioned schools at many of the missions, where Indians were instructed in various crafts, including carpentry, presumably by the friars. Two New Mexican Indian pueblos,

Pecos and Cochiti, continued as furniture-producing areas into at least the late eighteenth and mid-nineteenth centuries, respectively.[28]

No remaining furniture can be traced to the early part of the eighteenth century. Alan Vedder has suggested that this is "no doubt due to constant reusing and reworking of every piece of furniture until it was literally worn out, as was the case with the tools used."[29] From the later eighteenth century, the furniture forms most common in New Mexico were the same standard forms used in Spain and Mexico—chests, benches, armchairs, side chairs, tables, cupboards, and shelves.

Chests

As in Mexico and Spain, chests were the most common furniture form used in New Mexico during the colonial period. In inventories of New Mexican estates, the chest is the most frequently listed furniture item, every household owning at least one and some having as many as fourteen.[30] In the New Mexican inventories studied by Taylor and Bokides, more than a third of the chests were imported, mostly from the Michoacán area of Mexico; the rest were of local manufacture.

Three types of chests were constructed in New Mexico: board chests, with six boards joined together by dovetail joints and pegs; framed chests, with panels set into a framework of rails and stiles with pegged mortise-and-tenon joints; and false-framed chests, basically board chests disguised as framed chests by applied strips of molding.[31] All types occasionally contained sections of small drawers in the interior.

The dovetailed board chests were decorated with relief carving created by chiseling away the background area to leave the design raised (cat. no. 74). Just as these chests have a uniform construction, so they have a standard vocabulary of decorative motifs—rosettes, pomegranates, lions, scallops, vines or branches, birds, circles—in various combinations. Many Spanish Gothic chests were constructed in the same manner, the dovetail joinery being exposed and the background carved away to leave raised patterns of rosettes, fleurs-de-lis, coats of arms, tracery, and geometric designs. This type of board construction with relief design was in use in Spain and Mexico for several hundred years. An example from the seventeenth century exhibits elaborate dovetail joinery and carving depicting the Hapsburg double eagle, vines, and quarter rosettes (cat. no. 75).

According to inventories of estates in New Mexico, chests were often placed on stands. The few extant chest stands from the late eighteenth century consist of two separate stands of three boards each.[32] Chests with built-in legs apparently were not made in New Mexico until the late eighteenth century; they are all of framed construction.[33] Eighteen examples of framed chests-on-legs from New Mexico are so similar in construction that they have been attributed to the same late eighteenth-century workshop or community, probably the Valdez family of Velarde (cat. no. 76).[34] All eighteen were made by joining two side panels, two front panels, and a back panel into a framework of eight horizontal rails and five vertical stiles. The four end stiles are extended to form legs, and two angular braces, like the iron braces on some Spanish benches and tables, connect the front legs to the front rail. The decorative carving on all eighteen chests is also similar, with chip-carved motifs on rails and stiles and geometric patterns, often with circles, on the front panels.

The lengthening of end stiles to form short feet on chests is a method of construction peculiar to northern Spain, particularly Asturias and Navarra.[35] The type of decoration on chests of this construction includes chip carving, geometric panels, rosettes, and circles on the front face. Many of these chests contain small compartments or drawers in the interior. This similarity of construction techniques and decorative motifs suggests that possibly a member of the Valdez family came to New Mexico from northern Spain, was trained by a carpenter from there, or was inspired by a chest imported from that area. The extension of stiles to form long legs, however, is not characteristic of the regional chests from northern Spain and may reflect influence, in form if not in function, from the famous *vargueños*, or writing desks, of Spain (fig. 1).

The *vargueño* is actually a chest of drawers that rests on a separate piece of furniture serving as a stand and known as a *pie de puente*.[36] When assembled, the *vargueño* and *pie de puente* resemble the New Mexican chest-on-legs in outlines and proportions. On a *vargueño*, it is the front panel, rather than the top panel, that opens to form a writing surface. Like the New Mexican chest-on-legs, the *vargueño* is decorated on the front face. The development in New Mexico of the tall chest-on-legs as a furniture form in the late eighteenth century may have been inspired by actual Spanish *vargueños* or by similar Mexican writing desks imported to New Mexico. Writing desks are listed in estate inventories from New

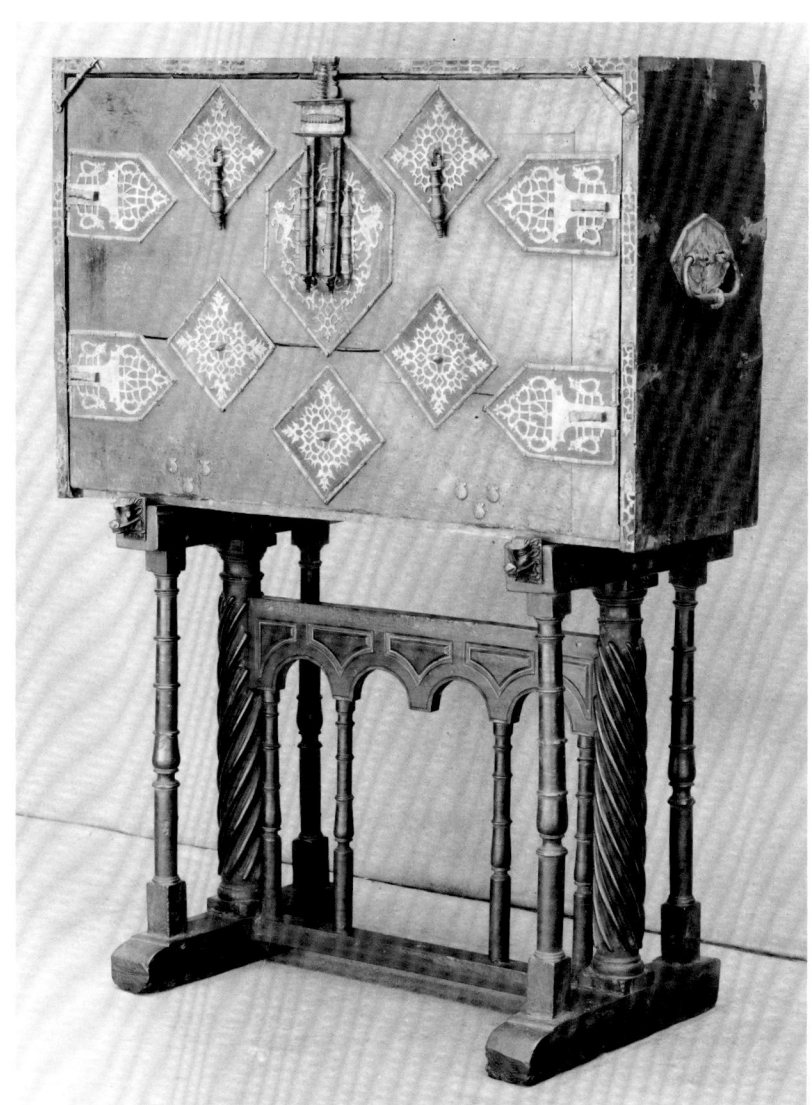

Fig. 1. *Vargueño*. Spanish, 17th century. Walnut. H. 61 in (155 cm), W. (top) 43⅞ in (111.5 cm), W. (base) 34¼ in (87 cm), D. (top) 15¾ in (40 cm), D. (base) 21⅝ in (55 cm). Courtesy of The Hispanic Society of America, New York, S43.

Mexico in the late eighteenth and early nineteenth centuries.[37]

The *vargueño* itself, with its numerous drawers, was descended from a particular type of bride's chest, or *hembra*, with a section of drawers on one side, that was developed in Cataluña in the late fifteenth century.[38] Several New Mexican chests also contain a section on one side with drawers for small items and are distantly related to the Catalonian prototype.[39] In New Mexico, chests of this type probably also served as bride's chests.

Numerous board-construction chests with colorfully painted surfaces have been collected in New Mexico (cat. nos. 77, 78).[40] In the New Mexican inventories surveyed by Taylor and Bokides, among the 150 chests listed, 49 were described as being "from Michoacán," 2 from "outside the region," and 1 from Mexico.[41] Thus, more than a third of the total were imported. Other furniture from Michoacán appears in inventories, with 2 writing desks listed as "from Michoacán" and a missal stand described by Father Domínguez in 1776 as "painted, from Michoacán."[42] That furniture from Michoacán was decorated, probably painted, is often implied in New Mexican documents by such statements as "three chests in which clothing is kept, two from Michoacán and one plain."[43] Beginning in the second half of the sixteenth century and continuing into the mid-nineteenth century, furniture from Michoacán is listed in the inventories of households and convents in central Mexico, and many examples survive in Mexican collections.[44]

During pre-Hispanic times, a type of lacquerware was produced in Mexico, notably small utensils such as bowls and trays.[45] When the China trade passed through Mexico beginning in the late sixteenth century, oriental lacquer products greatly influenced the production of lacquerware in Mexico. The lacquer industry seems to have reached its peak in Mexico during the eighteenth century, when all types of furniture were decorated in this manner. Areas known for producing lacquerware included Michoacán, Guerrero (part of Michoacán during the colonial period), and Chiapas. An offshoot of the lacquer industry in Mexico was a simplified technique for making inexpensive objects, consisting of designs painted on poorer quality woods (usually pine) that were then covered with a varnish or shellac (cat. no. 78). The towns of Cuanajo, Michoacán, and Toluca are still known for this type of painted furniture.

These inexpensive painted chests were evidently imported to New Mexico from Michoacán. According to New Mexican oral history, families acquired such chests when their ancestors brought them back from trade fairs in Chihuahua.[46] The chests apparently inspired local artists to paint their own chests and other furniture from time to time.[47] Two board chests from New Mexico are painted with geometric designs and may be the work of Pueblo Indian artists (cat. no. 77; fig. 2).[48] In his 1776 description of the interior of an Indian home in Tesuque Pueblo, Father Domínguez stated, "They usually have . . . some kind of chest, either plain or painted."[49] The designs on these chests are reminiscent of those on some Pueblo Indian pottery; both the designs and the colors are similar to those on Plains Indian parfleches (traveling pouches).[50] These chests may represent a synthesis of Spanish (both Mexican and New Mexican), Pueblo, and Plains Indian traditions and may indicate a distant influence of oriental lacquerware traditions on southwestern Indian material culture.

Chairs

Next to the chest, the chair is the furniture form that appears most frequently in New Mexican estate inventories.[51] Both armchairs and side chairs were made in New Mexico and imported from Mexico. Armchairs made in New Mexico are of mortise-and-tenon construction and are based on the simple lines of the early *sillón de frailero* (priest's chair) of Spain and Mexico rather than the more curvilinear armchairs of the baroque period. Now popularly known as the *sillón de frailero*, these simple rectangular armchairs replaced the hip-joint chair as the most popular type of armchair in Spain around the middle of the sixteenth century (cat. no. 80).[52] Early *fraileros* were slung with leather or fabric and were collapsible for portability. Later ones were of solid wood construction and often upholstered with embroidered and fringed velvet or *guadamecil* (a Moorish technique of embossed leather), and were often painted or gilded as well.

These Spanish chairs of mortise-and-tenon construction had slightly raked back posts topped with bracket-shaped or ball finials, narrow arms resting on extended front legs, low side stretchers, and a distinctive high, wide front stretcher often carved or fretted and known as a *chambrana*. One of the most famous examples of a *sillón de frailero* including a fretted *chambrana* is the leather-covered one that was converted into a sedan chair for use by Philip II, now at the Escorial near Madrid.[53] The *sillón de frailero* remained widely popular in Spain and Mexico throughout the seventeenth and on to the end of the eighteenth century. Beginning in the mid-seventeenth century, the legs, side stretchers, and eventually the arms were turned and blocked, reflecting influences from the styles of Louis XIII and Louis XIV, and later were carved and scalloped, reflecting rococo tastes.

Several New Mexican armchairs have wide front and

Fig. 2. *Chest.* New Mexican, late 18th or early 19th century. Pine. H. 17⅛ in (43.5 cm), W. 29 in (73.7 cm), D. 15 in (38.1 cm). Spanish Colonial Arts Society Collection on loan to the Museum of International Folk Art, Museum of New Mexico, Santa Fe, L.5.78-3.

Fig. 3. *Armchair*. New Mexican, Taos Pueblo, 18th century. Pine. H. 40½ in (103 cm), W. 23⅝ in (60 cm), D. 21¼ in (54 cm). Collection of Dr. and Mrs. Ward Alan Minge.

back stretchers reminiscent of the *chambrana* of the Spanish *sillón de frailero* (cat. no. 79). The stepped geometric patterns on the rails and stile finials of many New Mexican chairs have been related by some authors to Pueblo Indian designs such as the cloud-terrace motif.[54] It should be noted, however, that similar stepped and bracketed designs can also be found on Mexican and Spanish chairs of the sixteenth through the nineteenth centuries, especially in provincial areas, and derive from Moorish prototypes.

A possible prototype for the *sillón de frailero* in New Mexico could have been the governor's chair in the church of St. Francis in Santa Fe, described by Father Domínguez in 1776:

On the wall opposite the altar of Our Lady of Guadalupe and toward the mouth of the nave of the church is the lord governor's seat. This is an armchair (it belongs to the government, but I mention what is there) of fine wood upholstered in crimson velvet with galloon and fringe of fine gold, all affixed by nails of gilt metal. The cushion matches the chair, with tassels at the corners. The whole thing stands on a little dais facing the high altar.[55]

This may be the same chair described by Lieutenant Colonel W. H. Emory in August 1846:

Today we went to church in great state. The governor's seat, a large well stuffed chair, covered with crimson, was occupied by the commanding officer.[56]

This chair, obviously an import, sounds similar to the type of embroidered red-velvet *frailero* chair popular in both Spain and Mexico from the sixteenth through the eighteenth centuries (cat. no. 80).

In the sacristy at the mission church of San Ildefonso, Father Domínguez noted in 1776 "three armchairs upholstered in painted buffalo skin."[57] A chair collected from Taos Pueblo has a piece of hide stretched across the back rail, secured with hand-forged nails (fig. 3). The leather strip is nonstructural and was probably added in imitation of imported leather-backed or upholstered Spanish and Mexican chairs. Painted dots and rectangles similar to Pueblo Indian pottery designs decorate the wooden elements of the chair.[58] The absence of other such "upholstered" chairs, so common in Spain and Mexico, may be due to the lack of both fabrics for upholstery and brass tacks, or even nails, to attach leather hides adequately.

Side chairs (*taburetes*) and benches made in New Mexico are similar in construction and decoration to the armchairs (figs. 4, 5). In some New Mexican chairs, splats or spindles link the stretchers and rails, a construction element common in Spanish and Mexican chairs of the late sixteenth and seventeenth centuries (figs. 5, 6). Several side chairs are decorated with a distinctive gouge-carved design that has been connected to Cochiti Pueblo (fig. 4).[59] Gouge-carved designs can also be found on chairs in Spain and Mexico. A seventeenth-century example from Santander in Spain includes back splats, rosette or Romanesque wheel shapes, scalloped stretcher skirts, and overall gouge or chip carving, all elements found in New Mexican chairs (fig. 6). The cornhusk motifs on the back posts of the New Mexican side chair have been related to Indian designs by Taylor and Bokides (fig. 4).[60] It should be noted that repetitive wheat and cornhusk patterns were common

Fig. 4. *Side chair.* New Mexican, 19th century. Pine. H. 33 in (83.8 cm), W. 18⅞ in (48 cm), D. 14½ in (36.9 cm). Historical Society of New Mexico Collection in the Museum of International Folk Art, Museum of New Mexico, Santa Fe, 83/84.

Fig. 5. *Chair.* New Mexican, early 19th century. Pine. H. 37¾ in (95.9 cm), W. 20¾ in (52.7 cm), D. 18⅞ in (48 cm). Museum of International Folk Art, Museum of New Mexico, Santa Fe, A.62.23-2.

Fig. 6. *Side chair.* Spanish, Santander, 17th century. Mahogany. H. 34 in (86.4 cm), W. 15½ in (39.4 cm), D. 16¼ in (41.3 cm). The Minneapolis Institute of Arts, 13.8.

motifs on furniture during the neoclassical period, particularly on examples by Sheraton and Hepplewhite, which were copied in Spain and Mexico. In Mexico, one type of late colonial marquetry is referred to as *elote*, or corn-style, furniture because of such motifs.[61] Boyd has pointed out that some pieces of New Mexican furniture show evidence of neoclassical influence in decoration.[62]

In the late eighteenth and early nineteenth centuries in New Mexico, chair construction followed the same basic formula used for the sixteenth-century Spanish *sillón de frailero*. The reliance on this simple form was probably a result of old craft traditions being passed from generation to generation in New Mexico. The baroque and rococo elaboration added to the *sillón de frailero* in Spain and Mexico in the seventeenth and eighteenth centuries was not obvious in New Mexico. Instead, decoration was limited to shallow surface carving, painted motifs, and geometric cutouts—probably due to the limitations imposed by the crude tools and soft wood available in New Mexico. The geometric cutout forms used in New Mexico may be reminiscent, at least in outline, of the blocked and turned elements of seventeenth-century baroque chairs (fig. 5). Similarly, the stepped rails and stretchers on New Mexican chairs may represent a simplification of the scalloped valances and crests of the eighteenth-century rococo style (cat. no. 79).

Tables

During the late Gothic and early Renaissance periods, Spanish tables consisted of boards supported by crude trestles or chests. When portability became of less concern, the table developed into two forms that were built in great numbers during the seventeenth century and are still used today. In one form the tabletop is supported by either lyre-shaped or splayed trestles connected by iron braces. In the other form, the tabletop is supported by fixed legs braced by side or box stretchers (cat. no. 82). These tables often had one to three drawers set in an underframing between the top and legs and carved with geometric or floral decoration. Probably a holdover from the days when portability was essential, the tabletops and legs were joined by a method uniquely Spanish—cleats or crosspieces were mortised into the underside of the tabletop and the legs were then attached to these.[63]

Later furniture in Spain and Mexico was often constructed along the traditional rectangular Spanish lines with the addition of baroque and rococo decoration. Beginning in the mid-seventeenth century, the legs and side stretchers of tables were turned and blocked, reflecting influences from the baroque styles of Louis XIII and XIV. During this period, valances were often scalloped—a motif that was continued and exaggerated during the rococo period in the eighteenth century.

If the trestle table was used in New Mexico, no examples have survived. Fixed-leg tables were constructed in New Mexico with a solid framework of four legs with rails or stretchers topped by boards either pegged or nailed to the framework (cat. no. 81).[64] The Spanish tradition of inserting crosspieces or cleats between the legs and the tabletop was continued in New Mexico into the nineteenth century. On some New Mexican tables, splats or turned spindles connect the upper and lower rails. Many New Mexican tables, like their Spanish predecessors, include drawers supported by a central runner between upper rails. Like Spanish tables, New Mexican tables are often decorated with grooves or chip-carved designs on the drawers and rails. The angular scalloping on the rails of some tables is reminiscent of baroque and rococo decoration on Spanish and Mexican tables (cat. no. 81).

Other Furniture Types

In Spain, cabinets were rare during the Gothic period, but during the Renaissance, when portability was no longer essential, the convenience of the chest-on-chest was recognized. The first use was in church sacristies.[65] Various wardrobes and cupboards evolved from the chest-on-chest. Tall cabinets, known as *fresqueras*, were built in Spain in the seventeenth century and included a spindled top story forming a ventilated food cupboard for storing fruit, cheese, and bread.[66] Large cabinets with wire grille doors are listed in inventories of homes in Mexico in the seventeenth and eighteenth centuries.[67] Tall freestanding cabinets were made in New Mexico of framed construction (fig. 7). Some had solid double doors; others were made with spindles or pierced panels in at least the upper portion of the doors. Most cabinets were constructed with a grooved top section to hold a decorative crest, usually a half rosette or scallop.

Cresting on cabinets became popular in Spain and

Fig. 7. *Cabinet.* New Mexican, 19th century. Pine. H. 89½ in (227.3 cm), W. 38½ in (97.8 cm), D. 15¾ in (40 cm). School of American Research Collection in the Museum of International Folk Art, Museum of New Mexico, Santa Fe, A.7.49-28.

Mexico in the eighteenth century. According to Burr, heavy cresting is a characteristic of furniture in the Spanish colonies during the eighteenth century.[68] The use of half-rosettes and scalloping on New Mexican cabinets was probably influenced by similar crests on Mexican prototypes. Some New Mexican cabinets have secret or hidden drawers, a motif borrowed from the Spanish *vargueño*.

Among other furniture forms used in New Mexico during the colonial and Mexican periods were two kinds of wooden wall shelves, *repisas* and *alacenas*. The *repisa* was a free-hanging single or double shelf; the *alacena* was built into the adobe wall and covered with double puncheon shutters. Other types of built-in furniture used frequently in New Mexico included adobe benches along the walls, used for sitting and sleeping, and adobe tables along the walls in homes and also in churches, where they served as altar tables.[69] In Spain, built-in furnishings seldom appeared after the Gothic period in the town homes of the wealthy, but they continued in use in the homes of the lower classes and in the provinces.[70] Built-in furniture in adobe homes was also a Moorish tradition.

With the independence of Mexico from Spain in 1821, New Mexico soon became the northern frontier of the new Republic of Mexico rather than the colony of New Spain. The opening of the Santa Fe Trail and trade with the eastern United States introduced new tools, materials, and styles to the New Mexican craftsmen. Occupation by the American army in 1846, the Civil War, and ultimately the arrival of the railroad in the 1880s made the nineteenth century a period of rapid change in New Mexico.

New Mexican furniture of this late period often combines traditional colonial elements with techniques made possible by the availability of milled lumber and new tools, particularly jigsaws and molding planes. Elements of new styles introduced by Anglo tastes and imports, such as Victorian, Queen Anne, American federal, Italian Renaissance, and Gothic revival, were often grafted onto traditional Spanish furniture forms, creating a lively folk style.[71]

Summary

Furniture making in New Mexico during the colonial period was based, in both construction and form, on Spanish prototypes from the sixteenth century. These models were repeated through the years in provincial areas of Spain and in the New World with regional variations. In Spanish furniture, often the construction and form remained constant through several centuries, with only the decorative motifs reflecting changing fashions.

In New Mexico, furniture construction followed Spanish and Mexican prototypes with the exception of the innovative chest-on-legs, which may be a synthesis of two Spanish chests, the *vargueño* and the northern chest with extended stiles. Carved decorative motifs in New Mexico can be traced to Spanish and Mexican predecessors, but the prevalence of certain forms, such as stepped patterns and gouge or chip carving, may also reflect Pueblo Indian traditions. These designs may result in part from the crude tools and brittle wood available in New Mexico, which made the execution of more curvilinear patterns difficult at best. Painted furniture in New Mexico appears to have been inspired by the painted furniture imported from Michoacán, which was in turn influenced by oriental lacquerware. The geometric patterns on two painted chests in New Mexico are probably the work of Indian artists, since they resemble both Pueblo and Plains Indian designs.

In the early colonial period, Indians in the New Mexican pueblos were instructed in carpentry by either Spanish master carpenters or the friars themselves. The apparent absence of formal craft guilds, the geographical distance from Mexico City, and the Spanish Crown's trade restrictions forced New Mexican carpenters to rely on craft formulas probably passed from father to son. Furniture imported from Spain or Mexico served as models. This artistic isolation probably reinforced the Spanish tradition of grafting new or regional decorative motifs onto traditional furniture forms constructed according to archaic formulas.

Furniture in New Mexico from the late eighteenth and early nineteenth centuries presents a synthesis of elements spanning vast geographical distances, three centuries of time, and various cultures. Some construction techniques and forms date to the fifteenth and sixteenth centuries in Spain and show Moorish influence. Certain decorative motifs can be traced to Renaissance and baroque furniture in Spain and Mexico. Some pieces reflect oriental and American Indian traditions. Whether the furniture was made by Indian or Spanish craftsmen, all of the various influences were tempered by the tools and materials available on the northern frontier of New Spain.

NOTES

1. Gertrude Hardendorff Burr, *Hispanic Furniture* (New York: Archive Press, 1964); Luis Feduchi, *Historia de los estilos del mueble español* (Madrid: Editorial Abantos, 1969); Luis Feduchi, *El mueble español* (Barcelona: Ediciones Poligrafa, 1969).

2. Burr, *Hispanic Furniture*, pp. 1–3.

3. Examples can be found in the Codex Duran, Codex Kingsborough, Codex Yanhuitlan, and the Lienzo de Tlaxcala, among others. See Abelardo Carrillo y Gariel, *Evolución del mueble en Mexico* (Mexico: Instituto National de Antropologia e Historia, 1957); and Federico Gómez de Orozco, *El mobiliario y la decoración en la Nueva España en el siglo XVI* (Mexico: Universidad Nacional Autónoma de Mexico, 1983).

4. Manuel Toussaint, *Colonial Art in Mexico* (Austin: University of Texas Press, 1967), p. 69.

5. Francisco Santiago Cruz, *Las artes y los gremios en la Nueva España* (Mexico: Editorial Jus, 1960); and Toussaint, *Colonial Art*, pp. 158–60.

6. Diego Basalenque, *Historia de la Provincia de San Nicolas Tolentino de Michoacán* (Mexico: Editorial Jus, 1963), pp. 59–60; Fray Juan de Grijalva, *Crónica de la Orden de N. P. San Agustín en las provincias de Nueva España* (1624) (Mexico: Victoria, 1924), pp. 223–25; George Kubler, *Mexican Architecture of the Sixteenth Century*, 2 vols. (New Haven, Conn.: Yale University Press, 1948) 1:154; 2:220; Constantino Reyes-Valerio, *Arte indocristiano* (Mexico: Instituto Nacional de Antropologia e Historia, 1978), pp. 69–110, 301–5.

7. Burr, *Hispanic Furniture*, p. 108. See also Sali Barnett Katz, *Hispanic Furniture: An American Collection from the Southwest* (Stamford, Conn.: Architectural Book Publishing Co., 1986), p. 36.

8. Marita Martinez del Rio de Redo, et al., *El galeon de Acapulco* (Mexico: Instituto Nacional de Antropologia e Historia, 1988); and Francisco Santiago Cruz, *La nao de China* (Mexico: Editorial Jus, 1962).

9. Manuel Carballo, "Influencia asiática," in *El mueble mexicano: historia, evolución e influencias* (Mexico: Fomento Cultural Banamex, 1985), pp. 115–32; and Marita Martinez del Rio de Redo, "The Oriental Influence upon Mexican Furniture," in *Artes de Mexico* 16, no. 118 (1969): 15–33.

10. For examples see Feduchi, *El mueble*, pp. 154–214.

11. Teresa Castelló Iturbide and Marita Martinez del Rio de Redo, *Biombos mexicanos* (Mexico: Instituto Nacional de Antropologia e Historia, 1970).

12. Fray Alonso de Benavides, *Benavides' Memorial of 1630*, trans. Peter P. Forrestal (Washington, D.C.: Academy of American Franciscan History, 1954), p. 36.

13. France V. Scholes, *Church and State in New Mexico, 1610–1650* (Albuquerque: Historical Society of New Mexico, 1937).

14. Fray Angélico Chávez, *Our Lady of the Conquest* (Santa Fe: Historical Society of New Mexico, 1948).

15. Lonn Taylor and Dessa Bokides, *New Mexican Furniture, 1600–1940* (Santa Fe: Museum of New Mexico Press, 1987). Photographs of roof beams from Quarai (p. 11) and Pecos (p. 14) are reproduced. Roof beams from the seventeenth-century church at Acoma survive and have been reused in homes in the pueblo. See Viviana Nigro Holmes, "Architectural Woodwork of Spanish Colonial New Mexico," *New Mexico Studies in the Fine Arts* 10 (1985): 22. The seventeenth-century church of Our Lady of Guadalupe in El Paso del Norte (now Ciudad Juarez, Mexico) was part of the Province of New Mexico during the colonial period and retains its original carved-beam ceiling.

16. Joseph H. Toulouse, Jr., *The Mission of San Gregorio de Abó: A Report on the Excavation and Repair of a Seventeenth-Century New Mexican Mission* (Albuquerque: University of New Mexico Press, 1949), pp. 23–24.

17. Ibid., pp. 41–42; Taylor and Bokides, *New Mexican Furniture*, p. 11.

18. Fray Alonso de Benavides, *Revised Memorial of 1634*, ed. Frederick Webb Hodge, George P. Hammond, and Agapito Rey (Albuquerque: University of New Mexico Press, 1945), pp. 109–24; and France V. Scholes and Eleanor B. Adams, "Inventories of Church Furnishings in Some of the New Mexico Missions, 1672," in *Dargan Historical Essays*, ed. William M. Dabney and Josiah C. Russell (Albuquerque: University of New Mexico Press, 1952), pp. 27–38.

19. George P. Hammond and Agapito Rey, eds., *Don Juan de Oñate, Colonizer of New Mexico, 1598–1628*, 2 vols. (Albuquerque: University of New Mexico Press, 1953), pp. 231–43, 266.

20. Benavides, *1634*, p. 67.

21. Fray Angélico Chávez, "The Carpenter Pueblo," *New Mexico Magazine* 49 (September–October 1971), pp. 26–33; and John L. Kessell, *Kiva, Cross, and Crown: The Pecos Indians and New Mexico, 1540–1840* (Washington, D.C.: The National Park Service, 1979), pp. 132–33, 177–78, 292, 305, 321–22, 336, 346, 379, 474–75.

22. E. Boyd, *Popular Arts of Spanish New Mexico* (Santa Fe: Museum of New Mexico Press, 1974).

23. Max Moorehead, *New Mexico's Royal Road: Trade and Travel on the Chihuahua Trail* (Norman: University of Oklahoma Press, 1958).

24. Boyd, *Popular Arts*, p. 246.

25. Taylor and Bokides, *New Mexican Furniture*, pp. 6, 12, 23, 98.

26. Burr, *Hispanic Furniture*, pp. 99–100.

27. Benavides, *1634*, p. 67; and Taylor and Bokides, *New Mexican Furniture*, pp. 14–15.

28. Taylor and Bokides, *New Mexican Furniture*, pp. 9, 18–19, 22, 25, 67, 80–81, 96. Inquisition documents from the 1660s mention Indian carpenters from the pueblos of Sandia, Isleta, Alameda, Jemez, Zia, and Santa Ana (Archivo General de la Nación, Mexico City, Tierras, 3268).

29. Alan C. Vedder, *Furniture of Spanish New Mexico* (Santa Fe: Sunstone Press, 1977), p. 9.

30. Taylor and Bokides, *New Mexican Furniture*, p. 21.

31. Ibid., p. 23.

32. Vedder, *Spanish New Mexico*, p. 25.

33. Boyd, *Popular Arts*, pp. 250, 258; Vedder, *Spanish New Mexico*, p. 21.

34. Taylor and Bokides, *New Mexican Furniture*, p. 24.

35. Burr, *Hispanic Furniture*, pp. 63–66.

36. These writing desks, or *escritorios*, have been known as *vargueños* since the late nineteenth century. When the stand is paneled, it is known as a *taquillón*. Burr, *Hispanic Furniture*, pp. 35–37; Feduchi, *Estilos*, pp. 130–40; and Feduchi, *El mueble*, pp. 134–44.

37. Boyd, *Popular Arts*, p. 251; Taylor and Bokides, *New Mexican Furniture*, pp. 19–21.

38. Burr, *Hispanic Furniture*, pp. 32–37.

39. For examples see Taylor and Bokides, *New Mexican Furniture*, pp. 44–45.

40. On the basis of tests proving the wood used to be a type of pine common in New Mexico, Boyd and Vedder considered the chests to be of local manufacture. As a result of the use of oil paint and motifs foreign to New Mexico, however, they attributed the chests to an itinerant Mexican artist. Taylor and Bokides have pointed out the similarity of forest growth in New Mexico and the Sierra Madre of Mexico, making wood analysis less conclusive. Boyd, *Popular Arts*, p. 258; Vedder, *Spanish New Mexico*, pp. 32–33; Taylor and Bokides, *New Mexican Furniture*, p. 15.

41. Taylor and Bokides, *New Mexican Furniture*, p. 21.

42. Ibid., pp. 19–21; Fray Francisco Atanasio Domínguez, *The Missions of New Mexico, 1776*, trans. and ed. Eleanor B. Adams and Fray Angélico Chávez (Albuquerque: University of New Mexico Press, 1976). p. 65. Adams and Chávez commented in a footnote that this description may refer to Michoacán lacquerware.

43. This page from the original 1752 document is reproduced by Taylor and Bokides *(New Mexican Furniture*, p. 16), but the phrase

is incorrectly translated in the caption on this same page. The correct translation is used in the text of the book on page 21.

44. Toussaint, *Colonial Art*, p. 168. Examples of painted or "lacquered" furniture from Michoacán dating from the eighteenth and nineteenth centuries can be found in the Franz Mayer Museum, Mexico City; Felipe Seigal Collection, Mexico City; Museo de Historia, Mexico City; Museo Regional de Pátzcuaro, Pátzcuaro, Michoacán; Museo de la Guatapera, Uruapan, Michoacán; Museo Bello, Puebla; and many private collections.

45. Teresa Castelló Iturbide and Marita Martinez del Rio de Redo, *El arte del maque en Mexico* (Mexico: Fomento Cultural Banamex, 1980); Teresa Castelló Iturbide, "Maque," *Artes de Mexico* 18, no. 153 (1972): 92–101.

46. E. Boyd, unpublished accession records, Museum of International Folk Art, Museum of New Mexico, A.5.53-36 and A.8.60-1.

47. One of the Valdez chests-on-legs has red, green, black, and white painted patterns outlining the carved designs. This chest is reproduced in color in Taylor and Bokides, *New Mexican Furniture*, p. 35. A board-construction chest in the collection of the Taylor Museum of the Colorado Springs Fine Arts Center has delicate painted designs of scallops, rosettes, plants, and birds in pastel colors. The painting has been attributed to an early nineteenth-century New Mexican folk artist known as the Santo Niño Santero. See Vedder, *Spanish New Mexico*, p. 31.

48. Both are reproduced in color in Taylor and Bokides, *New Mexican Furniture*, p. 48.

49. Domínguez, *Missions 1776*, p. 50.

50. Mable Morrow, *Indian Rawhide: An American Folk Art* (Norman: University of Oklahoma Press, 1975).

51. Taylor and Bokides, *New Mexican Furniture*, p. 21.

52. Burr, *Hispanic Furniture*, pp. 26–27; Feduchi, *Estilos*, pp. 105–19; Feduchi, *El mueble*, pp. 102–10.

53. Feduchi, *Estilos*, pp. 65–72; and Feduchi, *El mueble*, pp. 104–7.

54. Taylor and Bokides, *New Mexican Furniture*, p. 25.

55. Domínguez, *Missions 1776*, p. 17.

56. Lt. Col. W. H. Emory, *Notes of a Military Reconnaissance from Ft. Leavenworth, in Missouri, to San Diego, in California*, Report of the Secretary of War, 30th Congress, Exec. Doc. No. 41 (Washington, D.C.: Wendell and Van Benthuysen, 1848).

57. Domínguez, *Missions 1776*, p. 67.

58. Taylor and Bokides, *New Mexican Furniture*, p. 90.

59. Ibid., pp. 96–99.

60. Ibid., p. 99.

61. Marita Martinez del Rio de Redo, "El mobiliario novohispano," *New Mexico Studies in the Fine Arts* 10 (1985): 7. For examples of the cornhusk motif in Spain and Mexico, see Feduchi, *Estilos*, pp. 241–86; Luis Ortiz Macedo, "Mueble neoclásico," in *El mueble mexicano* (Mexico: Fomento Cultural Banamex, 1985), pp. 93–102; and *Artes de Mexico* 16, no. 118 (1969): 50–75.

62. Boyd, *Popular Arts*, pp. 248–49.

63. Burr, *Hispanic Furniture*, pp. 48–52.

64. Taylor and Bokides, *New Mexican Furniture*, pp. 25–26; Vedder, *Spanish New Mexico*, pp. 61–74.

65. Burr, *Hispanic Furniture*, p. 34.

66. For examples, see Burr, *Hispanic Furniture*, pp. 73, 78–79.

67. Toussaint, *Colonial Art*, pp. 168–69.

68. Burr, *Hispanic Furniture*, p. 107.

69. Domínguez, *Missions 1776*, pp. 62, 106; Emory, *Military Reconnaissance*, p. 7; and unpublished documents, Archive of the Archdiocese of Santa Fe, New Mexico State Records Center and Archives, Reel 54 (1798 and 1821) and Reel 45 (1818).

70. Burr, *Hispanic Furniture*, p. 22.

71. For examples, see Taylor and Bokides, *New Mexican Furniture*, pp. 119–210; and Vedder, *Spanish New Mexico*, pp. 89–94.

Catalogue Objects

74. *Board chest*
Spanish colonial, New Mexico, late 18th century
Pine
H. 25⅜ in (65 cm), W. 49 in (124.5 cm), D. 24 in (61 cm)
School of American Research Collections in the Museum of New Mexico, Museum of International Folk Art, Santa Fe, Bfmc 91/nb-1

74. Board chest / 75. Board chest

Chests were the earliest and most common furniture items made in Europe. They were extremely portable and used for multiple purposes, such as transporting and guarding valuables, storing food and clothing, seating, a writing surface, and even for supporting boards on which to sleep or eat. Lavishly decorated chests were the most important possessions of brides and ladies of the court.

From the Middle Ages on, some of the chests made in Spain consisted of six boards joined by dovetailed joints and pegs. These board-construction chests were often decorated with relief carving created by chiseling away the background to leave a raised design. In the thirteenth to fifteenth centuries, and later in provincial areas of Spain, the designs were usually geometric (reflecting Moorish influence) or Gothic in style. By the late sixteenth century and throughout the seventeenth century, florid baroque motifs appeared in the relief carvings of board chests, as seen in the Spanish example here. Spanish furniture, including the six-board chest, often retained the traditional form of construction while being overlaid with decorative motifs of later fashions.

The basic six-board chest was reproduced throughout the Spanish empire during the colonial period, including the far northern frontier which is now in the southwestern United States. Here metal tools had to be imported over thousands of miles of rough terrain from Mexico City. As a result, the tools were often scarce, frequently reworked, and rather crude. The only wood

75. *Board chest*
Spanish, late 17th century
Mahogany
H. 28¾ in (73 cm), W. 53⅛ in (135 cm), D. 27 in (68.6 cm)
Pueblo I

available in New Mexico was soft, dry Ponderosa pine, not the good hardwoods of Spain and Mexico. Consequently, the furniture of New Mexico was of sturdy design with simple decorative carving.

The dovetailed joinery on this New Mexican chest is very elementary in comparison with the delicately stepped joinery of the Spanish chest. The relief carving is also less elaborate, but it retains many baroque motifs. The Spanish chest displays the double-headed Hapsburg eagle flanked by baroque vines on the front panel. On the New Mexican chest, stylized baroque vines flank a small rosette with four rampant lions and two rabbits above and three pomegranate or fleur-de-lis forms below. The center panel on the Spanish chest is framed by a border filled with S curves; on the New Mexican chest the panel is surrounded by a border of scallops. Four quarter-rosettes appear in the corners of the front and end panels of the Spanish chest. The rosette is one of the most common decorative motifs in New Mexican furniture, and there is a small one in the center of this chest.

Just as the construction of the six-board chest was uniform, so a standard vocabulary of decorative motifs in various combinations was used in New Mexico. The motifs included rosettes, pomegranates, lions, scallops, vines and branches, birds, and circles. All are found also in European baroque ornament, but in New Mexico the motifs were spread out over the surface rather than being tightly arranged in an intricate composition. In New Mexico the handicaps of crude tools and brittle wood resulted in furniture that was less finely constructed than Spanish or Mexican examples but still strongly based on European tradition in both construction technique and decoration.

76. Framed chest-on-legs

Framed chests, constructed with panels set into a framework of rails and stiles with pegged mortise-and-tenon joints, were made in Spain and the New World. The lengthening of the end stiles to form short legs on chests is a method of construction developed in northern Spain, particularly in Asturias and Navarra. Chests with built-in legs were apparently not made in New Mexico until the late eighteenth century; they are all of framed construction. This New Mexican chest-on-legs is one of eighteen examples so similar in construction that they have been attributed to the same workshop or family, probably the Valdez family of Velarde.[1]

In Spain and Mexico carpentry techniques were transmitted through formal guild systems regulated by ordinances and inspections. If formal guilds existed in New Mexico, their ordinances have not survived. In both Spain and Mexico, master craftsmen often accepted members of their own families into apprenticeship. This practice of passing on craft traditions within a family was probably continued in New Mexico in an informal manner.

Framed chests were made by joining two front panels, two side panels, and a back panel into a framework of eight horizontal rails and five vertical stiles. In New Mexico the four end stiles were extended to form legs, and two angular braces connect the front legs to the front rail. The decorative carving on the New Mexican framed chests includes chip-carved motifs on rails and stiles, zigzag borders around panels, and geometric patterns, often with circles, on the front panels. Variations of these motifs are also common on regional chests from Spain, particularly the chip carving. Extension of the stiles to form tall legs, however, is not characteristic of the chests from northern Spain and may reflect influence, in form if not in function, from the famous *vargueños*, or writing desks, of Spain (fig. 1, p. 184).

The *vargueño* is actually a chest with drawers that rests on a separate piece of furniture that serves as a stand, known as a *pie de puente*. Derived from Moorish woodworking techniques, the distinctively Spanish *vargueño*

76. *Framed chest-on-legs*
Spanish colonial, New Mexico,
late 18th century
Attributed to the Valdez family,
Velarde, New Mexico
Pine
H. 27¾ in (70.5 cm),
W. 32½ in (82.5 cm),
D. 16 in (40.6 cm)
Millicent Rogers Museum,
Taos, N.M., MRM 1967-3-53

became especially elaborate in the seventeenth century, with intricate ivory carvings, *salomonic* (twisted) columns, filigreed ironwork, and polychromed and gilded details. When assembled, the outlines and proportions of the *vargueño* and *pie de puente* resemble the New Mexican chest-on-legs. On a *vargueño*, it is the front panel rather than the top panel that opens to form a writing surface. Like the New Mexican chest-on-legs, the *vargueño* is decorated on the front face. The development in New Mexico of the tall chest-on-legs as a furniture form in the late eighteenth century may have been inspired by actual Spanish *vargueños* or similar Mexican writing desks imported to New Mexico.

1. Lonn Taylor and Dessa Bokides, *New Mexican Furniture, 1600–1940* (Santa Fe: Museum of New Mexico Press, 1987), p. 24.

77. Board chest / 78. Board chest

In 1565 a trade route was established between the Orient and Spain via the Philippines and Mexico. The galleons of the king of Spain sailed from Manila to Acapulco. From there goods were carried overland to Mexico City and eventually to Veracruz, on the Gulf Coast, where they were loaded onto galleons for the trip to Spain. Many oriental products remained in Mexico. These, along with oriental craftsmen who immigrated there, exercised a direct influence on the decorative arts of New Spain, including lacquerware. Lacquered objects had been produced in Mexico since pre-Hispanic times. The lacquer industry seems to have reached its peak in Mexico during the eighteenth century, when all types of furniture were decorated in this manner.

From the late sixteenth century on, the Michoacán area of Mexico became well known for its furniture, particularly chip-carved, brightly polychromed, and lacquered pieces. An offshoot of the lacquer industry in Mexico was a simplified technique for producing inexpensive objects. Painted designs on poorer quality woods (usually pine) were covered with a varnish or shellac in imitation of true lacquerware. Michoacán furniture often depicted rather whimsical scenes of daily life, as does this chest decorated with a private coach pulled by two white horses with a footman and driver (cat. no. 78). Painted board chests of this type were imported to New Mexico from Michoacán.

According to local oral history, New Mexican families acquired Michoacán chests when their ancestors brought them back from trade fairs in Chihuahua, Mexico. In a study of New Mexican estate inventories, a third of the chests listed were from Michoacán.[1] Apparently these imported chests inspired local artists to paint chests and other furniture from time to time. Two board chests from New Mexico are painted with geometric designs; they may be the work of Pueblo Indian artists (cat. no. 77; fig. 2, p. 185). The designs on these chests are reminiscent of those on some Pueblo Indian pottery. Both the designs and colors are similar to those on Plains Indian parfleches (traveling pouches). These chests may represent a synthesis of Spanish (both Mexican and New Mexican), Pueblo Indian, and Plains Indian traditions and may indicate a distant influence of oriental lacquerware traditions on southwestern Indian material culture.

In the early colonial period in Mexico, Indians were trained in various crafts, including woodworking, under the direction of Franciscan friars in convent schools and by Spanish master carpenters during the construction of churches. Initially not admitted to the guilds, Mexican Indians were allowed to practice carpentry outside of the guilds and unrestricted by their ordinances. The same pattern apparently prevailed on the northern frontier, where Franciscan friars with the occasional assistance of Spanish master carpenters trained New Mexican Indians in European woodworking techniques. The Indians of Pecos Pueblo became especially adept at carpentry, and their skills and products were in demand by Spaniards and Indians alike throughout the colonial period.

1. Taylor and Bokides, *New Mexican Furniture*, p. 21.

77. *Board chest*
New Mexican, 19th century
Pine; tempera paint; gesso; iron hardware
H. 13 in (33 cm), W. 27¾ in (70.5 cm), D. 13½ in (34 cm)
School of American Research, Santa Fe

78. *Board chest*
Mexican, Michoacán, early 19th century
Imported to New Mexico
Pine; oil paint; iron hardware
H. 13¾ in (35 cm), W. 24¹³⁄₁₆ in (63 cm), D. 13 in (33 cm)
Spanish Colonial Arts Society, Inc., Collection on loan to the Museum of New Mexico, Museum of International Folk Art, Santa Fe, L.5.58-28

79. *Armchair*
New Mexican, late 18th century
Pine
H. 29¼ in (74.3 cm), W. 17¾ in (45.1 cm), D. 17 in (43.2 cm)
Collection of Mr. and Mrs. J. Paul Taylor

80. *Armchair* (sillón de frailero)
Spanish, late 16th century
Walnut; modern silk upholstery
H. 47½ in (120.7 cm), W. 25½ in (64.8 cm), D. 25 in (63.5 cm)
The Minneapolis Institute of Arts,
gift of Mrs. Keith Merrill in memory of Mr. Merrill,
63.63.2

79. Armchair
80. Armchair (sillón de frailero)

The armchair, popularly known as a *sillón de frailero*, or priest's chair, developed in Spain during the early sixteenth century. Made with mortise-and-tenon construction, these chairs are often upholstered with embossed leather or silk. They usually have slightly raked back posts topped by bracket or ball finials, narrow arms resting on extended front legs, and low side stretchers (cat. no. 80). The most distinctive characteristic of the *sillón de frailero* is the high, wide front stretcher, or *chambrana*, which is often carved or fretted. The *sillón de frailero* remained widely popular in Spain and Mexico into the nineteenth century. In the seventeenth century the legs, arms, and side stretchers were blocked and turned, reflecting influence from the styles of Louis XIII and Louis XIV; later they were carved and scalloped, in the rococo taste. The basic form of the *frailero* remained constant, however.

Next to the chest, the chair was the most common furniture item in New Mexico. Throughout the colonial period, the Spanish Crown maintained a monopoly on many important goods and prohibited independent trade with foreign countries. As a result, New Mexico remained cut off from European settlements on the East Coast and Mississippi River valley. Imported goods for New Mexico generally had to come from Europe or the Orient by ship and then be hauled overland through Mexico City and north on the Camino Real to Chihuahua. New Mexican traders went south with blankets, tanned hides, wool stockings, and sheep to trade for imported goods at the trade fairs in Chihuahua and elsewhere in northern Mexico. The journey was long and dangerous, with the result that imported goods were expensive.

Several armchairs were imported to New Mexico, including one described in 1776 as "an armchair of fine wood upholstered in crimson velvet with galloon and fringe of fine gold, all affixed by nails of gilt metal."[1] The imported *fraileros* must have inspired local carpenters, since New Mexican armchairs are constructed according to the same basic formula. Several include wide front and back stretchers placed in high positions like the Spanish *chambranas* (cat. no. 79). The bracketed back post finials of the Spanish chair are stair stepped on the New Mexican version. The stepped geometric patterns that appear on the finials and rails of New Mexican chairs may be related to Pueblo Indian designs, but they can also be found on provincial Spanish and Mexican chairs of the sixteenth through the nineteenth century and are derived from Moorish prototypes. The soft, dry quality of pine and the crude tools available in New Mexico would have precluded intricately carved and curvilinear decorations on most furniture.

1. Fray Francisco Atanasio Domínguez, *The Missions of New Mexico, 1776*, trans. and ed. Eleanor B. Adams and Fray Angélico Chávez (Albuquerque: University of New Mexico Press, 1976), p. 17.

81. *Table*
New Mexican, early 19th century
Pine
H. 29½ in (75 cm), W. 57 in (144.8 cm), D. 34¼ in (87 cm)
Collection of Shirley and Ward Alan Minge

81. Table / 82. Table

During the late Gothic and early Renaissance periods, Spanish tables consisted of boards supported by crude trestles or by chests. As portability became of less concern, the table developed into two forms that were built in great numbers during the seventeenth century and are still used today. In one form, the tabletop was supported by either lyre-shaped or splayed trestles connected by iron braces. In the other, the tabletop was supported by fixed legs braced by side or box stretchers (cat. no. 82). These tables often had one to three drawers set in an underframing between the top and the legs and carved with geometric or floral decoration. Probably a holdover from the days when portability was essential, the tabletops and legs were joined by a method uniquely Spanish—cleats or crosspieces were mortised into the underside of the tabletop and the legs were then attached to these.

Later furniture in Spain and Mexico was often constructed along the traditional rectangular Spanish lines with the addition of baroque and rococo decoration. Beginning in the mid-seventeenth century, the legs and side stretchers of tables were turned and blocked, reflecting influences from the baroque styles of Louis XIII and Louis XIV. During this period, valances were

82. *Table*
Spanish, 17th century
Walnut
H. 35 in (88.9 cm), W. 27¾ in (70.5 cm), D. 74 in (188 cm)
The Metropolitan Museum of Art, New York, gift of Russell Cowles, 1954, 54.104.1

often scalloped—a motif that was continued and exaggerated during the rococo period in the eighteenth century.

If the trestle table was used in New Mexico, no examples have survived. Fixed-leg tables were constructed in New Mexico with a solid framework of four legs with rails or stretchers topped by boards either pegged or nailed to the framework (cat. no. 81). The Spanish tradition of inserting crosspieces or cleats between the legs and the tabletop was continued in New Mexico into the nineteenth century. On some New Mexican tables, splats or turned spindles connect the upper and lower rails.

Many New Mexican tables, like their Spanish predecessors, have drawers supported by a central runner between the upper rails. Like Spanish tables, New Mexican tables are often decorated with grooves or chip-carved designs on the drawers and rails. The angular scalloping on the rails of this table recalls baroque and rococo decoration on Spanish and Mexican tables.

Arlene Palmer

"To the Good of the Province and Country"

Henry William Stiegel and American Flint Glass

Henry William Stiegel was among the handful of entrepreneurial spirits in colonial America who determined to undertake the manufacture of glass even though "it was not for the Honour of England to Suffer Manufactories in the Colonies."[1] This was no inexpensive or easy decision: the would-be glass manufacturer had to construct a sizable factory, have access to tremendous amounts of fuel, acquire raw materials of a very specific nature, and find and hire a team of highly skilled craftsmen. Nevertheless, Stiegel, a successful ironmaster, opened a glasshouse in Manheim, Lancaster County, Pennsylvania, in 1764.

Like his rivals in New Jersey and Massachusetts, Stiegel succeeded in engaging German-born glassblowers to make bottles, windowpanes, and other utilitarian goods for a local market. He was alone, however, in seizing the opportunity created by the growing tension between Great Britain and the colonies: when nonimportation agreements removed fashionable English table glass from the market, Stiegel revamped his operation to fill the void. He recruited English artisans to produce what he called "American Flint Glass" and marketed it throughout the colonies. Although the business did not prosper in the economic climate of the prewar years and failed in 1774, Stiegel did succeed in introducing important technological changes, in turning out creditable imitations of English glass, and in offering luxury cut and engraved glassware. The German traditions on which Manheim was founded did not disappear but evolved in a way that reflected the English influence.

The European Background of Colonial Glassmaking

Throughout the history of glassmaking, distinctive styles have emerged as a result of technological considerations and market demands. Furnace construction and fuels, raw materials, and methods of shaping and decoration have largely determined the style and quality of the glass produced. At the same time, cultural traditions and consumers' needs have influenced the design of table and ornamental wares.

Glassmaking centers evolved as technical advances or stylistic sophistication secured a market beyond the factory environs. Their success in turn spawned rival centers. The glass industry of Venice, which came to dominate the world market in the Renaissance, exemplifies this process. Intrigued by the "art and mistery" of glassblowing as well as its potential for profit, foreign entrepreneurs and princes persuaded craftsmen to leave the Venetian glassmaking center of Murano and operate rival establishments elsewhere.

Something of the importance attached to glassmaking in the early seventeenth century can be understood by the role it played in the founding of the Virginia colony: the Jamestown glasshouse of 1608 was the premier industrial endeavor in North America. The reasons for establishing this factory and its successor of 1621 had more to do with the state of English glassmaking, however, than with any vision of a colonial market. Henry VIII's household inventory reveals how highly Venetian glass was esteemed in Tudor England,[2] and Venice and its offspring were still England's major sources of glassware at the time Virginia was settled. The Jamestown glasshouses represented one part of the complicated process by which England eventually freed its glass trade from the hegemony of Venice.

With the landmark development of lead oxide crystal by George Ravenscroft in the last quarter of the seventeenth century, England's dependence on the Continent for glassware decreased sharply. At the same time, desirous of expanding the market for this new glass, the British government actively discouraged colonial attempts at glassmaking and instituted trade policies that would assure English manufacturers of a substantial overseas market.

This did not deter several colonists from setting up glasshouses, although British emigration restrictions, along with the reluctance of good workmen to abandon their secure positions, meant that would-be glass manufacturers turned to the German principalities and countries of the Austro-Hungarian Empire for experienced craftsmen. Indeed, there is some evidence that unemployed or discontented glass artisans from those regions, wishing to join the general migration to America, may have proposed the idea for Wistarburgh, the first commercially successful and also the longest-lived colonial glasshouse.[3]

Wistarburgh was built near Alloway, New Jersey, by Palatine immigrant Caspar Wistar in 1739 and continued in operation under Caspar's son Richard until about 1777. Four German glassblowers built and operated the works for the production of bottles and windowpanes. Some tablewares also were made there, but they were mostly fashioned from unrefined, nonlead-formula bottle and window glass and they exhibited the German forms and ornamentation familiar to the workers.[4] Thus in both technique and style the New Jersey products differed significantly from English imports.

Wistarburgh's German orientation in a market dominated by English glass typified the colonial glass trade. All of America's glasshouses established between 1700 and 1770 were operated by craftsmen of continental European background; yet a vast majority of the glasswares available in America were British-made, and many colonial consumers, regardless of their national origins, preferred the glass manufactured in London, Bristol, or Newcastle upon Tyne.

Though not as widely admired as Venetian glass, glass *à la façon d'Angleterre* enjoyed international renown in the eighteenth century.[5] The sturdiness of England's dark green wine bottles and the brilliance of English lead crystal tablewares commanded such respect that several Continental glass manufacturers enticed English artisans to their factories to produce glass of comparable style and quality.[6]

The Study of Stiegel Glass

The story of the Lancaster County glassworks and its flamboyant proprietor has been the subject of speculation since at least 1844, when a local historian, I. Daniel Rupp, reported on the "eccentric German Baron" and his "singular career."[7] Armed with his discovery of Stiegel's factory record books, Frederick William Hunter determined to set the record straight with his 1914 publication, *Stiegel Glass*, and since then his version of the factory's history has been generally accepted.[8] Hunter correctly isolated some of the European influences on Stiegel's operation, but his conclusions about how those influences were expressed in the products have raised many questions concerning attributions.

Recognizing the difficulties of distinguishing between Stiegel glass and glass made in Europe, scholars have resorted to the designation "Stiegel-type" even in the absence of any firmly attributed Stiegel product. The first object that can be documented to Manheim, a goblet made for Stiegel's daughter (cat. no. 93), surfaced only recently, and it challenges the long-accepted notions of the designs and styles of Stiegel output. Furthermore, examination of the factory record books shows that Hunter ignored or misinterpreted key data. My discussion of Stiegel glass and its relationship to European glass will therefore be based on a revised analysis of the primary evidence and not on the traditional identification of "Stiegel-type" glass.

In framing a discussion of Stiegel glass, it is necessary to determine what objects or type of objects can reasonably be attributed to the Manheim enterprise. For both the German-oriented period of 1764 to 1769 and the English-dominated years of 1769 to 1774, distinguishing Stiegel's products from contemporary European glass is problematical at best. The mutual influences of the German and English traditions, difficult to measure, were always present. Even though no English artisans were employed at Manheim in the early years, there may have been some pressure on the Germans to imitate English imports. Since German glassblowers remained in Stiegel's employ after the English workers arrived, they in turn could have influenced the work of the British craftsmen.

Beginnings

In 1750, at the age of twenty-one, Stiegel arrived in America from Cologne. He soon became involved in ironworks, learning the business under John Jacob Huber. By 1757 he had assumed control of Huber's Elizabeth Furnace in Lancaster County and apparently prospered in this undertaking.[9] Although he resided in a Pennsylvania-German area, Stiegel evidently became fluent in English and was at ease in Philadelphia's business community. How he came to glassmaking is not known; he seems to have had no previous association with the industry. The factory may well have been part of the master plan for the settlement of the town of Manheim, a project which he undertook in partnership with Charles and Alexander Stedman of Philadelphia.[10] Even though Stiegel was not, as has been claimed, a baron, his proprietary role in the establishment of the town, symbolized by his rather grand dwelling, suggests that his interest in glassmaking may owe something to the practice of German princes, who sponsored glasshouses in their principalities. Yet Stiegel would not have gone into the glassmaking business unless skilled labor was available, so either he enticed a glassblower away from another factory, or the scheme was initiated by a skilled glassworker in need of employment.[11]

Such a man was Martin Greiner, who traveled from Saxe-Weimar in 1752 to make bottles at the behest of some investors in New York.[12] Glassmaking seems to have ceased in New York by the spring of 1763, and in the fall of 1764 Greiner was blowing glass for Stiegel. Something of Greiner's experience can be inferred from his contract with his New York employers. He consented to "Instruct & Inform" his backers in "Ev'ry respect in the art & Mistery of Erectg & Buildg a Glass House & allso in Blowing and Makeing of Glass." Greiner was to help construct the glasshouse and fabricate the ovens and pots needed to melt the glass batch. Besides underwriting the cost of his voyage and providing housing and land, the investing partners agreed to pay Greiner a wage based on the number of quart bottles and half-gallon flasks he produced.[13]

After six years, two of the partners, Samuel Bayard and Matthew Earnest, announced their intention of building a new glasshouse four miles from New York City at a place called Newfoundland, but both factories seem to have closed by the early 1760s.[14] In Governor Moore's view, the manufacturer's ruin had "no other cause than being deserted . . . by his servants, which he had Imported at a great expence."[15] Although the governor claimed the lure of the land drew many artisans to agricultural pursuits, it may have been the attraction of better wages that led Greiner to Manheim.

A glassworks needed more than one blower, however, and Stiegel managed to hire Christian Nassel, and possibly Christian Gratinger, away from the rival glasshouse of Caspar Wistar.[16] Stiegel's fourth glassblower, Jacob Halder, does not seem to have been directly related to the Halters (Caspar, Hans Martin, and Peter) who were in Wistar's employ. In Greiner, Nassel, and possibly Gratinger, Stiegel had German-born and -trained glass craftsmen whose experience had already been affected by a decade of life in the colonies — how, exactly, cannot be said. Certainly, given the overlap of factory work, the Manheim products can be expected to share certain features with South Jersey and New York glass.

Study of the Stiegel records indicates that glassmaking commenced late in 1764 at Manheim, not in the fall of 1763 at Elizabeth Furnace as Hunter believed. Stiegel first publicized the undertaking in the February 7, 1765, *Pennsylvania Gazette*: "Notice, that the Glasshouse, which he has erected in the Town of Manheim, is now compleatly finished, and the Business of Glassmaking in it carried on; where all Persons may be suited in the best Manner, with any Sort of Glass, according to their Order."[17]

Production from 1764 to 1769

In the early years, Stiegel concentrated production on green glass bottles. The quart size must have been in greatest demand because between December 1764 and April 1767 the workmen made 22,561 of them, which constituted 59 percent of the total output.[18] The scale of production and the types of bottles made can be seen from the records of the 1765–66 blowing season, when another glassblower, Conrad Waltz, joined the factory. During that November-to-April season, the five gaffers made five 8-quart bottles, three 6-quart, 270 gallon, 2,901 half-gallon, 9,677 quart, 4,281 pint, 344 pocket bottles, and also 112 bottles of unspecified capacity. While these descriptions imply that bottle sizes were standardized, the Manheim bottles probably varied in capacity within each given measure as did the English imports.[19]

Technological differences ensured that Stiegel's green bottles would not have resembled their imported English counterparts. As represented by the bottle made about 1765 for the New York merchant Sidney Breese (cat no. 84), the English product was thick-walled, heavy, and very dark green; these traits, renowned in their day, were the result of an English technology based on coal-fired furnaces. There is no evidence that Manheim's furnaces were ever fired with anything but wood. Although no green bottle has documentation unequivocally associating it with Stiegel's works, an American-made eighteenth-century bottle that has a history of ownership in Lancaster County can be attributed with some confidence to Manheim (cat. no. 83). Its light green, thin-walled body distinguishes it from standard English issue, and its irregular shape owes nothing to the straight-sided English bottle. Stiegel's sales records indicate that his bottles sold well in spite of differing from the imported ones. Their lighter, more transparent color might have discouraged some people from storing wine in them, but these utilitarian vessels would certainly have served many other functions as satisfactorily as imported bottles.

The first window glass was made at Manheim between December 16 and 21, 1765, by means of the cylinder process. Long, hollow cylinders of glass were blown, slit, and placed on iron shovels which were inserted into the arched openings of a flattening oven.[20] The heat caused the cylinders to unfurl into flat sheets of glass, which when cooled were cut into panes of the desired sizes. This was traditional practice on the Continent, whereas many English eighteenth-century glasshouses manufactured window glass by the crown process, which did not require flattening ovens.[21] English crown glass was considered superior to cylinder glass and was enjoyed by the wealthier colonists.[22] Stiegel apparently never aspired to that market: even though English craftsmen would significantly alter the tableware production at Manheim, there is no evidence that they ever made crown glass at the Lancaster County works.[23]

In the three-year period that is documented in detail, it is clear that Greiner alone was responsible for table glass and chemical wares. For the 1764–65 season, the shapes of these objects are not named, but their sizes ranged from "extraordinary" to gill (4 fluid ounces). Of the 996 objects Greiner created during the 1765–66 blast—about 5 percent of the total output—50 were identified as retorts and receivers. Sales records note an "electer glass," probably an "electerising" tube, globe, or jar designed for electricity experiments.[24]

The other "small" or "sundry" glass created by Greiner included tumblers, mugs, salts, cream jugs, plates, sugar bowls, jugs, bowls, cruets, inkstands, candlesticks, and horns. Unusual utilitarian forms also blown by Greiner were flowerpots and candlemolds. In April 1767, the other glassblowers joined Greiner in making "garden bells."[25] No description of these items is given, but most would have been of green bottle glass, the color resulting naturally from iron impurities in the raw materials. There is, however, a single reference to payment to Greiner for "making white glass," and in March 1769 a "white ½ pt milk pot" was sold.[26] In eighteenth-century parlance, "white glass" generally meant colorless glass, so at Manheim in this period there was apparently some interest in making more refined tableware. Regardless of their color, these objects were probably German in style (cat. no. 85; fig. 2).

Greiner's exact lineage has not been traced, but Greiners had long been involved in the glass industry of Thuringia. A large mug or jug (fig. 1), blown in a shape that was common in Thuringia, may have been made by Greiner in this early period.[27] Sales records show that he made pint- and quart-size mugs, and the different prices for mugs of the same size indicate that some were embellished. This one, however, is very plain except for its boldly ribbed handle and pincered foot. Greiner's tumblers may have been of a basic cylindrical form with a flat bottom; like any glass object, they could have been made with pattern-molded or applied ornamentation. Both English and Continental glassmakers adopted a barrel shape for tumblers and mugs, enhanced with vertical rib molding and applied threading.[28] The capacities of Greiner's tumblers ranged from gill to quart; though size difference may explain the price variations, so would the amount of ornamentation.

The Manheim ledgers of the 1760s supply no hint of the style of Greiner's glass salts. Again, the price varies widely, from 6d to 2s 6d for a single salt, indicating some degree of elaboration (saltcellars tended to be of uniform size). Cream pots and cream jugs varied in price from 6d to 1s apiece. Though often acquired separately,

Fig. 1. *Jug*. American, possibly glassworks of H. W. Stiegel, Manheim, Pa., 1764–74. Blown green glass. H. 7¼ in (18.5 cm). Hershey Museum of American Life, Hershey, Pa., 75.010.80.

cream containers may have been made en suite with sugar bowls, since both were necessary accoutrements of the tea table.

Eighteenth-century European sugar bowls typically had high, inset covers with a pulled-out and folded flange designed to rest on the rim of the bowl. For the German blower, the finial of the cover offered an irresistible opportunity for creative expression. A popular technique was to apply blobs of glass to a knop and then tool and pincer them into fantastic bird and animal shapes (cat. no. 86). German craftsmen followed the tradition of Venice and made handles with pincered or applied decoration.[29] In both Continental and English traditions, bowls and covers might be pattern-molded.

Several covered bowls of German style have been attributed to Wistarburgh, but the identification of Stiegel examples remains conjectural.[30] Certainly Greiner's sugar bowls must have reflected his German heritage. Ranging from 1s 6d to 3s each, they were the most expensive objects he made, due to their technical difficulty and the amount of ornamentation. Two sugar bowls that have been attributed to the New Geneva glassworks of western Pennsylvania may instead represent Greiner's work in Lancaster County (fig. 2).[31] Blown of nonlead green glass, both have deep bowls; one is pattern-molded with twenty-four vertical ribs. Following German fashion, the bowls have large ear-shaped handles and the high-domed lids carry handsome swans. Their attribu-

Fig. 2. *Covered sugar bowl.* American, possibly glassworks of H. W. Stiegel, Manheim, Pa., 1764–74. Blown and pattern-molded green glass (24 ribs). H. 8½ in (21.6 cm). Cincinnati Art Museum, bequest of Grace Spiegel, 1955.810.

tion to Manheim is suggested by their similarities to another sugar bowl fashioned of colorless lead glass (cat. no. 91). Other contenders for Greiner's sugar bowls are five colorless bowls that have never been associated with any particular factory (cat. no. 85). The inset lids have different profiles but sport swan finials that appear to have been executed by the same hand and that vary only slightly from those on the green glass examples.

A form made by Greiner but hitherto unrecorded in the literature about Stiegel is the glass horn. In the eighteenth century, the term "glass horn" was applied to three types of objects. One was a crescent-shaped vessel inspired by animal horns, which goes back to the late Roman Empire and was typically decorated with applied ornament. It continued to be made in green glass in medieval times as a ceremonial drinking vessel. Several sixteenth-century examples from the southern Netherlands are known, made of decorated colorless glass, and similar horns of less refined style were probably made throughout northern Europe (fig. 3).[32] At some point the crescent-shaped glass horn, like its animal-horn counterpart, became a container for gunpowder. That Greiner's glass horns may have functioned in this way is suggested by Stiegel's own purchase of "1 lb. Powder" and a "Glasshorn," the latter costing three shillings.[33] Another kind of glass horn was made both in England and on the Continent. Curving back on itself in the manner of the musical instrument, this horn

Fig. 3. *Drinking horn*. Probably northern European, late 16th–early 17th century. Blown and gilded colorless glass. L. 10½ in (26.7 cm). Wadsworth Atheneum, Hartford, Conn., Edith Olcott Van Gerbig Collection, 1956.3468.

could have served as a whimsical drinking vessel but is more often interpreted as a conceit to be carried in glassmakers' parades.[34] A third possibility for Greiner's object was a horn-shaped pocket designed to hang on a wall and hold flowers. This was more common in ceramics than in glass, but English ones of opaque white glass are known from this period.[35]

A most unusual form produced by Martin Greiner at Manheim is the candlemold, an object better known in metal. No other reference to glass candlemolds in America, either imported or native-made, has been found. As the name suggests, these were long, rounded tubes of glass in which molten wax was cooled for candles. A nearly contemporary illustration of glass candlemolds can be seen in the 1763 pattern book of Norwegian glass. Made in two sizes, those sold for the equivalent of 3*d* and 4½*d* each.[36] Glass candlemolds must have been made elsewhere in continental Europe but do not seem to have been known in England. The set shown in figure 4 may be the only set in existence.

The Effect of the Townshend Acts

Because a fundamental purpose of colonies was to provide a guaranteed market for the manufactured goods of the mother country, it was official British policy to discourage, if not prohibit, colonial manufactures. Concerned that American manufactures were on the rise and would threaten home industries, the Lords Commissioners for Trade and Plantations instructed each colonial governor in 1766 to assess the manufactures under his jurisdiction. In his response for Pennsylvania, dated January 21, 1767, Lieutenant Governor John Penn stated that he knew of only two manufactures, neither of which in his opinion represented a threat to British industry. According to Penn, the "Glass Manufactory, . . . was erected about four Years ago in Lancaster County, . . . by a private Person: it is still carried on, tho' to a very inconsiderable Extent, there being no other Vent for their Ware, which is of very ordinary Quality, but to supply the small demands of the Villages and Farmers in the adjacent inland Country."[37] Benjamin Franklin reiterated this assessment, noting that Stiegel's undertaking made "only a little coarse wear [*sic*] for the country neighbours."[38] Recognizing that it was to their advantage to cite only minor manufacturing efforts, colonial officials may have deliberately belittled Stiegel's achievements. However, Stiegel's own sales records indicate that his role in the urban marketplace was indeed negligible. Soon this would change; ironically, it changed because of the policy of the British government.

As William Pitt's health declined during 1767, Charles Townshend, chancellor of the exchequer, assumed a leading role in the government. The Whigs had pushed through a reduction in British land taxation that cut revenues by £500,000, while the army estimated its cost of keeping troops in America would be £400,000. This situation prompted Townshend to propose measures that would raise money in the colonies to pay for British support. Among them were import duties on manufac-

Fig. 4. *Set of twelve candlemolds*. Northern European, 18th century. Blown green and yellow glass, wood frame. L. 11 in (28.1 cm). Wadsworth Atheneum, Hartford, Conn., Edith Olcott Van Gerbig Collection, 1956.n.r.

tured goods that were in high demand: paints, sixty-seven grades of paper, tea, white and red lead, and five grades of glass. For "crown, plate, flint and white glass" the tax rate was 4s 8d per hundredweight; on green utilitarian glass, 14d per hundredweight. The expected annual revenue from these duties, however, was only £40,000.[39]

The Townshend Acts were scheduled to take effect November 20, 1767, but news of the measures had crossed the Atlantic by August. Some Boston citizens immediately began to clamor for nonimportation, but few merchants were willing to risk this significant portion of their trade. The result of a meeting held in Boston in October 1767 was to urge voluntary nonconsumption of British goods and to encourage local manufactures, especially American paper and glass.[40]

It was the reasoning of John Dickinson, Stiegel's friend and legal adviser, that helped mold public opinion and spur action. Beginning in December 1767, Dickinson's famous "Letters from a Farmer" appeared in the *Pennsylvania Chronicle*. He disputed the legality of the Townshend Acts, claiming they constituted a violation of colonial rights. He did not recommend nonimportation but urged Americans to petition for repeal of the acts and to reduce their reliance on British goods by adopting personal habits of frugality and supporting domestic manufactures. Nonetheless, nonimportation eventually became the uniform response in the colonies.

Unable to act in concert, the merchants in the major ports set their own timetables for nonimportation. In New York, articles of nonimportation took effect November 1, 1768. Boston's merchants agreed on January 1, 1769. Philadelphia's commercial community finally followed suit, so that by April 1, 1769, most British goods were banned in colonial America—not just the enumerated items of the Townshend Acts.

Although the merchants who signed the nonimportation agreements risked considerable financial loss by their action, manufacturers like Stiegel, who had struggled to compete with imported wares, stood to gain. With British goods no longer available, consumers would, in theory, turn to domestic products. The hope was that they would find them fairly priced and of good quality; they would, moreover, be doing their patriotic duty—as glassmakers were quick to remind them.

The glass industry adapted in three ways. Several entrepreneurs built new glasshouses. Others, like Richard Wistar, now advertised with a "buy American" slant, but Wistar apparently did not greatly adjust production to cater to the changed marketplace.[41] Finally, there was Stiegel. Motivated by patriotism as much as by the promise of profit, he completely revamped his business to accommodate the new market. Stiegel realized that the German-style tablewares Greiner had been making for the rural Pennsylvania communities would not appeal to urban consumers accustomed to English table glass. To fill the void created by nonimportation, Stiegel had to replicate both the quality and the styles of contemporary English wares, and he recognized that only English-trained craftsmen could effect the necessary changes in the Manheim operation.

Technological Changes

The English glass so widely admired and purchased was of a lead-formula composition not known to American manufacturers. This lead glass (or flint glass, as it was sometimes called) was heavy and brilliant and when struck had a wonderful resonance. Its production required more than merely a change in raw materials and recipes. As R. J. Charleston has pointed out:

> It was not sufficient in the 18th century merely to know that English crystal was made by the addition of lead-oxide to the batch: nor even that it was fired with coal. It was necessary to obtain the services of an English glassman, or one trained in England, to impart the whole secret, the innermost *arcanum* of which was no doubt the use and structure of the covered pot, used to protect the lead metal from discoloration by coal fumes.[42]

With red and white lead among the enumerated items of the Townshend Acts, Stiegel may have had some problems obtaining raw lead. The English glassmen who joined the factory in 1769 may not have been sufficiently familiar with the process of making flint glass from raw materials, or perhaps they were unable to adapt the available raw materials to the formulas they knew. Stiegel's solution is revealed by the entry on Friday, November 10, for the "first flint glass made of Cullet." Three days later the blowers made "The first Produce of America flint Glass."[43] In other words, Stiegel's first flint glass seems to have been fashioned entirely from remelted broken glass. Its lead content would have depended on the type and amount of cullet used. Conceivably, some of the products of the 1769–70 years could have been of a high-lead glass chemically indistinguishable from imports. Other products might have been of a highly refined but nonlead or low-lead composition and still have been called "flint" by Stiegel and his customers. The only advertisement from this period describes the Manheim glass as a "very necessary, useful and curious variety of white and blue Flint."[44]

Although Stiegel may not have achieved his technical aims as quickly as he would have liked, the five English glassblowers he secured for 1769–70 were able to blow glass of English styles, regardless of the exact lead content of the batch. How Stiegel found George Allen, Thomas Williamson, William Rego, Felix Farrill, and William Green is something of a mystery, because there was a long history of restrictions on the emigration of glass craftsmen from Great Britain. Records of the overseas passage of these workers have not been found, but in his published statement in 1771, the errant Farrill implies that his coming to America to make glass had been on his own initiative: "I and several other men came to America to pursue the business of making glass-ware; Mr. Stiegal persuaded us to enter into articles of agreement with him, to carry on the said business; we, being strangers in America, and pleased with the civility of Mr. Stiegal's then behaviour to us, we executed the articles. . . ."[45]

Whether they came from Newcastle, London, or Bristol, these men would have been familiar with the kinds of glass exported to the colonies. Importers' advertisements spell out the range of form and decoration that was sent from British glasshouses, and surviving examples provide specific details of manufacturing technology and quality. Forms ran the gamut from hock glasses to hyacinth glasses, from punch bowls to dessert pyramids. The finer wineglasses had remarkable stems containing air twists or twisted rods of opaque glass. Most objects were blown of a sparkling colorless glass, but some were colored a rich blue or amethyst or made of opaque white glass that rivaled porcelain in appearance. The most expensive items were embellished with cutting and engraving.

Stiegel faced a tremendous challenge in trying to meet the standards imposed by such imports, but his production record for the 1769–70 season proves his commitment to doing so. Between November 18, 1769, and May 5, 1770, the workers blew 37,206 objects, representing 38 different forms. Many of these were new forms for Manheim—decanters, wineglasses, mustard pots, and dessert wares. Some of the forms Greiner had made continued to be offered, such as cream jugs, salts, sugar bowls, tumblers, and mugs; presumably the Englishmen's interpretation of these forms differed radically from Greiner's in shape, ornamentation, and composition. Greiner and the other Germans were still employed, however, and doubtless participated in the revised production plan.

In spite of his imported workmen, the improved materials and processes they must have been using, and, most important, the removal of British competition, Stiegel's first year in the manufacture of flint glass can only be called a failure: as of April 17, 1770, only 9,863 objects—27 percent of the total number and 36 percent of the total value—had been sold. Whether the glass simply did not meet the public's expectations is not known; perhaps consumers were merely taking to heart John Dickinson's pleas for frugality.

While Stiegel was struggling for acceptance in the market that had spurred his effort in the first place, pressure was being placed upon Parliament to repeal the Townshend Acts.[46] Lord North, who became prime minister early in 1770, proposed a bill for the withdrawal of all duties except that on tea. This measure took effect with the king's approval April 12.

Sensing that the end of nonimportation was nigh and fearing the public would completely abandon even lip-service support of domestic manufactures, Stiegel published a somewhat desperate appeal in July 1770. Noting that he had "been at immense expence in erecting said works, and engaging some of the most ingenious artists in said manufacture, which is now arrived at great perfection," he claimed it was the "indispensible duty" of "every real well wisher of America" to support his endeavor. This would be particularly to their interest because he claimed his goods were cheaper than imported ones.[47] The following month he was among the Lancaster businessmen who signed a letter urging the continuation of nonimportation. Nonetheless, Philadelphia's merchants followed the lead of other cities and lifted the ban on importation in September 1770.

Stiegel must have been horrified by the reopening of trade with Great Britain, but he had invested too much —and had too much pride—to turn back. Relying on those citizens who still hoped American manufactures would flourish, Stiegel set out to wean the public away from foreign glass. His first task was to fabricate a lead-formula glass using raw materials.

The secret of making lead glass from local raw materials seems to have become known at Manheim sometime in 1771. In September of that year, Stiegel petitioned the Pennsylvania Assembly for monetary recognition of his accomplishment, but John Allman, the technician he had engaged, claimed that "without his Assistance and particular Management of *American* Materials at the Glass-Work of *Henry William Stiegel*, in *Lancaster* County, the Manufacture of white Flint Glass could not have been brought to its present Degree of Perfection in this Province."[48] These documents suggest that lead glass had only recently been manufactured "from scratch" at Manheim, a suggestion supported by advertisements for Stiegel's "greatly improved" products. The factory records contain references to changes in the physical plant, specifically to the "Building of Flint work."[49] Purchases of red lead and litharge appear throughout the records for 1772 and 1773, and the covered crucible, necessary to protect the molten glass from discoloration, was certainly part of the factory's equipment. Coal was never burned at Manheim, but that did not preclude the successful manufacture of lead glass.[50]

Having accomplished the manufacture of lead glass, Stiegel had to convince the public that his glassware was truly as good as imported lead glass. He embarked upon an ambitious advertising program and secured the agencies of key glass merchants in several cities. Recognizing the value of independent endorsement for his improved product, Stiegel presented samples of his glass to the June 21, 1771, meeting of the American Philosophical Society. In the opinion of the committee, published a few days later, the Manheim-made "FLINT GLASS, viz, decanters, wine glasses, tumblers, Etc. . . . was . . . equal in beauty and quality to the generality of Flint Glass imported from England; and entitles the ingenious and public-spirited manufacturer to the particular encouragement of this province and country."[51] This announcement was soon carried in the papers of other colonies. It also appeared overseas in a Bristol newspaper, where it no doubt caused consternation among the glass manufacturers who depended on the American trade.[52]

A second part of his plan was to explain how supporting American manufactures was a patriotic act and duty. Stiegel turned to his influential friends in Philadelphia society. On June 24, 1771, he wrote to the famous "Farmer," John Dickinson: "I make no Doubt but you Recomand and Encourage the Manufactory all you can as an undertaking so advantagious to the Good of the province and Country."[53] An anonymous "Pennsylvania Planter" then addressed these issues quite eloquently in the August 1, 1771, issue of the *Pennsylvania Gazette*:

Every Inhabitant of *Pennsylvania* must observe, with Pleasure, the Progress we make in this Province, towards Perfection in useful Arts . . . Every Person seems pleased with the late Success of Mr. *Stiegel*, who has erected the first House in *America* for making white Flint Glass. We have already seen that Work brought to Perfection; Decanters, Wine Glasses, etc. etc. now manufactured in this Province, equal in Whiteness, Transparency and Figure, to those which are imported from *Europe*; that many Thousands of Pounds must be saved to Pennsylvania by this Manufacture alone, will readily be granted.

The author maintained that Stiegel had "some Claim to a public Reward, who had the Spirit and Fortitude to risque his Estate in erecting such a Manufacture, by which the Province will presently save Twenty or Thirty Thousand Pounds *per Annum*." Like the American Philosophical Society judgment, this recommendation was publicized throughout the colonies.[54] Buoyed by these endorsements, Stiegel did apply for "Notice and Encouragement" from the Pennsylvania legislature. His petition, presented September 19, 1771, was tabled until the following September when the paltry sum of £150 was granted.

The English Style at Manheim, 1769–74

Documentation for these years of Stiegel's operation is sadly incomplete, so making the connection between the scattered written sources and existing objects is difficult at best.[55] It involves assessing the influences of German and English glassblowers, technical limitations, the urban market and local Pennsylvania-German taste, and Stiegel's personal aspirations.

The problem is perhaps best illustrated by Stiegel's "enamelled" glasswares advertised in 1772 by Cauffman and Fegan of Philadelphia.[56] These descriptions have long been interpreted as enamel-painted nonlead glasses of the Continental peasant style (cat. no. 95), the assumption being that Stiegel's German craftsmen catered to the taste of the local Pennsylvania-German community. This interpretation becomes impossible, however, when the notices are considered in their context: they appeared at the height of Stiegel's "English" phase and in the newspapers of New York and Philadelphia.

Though "enameled" could have indicated decoration painted in enamel colors, "painted" seems to have been the preferred term of the period. As used by contemporary British glass merchants and manufacturers, "enameled" had two meanings. It described the stems of wineglasses and other forms that contained twisted threads of opaque white glass or enamel (fig. 5; cat. no. 94), a style that "must always be regarded as a symptom of English influence."[57] Secondly, "enameled" described objects fashioned entirely of opaque white glass (fig. 12). In the eighteenth century glass was treated as a substitute for porcelain and was made in traditional ceramic shapes like teacups and painted in the manner of porcelain. The opaque white glass made in Germany and Bohemia was of the "milk glass" type, having a thin and watery aspect and often a fiery opalescence, whereas English white glass was a better pseudo-porcelain because of its denser, dead-white appearance. Advertisements indicate that glasshouses in Warrington, Bristol, Tyneside, south Staffordshire, and London were all producing opaque white glass as well as colored glass during the third quarter of the eighteenth century.[58]

There is no documentary proof that enamel-painted glasses of continental European style were ever made in Lancaster County, nor have any such glasses been identified that could be distinguished from known Continental examples.[59] The interpretation of Stiegel's enameled glass in the first English sense, however, is strengthened by the inclusion of "twisted wines" in his sales records and by the fact that the documented Stiegel family goblet features a twist stem of opaque white glass (cat. no. 93). Some enamel-painted glasswares were made in England, but as with those from central Europe, the decoration was often the handiwork of independent artisans working outside of the factory.

During the eighteenth century, many table forms were popular in blue or purple glass (cat. nos. 92, 95), and this taste is reflected in Stiegel's output. Blue glass flower jars, mugs, bowls, and salts were made in Manheim. Purple glass is not specified in the documents, but it was a color derived from the same manganese needed to make colorless glass.[60] Achieving a truly colorless glass free of imperfections was extremely difficult, so making opaque white, blue, or purple glass at Manheim may have been a convenient means of concealing technical flaws.

Fig. 5. *Goblet.* English, dated 1770. Blown colorless glass, white enamel-twist stem and engraved bowl. H. 7⅝ in (19.5 cm). Private collection. Courtesy of Christie, Manson & Woods, Ltd.

Fig. 6. *Pocket bottle*. American, attributed to glassworks of H. W. Stiegel, Manheim, Pa., 1769–74. Blown and pattern-molded amethyst glass ("nipt" diamonds). H. 5 1/16 in (12.7 cm). Private collection.

Cross-Influence of English and German Styles, 1769–74

Although no longer advertised after 1769, some green glass bottles and apothecary ware continued to be made at Manheim and were the responsibility of Greiner, Halder, and Nassel. The "common" tablewares mentioned in this period were probably blown of the green bottle glass. Entries in the records for 1773 prove that flint and bottle glass were worked from the same furnace, so there was ample opportunity for the German and English craftsmen to observe each other at work and to learn each other's styles and techniques. Indeed, the differences in the two traditions would be most readily seen in the two types of glass batch. This is well demonstrated by a cream jug (cat. no. 89) with a stylish English shape rendered in common green glass. The cabriole legs follow English prototypes (cat. no. 90), whereas the waffle-pincering of the feet is decidedly German and is seen on Wistar products. By the same token, the Stiegel oeuvre should include objects like catalogue number 91, which is of German style but blown of lead-formula glass.

The ongoing influence of the German glassblowers at Manheim between 1769 and 1774 is perhaps best illustrated by a large group of pattern-molded pocket bottles commonly in amethyst nonlead glass but also recorded in colorless and blue (cat. no. 87; fig. 6). In spite of the number that survive, only one has a history (cat. no. 87): it descended in the family of Elizabeth Shinn Armstrong of Medford, New Jersey, whose initials are scratched on the side. These pocket bottles hark back to Continental prototypes (cat. no. 88), but their puffy form is distinctive. Their occurrence in colored glass may reflect the English influence in Stiegel's production at this time, although amethyst glass was blown in Continental glasshouses as well (cat. no. 95). No exact prototypes for the Stiegel patterns have been uncovered, yet the combination of floral and geometric patterns in the so-called diamond-daisy and daisy-in-hexagon designs is curiously reminiscent of some Venetian designs.[61] Pocket bottles mold-blown with rows of large flowers were made in German glasshouses (cat. no. 88).

An analysis of the products of the 1769–74 period shows that some of the table glass forms Greiner had made earlier were still offered, while others were new to the Lancaster County works. The term "German" appears once in the Stiegel documents, when "German cans with covers" were sold.[62] What these looked like is not clear, but the designation does indicate a conscious differentiation between English and German styles.

Tumblers remained popular in this period, ranging in capacity from half-gill to one quart. Some were "tall" and some were sold with covers. Stiegel's workers made mugs in half-pint, pint, and quart sizes, but what made half-pint mugs different from canns of the same capacity is not known.

What distinguished the "German" canns is also unclear. Although covers are commonly associated with German glass, a 1752 shipment of English glass to Charleston included canns with handles and covers. An English price list illustrates the variety of the form, mentioning both one- and two-handled canns without covers, and three sizes of one-handled canns with covers.[63] Barrel shapes were used in both traditions, but perhaps Stiegel's "German" canns had the distinctive thumbpiece found on Continental glass (fig. 7).

Fig. 7. *Covered mug or cann.* European or possibly American, 1765–1800. Blown colorless glass with threaded decoration. H. 10 in (25.5 cm). The Newark Museum, Newark, N.J., 40.182.

Vinegar and mustard cruets with stoppers were produced in the 1769–74 period in both twisted and plain styles. Here, "twisted" must refer to a technique of pattern-molding in which a vertically ribbed mold imparts a ribbed pattern that is twisted when the gather is removed from the mold before being blown to its ultimate shape and size. This type of pattern-molding was universal, but the enameled cruets advertised in 1772 were probably blown of opaque white glass in the English manner.[64] Stiegel's "vinegar and oil cruits joined together" were in the German taste, the so-called crossbill that was produced in all regions of Germany.[65]

Greiner had made cream jugs in the 1760s, but new fashions emerged with the introduction of flint glass. The most telling indication of the style change is the description of "three feeted" cream jugs, recalling the silver, ceramic, and glass creamers with cabriole legs that were in vogue during the rococo period of the mid-eighteenth century (cat. no. 90). The American example shown as catalogue number 89 is refined in shape but, being blown of green glass, may represent the "common" or "plain" three-footed jugs of Stiegel's advertisements. Creamers were also among the enameled wares presumably of opaque white glass, but none have been identified. Hundreds of pattern-molded cream jugs blown in blue, green, and colorless glass, however, have been assigned to Manheim over the years. Patterned with diamonds and ribs, most are of lead glass, but some are nonlead glass and may represent some of Stiegel's output, particularly in the years 1769 to 1771. That such jugs were widely imported from England is seen in the import records of Frederick Rhinelander, who in 1773 sold English "blue milk jugs" in the New York City market. Just after the Revolution, Thomas Tisdale carried in his Hartford store both "plain and moulded blue glass creamers."[66] Not only was glass of this kind exported to America in the eighteenth and early nineteenth centuries, but even more was shipped over in the twentieth century, when it could command high prices as "Stiegel glass."

As discussed earlier, sugar bowls were among the most ambitious forms made in Manheim by Martin Greiner. The examples made by the English blowers would have been very different, although few English sugar bowls of this period can be documented. It is believed, however, that they rarely had handles or animal finials, and some were made without covers. Sugar bowls as such are not listed in a contemporary English price list, though perhaps the "basons with covers" served this function. "Moulded" sugar basins and covers of the sort Stiegel might have emulated were made in Liverpool in the 1770s, while in New York Rhinelander sold Bristol-made blue and purple ones, some of a "low, flat shape."[67]

These importers' descriptions fit the blue diamond-molded sugar bowls, blown of lead glass, that have been attributed to Stiegel for decades (cat. no. 92). A few of these bowls have histories in America, but given the records of importation that is no guarantee of American manufacture. The detection of mold defects in certain patterns has resulted in the firm English attribution of at least one design, the eleven-diamond-over-flute.

Decanters and wineglasses were appropriate choices for the American Philosophical Society's consideration because they were new forms for Stiegel and were closely associated with the English life-style. Decanters ranged in size from half-pint to gallon, and some were mold-blown. No details of the patterns are given, but ribbed and diamond designs were known in England. Stiegel's decanter shapes included champagne, sugar-loaf, and round, all English styles of the period.[68] When he offered sugar-loaf decanters in 1769, Stiegel was at the height of fashion; indeed, his is the earliest use of that term recorded in colonial sources.[69] It describes a tapered form like that of the cones in which refined sugar was molded. The curious "bubbled stopers" produced in the 1769–70 blast were presumably decanter stoppers of ball-knop form containing air bubbles, a style common in English ware of 1750 to 1775.[70]

The 1769–70 production records show that "Common," "tale," and "fine" wineglasses were made, and the least expensive, tale, outnumbered the fine by nineteen to one. The fancier rococo styles of twist-stem English wineglasses were probably only introduced with the improved formula in 1771; both air- and enamel-twist stems may have been produced by Stiegel's workers.

Wine-and-water glasses were also among the Manheim products. Scholars disagree on the interpretation of this term, some taking it to mean a finger bowl / wineglass cooler and others believing it refers to a stemmed form designed to accommodate the practice of diluting wine with water. The English-import records of Frederick Rhinelander support the latter idea, because his wine-and-water glasses all had "cut shanks" and lemon bowls. On an English price list of the period, wine-and-water glasses are equated with beer glasses and are definitely stemmed.[71]

The exact appearance of the thirty-two beer glasses made by Stiegel's workers in 1769–70 cannot be determined, because the form took different shapes, as demonstrated by a Salem merchant's 1773 advertisement for beer glasses "of all sizes and shapes." That they could be flat-bottomed like tumblers is evidenced by the notice of Hartford importer William Ellery, who in 1771 sold "Tumblers or beer glasses, one-half gill to one pint." Stemmed ones were offered by Boston's Joseph Barrel, who advertised "Beer glasses with cut shanks [stems]" the following year.[72] Beer was also associated with "free masons" glasses. In a 1763 price list of Norwegian glass, beer glass was the name given to firing glasses—the short, thick-footed glasses designed for multiple toasting and popular with the Masons.[73] Stiegel's references to firing glasses indicate that some of the ones he offered had enamel-twist stems (fig. 8).

Most closely associated with English traditions are glasses designed for the dessert table. Jelly and syllabub glasses appear in colonial inventories from the early 1700s. These small glasses were often arrayed on glass salvers that were stacked one upon the other to create a pyramid. Stiegel's 1772 advertisement gives unusually detailed descriptions. Both his "bell bowl" and "bubbled button" jellies imitated English styles. A standard trade term, "bubbled button" denoted a glass with a compressed knop, or "button," that contained decorative air beads, or "bubbles" (fig. 9). Stiegel's "common acorn" jellies suggest an English shape that in America is believed to be a saltcellar and in England is known as a "bonnet" glass (fig. 10).[74] "Common" could refer to unrefined green or aqua glass or to plain colorless glass, perhaps of nonlead formula.

Fig. 8. *Mason's or firing glass*. English, about 1770. Blown colorless glass, white enamel-twist stem and engraved bowl. H. 4³⁄₁₆ in (10.75 cm). The Corning Musem of Glass, Corning, N.Y., 50.2.76.

Fig. 9. *Jelly glass with "bubbled button."* English, 1750–75. Blown and pattern-molded colorless glass. H. 3⅝ in (9.2 cm). Private collection.

Fig. 10. *Jelly glass or salt dish of "acorn" form.* English, 1760–90. Blown and pattern-molded colorless glass (10 diamonds over flutes). H. 2⅝ in (6.6 cm). Private collection.

Fig. 11. *Salt.* English or possibly Norwegian, 1750–70. Blown colorless glass. H. 2 1/16 in (5.2 cm). Courtesy of The Henry Francis du Pont Winterthur Museum, Winterthur, Del., 73.295.

Several salt styles were made at Manheim. In contrast to the flat-based trencher salt, Stiegel's salts had either a round, applied foot or three legs, in the manner of silver and ceramics (fig. 11). (The latter style, advertised in 1772, was also popular in Norway, where German and English traditions were blended).[75] In the 1769–70 accounting at Manheim, more tale salts were made than any other style. These were probably plain but differed from "common" salts, which may have been of green glass. That pattern-molded salts were made is suggested by the listing for "chain salts," a term not found in other documents of the period. The salt traditionally attributed to Stiegel is pattern-molded with a diamond design. As mentioned above, however, these may have functioned as jellies rather than salts. In either case, it is a characteristically English form, even to the irregularly petaled foot.[76]

Smelling bottles, a new form at Manheim after 1769, were available in enameled, common, and twisted varieties. In 1768 a Philadelphia merchant was advertising "enameled smelling bottles from London."[77] Opaque glass was a favored material for this form, and the fanciest were enamel-painted. Rib-molded and twisted bottles were also made in England in a range of colors (fig. 12).

Luxury Decoration: Cut and Engraved Glass, 1773–74

Although Stiegel attained his goal of producing lead-formula glass in the English manner, he was not able to offer tablewares to satisfy the most discriminating colonists for want of an artisan who could cut and engrave. It was not until 1771, however, long after the repeal of the Townshend Acts and the renewal of importation, that Stiegel actively sought such a craftsman. Perhaps he believed that decorated glass would bring more customers, especially when sales of his "American Flint Glass" were flagging. It may also have been a matter of personal pride, because he had not secured the top of the market—such Philadelphians as John Cadwalader, who ordered cut glass from London's leading glasscutter.[78] Finally, Stiegel may have remembered that the most prestigious of the princely glass manufacturers on the Continent enjoyed the services of a court glasscutter or engraver. Whatever his reasons, in the summer of 1771 Stiegel notified the public that "A glass-cutter and flow-

218 Arlene Palmer

Fig. 12. *Scent bottle*. English or possibly American, 1770–1800. Blown and pattern-molded opaque white glass. L. 3¼ in (8.29 cm). The St. Louis Art Museum, bequest of Christine Graham Long, 547:1961.

erer, on application, [would] meet with good encouragement" at the Manheim glasshouse.[79]

Cutting glasswares with decorative scallops and facets was a technique which exploited the refractive properties of lead-formula glass for a brilliant effect. In England cut glass gained favor as a luxury item after 1750. "Flowerer" was the eighteenth-century designation for glass engraver and was first recorded in England in 1742. The art of wheel-engraving had been introduced into England in the early 1700s by German craftsmen. The formal baroque style of engraving they favored gave way during the rococo period to a peculiarly English style marked by an "easy naturalism . . . the main inspiration of which came from the garden."[80] Hence "flowering" became synonymous with "engraving."

Stiegel's notice elicited no response; only in June 1773 was he able to engage a glasscutter and flowerer. Lazarus Isaac had been working independently in Philadelphia, according to an advertisement he placed in the newspapers:

Glass Cutter—Lazarus Isaac. At the house of Mrs. Mary Wood, nearly opposite to Mr. John Elliott's Looking Glass store. . . . Being just arrived . . . from London, takes this method of acquainting the Public in General, that he undertakes to cut and engrave on glass of every kind, in any figure whatsoever, either coats of arms, flowers, names, or figures, to the particular fancy of those who may please to employ him. Patterns of his work may be seen at his dwelling, He cuts upon decanters a name of the wine, &c. for 1s. tumblers for 6d each, wine glasses for 2s per dozen, and the stems cut in diamonds at 2/6 per dozen . . .[81]

Isaac's location is interesting because John Elliott was at that time an owner of the Kensington glassworks, to which concern John Allman had also transmitted the secrets of lead glass technology. This raises the sticky issue of distinguishing between Stiegel's flint glass and that of the Kensington factory. Moreover, Elliott had apparently hired glasscutters and engravers before Stiegel.[82] Isaac may have been one of the Kensington cutters and for some reason chose to leave Elliott's employ. His advertisement implies he was fresh from London, but British records reveal that a man of this name was transported to America as a convict in February 1769.[83] Regardless of Isaac's possibly criminal past and the questionable date of his arrival in America, it is clear that he had received his training in England.[84]

The engraving tradition in which Isaac was schooled was a full-blown English rococo style rooted in nature. Large roses and rosebuds on branches, and grapevines, insects, and birds—these formed the repertory of the English flowerer (cat. no. 94; fig. 5). In the 1750s a new fashion was introduced that became a standard offering of glass engravers. This was the practice of inscribing a decanter with the name of the liquor it would contain. Lettering skills were also required to fulfill the many commissions for presentation pieces, commemoratives, and drinking glasses for special occasions both private and public. There would also have been an occasional demand for heraldic engraving and figural designs.

Cutting was a feature of the most costly English glass made in the second and third quarters of the eighteenth century, but only about 1770 did cut stems displace the popular twist stems.[85] A solid stem was cut all over with shallow hexagons or diamonds for a textured and light-catching effect; often the bases of bowls sported panel cuts or other devices to soften the transition from stem to bowl (cat. no. 97). By adapting the glasscutter's art to tableware, the English glass industry responded to the new interest in classicism that was sweeping England. Engraving styles began to change, too, and by the 1780s a new vocabulary had emerged. Delicate beaded chains and swags or floral festoons and garlands were now symmetrically disposed around the rim of a wineglass bowl.

That Lazarus Isaac was familiar with the changing styles is evident from his notice that he would cut the stems of wineglasses "in diamonds." Stiegel's determination to compete with imported table glass, most of which was English, would have dictated that he provide his market with drinking glasses of both cut and twisted stem styles, with bowls engraved with the new neoclassical motifs as well as in the naturalistic rococo manner. With Isaac on staff he was able to do so. Sales records indicate that wineglasses, decanters, and bottles were among the items Isaac engraved for Stiegel.

Two glasses survive that attest to Stiegel's achievements in decorated glass. The first is a large goblet or wineglass inscribed to commemorate the marriage of Stiegel's daughter Elizabeth to William Old, Jr., on March 23, 1773, and handed down in the Stiegel family (cat. no. 93). The engraving may be viewed as the handiwork of Isaac, who was in Manheim by early July, only a few months after the wedding ceremony.[86] The other glass is an impressive covered goblet made as a presentation piece for Emmanuel Carpenter (cat. no. 96). Its curious blend of German and English stylistic features lends credence to its Manheim attribution. In form, this goblet bears a resemblance to the traditional German pokal (fig. 13), a covered vessel with a tallish stem and capacious bowl. Documentary evidence indicates that some large English goblets and tumblers were meant to have lids, but the handful that survive suggest this was not common, especially by 1770. Certainly the angle-knop faceted stem and the cutting around the bowl have a precedent in several English glasses of about 1760.[87]

Carpenter was a leading citizen of Lancaster County, serving for sixteen years as the county's representative to the Pennsylvania Assembly. The sentiment expressed on the goblet leaves little doubt that it was a gift to Carpenter from a grateful constituent; indeed, it may have been a gift from Stiegel himself, because one of the first matters to be discussed in Carpenter's final session of 1771–72 was Stiegel's petition for support from the legislative body for his achievement of bringing the manufacture of flint glass to "such a Degree of Perfection as may prove advantageous to the Public." The assembly records do not state who presented the petition, but it may well have been Carpenter. Although the assembly tabled the matter, Stiegel's petition did receive favorable if nominal action in the fall of 1772. It would have been fitting that Stiegel present his supporter the following year with an example of his new, stylishly decorated glass, as proof that the assembly's support was not ill founded.

With the attribution of these two decorated glasses to Manheim's final years, and specifically to the hand of the engraver Lazarus Isaac, certain characteristics can be put forward as evidence of Manheim production and as a basis for additional attributions.

It is significant that these engraved glasses in the English style bear no relation whatsoever to the traditional "Stiegel-type" glasswares with their crude, shallow engraving and stylized tulips and baskets of flowers. Of course, it was the obvious German character of those wares that led the early students of American glass to link them with Stiegel on account of his German workers, his "flowerer," and his location in the heart of Pennsylvania-German country. However, Stiegel's records prove that no engraver of German or Bohemian origin practiced his art at Manheim, and Isaac's sharply different English style is well demonstrated by the Old and Carpenter goblets. No documentation exists to associate Stiegel with the engraved glasses of continental European style, but that they were popular export items sent to the post-Revolutionary American market is well documented.[88]

The Stiegel Legacy

Stiegel had but a short time to savor the success of his luxury decorated glass. By the end of 1774 the factory was shut down and Stiegel himself committed briefly to debtor's prison. His determination to make flint glass led to his downfall, because the cost of converting the factory and enlarging the work force was well beyond his means. As a land speculator and developer of the town of Manheim, partner in the Elizabeth Furnace and Charming Forge, and proprietor of the glassworks,

Fig. 13. *Covered goblet*. German, Saxony, about 1730. Blown, cut, and engraved colorless glass. H. 11⅞ in (30.2 cm). The Art Institute of Chicago, gift of Julius and Augusta N. Rosenwald, 1927.1244. ©The Art Institute of Chicago. All rights reserved.

Stiegel was already overextended. When he tried to liquidate his holdings he was offered but a fraction of their value, so he mortgaged his properties heavily in order to finance the glassworks expansion. Stiegel turned to the legislature for help in making up his losses. Receiving only token support from that quarter, he initiated a lottery as a means of raising capital, a scheme he said had originated with numerous "Wellwishers to this Beneficial Manufactory" who relished the opportunity to "shew their Zeal of Promoting the same."[89] Records show, however, that the lottery was an abysmal disappointment; Stiegel's creditors could not be forestalled any longer.

Stiegel's original plan for the glassworks, which emphasized utilitarian wares and a sideline of German-style tablewares, seems to have been successful within the Pennsylvania-German market. He may have lost that market, however, when he decided to cater to the urban taste for English wares.

Although the records are incomplete after 1769, it is obvious that sales of his "American Flint Glass" in the cities did not meet Stiegel's expectations. Exactly how the Manheim products did not meet the public's expectations is not clear. Certainly Stiegel had done his utmost to match the quality and style of popular imports: he achieved the lead oxide composition and offered a range of color, form, and decoration comparable to that of English imports. Indeed, the very difficulty of distinguishing Stiegel's glass from contemporary imports is perhaps the greatest testimony to its technical success.

The identification of Stiegel glass will most likely remain problematical, given the complexity of the factory's history. For his tablewares Martin Greiner would have worked from a memory of German glass rather than from German glass present in the colonies, but his style could also have been influenced by English imports and by the work of colleagues who had come to Manheim from New Jersey. The English artisans, on the other hand, were fresh to these shores; as the Old goblet with its fashionable twist stem attests, they well understood the styles with which they were to compete. With its German overtones, however, the Carpenter presentation piece must have been tailored to the man it was to honor.

Quite naturally, the colonial glass industry did not attract the most skillful craftsmen from either Britain or the Continent. The engraving of Lazarus Isaac, for example, met only average standards of English production in both vocabulary and execution. On one occasion, Stiegel confessed, "my workmen are such bunglers."[90] This level of craftsmanship, combined with the uncertain performance of raw materials and fuels, made it hard for Stiegel as well as other manufacturers to reach and maintain the quality they desired.

Throughout his advertising campaign for "American Flint Glass," the Pennsylvania manfacturer pinned his hopes on "the glorious spirit of patriotism" within the consumer, investor, and legislator.[91] Dissatisfied as they may have been with Great Britain's policies, however, the colonists were reluctant to abandon English goods. Whether this was the result of habit or thoughtful choice is not known. Given the rhetoric of the pre-Revolutionary era, Stiegel cannot be blamed for his overambitious assessment of the colonial market. Later glassmakers would follow his path in the same vain hope that the American consumer truly wanted independence from foreign manufacturers, and, like Stiegel, they would continue to be disappointed. Moved by the same vision as Stiegel, entrepreneurs hastened to build or expand glass factories when the War of 1812 interrupted trade with Great Britain, but half of America's glasshouses failed between 1815 and 1820.

In setting out to produce bottle and window glass using German-trained glassblowers, Stiegel was following much the same course as other American glass manufacturers, but in his commitment to making table glass in the English manner, the Pennsylvania ironmaster boldly trod new ground. He can be credited with founding the American table glass industry, and in Manheim's peculiar mix of German and English traditions can be seen the beginnings of an American style. When Stiegel's glassblowers left to find employment elsewhere, they carried their knowledge and experience with them. Much has been made of the "Stiegel tradition" over the years, but it is a legacy that will only be fully appreciated as more objects come to light that can be attributed with confidence to this pioneer venture in manufacturing "American Flint Glass."

NOTES

For their assistance and advice, I am grateful to Bert Denker, Rachel Russell, Lynne Stair, Jonathan Coxe, Lynn Springer Roberts, Jessie McNab, Linda Stanley, and David Cassedy.

1. New Jersey glass manufacturer Richard Wistar to Daniel Taylor of Bristol, October 21, 1760, Richard Wistar Letterbook (microfilm), Joseph Downs Manuscript and Microfilm Collection, Winterthur Museum Library.

2. R. J. Charleston, "Pottery, Porcelain and Glass," in *The Connoisseur's Complete Period Guides*, ed. Ralph Edwards and L. G. G. Ramsey (1956–58; reprint, New York: Bonanza Books, 1968), pp. 122–23.

3. Arlene Palmer, "Glass Production in Eighteenth-Century America: The Wistarburgh Enterprise," *Winterthur Portfolio* 11 (1976): 77.

4. Ibid., pp. 75–101.

5. R. J. Charleston, "English Glass-Making and Its Spread from the XVIIth to the Middle of the XIXth Century," *Annales du 1er Congrès des "Journées Internationales du Verre"* (Liège) 1960:155–72.

6. The emergence in Norway of a distinctive style combining elements of both the German and the English traditions may in some ways parallel the Stiegel phenomenon, but a comparative study must await further documentation of Manheim products. See Ada Buch Polak, *Gammelt Norsk Glass* (Oslo: Gyldendal Norsk Forlag, 1953), pp. 223–32, and Ada Polak, "The 'Ip Olufsen Weyse' Illustrated Price-List of 18th-Century Norwegian Glass," *Journal of Glass Studies* 11 (1969): 86–104.

7. I. Daniel Rupp, *History of Lancaster County* (Lancaster, Pa.: Gilbert Hills, 1844), p. 347.

8. Fifteen volumes of H. W. Stiegel's records survive in the Historical Society of Pennsylvania (hereafter HSP). Study of these records in preparation for this exhibition yielded information that substantially contradicts much of what Frederick William Hunter published about the operation, laborers, and products of Stiegel's factory in *Stiegel Glass* (1914; reprint, New York: Dover, 1950).

9. Time and space do not permit a consideration of Stiegel's iron products, though like the glassware, they also underwent a dramatic stylistic change in 1769.

10. Rupp suggested this motive in his *History*, pp. 347–48. Hunter misinterpreted the records of shipments of bar iron from Elizabeth Furnace to London in 1763 as voyages made by Stiegel to learn about the glass industry and to secure workmen (Hunter, *Stiegel Glass*, p. 46).

11. See Arlene Palmer Schwind, "The Glassmakers of Early America," in *The Craftsman in Early America*, ed. Ian M. G. Quimby (New York: W. W. Norton, for the Henry Francis du Pont Winterthur Museum, 1984), pp. 164–65.

12. Stiegel may have read about the arrival of Greiner and his team because news of the event was published in the Philadelphia newspaper, *Pennsylvania Journal*, August 6, 1752.

13. M. Earnest et al., Draft agreement with Johan Martin Greiner, New-York Historical Society. Greiner also made "all sorts of Bottles from 1 Quart to 3 Gallons and upwards, as also a Variety of other Glass Ware too tedious to mention" (*New York Gazette*, October 14, 1754).

14. The Newfoundland works was advertised for sale in July 1762, and by May 1763 it was functioning as a tavern (*New York Gazette*, July 22, 1762, and *New York Mercury*, May 23, 1763).

15. Governor Henry Moore to Lords of Trade, January 12, 1767, quoted in John Romeyn Brodhead, ed., *Documents Relative to the Colonial History of the State of New-York*, vol. 7 (Albany, N.Y.: Weed, Parsons & Co., 1856), pp. 888–89.

16. Palmer, "Glass Production," p. 78. A Gratinger is also mentioned in the Wistar records.

17. The book Hunter cites (p. 43) is dated September 1764, not 1763. The same notice appeared in the German paper, the *Staatsbote*, February 4, 1765.

18. Journal, Ledger B, and Elizabeth Furnace Store Daybook, Stiegel Records, HSP. In computing the numbers of vessels made in a given blowing season, I found that Stiegel's totals were often inaccurate. The numbers cited here are the corrected totals.

19. Olive R. Jones, *Cylindrical English Wine and Beer Bottles, 1735–1850* (Ottawa: Environment Canada—Parks, National Historic Parks and Sites Branch, 1986), pp. 107–14.

20. "Flatt[en]ing arches" are mentioned in a March 14, 1771, entry, Ledger C, Stiegel Records, HSP.

21. For an illustration of the cylinder process, see Denis Diderot, *Encyclopédie, ou Dictionnaire raisonné des sciences, des arts, et des métiers*, 17 vols. (Paris: Briasson [etc.], 1751–65), vol. 4, pls. 36–38. The crown process is well illustrated in William Cooper, *The Crown Glass Cutter and Glazier's Manual* (Edinburgh: Oliver & Boyd, 1835), pp. 23–34.

22. See, for example, the account book of Philadelphia merchants Christopher and Charles Marshall, Joseph Downs Manuscript and Microfilm Collection, Winterthur Museum Library.

23. John Elliott & Co., operating a rival glassworks at Kensington, Philadelphia, advertised for "A person who understands the making of Window Glass in the English method," but there is no evidence that they found one (*Pennsylvania Journal*, December 7, 1774).

24. Arlene M. Palmer, "Benjamin Franklin and the Wistarburg Glassworks," *Antiques* 105, no. 1 (January 1974): 208–9, figs. 3, 4.

25. Daybook, p. 122, Stiegel Records, HSP.

26. March 8, 1769, Ledger B, p. 13, Stiegel Records, HSP.

27. Herbert Kühnert, *Urkundenbuch zur Thüringischen Glashüttengeschichte* (Wiesbaden: Franz Steiner Verlag, 1973), pp. 187–95, 394–95. For an enamel-painted jug of this shape dated 1684, see tafel 5, no. 8. That the form was made elsewhere in Germany is seen by a green glass one with a thumbpiece handle in Karl Greiner, *Die Glashütten im Wurttemberg* (Wiesbaden: Franz Steiner Verlag, 1971), pl. 13, no. 30.

28. A dated 1760 example made in Bristol for Martha Goldham is shown in Cleo Witt, Cyril Weeden, and Arlene Palmer Schwind, *Bristol Glass* (Bristol: Bristol & West Building Society in conjunction with City of Bristol Museums and Art Gallery, 1984), pl. 34. For Continental examples see *Spanish Glass in the Hermitage* (Leningrad: Aurora Art Publications, 1970), nos. 220, 221.

29. Hugh Tait, *The Golden Age of Venetian Glass* (London: British Museum Publications, 1979), pp. 108–9, no. 174.

30. Palmer, "Glass Production," pp. 91–92. Arlene M. Palmer, *The Wistarburgh Glassworks: The Beginning of Jersey Glassmaking* (Alloway, N.J.: Alloway Township Bicentennial Committee, 1976), pp. 20–23.

31. Neither of these sugar bowls bears any relationship to the documented New Geneva objects, nor do they relate to the wares made at New Bremen, where New Geneva workers had previously been employed. The documented New Geneva goblet is in Helen and George S. McKearin, *Two Hundred Years of American Blown Glass* (New York: Bonanza, 1950), pl. 69, pp. 258–59.

32. Donald B. Harden et al., *Glass of the Caesars* (Milan: Olivetti, for Corning Museum of Glass, British Museum, and Romisch-Germanisches Museum, 1987), pp. 116–17; D. B. Harden et al., *Masterpieces of Glass* (London: Trustees of the British Museum, 1968), p. 141, no. 184.

33. May 11, 1769, King of Prussia Tavern Accounts, HSP. What may be an eighteenth-century American glass horn for gunpowder is illustrated in *Antiques* 6, no. 2 (July 1924): 20.

34. Keith Vincent, *Nailsea Glass* (London: David & Charles, 1975), p. 93, fig. 102; Harold Newman, *An Illustrated Dictionary of Glass* (London: Thames & Hudson, 1977), p. 248. Each glassmaker who paraded in Newcastle upon Tyne in 1823 "carried a glass ornament in his hand. Among the articles in the procession were many swords; a bugle; a windmill at work; . . ." (*Newcastle Courant*, September 20, 1823, quoted in Ursula Ridley, "The History of Glass Making on Tyneside," *Circle of Glass Collectors Paper*, no. 122 [January 1961], p. 5).

35. See an example in the High Museum of Art, Atlanta.

36. Polak, "The 'Ip Olufsen Weyse,'" p. 98, fig. 31.

37. Minutes of the Provincial Council of Pennsylvania, *Colonial Records*, vol. 9 (Harrisburg, Pa.: Theo. Fenn & Co., 1852), p. 354.

38. Letter to William Franklin, March 13, 1768, in *The Papers of Benjamin Franklin*, vol. 15, ed. William B. Willcox (New Haven, Conn.: Yale University Press, 1972), p. 77.

39. "The Townshend Revenue Act, June 29, 1767," in *Documents of American History*, ed. Henry Steele Commager, 7th ed. (New York: Appleton-Century-Crofts, 1963), p. 63; Robert Middlekauff, *The Glorious Cause: The American Revolution, 1763–1789*, vol. 2 of *The Oxford History of the United States* (New York: Oxford University Press, 1982), pp. 142–51.

40. Middlekauff, *The Glorious Cause*, p. 157. There was a glassworks in operation at Germantown (Braintree), Massachusetts. See Kenneth M. Wilson, *New England Glass and Glassmaking* (New York: Thomas Y. Crowell, 1972), pp. 41–51.

41. Advertisement, *Pennsylvania Chronicle*, July 31, 1769, reproduced in Palmer, "Glass Production," p. 85, fig. 4.

42. Charleston, "English Glass-Making and Its Spread," p. 157.

43. Back pages of Ledger C, no. 3, 1773, Stiegel Records, HSP.

44. *Pennsylvania Journal*, July 5, 1770.

45. *Pennsylvania Packet*, November 11, 1771, quoted in George S. and Helen McKearin, *American Glass* (New York: Crown, 1941), pp. 95–96. The English background of these men has not been tracked down. Glassmakers named Green worked in the flint tableware factories near Dudley in the eighteenth century; see Francis Buckley, "The Glasshouses of Dudley and Worcester," *Journal of the Society of Glass Technology* 11 (1927): 287–93. In 1755 an agent sent by the Norwegian glass industry was convicted for "seducing 7 persons, artificers in the glass manufacture to depart this kingdom. The penalty for every person seduced . . . is £500 and 12 months' imprisonment" (*The Gentleman's Magazine*, July 19, 1755, quoted in Charleston, "English Glassmaking and Its Spread," p. 158).

46. For example, the appeal of the merchants of Bristol, a major glassmaking center, published in the *London Chronicle*, March 14, 1769, quoted in Fred Junkin Hinkhouse, *The Preliminaries of the American Revolution as Seen in the English Press, 1763–1775* (New York: Columbia University Press, 1926), p. 152.

47. *Pennsylvania Journal*, July 5, 1770.

48. *Pennsylvania Archives*, 8th ser., vol. 8 (January 7, 1771–September 26, 1776), ed. Charles F. Hoban (1935), pp. 6681–82. Allman's background has not been traced; that he was English is known from Joseph Leacock, who employed him at the Kensington Glassworks in 1771 (Letter to John Nicholson, December 23, 1794, John Nicholson Collection, Manuscript Group 96, Division of History and Archives, Pennsylvania Historical and Museum Commission, Harrisburg).

49. August 30, 1771, Daybook, Stiegel Records, HSP.

50. William Rego made all the "flint pots." The February 24, 1774, entry in the daybook records, "This day where [sic] set the 4 large Flint pots the Hoods being taken of[f] them for to melt botle mettal in them." In 1781 the royal glassworks at St.-Louis achieved lead glass using wood-fired furnaces; James Barrelet, *La verrerie en France de l'époque gallo romaine à nos jours*, Arts, Styles et Techniques, ed. Norbert Dufourcq (Paris: Librairie Larousse, 1953), pp. 108–9.

51. American Philosophical Society, *Proceedings, 1744–1838* (Philadelphia, 1884), p. 65. *Pennsylvania Journal*, June 27, 1771. At least one member of the committee, David Rittenhouse, was already a satisfied customer of Stiegel's, having purchased a barometer from him (G. A. R. Goyle, "Contemporaneous Estimations of Stiegel Glass," *Antiques* 13, no. 3 [March 1928]: 225).

52. *South Carolina Gazette*, July 8, 1771; *F. F. Bristol Journal*, August 31, 1771, quoted in *Glass*, July 1934, p. 267.

53. Letter, Logan Papers, vol. 38, HSP.

54. *Virginia Gazette*, August 22, 1771, reference courtesy Museum of Early Southern Decorative Arts, Winston-Salem, N.C.

55. For this period there are no accounts for the output of individual workers. For the 1769–70 blast there is a weekly accounting of the forms and quantities of tablewares made and sold. Information about production when full-lead glass was made comes primarily from newspaper advertisements and the occasional sales record.

56. *Pennsylvania Gazette*, June 4, 1772; *Pennsylvania Packet*, July 6, 1772.

57. Charleston, "English Glass-Making and Its Spread," p. 161.

58. R. J. Charleston, Foreword to *Gilding the Lily: Rare Forms of Decoration on English Glass of the Later 18th Century* (London: Delomosne & Son, 1978), pp. 2–3.

59. The factory record books contain no mention of enameled glass, but in one instance, on December 28, 1771, the factory purchased "Colours" from Alexander Bartram for 7s 6d (see Daybook, Stiegel Records, HSP). No one is described as an enameler; the men Hunter designated as such are in fact credited with construction-related tasks at Manheim.

60. Stiegel purchased 89 pounds of "Magness" from Ludwig Lauman, October 7, 1771 (Legal Accounts, Jasper Yeates Papers, Division of History and Archives, Pennsylvania State Museum and Historical Commission).

61. There are Venetian glasses of the late fifteenth century that have enamel-painted stylized flowers within pincered or "nipt" diamonds. See Tait, *The Golden Age*, pl. 1, p. 28, and Giovanni Mariacher, *Italian Blown Glass* (New York: McGraw-Hill, 1961), pl. 34.

62. Purchased by Reynoldus Keller in 1774 (Daybook, Stiegel Records, HSP).

63. Advertisement of Middleton and Brailsford, *South Carolina Gazette*, May 20, 1752.

64. *Gilding the Lily*, pp. 11, 17.

65. Newman, *An Illustrated Dictionary*, p. 97; Gustav E. Pazaurek, "A German View of Early American Glass," part I, *Antiques* 21, no. 4 (April 1932): 164, 167.

66. Arlene Palmer Schwind, "English Glass Imports in New York, 1770–1790," *Journal of Glass Studies* 25 (1983): 184. Tisdale advertisement, *Connecticut Courant*, June 30, 1788.

67. Sample invoice of Josiah Perrin, Liverpool, June 2, 1774, sent to Frederick Rhinelander; this sort sold for 6s 6d a dozen. Rhinelander purchased sugars of a "low, flat shape" on several occasions (Letter and Order Book, Frederick Rhinelander Papers, New-York Historical Society).

68. Thomas Betts sold champagne decanters in London as early as 1755; see W. A. Thorpe, *A History of English and Irish Glass*, vol. 1 (London: Medici Society, 1929), p. 308. In New York, James Gilliland sold them in 1763 (*New York Mercury*, April 4, 1763).

69. This new-fashion decanter may only have been introduced a year or so before, as indicated by an English advertisement of 1768 for the "newest fashion" decanters. Rhinelander purchased Bristol-made sugar-loaf decanters in 1770, and by 1781 he was offering a variant described as "new sugar loaf." See Schwind, "English Glass Imports," p. 183.

70. Olive R. Jones and E. Ann Smith, *Glass of the British Military, ca. 1755–1820* (Ottawa: Parks Canada, Environment Canada, National Historic Parks and Sites Branch, 1985), p. 28, fig. 18.

71. Price-List of English Glass, Whitefriars Glassworks Collection Museum of London, reference courtesy Wendy Evans.

72. Advertisement of Stephen Higginson, *Essex Gazette*, September 14–21, 1773; Ellery notice, *Connecticut Courant*, October 15–22, 1771; Barrel advertisement, *Boston Evening Post*, October 26, 1772.

73. Polak, "The 'Ip Olufsen Weyse,'" p. 104.

74. An advertisement for English glass sold in Boston includes "round and oval Pillar Cut Salts, and bonnet ditto" (*Boston News-Letter*, November 28, 1771, in George Francis Dow, *The Arts and Crafts in New England, 1704–1775* [Topsfield, Mass.: Wayside Press, 1927], p. 94).

75. Polak, "The 'Ip Olufsen Weyse,'" p. 97, fig. 25.

76. Derek C. Davis and Keith Middlemas, *Coloured Glass* (London: Herbert Jenkins, 1968), p. 48.

77. Timothy Barret, *Pennsylvania Chronicle*, February 22–29, 1768.

78. Nicholas B. Wainwright, *Colonial Grandeur in Philadelphia: The House and Furniture of General John Cadwalader* (Philadelphia: Historical Society of Pennsylvania, 1964), pp. 55, 82.

79. *Pennsylvania Gazette*, June 20, 1771, and *New York Gazette and Weekly Mercury*, July 9, 1771.

80. R. J. Charleston, *English Glass and the Glass Used in England, circa 400–1940* (London: George Allen and Unwin, 1984), p. 154.

81. *Pennsylvania Packet*, May 17, 1773. The contract is in the collection of the Hershey Museum of American Life, Hershey, Pennsylvania; it is published in facsimile in Hunter, *Stiegel Glass*, after p. 72. Although his name appears there as Isaacs, it is more often recorded as Isaac.

82. William Logan to Cornelius Frye, [May 17], 1773, Smith Papers, Library Company of Philadelphia.

83. Old Bailey Sessions Papers, *The Whole Proceedings on the King's Commission of the Peace . . . for the City of London . . . held at Justice Hall in the Old Bailey*, II, pt. IV (London: S. Bladon, 1769): 109–10, case no. 126. His crime was stealing a linen handkerchief valued at ten shillings. The Old Bailey records reveal that another Londoner of the same name was sentenced to transportation for stealing a 24-pound cheese in February 1773, but there is no evidence that the sentence was carried out.

84. On the contract with Stiegel, Isaac signed his name in Hebrew. There were a number of Jewish glass decorators working in England in the eighteenth century, the most famous of whom was Isaac Jacobs of Bristol. An Isaac Isaacs, possibly a relation, is recorded as a glass engraver in Bristol in 1775. See Zoë Josephs, "Jewish Glass-makers," *Transactions, Jewish Historical Society of England* 25 (1977): 107–19.

85. In an invoice of Thomas Betts, London, 1757, twist-stem wines sold for six pence each, while wines with cut stems were two shillings (quoted in Charleston, *English Glass*, p. 178).

86. "The Furnace Team came home this Evening & brought the Glasscutter & his tools & furniture from Philadelphia" (July 3, 1773, Daybook, Stiegel Records, HSP). There is no evidence of another engraver ever working at Manheim.

87. Covered tumblers were among the forms imported from Bristol by Frederick Rhinelander; see Schwind, "English Glass Imports," p. 181. For an English covered goblet with twist stem, see Ada Polak, *Glass: Its Makers and Its Public* (London: Weidenfeld & Nicolson, 1975), p. 141, fig. 60. Charleston, *English Glass*, pl. 50d, f, illustrates the English angle-knop faceted stem.

88. The illustrated trade catalogue of a Bohemian glass manufacturer proves that in spite of their naïve charm such wares were standard commercial products. They were exported to America in great numbers in the post-Revolutionary years and again in the twentieth century, when they could be sold as "Stiegel-type." See Arlene Palmer Schwind, "Pennsylvania-German Glass," in *Arts of the Pennsylvania Germans* (New York: W. W. Norton for the Henry Francis du Pont Winterthur Museum, 1983), p. 207.

89. Letter to John Dickinson, June 22, 1772, Logan Papers, vol. 38, p. 89, HSP.

90. Letter to John Dickinson, December 2, 1772, Logan Papers, vol. 38, p. 91, HSP. Schwind, "The Glassmakers," pp. 163–67.

91. *Pennsylvania Journal*, July 5, 1770.

Catalogue Objects

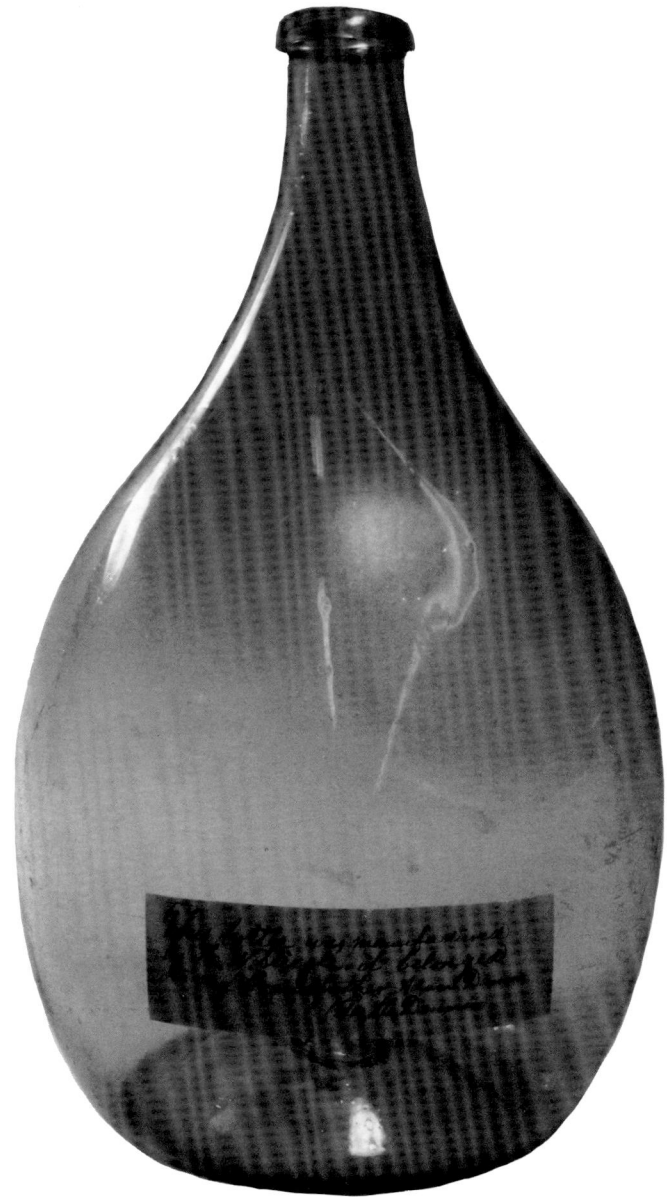

83. *Bottle*
American
Possibly glassworks of H. W. Stiegel, Manheim, Pa., 1764–74
Blown green glass
H. 13¼ in (33.7 cm)
Hershey Museum of American Life, Hershey, Pa., 75.009.064

83. Bottle / 84. Bottle

It was the technology of England's coal-fired furnaces that made possible the sturdy type of bottle shown here (cat. no. 84). Glass manufacturers adapted their furnaces to coal in the early 1600s, but the successful formula for a bottle glass high in silica was not developed until midcentury.[1] From the squat, globular bottles of that era, the English bottle changed in shape over time; by the 1730s a cylindrical dip mold was widely used to achieve the straight sides desirable for binning and storing wines. As seen here, the typical English bottle in the 1760s had a fairly broad, straight-sided body. Its tapered cylindrical neck had an applied string rim near the lip and the bottom had a high, dome-shaped push-up with a large sand pontil mark.[2] Archaeological evidence, as well as the written record, shows that thousands of English bottles of this kind were shipped to colonial America. Consumers both here and in England paid more to have their bottles personalized with a seal bearing their name, initials, or coat of arms, and often a date. This one was made for Sidney Breese (1709–67), a New York merchant.

The technical and stylistic differences between these two bottles account for the attribution of catalogue number 83 to the Stiegel enterprise. Its pale green, transparent glass is thinly blown, unlike the thicker, dark green glass of the English import. Moreover, the manufacturing details indicate that its maker was not familiar with the production methods of English glasshouses. The lip is turned or folded over and lacks the applied string rim seen in the English bottle. Its push-up is narrow and irregular, and a blowpipe, used in lieu of a pontil, left a thick, ring-shaped mark on the bottom. In its bulbous, almost misshapen body, this bottle pays no

84. *Bottle*
English, about 1765
Blown dark olive green glass; applied seal with relief inscription *Sidney / Breese / 1765*
H. 11¼ in (28.6 cm)
The Henry Francis du Pont Winterthur Museum, Winterthur, Del., 65.2337

court to the symmetrical and straight-sided British bottle. In short, it is exactly what would be expected of German workmen charged with the task of producing large quantities of these utilitarian forms.

Although no mention of seal bottles occurs in the Stiegel records or advertisements, the lack of a seal does not enhance the Manheim attribution of catalogue number 83. Seal bottles in the English manner were made at the Wistarburgh glassworks in New Jersey, even though they were never advertised or mentioned in any records of that factory. In 1754 the New Windsor, New York, glassworks notified "all Gentlemen that wants Bottles of any size with their Names on them."[3] Since Stiegel's chief gaffer, Martin Greiner, was probably responsible for the seal bottles made in New York, it is reasonable to assume that seal bottles could have been made at Manheim. That development, however, may only have occurred after 1769, when Stiegel had crystallized his goal of providing glass equal in style and quality to British imports.

1. Eleanor S. Godfrey, *The Development of English Glassmaking, 1560–1640* (Chapel Hill: University of North Carolina Press, 1975), pp. 229–30. R. J. Charleston, *English Glass and the Glass Used in England, circa 400–1940* (London: George Allen and Unwin, 1984), pp. 94–96.
2. For a visual chronology of English bottle shapes see Ivor Noël Hume, *A Guide to Artifacts of Colonial America* (New York: Alfred A. Knopf, 1970), pp. 63–68. Olive Jones, "Glass Bottle Push-Ups and Pontil Marks," *Historical Archaeology* 5 (1971): 69.
3. *New York Gazette* (October 14, 1754), quoted in Rita S. Gottesman, comp., *The Arts and Crafts in New York, 1726–1776* (1938; reprint, New York: Da Capo Press, 1970), p. 93. A Wistarburgh seal bottle, now in the Corning Museum of Glass, is illustrated in Arlene Palmer, "Glass Production in Eighteenth-Century America: The Wistarburgh Enterprise," *Winterthur Portfolio* 11 (1976): 86, fig. 6, and was featured on the cover of *The Glass Club Bulletin*, no. 155 (Spring 1988).

85. *Covered sugar bowl*
American
Possibly glassworks of H. W. Stiegel, Manheim, Pa., 1764–74
Blown colorless nonlead glass
H. 7 in (17.8 cm)
The Corning Museum of Glass, Corning, N.Y., 50.4.4

85. Covered sugar bowl
86. Covered sugar bowl

Blown of green glass and featuring a large swan finial on a domed, inset cover, catalogue number 86 well represents the style of sugar bowls made at glasshouses throughout Germany in the seventeenth and eighteenth centuries. Whether plain or pattern-molded, these bowls had intricate applied and tooled decoration, with the swan especially favored as the crowning ornament.[1] Immigrant glass craftsmen carried the tradition to colonial America.

Martin Greiner, who emigrated from Saxe-Weimar in 1752, was making green glass sugar bowls in the

86. *Covered sugar bowl*
Probably German, 1750–1800
Blown pale green glass
H. 7⅞ in (20 cm)
The Metropolitan Museum of Art, New York, gift of Henry G. Marquand, 1883, 83.7.17

1760s for Stiegel and the example shown in figure 2 (p. 207) may be his work. The Stiegel records prove that Greiner also made some colorless glass in the 1760s; the use of cullet (broken glass) to achieve this may explain the low amounts of lead found in two of four examples related to catalogue number 85.[2] Stylistically, the American sugar bowls do not reflect the influence of English imports, unless the foot of figure 2 is viewed as an interpretation of the popular English scalloped foot, cut or tooled (fig. 10, p. 218).

There is little doubt that such bowls were intended to hold lumps of sugar cut from the loaf, but why the form became so important in colonial America and what was the symbolism, if any, of the ubiquitous swan finial remain to be explained.

1. The rings on this bowl recall late medieval *waldglas* and are not recorded in American production: see Rudolf von Strasser, *Masterpieces of Germanic Glass, 15th–19th Centuries* (Neenah, Wis.: John Nelson Bergstrom Art Center and Museum, 1979), p. 21, no. 6.

2. The other bowls are at Winterthur (59.30.1, 59.3028), the Metropolitan Museum of Art (30.120.211), and the Henry Ford Museum of the Edison Institute (78.73.43). The swan finials appear to have been tooled by the same hand. Four of the five bowls have the distinctive squared foot with pincered corners.

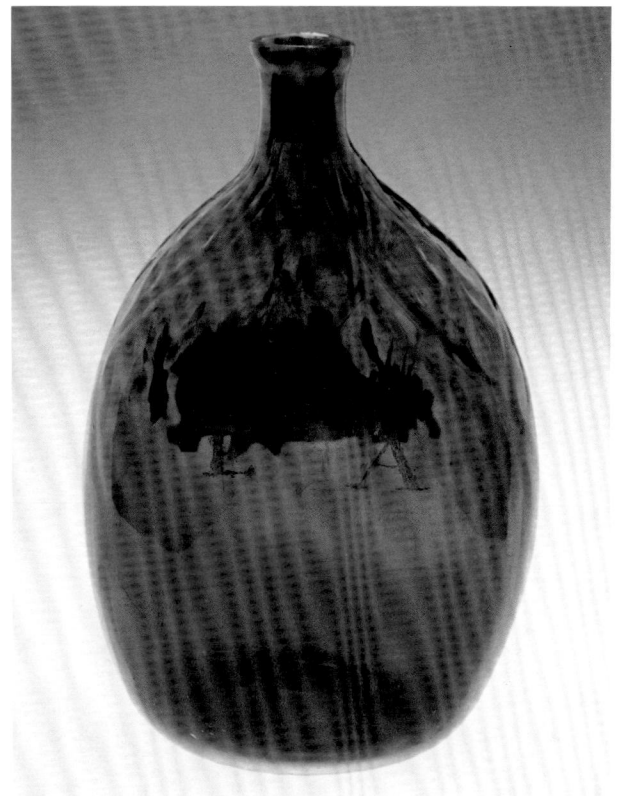

87. *Pocket bottle*
American
Attributed to the glassworks of H. W. Stiegel, Manheim, Pa., 1769–74
Blown amethyst glass, molded with diamond-daisy design; initials *E.A* engraved in diamond-point
H. 5½ in (14 cm)
Los Angeles County Museum of Art, Museum Associates Acquisition Fund, M.84.95

87. Pocket bottle / 88. Pocket bottle

Mold-blown bottles and flasks of floral design (cat. no. 88) were probably made as less expensive alternatives to glasswares cut with similar patterns.[1] Although their flowers seem out of scale for their size, such flasks were probably the inspiration for Stiegel's more restrained diamond-daisy (cat. no. 87) and daisy-in-hexagon patterns. However, the Continental model differs in technique from the American bottles in that it was made by the so-called half-post method, in which the gather or post was dipped again into the melting pot and covered part way with a second gather of glass. Catalogue number 88 is flatter and more ovoid in shape than its American counterparts and has a distinctive horizontal lip.

Several Stiegel pocket bottles are recorded in colorless glass, but the vast majority were made in amethyst (see fig. 6, p. 214). Although amethyst glass was made in central Europe (cat. no. 95), it may have been the growing taste for that color in England that influenced Stiegel. As containers for "spirituous beverages," pocket bottles were often colored so as to protect the contents from the adverse effects of light.

The well-known amethyst pocket bottles pattern-molded with ribs, diamonds, and floral patterns, represented here by catalogue number 87 and figure 6, probably constituted the 6,251 pocket bottles of "flint glass" which Stiegel's workers made between November 1769 and May 1770. No examples are known in lead glass, however, so the term flint was apparently used merely to indicate they were blown of refined colored glass rather than green bottle or window glass.

Of the many pocket bottles known, catalogue number 87 is the only one with a documented history.[2] It was originally owned by Elizabeth Shinn Armstrong (1748–1813) of Medford, New Jersey, and descended through her family.

1. Ludwig Moser, *Badisches Glas: Seine Hütten und Werkstätten* (Wiesbaden: Franz Steiner Verlag, 1969), tafel 9, no. 13.
2. Leslie Greene Bowman, "An Engraved Stiegel Pocket Bottle," *The Glass Club Bulletin*, no. 147 (Fall 1985): cover, pp. 3–5.

88. *Pocket bottle*
Probably South German, 1750–1800
Blown colorless glass, molded with four large daisies
H. 8⅞ in (22.5 cm)
Private collection

89. Cream jug / 90. Cream jug

With its cabriole legs, lion masks, and paw feet, this English creamer (cat. no. 90) parallels silver and ceramic designs of the second quarter of the eighteenth century.[1] That this shape was still being made in English glass in the 1770s is seen in a contemporary manufacturer's price list which included, at 6d each, "Milk Pots with 3 Legs." "Best" ones without legs were 4½d each, and tale ones of that form were 3½d.

Such English jugs doubtless inspired the production of American cream jugs like catalogue number 89. The variation in this example can be explained by the cross-influences of German and English glassmaking that affected Stiegel's production after 1769. With his move to create flint glass, Stiegel turned to fashionable English-style tableware forms, including "three-feeted creams." Stylistically sophisticated in form, this American creamer has traditional German embellishment in its swirl ribbing and waffle-pincered feet. Because similar pincering is seen in the finials of sugar bowls attributed to Wistarburgh, this feature can perhaps be traced to the influence of Wistar workers at Manheim.[2] Blown of nonlead green glass of the kind used for utilitarian ware, the creamer could have been described by Stiegel as "common."

1. For example, see Arnold R. Mountford, *The Illustrated Guide to Staffordshire Salt-Glazed Stoneware* (New York: Praeger, 1971), fig. 67.
2. Palmer, "Glass Production," pp. 91–92.

89. *Cream jug*
American
Probably glassworks of H. W. Stiegel, Manheim, Pa., 1769–74
Blown green nonlead glass, pattern-molded
H. 4½ in (11.4 cm)
Yale University Art Gallery, New Haven, Conn., The Mabel Brady Garvan Collection, 1930.1648

90. *Cream jug*
English, 1735–55
Blown colorless lead glass
H. 3¼ in (8.3 cm)
Collection of Lynne Stair

91. *Covered sugar bowl*
American
Possibly glassworks of H. W. Stiegel, Manheim, Pa., 1769–74
Blown colorless lead glass
H. 6⅝ in (16.8 cm)
Cincinnati Art Museum, bequest of Edith B. Tranter, 1951.501

92. *Covered sugar bowl*
English, 1760–1800
Blown blue lead glass, pattern-molded
H. 5½ in (14 cm)
Cincinnati Art Museum, bequest of Edith B. Tranter, 1951.352

91. Covered sugar bowl
92. Covered sugar bowl

The blue pattern-molded sugar bowl (cat. no. 92) is of the kind that has been attributed to Manheim for decades. Its particular 11-diamond-over-flute design, however, carries a mold defect that has been found in several glasses that have never left England. Hence, the attribution of that pattern to England is well established. Nevertheless, this was the type of blue, mold-blown sugar bowl that was imported to America in the second half of the eighteenth century and that Stiegel's blowers might have emulated.

Catalogue number 91 owes little to English style except its lead-formula composition, suggesting it was made at Manheim by German workers during the period after 1769–71, that is, after Stiegel had introduced the technology of lead glass. While its petaled foot may derive from English tradition (fig. 10, p. 218), the finial resembles the finials on Wistarburgh bowls. German examples prove the origin of that feature.[1]

1. Arlene M. Palmer, *The Wistarburgh Glassworks: The Beginning of Jersey Glassmaking* (Alloway, N.J.: Alloway Township Bicentennial Committee, 1976), pp. 21–23, figs. 14–16. Moser, *Badisches Glas*, tafel 35, no. 61.

Henry William Stiegel and American Flint Glass   233

93. *Goblet*
American
Attributed to the glassworks of H. W. Stiegel, Manheim, Pa., 1773–74
Blown colorless lead glass; white enamel-twist stem; wheel-engraved bowl with inscription *W & E / OLD*
H. 6¾ in (17.1 cm)
The Corning Museum of Glass, Corning, N.Y., partial gift of Roland C. and Sarah Katheryn Luther, Roland C. Luther III, Edwin C. Luther III, Ann Luther Dexter, 87.4.55

93. Goblet / 94. Goblet / 95. Tumbler

The identification of the "enamelled" glass Stiegel's agents advertised in 1772 is a subject of controversy. It has generally been assumed that the descriptions referred to enamel-painted nonlead glasswares of the Continental type. Charming but crudely painted designs occur frequently on colorless glass of central European origin, but as the tumbler shown here (cat. no. 95) demonstrates, colored glass was also decorated in this way. The date of 1740 on this tumbler indicates that such glass was made well before Stiegel's factory was in operation; other dated glasses prove that the tradition continued long into the nineteenth century.[1]

Because Stiegel's enameled glasses were made during the period of mixed English and German influences and experimentation with raw materials at his glasshouse, they should, in theory, differ visually or chemically from European prototypes. However, no examples of Continental-style enamel-painted glass of lead oxide composition are known. Tumblers with English inscriptions could be interpreted as evidence of the English influence at Manheim, but glasses with inscriptions in other languages seem to point instead to a manufacturer who was catering to specific foreign markets.[2] Finally, it is significant that an overwhelming majority of

234 Arlene Palmer

94. *Goblet*
English, dated 1760
Blown colorless lead glass; white enamel-twist stem; wheel-engraved bowl with inscription *M. S. July 25th 1760*
H. 7 in (17.8 cm)
The Philadelphia Museum of Art, bequest of George H. Lorimer, 38-23-7

95. *Tumbler*
Central European, dated 1740
Blown purple glass; enamel-painted decoration and inscription *Gott sei mit Dir alle zeit*
H. 2¹¹⁄₁₆ in (6.8 cm)
The Corning Museum of Glass, Corning, N.Y., The Charles Helme and Alice B. Strater Collection, 75.3.133

enamel-painted glasswares that have been published as "Stiegel-type" are shapes that are not those specified as enameled in the Stiegel advertisements.[3]

In eighteenth-century English usage, "enameled" referred to glasses with enamel-twist stems or to wares blown entirely of opaque white glass. "Painted" appears in the written sources and must describe glass like the tumbler shown here. Stiegel's contemporary in Philadelphia, Joseph Stansbury, offered "Painted, flower [engraved] and plain mugs" for sale, and Elizabeth Drinker bought "three painted glass muggs" in 1795.[4]

Stiegel's avowed purpose was to meet the demand for

English imports, so it makes sense to assume he would produce glass in the archetypal English style of the day, the twist-stem drinking glass (cat. no. 94; fig. 5, p. 213). A differentiation between "enamelled" wines and "twisted" wines can be read into the Cauffman and Fegan advertisement and may be explained by the suggestion that Stiegel also offered that other popular style of English stem, the air-twist. The production records offer no clarification of this point; wines described merely as "twisted" were sold to Joseph Welch in 1774.[5]

That opaque enamel-twist stems were indeed made at Manheim is shown by catalogue number 93, which is

Henry William Stiegel and American Flint Glass   235

the first documented Stiegel object to come to light. Made to celebrate the 1773 marriage of Stiegel's daughter Elizabeth to William Old,[6] this large drinking glass has an ovoid bowl that varies somewhat in profile and proportion from the English standard. The twist-stem, with its pair of loosely spiraled tapes within a ten-ply spiral band, is not perfectly executed but is well within the norm for enamel-twist stems. As in English glasses, the foot is conical and has a rough pontil mark on the underside.

Stiegel's English-trained glass engraver, Lazarus Isaac, was practicing his craft at Manheim within a few months of the wedding in 1773. English precedent for combining rose engraving with an inscription is seen in catalogue number 94. Isaac's rendition, somewhat cruder, nevertheless proclaims that English inheritance.[7] Closely associated with vessels made for supporters of the Jacobite movement in the 1740s, the rose motif continued to be used long after its political significance had faded. As most often executed, the English rose has a six-petal outline with a center defined by polished circles around cross-hatching. Isaac's is a more naturalistic, many-petaled flower, an effect achieved with linear bars placed at right angles and coming right to the crosshatched center. He has the same triple fronds extending between the outermost petals that are evident in the English goblet.[8] Rose-engraved drinking glasses were not commonly inscribed. The branches on the Old goblet almost form a heart around the inscription, a conceit highly appropriate for the occasion.

1. For example, a flask dated 1812 in the Bennington Museum, Bennington, Vt.
2. Axel von Saldern, "Baron Stiegel and 18th Century Enamel Glass," *Antiques* 80, no. 3 (September 1961): 232–35.
3. Wines, Mason wines, smelling bottles, cruets, three-footed creams, three-footed salts, mustards, and servers are the forms available "enameled."
4. Stansbury advertisement, *Pennsylvania Evening Post*, April 30, 1776. Elizabeth Drinker Diary, HSP.
5. September 31 [*sic*], 1774, Daybook, Stiegel Records, HSP.
6. Sheldon D. Butts, "The Stiegel Old Wedding Goblet," *The Glass Club Bulletin*, no. 139 (Winter 1983): cover, pp. 1–2.
7. R. J. Charleston, "Some English Glass-Engravers: Late 18th–Early 19th Century," in *The Glass Circle 4*, ed. R. J. Charleston, Wendy Evans, and Ada Polak (London: Gresham Books, 1982) pp. 4–19.
8. G. B. Seddon, "The Jacobite Engravers," in *The Glass Circle 3*, ed. R. J. Charleston, Wendy Evans, and Ada Polak (London: Gresham Books, 1979), pp. 40–78. A many-petaled example is shown on pp. 74–75.

96. Covered goblet / 97. Covered goblet

The covered goblet was a presentation form more commonly seen on the Continent and in Continental traditions than in England, but its appearance on the trade card of London's leading glasscutter suggests it had a place in England's luxury cut glass market in the late 1760s.[1] Catalogue number 97 displays the neoclassical taste that began to replace the rococo style in England during that decade. Here is a new proportion, with a deep bowl, shorter stem, and flatter foot. Most significant, however, is the facet-cut stem, a style that superseded the twisted fashions in the 1770s. The lid has the same domed profile as that of the blue sugar bowl (cat. no. 92).

With its knopped and facet-cut stem, the Carpenter goblet (cat. no. 96) reflects a knowledge of this emerging English fashion. Stiegel's engraver, Lazarus Isaac, had advertised his ability to cut the stems of wineglasses "in diamonds." The tall stem with its facet-cutting and angle knop recalls English sweetmeat glasses of the period, but the proportion of the bowl and the height and shape of the lid owe more to German traditions than to English example.[2]

The decoration of the Carpenter goblet is dominated by the inscription, the letters of which are deeply engraved and poorly spaced. Comparison of the *E*'s, *L*'s and *O*'s with those of the Old goblet reveals a strong similarity in both conception and execution, especially in the large triangular serifs on the horizontal elements of the *E*'s and *L*'s. For the flowered decoration, Isaac chose for both bowl and cover the fruiting grapevine, a classic motif of eighteenth-century English glass that was suitable given the toastlike character of the sentiment. A small bird, another standard motif of the English glass engraver (fig. 5, p. 213; cat. no. 94), is engraved on the reverse.

96. *Covered goblet*
American
Attributed to the glassworks of H. W. Stiegel, Manheim, Pa., 1773–74
Blown colorless lead glass; cut; wheel-engraved decoration and inscription HEALTH & PROSPERITY / TO / EMANUEL * CARPENTER ESQ. / MY * MOST / GENEROUS × PROMOTER
H. 13½ in (34.3 cm)
Lancaster County Historical Society, Lancaster, Pa., gift of Mrs. Benjamin Shreiner, 1921.2.1

Henry William Stiegel and American Flint Glass 237

The inventory of Carpenter's estate taken in 1780 includes no mention of the covered goblet, only a listing for "Glasses," valued at £1.17.6, a substantial amount compared with the £1.15.0 appraisal of two walnut tables.[3] The goblet descended in the Carpenter family and was presented to the Lancaster County Historical Society in 1921.

1. Trade card of William Parker, No. 69, Fleet Street, London, accompanying June 2, 1769, invoice, Cadwalader Collection, General John Cadwalader, Box 1, HSP. Reference courtesy of Nancy Goyne Evans.
2. Charleston, *English Glass*, pl. 48d. The German tradition of covered presentation goblets is well illustrated by documented glass made at the New Bremen Glassmanufactory of John Frederick Amelung, Frederick County, Maryland, 1784–95; see Dwight P. Lanmon and Arlene Palmer, "John Frederick Amelung and the New Bremen Glassmanufactory," *Journal of Glass Studies* 18 (1976): 48–49, 82–85.
3. Carpenter Inventory, Lancaster County Historical Society. For information on Carpenter and his career, see D. F. Magee, "Emanuel Carpenter, the Law Giver," and Frank Eshleman, "The Legislative Career of Emanuel Carpenter," *Lancaster County Historical Society Papers* 24, no. 4 (April 1920): 144–52; 153–68.

97. *Covered goblet*
English, 1770–90
Blown colorless lead glass; cut; wheel-engraved coat of arms and JM
H. 12¹³⁄₁₆ in (32.5 cm)
The Corning Museum of Glass, Corning, N.Y., 67.2.3

Graham Hood

The American China

The production and marketing of porcelain known as "American China" in Philadelphia in the years 1770 to 1772 parallels, in many respects, that of other trades and manufactures in the American colonies in the third quarter of the eighteenth century. The new venture was established with a mixture of domestic and foreign capital. It was organized and managed with a combination of local and imported experience. The managers discovered that the necessary skilled labor was in short supply and, therefore, expensive. They used native materials as much as possible for the sake of economy—and these often proved equal, if not superior, to the materials used in England. The factory produced wares that were profoundly indebted technologically and stylistically to English models. And it had to contend with severe competition from imported English goods. Consumers seem to have been unable to quell their suspicions that imported products were of better quality and likely to be more fashionable. Yet some patrons were very encouraging and earnestly wished the new product some measure of success, provided that it was achieved in the competitive arena of the market and not sustained only by massive infusions of local money, public or private.

China manufacture was quite distinct from certain other trades, however, such as cabinetmaking, joinery, goldsmithing, and portrait painting. Like the glass and textile industries, the china trade required major capital funds for equipment, buildings, and land, and it lacked an experienced work force on which to draw. Moreover, it was an industry, precisely like those producing glass, textiles, and pewter, that lent itself to mass production, a new process that had developed rapidly in the previous decades in England and other areas within the compass of the English mercantile system. It was, therefore, particularly sensitive to economic and political pressures, especially in the relatively long period of starting up production.

It may be no accident that the American China Factory was founded in the period of the nonimportation agreements, which called for the boycotting of British goods in response to the Stamp Act of 1765 and the Townshend Acts of 1767, and which was enthusiastically supported until the repeal of the latter in 1770. Stiegel's American Flint Glass Manufactory was also significantly expanded in these years in nearby Manheim, Pennsylvania. Such endeavors seem to have quickly become part of the spirit of the times and, to those who looked for such portents, clear indications of burgeoning local, regional, even national pride. Benjamin Rush wrote to a friend in Philadelphia from Edinburgh, where he was completing his medical studies, in April 1768: "Go on in encouraging American manufactures. I have many schemes in view with regard to these things. I have made those mechanical arts which are connected with chemistry the particular objects of my study, and am not without hopes of seeing a china manufactory established in Philadelphia in the course of a few years. Yes, we will be revenged of the mother country." A few months later he noted, "from late intelligence I have had from America, I am now fully convinced of the possibility of setting up a china manufactory in Philadelphia." While the source of his information and optimism is unknown, it seems impossible that he knew of plans for, or foresaw the establishment of, the later American China Factory. But it was certainly no accident that the repeal of the Townshend duties in 1770 and the decision of certain Philadelphia merchants to resume importation (they called it economic necessity) quickly led to extreme financial hardship for the fledgling enterprises. Local consumers were faced with an uneasy choice—patriotic support of local industry at a cost, or reliance on the fashionably and technologically proven import at a saving, the latter, however, leaving them open to accusations of Toryism and selfishness.[1]

Patriotic political pressures could be very persuasive and cause real anguish in the minds of local consumers. At this point, the heavily vested interests overseas—"the vortex of an East India Company"—moved quickly to stifle competition by manipulating prices, a stratagem aided and abetted by certain Philadelphia merchants. Thus the American China Factory closed in 1772, while Stiegel's flint glass factory hung on precariously until 1774. The main losers in these trade wars were not the consumers or the merchants, but rather the mechanics and other workers, many of whom did "lose their all." It may be only coincidental but it is symbolic that the buildings in which the few "Emissions of [china] Wares" had taken place in 1771–72 were later converted into a foundry for casting brass cannon, to be used against those forces that had ruthlessly extinguished the nascent enterprise five years earlier.[2]

The Americanness of this unique colonial china factory probably lies less in the wares it produced (which are few in number and differ from English prototypes only in detail and occasional ingredients) than in the economic, political, and social forces leading to its inception and subsequently its demise. The latter may have prompted a general sense of malaise among the local population, a suspicion that they were being manipulated unconscionably by forces too far away and in which they had no effective voice. But it must not be thought that the wares are deficient in artistic or technological interest—quite the contrary. The objects themselves represent an important constituent of the consumer revolution (that remarkable development on the demand side of personal and household consumables that scholars are now realizing was as significant as the industrial revolution was on the supply side) in which the colonies played an essential part. They are tasteful, fashionable for their time, nicely made, and prettily decorated. But the period in which the china factory enjoyed "a flourishing posture" and brought its wares "into no contemptable Train of Perfection" was too brief, and the surviving wares too few, for us to judge the output as a major new artistic identity.[3]

By 1770 Philadelphia had become, after London, one of the largest and wealthiest cities in the British Empire and was consequently a most promising location for a porcelain factory. Its citizens had a great taste for luxuries that, in the third quarter of the eighteenth century, inevitably included porcelain. Philadelphians had long bought an enormous amount of imported delft and stoneware and by 1770 were turning eagerly to the novel Wedgwood queensware. They also had a taste for hard-paste porcelain, to judge from the frequent advertisements in Philadelphia newspapers for "India China," while Bow soft-paste porcelain was imported into America at least as early as 1754.[4]

The founders of the American China Factory were Gousse Bonnin and George Anthony Morris. Before they entered into partnership in 1769, neither Bonnin nor Morris is known to have had any connection with a pottery or porcelain factory. Morris was born between 1742 and 1745 into a prominent Philadelphia family, the son of Joseph and Martha Fitzwater Morris. In 1767 he was living with his father on Front Street. In the spring of 1772 he went to North Carolina, where he died on October 5, 1773. His participation in the factory was probably limited to a financial interest, although he doubtless had many influential and useful contacts in Philadelphia through his family. He presumably managed the affairs of the factory during Bonnin's absences in England.

Gousse Bonnin was born about 1741, the son of Henry Bonnin, a prosperous merchant in Antigua. He was educated at Eton College from 1754 to 1759 and seems to have led a life of leisure for the next six or seven years; his name is not found in university, Inns of Court, army, or apprentice records. In November 1771, when he was deeply involved in the Philadelphia porcelain factory, he wrote: "I frequently smile at the wide diffrence, between my former and present pursuits in life, as also at the futile presages of those, who confidently foretold the impracticability, of my ever becoming a proficient in industry, and application, to business. . . . you may rest assured, the lively sun of Gallantry and Jollity is set with me, and gives place, to the Calmer light of unremitted assiduity, in the furtherance of the China Manufactory." His letters suggest a man of volatile temperament, impetuous perhaps, opportunistic certainly, firmly in the mold of the English entrepreneurial characters of the time, but not necessarily the most successful ones.[5]

On October 4, 1766, Bonnin married Dorothy Palmer, the daughter of Sir Charles Palmer of Dorney, Buckinghamshire, a most advantageous match socially for him. Both Henry Bonnin and Sir Charles Palmer settled significant amounts of money on their children.

Shortly thereafter Bonnin applied to the Crown for a grant of twenty thousand acres in eastern Florida, a large territory that was one of the spoils of the recent Seven Years' War, and sailed for America with his wife and children in May 1768. He quickly lost interest in Florida; in the next six months he borrowed £600 above his regular income and the capital he received at his marriage and returned to London in 1769 to seek a patent for the manufacture of black lead crucibles. The patent was acknowledged July 27, 1769.[6] According to Bonnin's specification, the crucibles were to be made from "a species of clay hitherto only discovered near the city of Philadelphia" mixed with an equal quantity of prepared black lead or graphite. "Of this mixture or cement the crucibles are formed upon a potter's wheel in the same manner as glazed or other pots, and undergo the same operation of heat to harden them. It is easy to discover any flaw in the crucibles by sounding them, as is customary with china."

The patent seems to have been nothing but an expense to Bonnin: "This is no Country to assert the privileges of a Patent, without which the Crucibles could not be momentous, as the fabrication, when once begun, is so extremely open, and simple, as to render it impossible to be preserved a secret. If ever it is my fate to reside in Great Britain, there they will shine with proper lustre, duely supported by the Authority of the King, not so here." Indeed, from the advertisement in the *Pennsylvania Chronicle* (Philadelphia), October 9, 1769, it seems that Bonnin had not at that time discovered or acquired any notable source of supply of this black lead.[7]

Undaunted, Bonnin formed a partnership with Morris for the manufacture of "American China." Their first public announcement appeared in the *Pennsylvania Chronicle*, January 1, 1770, boldly headlined "NEW CHINA WARE." An appeal to the spirit of the nonimportation agreement is evident: "Notwithstanding the various difficulties and disadvantages, which usually attend the introduction of any important manufacture in a new country, the proprietors of the China Works now erecting in Southwark . . . have proved to a certainty, that the clays of America are productive of as good porcelain as any heretofore manufactured at the famous factory in Bow, near London. . . ." Since a year elapsed before the production of porcelain was actually broadcast, the announcement could well have been designed to forestall others who were experimenting with the American clay,

or at least knew of its existence. Benjamin Rush had stated in January 1769, "We have all the materials for making *china* or porcelain ware in our province and in New-Castle county." And Benjamin Franklin in Europe wrote to Humphrey Marshall that he had showed the specimens of "white Earths" that Marshall had sent him to the "ingenious skillful French chemist," Pierre Joseph Macquer, director of the "Royal Porcellane Manufacture" at Sèvres, near Paris, and had received a positive report. Whether or not the threat of local rivalry was real, Bonnin's impetuousness was in character with his hasty application for the crucible patent.[8]

Immediately after announcing the partnership Bonnin returned once more to England to raise capital for the factory. He also sought to attract skilled workmen from English porcelain factories to immigrate to Philadelphia. The partners further advertised for skilled workmen in the *South Carolina Gazette* (Charleston) of March 15, 1770, presumably hoping to entice workmen away from John Bartlem's newly established creamware factory near Charleston, as Bartlem himself had enticed his men away from the Staffordshire factories earlier.[9]

Bonnin's visit to England produced "nine master workers for the porcelain manufactory" who arrived in Philadelphia in October 1770. Their effect can be gauged by the announcement two months later that the partners "have in some measure, answered the expectation of their friends, by their first Emission of Porcelain." Bonnin confirmed this in a letter to his mother-in-law, dated January 15, 1771, five days after the public announcement: "I think I can now congratulate myself on the flourishing posture of our affairs, The China Factory is brought to a crisis and the first Emission of ware which took place the 24th of December was immediately bought up and most generally admired, I shall send forth another large quantity in ten days, which is already bespoke, nevertheless you may believe there are some faults in it, since no work was ever immediately brought to perfection."[10]

To attract the master workers to Philadelphia, Bonnin and Morris offered twice the wages Wedgwood paid—a weekly salary of a guinea and a half for a twelve-hour day plus passage to America. Although all the master workmen arrived on a ship from London, it is not known if they were all English. Only three are known by name: Thomas Gale, whose antecedents are unknown; Thomas Frye, an apprentice, nephew and namesake of one of the founders of the Bow factory; and, apparently, Thomas Byerley, nephew of Josiah Wedgwood. By the time of the first production the factory was fairly extensive, consisting of "three kilns, two furnaces, two mills, two clay vaults, cisterns, engines, and treading room."[11]

Once the initial production was achieved, Bonnin and Morris made a determined effort to speed things up "notwithstanding the designed importation of China ware by a few." Even at this early stage they offered "compleat sets for the dining and tea table together, or dining singly." These sets included such items as picklestands, fruit baskets, sauceboats in two sizes, pint bowls, and plates. Bonnin's letter to Lady Palmer indicated that the first batch was immediately sold and that the second batch, produced in January 1771, was spoken for. This is confirmed by a recently discovered letter from Joseph Shippen, Jr., dated February 26, 1771: "I have been at the American China Shop, to procure some of the China which Mammy has an inclination for; and find they have none left of the same kind of cups and saucers bought by Mrs. Penn, which were tea cups with handles and not coffee cups; they are quilted china, and have a border round the edges in immitation of Nanking China. There were only a dozen of that sort made, all of which Mrs. Penn bought; but I am told by the seller that more of it will be finished at the factory next week; . . . there is often a great deal of difference among the cups and saucers, as well as other articles, as to the goodness of painting and glazing. This china is in general esteemed preferable to that made in England, as to its fineness, or quality; but as yet it has rather too yellowish a cast, owing to the want of a particular ingredient used in the composition for glazing; which could not hitherto be imported from England on account of the Non-Importation agreement; but the owners of the factory expect a quantity of that article in the first spring vessels; and then they are in hopes of making a great improvement in that particular."[12]

The next batch, announced by the partners on March 14, included four- and six-quart bowls. Such large bowls were difficult to fire successfully, and their appearance indicates an unexpected technical proficiency in the new enterprise. By May 1771, according to Thomas Wharton's bill, the available range of objects also included plain cups, handled cups, quilted cups, sugar dishes in two sizes, cream ewers, and teapots in two sizes. Orders seem to have been fairly numerous and came from as far away as Albany—although they were not always promptly filled. Sir William Johnson's agent in Philadelphia, Carpenter Wharton, wrote to him in Albany on October 14: "Show'd long since have done my Self the honour of Writing to you, had I not been frequently disappointed by the Managers of the China Factory in the receiving a breakfast Set a China of the Manufactory of this City (Which I beg leave to Present You for the use of the Hall,) as I flatter my Self it is the very best kind of the Kind they have yet exhibited. . . . I am Senceable it would afford you a Peculiar Satisfaction in observing the progress made in the China and Glass Manufactories, the demand for them is So Great, that the proprietors of the Manufactories are not able to Supply the orders from different Colonies."[13]

The partners presumably intended to decorate their wares with underglaze blue, as their advertised request for "zaffera" (cobalt oxide) in January 1771 would indicate. Fine decoration was a necessary adjunct to their wares if they were to provide any real competition with the brilliantly colored delft, polychromed Chinese export porcelain, Staffordshire stoneware, and English blue and white, all imported from England. Although "Blue and White Ware, either useful or ornamental," was not mentioned until July 1771, it seems to have been available from the beginning, according to the previously quoted letter from Joseph Shippen, Jr.; in another to his father from Philadelphia dated March 15, 1771, he wrote, "There have been no China Cups and Saucers made at the Factory since my last, like those which Mrs. Penn bought (tho' great quantities of an inferior kind have been made)."[14]

Two months after the first blue and white ware was produced, the American China Factory advertised in September 1771: "There will shortly be an emission from this manufactory, an assortment of both useful and ornamental Enamelled China." Not until the following January, however, did it announce that enameled porcelain was actually available: "Complete sets of Dressing Boxes for the Toilet, either in Blue or Enamel." This represented an ambitious and sophisticated addition to the factory's regular production. Unfortunately, no complete pieces are known to have survived.

Prominent Philadelphians were among those purchasing the products of the factory, including the Penn, Franklin, Cadwalader, Shippen, and Wharton families. What they bought was quite similar to the products of the Bow, Lowestoft, Liverpool, Plymouth, and Bristol — perhaps even Worcester and Derby — factories. Some of the purchasers would have been conscious of the (often small) differences between the products of the various English factories. For example, Benjamin Franklin sent his wife from England a selection of English china in 1758: "To show the Difference of Workmanship, there is something from all the China Works in England."

The American wares were identified with a number of marks, as were the English, though the partners announced only one, an uppercase *S* in underglaze blue. Some of the known American pieces are marked with an uppercase *P* in underglaze blue, as well as a somewhat rounded uppercase *Z*.

Four pieces representative of the known wares from the American China Factory have been chosen for this exhibition. The sweetmeat dish (cat. no. 98) is one of three of this form to have survived, two of which are decorated in underglaze blue. It may be the form identified in the contemporary bills as a picklestand. It bears more than a passing resemblance to Bow models (cat. no. 99). The dish consists of three shell forms united by a column (resembling a mass of coral encrusted with smaller shells), which is surmounted by another shell. It stands on three small conical feet and is painted with floral sprays and, on the upper shell, a butterfly. The underglaze blue decoration of the sweetmeat dish is close in detail to that on the handsome fruit basket also in this exhibition (cat. no. 102) and to that on a broken openwork dish whose attribution to Bonnin and Morris dates from 1841.[15]

In form and decoration the fruit basket (cat. no. 102) resembles Lowestoft examples (themselves based on Worcester prototypes [cat. no. 103]). Even the tiny flower applied to the outside of the basket at each juncture of the open strapwork is similar to Lowestoft examples, as is the inner border decoration. One basket of this form is printed rather than painted, and the print parallels Bow and Lowestoft prototypes, though it apparently was not used on such basket forms at the Lowestoft factory. Another is painted with a most assured and distinctive landscape scene. These baskets are perhaps the most successful and sophisticated forms surviving from the American China Factory and are comparable in quality to many of the English wares.[16]

The charming little fluted sauceboat (cat. no. 100) has decoration similar to that of other objects from the factory: two Chinese-style houses with a generic tree between. Here the decoration resembles that used by Chaffers at his Liverpool factory (1754–65) and subsequently at the same factory by Philip Christian. Similarities to Bow and Lowestoft are also evident (cat. no. 101). Once again the quality is quite acceptable in the English context.[17]

Finally, the small openwork potpourri dish with cover (cat. no. 104) is perhaps the most idiosyncratic form. Its small size, neat pierced work, and attractive floral knop on the cover compensate for the slightly erratic and undistinguished border decoration at the base and at the edge of the cover. It appears to be an otherwise unknown form in British blue and white porcelain, with general similarities to Derby and Bow (cat. no. 105).[18]

Among all the known wares from the factory there is a fairly wide range of quality, as one would expect from such a short-lived enterprise. The "difference . . . as to the goodness of painting and glazing" mentioned by Joseph Shippen, Jr., and implied in Carpenter Wharton's comments is apparent. The "rather too yellowish a cast" remarked by Shippen can be seen in some of the wares, which, like early Bow, have a straw-colored translucency. The glaze, which Shippen found wanting in an ingredient prohibited by the nonimportation agreement, pooled easily and is sometimes pitted and bubbly. The finely detailed forms and decoration of the pieces are culled, as we have noted, from a variety of English factories where the master workmen had been employed. All of the above characteristics can be observed among the English wares, but as isolated instances rather than typical features of a large group of objects. Virtually all the ingredients of the porcelain body and glaze and all the details of the decoration are found in the English counterparts. What is absolutely unique to the American factory's products is revealed by modern scientific analysis: the presence of tiny amounts of alpha quartz sets them apart as a group and reveals their origin.

Toward the end of 1771 Bonnin and Morris faced acute financial difficulties despite an apparently substantial capital investment from Bonnin's father. The repeal of English duties caused many Philadelphians to wonder if their rejection of English imports for the sake of local pride and industry was not too great a sacrifice. It clearly was, for after tax repeal the nonimportation agreement collapsed quickly, with adverse results for many native enterprises. "Actuated as strongly by the sincerest Attachment to the Interest of the Public as to . . . private Emolument," Bonnin and Morris then appealed to the Pennsylvania legislature for a loan. They submitted a sample of the kind of work they had brought into "no contemptable Train of Perfection," but the application was refused. As a substitute the proprietors organized a lottery to help recoup their finances.[19]

Faced with the refusal of a loan from the legislature, the disintegration of the nonimportation agreement, the large amounts of porcelain coming into the country through the East India Company and private importers, and criticism of the quality of their wares, Bonnin and Morris published a broadside in the *Pennsylvania Gazette* (Philadelphia), August 1, 1771: "The Manufacture of China Ware in this Province, certainly deserves the serious Attention of every Man, who prays for the Happiness of his Fellow-subjects, or that the very Semblance of Liberty may be handed down to Posterity. . . ." Again the factory was equated, in its ambitions and accomplishments, with Stiegel's Manheim glass factory as a compliment to colonial enterprise and virtue. But the real fear of insurmountable competition from established importers such as the East India Company showed through only too clearly. The partners recognized the problems of cost and inconsistent quality in their wares and begged for a certain tolerance as well as a grace period of "a few Years" to refine them, otherwise "the Factories, Labourers and all" would "be swallowed up in the Vortex of an East-India Company." Just as serious was the raw fact that "Every Importer of China knows, and most retail Purchasers have observed with Pleasure, that the Price of China is fallen Five Shillings in the Pound, since the Commencement of a China Factory in this place." It is important to note that it was precisely such complaints of price-cutting by the East India Company (with governmental abetting in the form of the Tea Act) that led to the Boston Tea Party later. In other words, protests against mercantile monopoly and political tyranny were closely interwoven, and it is possible that the colonists did not forget the collapse of the porcelain and glass factories in the heat of the later conflicts.[20]

Production apparently continued until at least September 1772, despite Morris's absence in North Carolina from April onward. During that time, Bonnin advertised repeatedly for painters, trained or apprentice. He may also have begun experiments with a hard-paste body; the *Pennsylvania Packet* (Philadelphia), August 3, 1772, included the Philadelphia news "that the Proprietors of the China Manufactory in this city, have lately made experiments with some clay presented to them by a Gentleman of Charlestown, South-Carolina, which produces China superior to any brought from the East-Indies, and will stand the heat beyond any kind of crucibles ever yet made."

This interesting reference links the patriotic enterprise in Philadelphia with efforts in South Carolina extending back a quarter of a century to mine excellent white clay from the Cherokee territory and export it to England as a profitable local trade.[21] The "Gentleman of Charlestown" was Henry Laurens, a successful merchant and later a prominent patriot, who had hoped to exploit the commercial possibilities of the china clay since at least 1757, when he sent several barrels of it to England for testing. In 1770–71 Laurens actually took two kegs of clay to Philadelphia and delivered them to George Morris, but he was prevented by a riding accident from visiting the factory.[22] Probably because of the precarious financial situation of the factory, the Cherokee clay initiative went no further.

By November 1772 the writing was on the wall. The workmen rebelled against their working conditions and sought charity openly on the streets. Wedgwood, in his later *Address to the Workmen*, gave some details with relish: "Some [of the workmen] died immediately, of sickness occasioned by this great change in their prospects and manner of living. . . . A subscription was set on foot by the inhabitants for their relief, by which those who had weathered the first storm were supplied with daily bread . . . but not one was left alive, to return to give us any farther particulars of this affecting tale."[23]

On November 14, 1772, Bonnin announced in the *Pennsylvania Chronicle* that he was "under a necessity of embarking with his family for England, on board one of the first Spring ships." He was anxious to sell the factory and various lots of ground as speedily as possible. This was no easy matter, however, and they were still for sale two years later. Bonnin seems to have returned to England about September 1773, where he lived first in Bristol, then on a fashionable street in Worcester. The last advertisement for the property in Philadelphia newspapers was dated October 19, 1774. Thereafter the buildings presumably began their slow descent into the limbo of a "sailor's brothel and riot house on a large scale."[24]

The reasons for the failure of the porcelain factory are not hard to identify. Bonnin persistently complained that the frequent importations of porcelain would flood the market, and merchants' advertisements in Philadelphia newspapers of the period amply confirm his gloomy prognostications. Imported wares were ever desirable, and it was impossible to compete with the huge wholesalers when they cut their prices by 25 percent. Bonnin was surely aware, also, that the hard-paste Chinese export porcelain could withstand any amount of boiling without cracking or discoloration and, with normal wear and tear, was a great deal more serviceable than soft-paste porcelain. Quantities of Chinese export ware, as well as English blue and white, were shipped in; moreover, there was a growing fashion for Wedgwood's fine and durable stoneware.

In 1765 Wedgwood had been deeply concerned about possible American competition from John Bartlem's factory: "The bulk of our particular manufactures are . . . exported to foreign markets . . . and the principal of these markets are the Continent and Islands of North America. To the Continent we send an amazeing quantity of white stoneware. . . . This trade to our Colonies we are apprehensive of loseing in a few years as they have set on foot some Pot works there already." But by 1770 Wedgwood, in common with many other producers of goods, seemed so confident of his own superiority that he appears never to have mentioned the American China Factory in his correspondence. In any case, the taste of the time was changing toward creamware, or queensware: "The demand for the said Cream color alias Queens Ware . . . still increases. It is really amazeing how rapidly the use has spread almost over the whole globe and how universally it is liked. . . . I had with me yesterday an East Indian Captain, and another Gentleman and Lady from those parts who . . . told me it was already in use there, and in much higher estimation than the present Porcellain."[25]

Despite their patriotic pride in Bonnin and Morris's new china factory, local patrons were clearly concerned about the varying quality and the price of the wares. Shippen noted the "great quantities of an inferior kind," and Wharton wrote Sir William Johnson that he had been "frequently disappointed." In the absence of larger quantities of superior-quality wares at competitive prices, the partners' strong suit was patriotism, or local pride. They played it as forcefully and as commercially as they could, but it was not enough. When the china was "esteemed preferable to that made in England," local pride glowed and citizens acted appropriately. When questions about the china's quality *and* its price arose, patriotism was not enough.

Labor difficulties and the flood of imported ceramics that poured in after the collapse of the nonimportation agreement were insurmountable problems. And that is regrettable, for the wares have charm, a strong regional interest, and were fashionably up-to-date. The floral and foliate motifs, especially those in relief, the scrolled molded decoration, the pierced work, and the shells employed in this porcelain are precisely the motifs that characterize the work of three of the finest silversmiths active in America at this time—Richardson, Myers, and Revere. The decorative motifs found in the known wares of Bonnin and Morris were culled from a variety of contemporary English porcelain factories. Yet these few pieces do form a distinct group within the various British eighteenth-century blue and white porcelains, and the American China Factory is important as the unique American porcelain factory of the colonial period of which significant evidence survives.

NOTES

1. T. M. Doerflinger, *A Vigorous Spirit of Enterprise: Merchants and Economic Development in Revolutionary Philadelphia* (Chapel Hill: University of North Carolina Press, 1986), pp. 167, 172, 184–85, 189–94; *Philadelphia: Three Centuries of American Art* (Philadelphia Museum of Art, 1976), pp. 108–9 for Bonnin and Morris, and pp. 121–22 for Henry William Stiegel. I am grateful to Michael K. Brown for pointing out, in an unpublished article, the Benjamin Rush letters (L. H. Butterfield, ed., *Letters of Benjamin Rush* [Princeton, N.J.: Princeton University Press, 1951], pp. 1, 54, 60–61).

2. For details and quotes see G. Hood, *Bonnin and Morris of Philadelphia: The First American Porcelain Factory, 1770–1772* (Chapel Hill: University of North Carolina Press, 1971).

3. Hood, *Bonnin and Morris*, pp. 25–45.

4. C. Bridenbaugh, *Cities in Revolt: Urban Life in America, 1743–1776* (New York: Alfred A. Knopf, 1971) 217n, modifies his earlier statement that in the 1770s Philadelphia was the second largest city in the British Empire. S. B. Warner, Jr., in *The Private City: Philadelphia in Three Periods of Its Growth* (Philadelphia: University of Pennsylvania Press, 1968), chap. 1, calculates that the population of the city in 1775 was only about twenty-four thousand, which, according to Bridenbaugh's figures, would have made it the sixth and possibly even the seventh largest city in the empire. With reference to imported china: "A Variety of Bow China, Cups and Saucers, Bowls, etc. . . . just imported by Philip Breadnig, and to be sold at his House in Fish Street" (*Boston Evening Post*, November 11, 1754, in G. F. Dow, *The Arts and Crafts in New England, 1704–1755* [Topsfield, Mass.: Wayside Press, 1927], p. 88). From the same source it is noted that china figurines were also available in America: "A variety of curious fine China in Statuary: also some of the best enamel'd China, sold at public auction at the House next to the Orange Tree in Hanover Street" (*Boston Gazette*, May 17, 1762, quoted in Dow, p. 90).

5. Hood, *Bonnin and Morris*, pp. 8–9.

6. *Chronological Index of Patents of Invention* (London, 1854), vol. 165, no. 919. The index refers to Letters Patent of March 5, 1769, but the specification, signed by Bonnin on July 25, refers to the Letters Patent of May 5, 1769. The complete charge for the application and issuance of a patent at that time was about £60.

7. Only three days before Bonnin announced his crucible patent

in Philadelphia, the American Philosophical Society, meeting on October 6, 1769, agreed upon a motion "to publish an advertisement for specimens of the different clays to be sent to this society." This may have been prompted by, or in opposition to, Bonnin. At the society's meeting of November 3, 1769, it was agreed to defer for some time the publication of any such advertisement.

8. All the newspaper advertisements pertaining to the factory are given in full in A. C. Prime, comp., *The Arts and Crafts in Philadelphia, Maryland, and South Carolina, 1721–1785* (Topsfield, Mass.: Walpole Society, 1929), pp. 114–24. For the source of the "clays of America," see Hood, *Bonnin and Morris*, pp. 11–12. For the Rush and Franklin references I am grateful to Michael K. Brown: see Butterfield, *Rush*, pp. 74–75, and W. B. Willcox, ed., *The Papers of Benjamin Franklin* (New Haven, Conn.: Yale University Press, 1973), pp. 17, 109–10.

9. The South Carolina advertisement is given in full in Prime, *Arts and Crafts in Philadelphia*, pp. 115–16. The Bonnin and Morris advertisement is dated several months before Bartlem's first recorded advertisement in the *South Carolina Gazette* (Charleston) of October 4, 1770 (Prime, *Arts and Crafts in Philadelphia*, p. 112).

10. First quote is from *The Pennsylvania Staatsbote*, October 1770. See also Hood, *Bonnin and Morris*, pp. 13, 50.

11. Details of the factory are given in full in Prime, *Arts and Crafts in Philadelphia*, pp. 120–24. See also Wedgwood's *Address to the Workmen . . .* (full reference given in n. 25). There is no record of Thomas Gale in connection with Wedgwood, nor is there any record at Barlaston of any of the other potters whose names occur in connection with the Bonnin and Morris site after the closing of the factory. Of course, it is possible that Gale and the others were not master potters at all but rather skilled workmen. Even if the master workmen had not made porcelain at Wedgwood's factory, it is more than likely that they had migrated there from Derby, Worcester, or Bow. N. McKendrick, "Josiah Wedgwood and Factory Discipline," *Proceedings of the Wedgwood Society*, no. 5 (1963): 1–29. See also Prime, *Arts and Crafts in Philadelphia*, p. 117.

12. Shippen to Edward Shippen, February 26, 1771, Shippen Papers, manuscript group 375, New Jersey Historical Society, Newark (courtesy of Michael K. Brown).

13. Carpenter Wharton's letter is in the *Papers of Sir William Johnson* (Albany: State University of New York Press, 1933), 8:293–94. The glass factory mentioned was Stiegel's.

14. The remainder of the reference to the factory in this letter is as follows: "In the meantime Jenny begs her Acceptance of a Sugar Dish as a specimen of the Philadelphia China, which I shall forward by the first opportunity with one of the same sort which she sends for my sister." Shippen to his father, March 15, 1771, Balch Collection, Historical Society of Pennsylvania, Philadelphia.

15. Hood, *Bonnin and Morris*, pp. 27–30 and figs. 1–4, 11–13, 24, 26.

16. Hood, *Bonnin and Morris*, pp. 30–34 and figs. 1–7, 30–34. The landscape-decorated basket is illustrated in *American Art, 1750–1800: Towards Independence* (Boston: Published for the Yale University Art Gallery, New Haven, and the Victoria and Albert Museum, London, by the New York Graphic Society, 1976), p. 237.

17. Hood, *Bonnin and Morris*, pp. 31–34 and figs. 8, 14–15, 24, 27–29.

18. Ibid., pp. 31–33 and figs. 20–21, 35–36.

19. Ibid., pp. 53–54. A ticket for the lottery was known to E. A. Barber, *Pottery and Porcelain*, p. 95; John Cadwalader paid £135 for ninety tickets in November 1771 (Cadwalader Collection, Historical Society of Pennsylvania).

20. Stiegel also had his hopes raised by the nonimportation agreement in 1769. In that year he built his second Manheim glasshouse, the American Flint Glass Manufactory, the first in America to produce glass presumably equal in quality and content to lead glass. He added to his factory each year for the next three years. But as early as 1770 he was in financial difficulties; in September 1770 he too appealed for a provincial loan. A year later he was given the useless sum of £150. In 1773 he resorted to a lottery, and the following year he closed his factory. At its peak his factory employed 130 men, but Stiegel was only too conscious of the high cost of labor and the unbeatable competition of imported wares. Whoever the author of the broadside was, he might have expressed perhaps justifiable resentment at the widespread local support given to the attempted culture of silk worms, when glass and porcelain factories were allowed to founder.

21. Hood, "The Career of Andrew Duche," *The Art Quarterly* 31, no. 2 (1968): 173–79, and an article to be published in the future by the same author, "The Carolina Clay Again." In the mid-1760s, Caleb Lloyd of Charleston sent some clay to his brother-in-law, Richard Champion, who was making porcelain in Bristol that subsequently attracted the attention of Richard Holdship at the Worcester factory. Wedgwood, too, explored the commercial viability of this clay in the 1760s but concluded that the uncertain access to Indian land and the lengthy overland haul would make the product prohibitively expensive.

22. George C. Rogers, Jr., kindly drew my attention to a letter from Henry Laurens in London from William Williamson in Charleston, dated November 28, 1771, giving details of this matter (Lauren Papers, Letterbook no. 5, South Carolina Historical Society, Columbia).

23. Hood, *Bonnin and Morris*, pp. 71–72 nn. 20, 23, pp. 64–65.

24. A part of the factory was used as a brass foundry for casting cannons during the American Revolution; John Adams wrote on March 30, 1777: "I then went to the Foundry of Brass Cannon. It is in Front Street in Southware, Nearly opposite to the Sweedes Church. This Building was formerly a China Manufactory, but is now converted into a Foundery, under the Directon of Mr. Biers [Byers], late of New York" (L. H. Butterfield, ed., *Adams Family Correspondence* [Cambridge, Mass.: Harvard University Press, 1963], 2:190). The main building of the factory, according to deeds and tax records, was "destroyed" about 1801. During the next thirty years or so the site was divided by another large road, and houses were extensively built upon it.

25. A. Finer and G. Savage, eds., *Selected Letters of Josiah Wedgwood* (London: Cory, Adams, and Mackay, 1965) p. 29. Wedgwood was concerned about losing the extremely profitable colonial trade not only because his own workers rejected his strict disciplinary control and were tempted by the higher wages offered by Bartlem, but also because of his knowledge that the South Carolina clays were "equal, if not superior," to those available in England. Bow had experimented with these clays (called unaker) during the years 1744 to 1749, and Wedgwood himself conducted experiments with them at this time (Hood, "Career of Andrew Duche," p. 179). Bartlem, however, does not seem to have been able to use these clays with any degree of success: "Having opened his Pottery and China Manufactory . . . Will be much obliged to Gentlemen in the Country, or others, who will be so kind to send him samples of any Kinds of fine Clay upon their Plantations, etc., in order to make them Trials of. He already makes what is called Queen's Ware, equal to any imported" (*South Carolina Gazette* [Charleston], January 31, 1771, in Prime, *Arts and Crafts in Philadelphia*, p. 112). As this is Bartlem's last recorded advertisement, Wedgwood need hardly have worried for his vast overseas trade. Bartlem, however, was a subject upon which Wedgwood could become overheated with little effort. Twenty years later, in his *Address to the Workmen in the Pottery: On the Subject of Entering into the Service of Foreign Manufacturers* (Newcastle, Staffordshire, 1783), he vituperated against Bartlem at length, painting an idyllic picture of Staffordshire life and a horrifying one of life in America. He mentioned three other workmen who migrated to South Carolina, "Mr. Lymer, Mr. Allen of Great Fenton and William Ellis of Hanley." Ellis, who was the only one to return, found his way to Winston-Salem, North Carolina, where he helped the Moravians make queensware; see J. H. Craig, *The Arts and Crafts in North Carolina* (Winston-Salem, N.C.: Museum of Early Southern Decorative Arts, 1965), p. 88.

Catalogue Objects

98. *Sweetmeat dish*
American, Philadelphia, Pa., 1771–72
Bonnin and Morris factory
Soft-paste porcelain painted in underglaze blue; marked *P*
H. 5¼ in (13.3 cm), W. 7¼ in (18.4 cm)
The Brooklyn Museum, 45.174

98. Sweetmeat dish / 99. Sweetmeat dish

Catalogue number 98 is one of three surviving sweetmeat dishes made by the Bonnin and Morris factory. This form may be the one identified in contemporary bills as a picklestand. Since the workmen for the Philadelphia factory had been hired away from English competitors, it is not surprising that the Bonnin and Morris products bear very close resemblance to English examples of the form. One such piece (cat. no. 99) was made

99. *Sweetmeat dish*
English, London, about 1760–70
Attributed to the Bow factory
Soft-paste porcelain painted in underglaze blue
H. 5 in (12.7 cm), W. 8 in (20.3 cm)
The Brooklyn Museum, 86.3

by the Bow factory. Both of these sweetmeat dishes consist of three shell forms united by a column (resembling a mass of coral encrusted with smaller shells) which is surmounted by another shell. The underglaze blue decoration on the Bonnin and Morris dish pictured here is very close in detail to that on a fruit basket (cat. no. 102) also made by the factory.

100. *Sauceboat*
American, Philadelphia, Pa., 1771–72
Bonnin and Morris factory
Soft-paste porcelain painted in underglaze blue; marked *P*
H. 2¼ in (5.7 cm), L. 4⅝ in (11.7 cm)
Private collection

101. *Sauceboat*
English, London, 1765–75
Bow factory
Soft-paste porcelain painted in underglaze blue
H. 1⅞ in (4.8 cm), L. 4⅞ in (12.4 cm)
The Minneapolis Institute of Arts, gift of Mr. and Mrs. David Williams and Mr. and Mrs. Charles Spensley, 78.79.6.7

100. Sauceboat / 101. Sauceboat

The fluted sauceboat made at the Bonnin and Morris factory (cat. no. 100) is decorated with two Chinese-style houses with a tree between. This type of decoration, which appears on other Bonnin and Morris pieces, resembles that found on English wares produced by the Bow and Lowestoft factories and by Chaffers, and later Philip Christian, at the Liverpool factory. The English example shown here (cat. no. 101) is from the Bow factory. The Bonnin and Morris piece is comparable in quality to the English ware.

The American China

102. *Fruit basket*
American, Philadelphia, Pa., 1771–72
Bonnin and Morris factory
Soft-paste porcelain painted in underglaze blue
Diam. 6⅞ in (17.5 cm)
Museum of Fine Arts, Boston, Frederick Brown Fund, 1977.621

102. Fruit basket / 103. Fruit basket

The fruit baskets produced by the Bonnin and Morris factory are perhaps their most successful and sophisticated forms. They are comparable in quality to many English wares. In form and decoration they resemble Lowestoft examples, which were based on Worcester prototypes (cat. no. 103). The inner border decoration, and even the tiny flowers applied to the outside of the baskets and at each juncture of the open strapwork, are close to English examples.

103. *Fruit basket*
English, about 1765–70
Worcester factory
Soft-paste porcelain painted in underglaze blue
H. 2¹¹⁄₃₂ in (6 cm), Diam. 8⁷⁄₁₆ in (21.4 cm)
The Art Institute of Chicago, The Amelia Blanxius Collection, gift of Mrs. Emma B. Hodge and Mrs. Jene E. Bell, 1912.524

104. *Potpourri basket and cover*
American, Philadelphia, Pa., 1771–72
Bonnin and Morris factory
Soft-paste porcelain painted in underglaze blue; marked P
H. 3¾ in (9.5 cm), Diam. 4⅛ in (10.5 cm)
The Colonial Williamsburg Foundation, Williamsburg, Va., 1969-41

104. Potpourri basket and cover
105. Bowl

The small openwork potpourri dish and cover illustrated here is perhaps the most idiosyncratic form made by the Bonnin and Morris factory. Although it has general similarities to forms made by the Derby and Bow factories, it is an otherwise unknown form in British blue and white porcelain. Its small size, neat pierced work, and attractive floral knop on the cover compensate for the slightly erratic and undistinguished border

105. *Bowl*
English, London, about 1760–70
Bow factory
Soft-paste porcelain painted in underglaze blue
H. 2⅞ in (7.3 cm), Diam. 6⅜ in (16.2 cm)
The Colonial Williamsburg Foundation, Williamsburg, Va., 1975-233

decoration at the base and at the edge of the cover. This very decoration, however, resembles that found on a bowl by the Bow factory (cat. no. 105), suggesting the influence of Bow workmen at the Philadelphia factory. The molded and painted decoration of the bowl closely resembles that found on fragments from the Bonnin and Morris factory site, as well as the painted border of the potpourri basket.

Gregory R. Weidman

Baltimore Federal Furniture
In the English Tradition

One of the most remarkable instances of urban growth in the history of this country was the development of Baltimore in the late eighteenth century, described even by observers of the time as "the most rapid growth of any city in America."[1] Almost equally notable was the expansion of the Baltimore furniture-making trades during the same period. The one circumstance fueled the other, leading to the production of a unique group of decorative arts objects. In both quantity and quality the products of Baltimore's cabinet shops are outstanding. Their similarity to English furniture has long been recognized and deserves closer study.

This essay supplies the context of the federal furniture in Baltimore by first reviewing the economic and social background of the city in the post–Revolutionary War period and then laying out factors, such as immigration patterns and the lingering influence of English culture, that influenced both cabinetmakers' designs and clients' choice of furniture. It then analyzes the furniture itself to define its relationship to English prototypes and English pattern books. It concludes with a brief discussion of the distinct American interpretations of these sources.

Baltimore's Growth in the 1700s

Baltimore became a thriving, prosperous city from very modest beginnings. Founded in 1729, in 1752 Baltimore was still a village of about twenty-five buildings (only four of them brick) and about one hundred inhabitants. By the early 1760s, however, an important pattern of settlement was under way. Newcomers were attracted by the small town's location close to the fall line, the excellent harbor on the north side of the Patapsco River, and easy access to rich farmlands. Scots-Irish flour merchants from Pennsylvania began to arrive and establish mills, sending their products to markets down the Chesapeake Bay. Other enterprising settlers followed. Barely a decade later Baltimore was a strong competitor of Philadelphia for most of the trade of southern Pennsylvania. Its population had reached approximately three thousand, about double that of Annapolis, the colony's capital and cultural center.

The great boom period in Baltimore, however, took place after the close of the Revolutionary War. Indeed, the war was the impetus for its rapid development. According to Johann David Schoepf, a German surgeon who traveled extensively in America after the war:

> Nothing was so favorable to the commerce of the place [Baltimore] as the last war. The situation of the harbour assured it against the sudden attacks of hostile craft; ... So Baltimore became the general depot of imports and exports for the middle part of the American States.[2]

Schoepf particularly noted the enormous profits Baltimore's merchants reaped in the flour trade with the West Indies during the war as their sailing ships ran the blockades of the islands.[3] With peace, other merchants concentrated on the lucrative European markets, and still others sought to open trade with the Far East. Captain John O'Donnell's ship *Pallas* returned to Baltimore from Canton in 1785 "with a full cargo of China goods, being the first direct importation from thence into this port, the value of which he realized here."[4] The following year, 232 sailing vessels entered and 227 cleared the port of Baltimore on their way to and from foreign ports.[5]

By the 1790s Baltimore had expanded its American markets to the Western frontier; growth of the local iron industry and other manufacturing also helped to fuel the economy. The flood of immigrants had now swelled the population to 13,500, a figure that was to double by 1800. "Building in all quarters of the town" and "new houses building in every street" are just two comments that reflect the spread of the city outward from the harbor to the north, east, and west.[6] Baltimore looked "new, elegant, and prosperous in every part . . . in 1760 there were not ten brick houses, whereas in 1787 it had 2,000 houses. . . . The houses are newer and more handsome than in Philadelphia."[7] The city was formally incorporated in 1796. Those growing wealthy in trade and in related industries and real estate built large brick town houses; many built fine country estates on the hills surrounding the city as well.

Character of the Population

Many of the patrons of Baltimore cabinetmakers were wealthy businessmen who had recently immigrated. One significant group, the Scots-Irish flour merchants who came on from Pennsylvania, has already been mentioned. More Irish, predominantly Protestants from the northern counties, came particularly in the early to mid-1780s. This group was by far the most important —numerically, financially, and influentially—in the mix that made Baltimore prosper, producing more large fortunes than any other ethnic group.[8] Despite the predominance of the Scots-Irish, federal Baltimore attracted a rich mixture of other ethnic groups as well, among them English, German, and French.

The opportunities available in Baltimore also attracted people from American regions. Many came from Pennsylvania (most notably a substantial group of Quakers), some from New England. Perhaps the most significant group was from relatively close by: many of Maryland's landed gentry of the colonial period came to the city and made fortunes in real estate and mercantile pursuits, becoming important figures in the social, political, and economic life of Baltimore.

Despite their differences in origin and religion, Baltimoreans were alike in their interest in acquiring wealth. Comments from a British observer of the Baltimore scene in the mid-1790s are illuminating:

There are many respectable families who live genteelly. . . . But the bulk of the inhabitants, collected from all quarters, are bent on the pursuit of wealth; to get money honestly, if they can, but at any rate to get it.[9]

Although a number of citizens of Baltimore came from old, landed families in the state, clearly most of the wealth in town was "new money."

Preferred Furniture Style

The "nouveau-riche" quality of life in Baltimore was reflected in the elaborate, stylish, sophisticated furniture being produced in the city. Other important social and cultural factors, such as religious affiliation and political leaning, seem to have had only minimal influence. Although examples of plain-style furniture have descended in Quaker families, documented pieces have not yet been identified. Leading Quakers patronized fellow Friend Gerrard Hopkins, but surviving accounts indicate that he made for them the same stylish federal furniture that he made for his other wealthy clients. And although Baltimore became "the first important urban constituency for the Republican party,"[10] the furniture of the time appears to reflect just the opposite philosophy. Rather than finding the strong French influence that one might expect in such a Republican stronghold, Baltimore's Federalists and Republicans alike bought London-inspired furniture.[11]

Why did Baltimoreans show such a marked preference for English designs? An obvious reason is the influence the British had on the American colonies until the Revolutionary War. The old-money landed gentry tended to look to England for cultural leadership. This Anglo character of the moneyed classes did not abruptly disappear with the achievement of independence from England. English goods continued to be imported, and immigrants from Great Britain continued to arrive.

Although most immigrant patrons were not directly from London, many were from regions (e.g., northern Ireland) that saw London as the world's style center. Others wanted to be assimilated into the dominant Anglophilic culture. These nouveaux riches wanted to be part of the establishment and to have what was most stylish and elegant. The presence of even a few London-trained craftsmen and their apprentices made it possible to buy the most stylish goods locally.

Patronage of the most current English designs was possible because English furniture pattern books were readily available. These were important sources of ideas for cabinetmakers and clients alike. Baltimore cabinetmakers referred to their English design books for all sorts of pieces, from the most everyday to the most extraordinary. George Hepplewhite's *Cabinet-Maker's and Upholsterer's Guide* (London, 1788, 1794) was probably in use quite early; a copy is known to have been in the original collection of the Library Company of Baltimore, founded in 1795. Plates from Thomas Shearer's *Cabinetmaker's London Book of Prices* (London, 1788, 1793) clearly inspired early federal designs, although the earliest documented appearance in Baltimore of this pattern book is 1807.[12] Thomas Sheraton's *Cabinetmaker's and Upholsterer's Drawing Book* (London, 1791, 1793, 1803) has yet to be discovered in Baltimore's records, though its existence can be deduced from the numerous examples of Baltimore furniture that derive from its illustrations. Although these pattern books were influential in all American urban centers, they had perhaps their greatest and most pervasive impact in Baltimore.

Furniture Craftsmen

The number of furniture craftsmen in Baltimore exploded along with the city's population. Before the Revolution the town had supported only two principal cabinet shops, those of Gerrard Hopkins (active 1767–1800) and Robert Moore (active 1770–83). In the early 1780s, even before the end of the war, several new shops opened (e.g., those of William Askew, active 1780–86; Thomas Aiton, active 1780–84; and James Davidson, active 1780–1806). By 1790 there were approximately twenty-five cabinet and chair-making shops in the city, a number that continued to grow.

The social and ethnic background of many of the most successful cabinetmakers did not reflect the Scots-Irish predominance in the broader mercantile community of Baltimore. Nor did many come to the city directly from London. Indeed, the most important single group appears to have been those who moved to the city from other areas of Maryland. These persons were more significant in both numbers and importance (success and length of career, number of prominent patrons, business connections with other craftsmen, etc.) than those from abroad or from other areas of the country. Among them were Robert Wilkinson, Isaac Johns, John Rutter, William Gordon, and William Singleton.

The leading figure of the Maryland-born group had a flourishing career for over three decades and was the only principal Baltimore cabinetmaker to span both the late colonial and the federal eras. Gerrard Hopkins (1742–1800) left his home in Baltimore County in 1754 to go to Philadelphia, where he trained with fellow Quaker Jonathan Shoemaker.[13] In 1767 he set up shop in Baltimore on Gay Street, where he remained throughout his long and successful career. Hopkins trained or worked with other Maryland-born cabinetmakers (William Askew, William Harris) who became important locally. His numerous clients ranged from local Quakers to prominent landowners of old Maryland families to several of the newly wealthy Scots-Irish Presbyterians.[14]

Some strong competitors (and sometimes partners) of the native group came from outside the state. Of Irish extraction were William McFadon (active 1790–95), William Singleton's partner; Anthony Law (active 1796–1818) and his partner John Denmead (active 1800–1810); John Dougherty (active 1796–1808); and James McCormick (active 1786–1812). (The last is interesting in that even though he advertised his experience "in the first shops of Dublin," he was not able to make a living exclusively as a cabinetmaker.)

Despite the English urban character of the furniture popular in Baltimore, the only English immigrant of significance in the early federal period was Richard Lawson (1749–1803). Born in Yorkshire, Lawson spent thirteen years at the large and fashionable London cabinet warehouse of George Seddon before coming to America about 1776. He began a notable partnership with John Bankson in Baltimore in 1785. Lawson's importance lies not only in the fact that he was the sole major cabinetmaker in the city with London experience, but also in the type of shop and merchandise he and his partner had. Bankson and Lawson's operation was a "cabinet warehouse and manufactury," the first such large-scale establishment in Baltimore. They carried the most up-to-date goods "in the newest taste," and may have been the first in the city to make neoclassical furniture (the commode sideboard tables and ornamented wine coolers they advertised in 1788).[15] They also imported from London stylish items such as looking glasses, dressing glasses, and tea caddies. At least two of their clients are known—General Otho Holland Williams, who purchased expensive settees in 1790, and Richard Tilghman, who purchased a desk and bookcase in 1785. (Significantly, in the following year Tilghman ordered twelve elaborate vase-back chairs from London. Thus Lawson's training may have influenced those clients seeking the latest English taste.) An apprentice of Bankson and Lawson's, William Patterson, later specialized as an inlaymaker, which again reflects the importance of London trade practices in Baltimore.

French-trained cabinetmakers had little impact on the

Baltimore market, certainly nothing comparable to the influence of Charles-Honoré Lannuier in New York. The earliest known Frenchman working in the furniture trades in Baltimore, Francis Fouassier, had disappeared from public view within a few months of his arrival in 1781. Later French arrivals were somewhat more successful, though never numerous.

Several cabinetmakers from states other than Maryland were among the most successful and influential in Baltimore. In the early federal era, the most prominent was John Bankson (active 1783–93), originally from Pennsylvania. He worked with Richard Lawson (noted previously) until 1792, when Lawson departed.[16]

In the late federal era, a craftsman originally from Newark, New Jersey, became the acknowledged leader in the cabinetmaking business. His name has become synonymous with the best of Baltimore neoclassical-style furniture: William Camp (active 1801–22). Camp was renowned in his own day, and his fame continued in Baltimore even after his death. He opened a shop in Baltimore in 1801, possibly having worked in Philadelphia for a few years before. Within a very short time his business expanded; he bought property, began dealing in lumber, and became involved in numerous civic activities. Camp left substantial business records, and his known clients run the spectrum from old Maryland families to newly rich merchants of every ethnic background.

Federal Furniture

Baltimore furniture of the federal period is often described as more English than the products of any other American regional school. In overall design, proportion, and ornamentation it adheres most closely to English prototypes, and references to non-English sources, such as the French neoclassical motifs of furniture produced in federal New York and Philadelphia, are rare.

In the second part of the eighteenth century, the design of English furniture had undergone a revolution. It became architectural in inspiration, but had a refined lightness and elegance. This neoclassical taste was first popularized by Robert Adam in the 1760s. It emphasized geometric forms, flat surface treatments, and delicate ornamentation. This extraordinary change in style came to Baltimore just as the city was undergoing its great period of social and cultural growth. The examples of Baltimore furniture discussed here illustrate the neoclassical style and show the close relationship of Baltimore furniture to its English antecedents and the reliance of the Baltimore craftsmen on the English pattern books. It is important to remember, however, that Baltimore cabinetmakers were eclectic in their borrowing and often digressed from their English sources in both style and techniques of construction. Further, they chose not to interpret many English forms.

The English character of Baltimore federal furniture is evidenced first by the forms and designs that were locally favored in the city. The oval-back chair, for instance, was extremely popular in Baltimore, and many Baltimore-made examples survive. Yet this Adamesque neoclassical form is found only rarely in other American cities. The standard Baltimore example follows English precedent closely: double-beaded edges, three curved splats with teardrop-shaped piercings, and a broad bow-front seat upholstered half over the rails. (This unusual English style of upholstering was used in many Baltimore chairs but in few from other regions.) Whereas the shield-back chair was popular in all American regions, the shape of the shield of the standard Baltimore example (cat. no. 106) is typically English (cat. no. 107). This Baltimore chair has broad proportions, double-beaded edges, a gently curved crest rail, and a curved rather than pointed stay rail. The uniquely Maryland "modified shield-back," with its serpentine side and stay rails, also is based on an English chair form.[17]

A wide variety of sideboard forms were available in Baltimore, but the one that seems to have been most popular is distinctively English. It features full-size drawers or doors on either side of a shallow center section and is either serpentine with canted corners or has a straight front with a projecting center section. In a less common Baltimore variant of this form (fig. 1), the side sections are veneered and banded to appear to be two drawers, and double ovals with pictorial inlays flank the sections. This unusual form has very specific English prototypes; it is not often seen elsewhere in American furniture.[18] In general, the proportions of most Baltimore sideboards are closely related to standard English examples. Another dining-room piece, the tall-legged serpentine English sideboard table (now called a "huntboard"), found its most frequent American expression in Baltimore.

The decoration of Baltimore federal furniture is particularly close to the English style in two specific areas:

Fig. 1. *Sideboard*. American, Baltimore, Md., 1800–1810. Mahogany; satinwood, poplar, yellow pine, and light wood inlays. H. 42⅝ in (108.3 cm), W. 71⅝ in (181.9 cm), D. 26⅜ in (67 cm). Maryland Historical Society, Baltimore, bequest of Mr. and Mrs. Edgar Hinkel, 87.78.

painting and pictorial inlay. Baltimoreans were importing painted furniture from both England and New York by the late 1790s. By 1803, at least three major Baltimore firms (John and Hugh Finlay, active 1803–31; Robert Fisher, active 1795–1810; and Matthew McColm, active 1803–50) were supplying a growing local market for "fancy" furniture imitating the English taste and fashion of the previous decade. Painted furniture was certainly popular in other American cities at this time, but not to the extraordinary extent that it was in Baltimore. Numerous well-to-do Baltimoreans chose to furnish town and country houses with this stylish furniture.

Although used to some extent elsewhere in America, pictorial inlay found its richest expression on Baltimore furniture. The variety seen is enormous: bellflowers, conch shells, grapevines, urns, eagles, thistles, and many other motifs. Some, specifically the large ruffled conch shells, were popular in England and are used similarly on Baltimore examples: placed on the tops of card tables, for instance. Indeed, some of the pictorial inlays used in Baltimore were imported, as documented by the advertisement of Robert Courtney in the *Maryland Journal* of October 19, 1793.

The demand was so great, however, that some Baltimore craftsmen specialized in producing these elaborate ornaments. The first of the inlaymakers, Thomas Barrett (active 1795–1800), carried a huge inventory of "shells" and banding and did business with almost every major cabinetmaker then working in the city.[19] After his death, a large part of the stock was purchased by William Patterson (active 1796–1818, mentioned previously), who then advertised his intention to specialize as an inlaymaker.[20]

A related type of English-inspired decoration, the use of exotic wood veneers, also manifested itself very early in Baltimore. In addition to the highly figured mahoganies and satinwood from the West Indies, South American woods found favor. A number of very high-style Baltimore pieces, such as the Maryland Historical Society's tassel-inlaid card table and wing wardrobe (fig. 2), feature the use of an Australian wood of the genus

Fig. 2. *Wardrobe*. American, Baltimore, Md., 1800–1820. Attributed to William Camp. Mahogany; satinwood, poplar, white pine, and yellow pine. H. 95¼ in (241.9 cm), W. 94 in (238.8 cm), D. 20¼ in (51.4 cm). Maryland Historical Society, bequest of J. B. Noel Wyatt, XX.1.4.

Casuarina. The date of both of these pieces, about 1805, is remarkably early for this sort of wood import. A fine table of about the same date that was originally owned by shipping magnate Robert Oliver is boldly veneered with zebrawood.[21]

The construction of Baltimore furniture as well as its design speaks of its close reliance on English tradition. The use by local cabinetmakers of Honduran mahogany (then usually called "bay wood") for drawer sides is one example. Many sophisticated late federal case pieces, such as the lady's cabinet desk (cat. no. 108), demonstrate this. Most Baltimore federal chairs, which have broad upholstered saddle or serpentine seats in the English fashion, also use the so-called English brace,

Fig. 3. *Library secretary and bookcase*. American, Baltimore, Md., 1800–1810. Attributed to William Camp. Mahogany; poplar, oak, yellow pine, and white pine. H. 90½ in (229.8 cm), W. 85⅛ in (216.2 cm), D. 22½ in (57.1 cm). Maryland Historical Society, Baltimore, Eleanor S. Cohen Collection, 38.7.2.

a narrow diagonal glue block at the corners that is a standard English method of construction.

It was in their extensive and continuing reliance on English pattern books, however, that Baltimore's cabinetmakers most clearly showed their allegiance to English design sources. Camp's use of these books can be both documented and demonstrated. The earliest surviving receipt for Camp's furniture, an 1806 order from Baltimore merchant prince William Patterson, refers to an elegant mahogany clothespress with "two wings."[22] This probably means the type of "wing clothes press" illustrated in plate 3 of Shearer's *Cabinetmaker's London Book of Prices*.[23] Another federal wing wardrobe (fig. 2), now in the collection of the Maryland Historical Society, is attributed to Camp on the basis of both construction and design. A related piece, the Maryland His-

Fig. 4. *Easy chair.* American, Baltimore, Md., 1816. Attributed to William Camp. Mahogany; poplar, chestnut, and white pine. H. 40½ in (102.9 cm), W. 23 in (58.4 cm), D. 21¼ in (54 cm). Maryland Historical Society, Baltimore, gift of Mrs. Joseph Kolodny (Bernice Hendler), 62.101.1.

Fig. 5. *Lady's cabinet dressing table.* American, Baltimore, Md., 1800–1810. Attributed to William Camp. Mahogany; satinwood, poplar, and red cedar. H. 72 in (182.8 cm), W. 54⅜ in (138.1 cm), D. 25¼ in (64.1 cm). Maryland Historical Society, Baltimore, Eleanor S. Cohen Collection, 38.7.8.

torical Society's library secretary and bookcase originally made for Solomon Etting and attributable to Camp's shop (fig. 3), is similarly based on Shearer's designs.

Camp referred also to Hepplewhite's *Guide* and to Sheraton's *Drawing Book.* In 1816 he made a barrel-back easy chair (fig. 4) for J. I. Cohen, Jr., that was derived from the "confidant" illustrated in plate 27 of the *Guide.* His elaborate trade card featured illustrations of several pieces from the *Drawing Book,* and a highly important group of pieces that can be attributed to Camp's shop are based on plates from this book. They include the lady's cabinet dressing table made for Mrs. Solomon Etting (fig. 5, based on pl. 49, which is also the central illustration on Camp's trade card), three similar cabinet desks (figs. 6, 7, 8), and catalogue number 108 (based on pls. 48 [cat no. 109] and 50).

Baltimore Federal Furniture 263

Fig. 6. *Dressing table.* American, Baltimore, Md., 1795–1810. Mahogany. H. 62⅛ in (19.7 cm), W. 30⅞ in (78.4 cm), D. 22¼ in (56.5 cm). Courtesy of The Henry Francis du Pont Winterthur Museum, Winterthur, Del., 57.68.

Fig. 7. *Dressing table.* American, Baltimore, Md., about 1800. Mahogany; satinwood, holly, and ivory. The Metropolitan Museum of Art, New York, Fletcher Fund, 34.135.

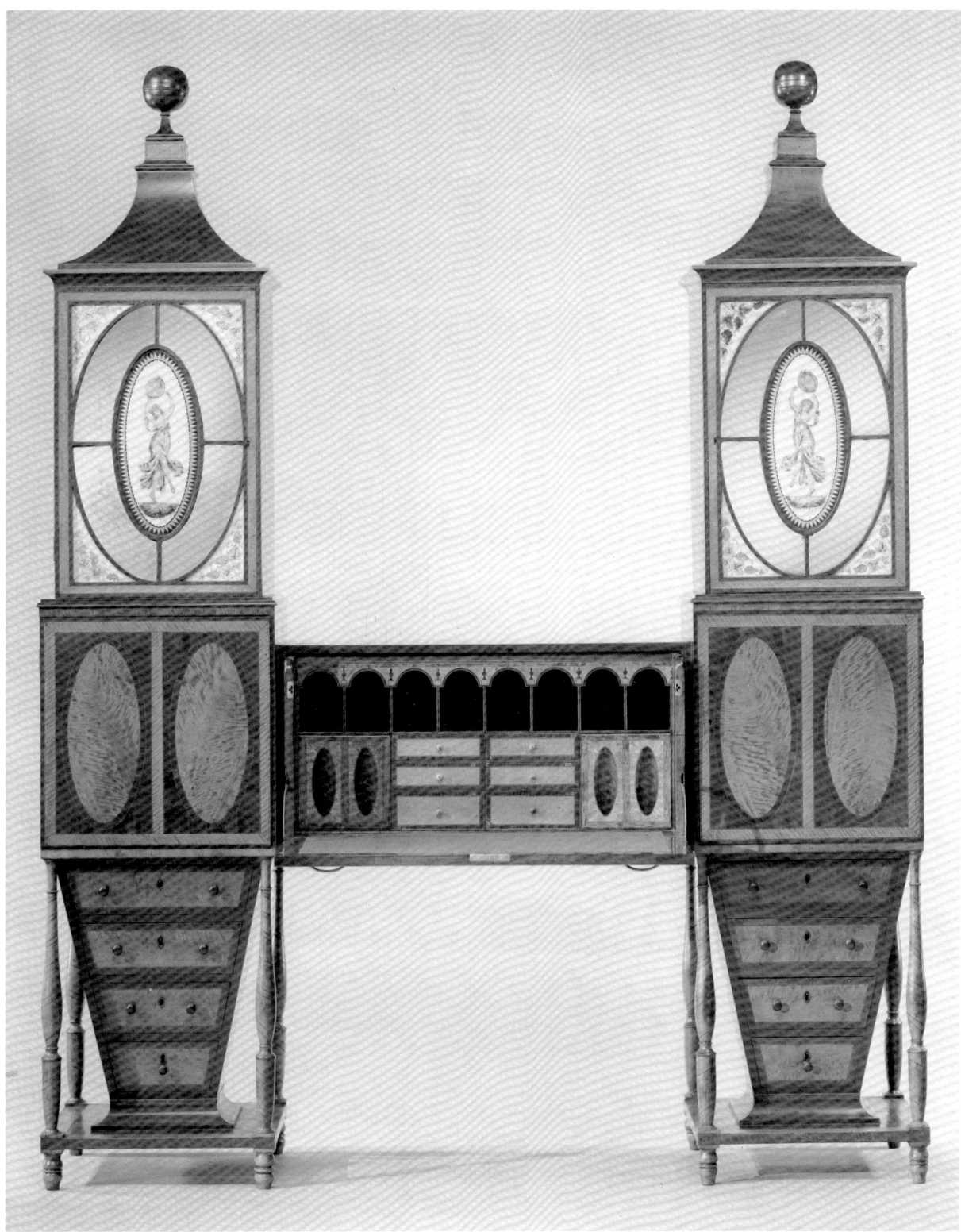

Fig. 8. *Desk and bookcase*. American, Baltimore, Md., about 1811. Mahogany; satinwood, maple, and cedar. H. 91 in (231.1 cm), W. 72 in (182.9 cm), D. 19⅛ in (48.6 cm). The Metropolitan Museum of Art, New York, gift of Mrs. Russell Sage and various other donors, by exchange, 62.203.

Fig. 9. *Side chair*. American, Baltimore, Md., 1790–1810. Mahogany; chestnut and ash. H. 36 in (91.5 cm), W. 20⅜ in (51.8 cm), D. 20¾ in (52.7 cm). Baltimore Musueon of Art, Philip B. Perlman Bequest Fund, 64.9.

Fig. 10. *Side chair*. American, Baltimore, Md., 1800–1810. Mahogany; poplar. H. 36⅝ in (93 cm), W. 21 in (53.3 cm), D. 20 in (50.8 cm). Maryland Historical Society, Baltimore, gift of Mrs. Dexter Pennington, 87.121.

Furniture by other Baltimore cabinetmakers also showed the influence of the three major pattern books. Among the original furnishings of Druid Hill, the splendid country house of Colonel Nicholas Rogers IV completed in 1801, was a beautiful Hepplewhite-derived sofa (cat. no. 110) and a square-back chair with racquet splat based on plate 28 of Sheraton's *Drawing Book* (fig. 9).[24] Similarly, two shield-back chairs owned by Charles Carroll of Carrollton may originally have been used at Homewood, completed in 1804. One chair is derived from plate 5 in Hepplewhite's *Guide* (cat. no. 107), the other from plate 36 in Sheraton's *Drawing Book* (fig. 10).[25]

The more expensive form of seating furniture, the sofa, began to be made with some frequency by the late 1790s, and most Baltimore examples are closely related to either plate 22 or 24 in Hepplewhite's *Guide* (see cat. no. 112). The standard Baltimore square-back reeded sofa of the 1815–20 period derived ultimately from plate 35 of Sheraton's *Drawing Book*.

Other than side chairs, the most frequently surviving form in American federal furniture is the card table, and the most typical form in Baltimore is derived from Hepplewhite's *Guide*. The standard example has a half-round top, a veneered and banded apron, and square tapered legs with chains of bellflowers (pl. 60). Although

Fig. 11. *Card table*. American, Baltimore or Annapolis, Md., 1790–1810. Mahogany; yellow pine, tulip poplar, and oak. H. 29¼ in (74.3 cm), W. 34⅞ in (88.6 cm), D. 17⅜ in (44.1 cm). Collection of Dorothy McIlvain Scott.

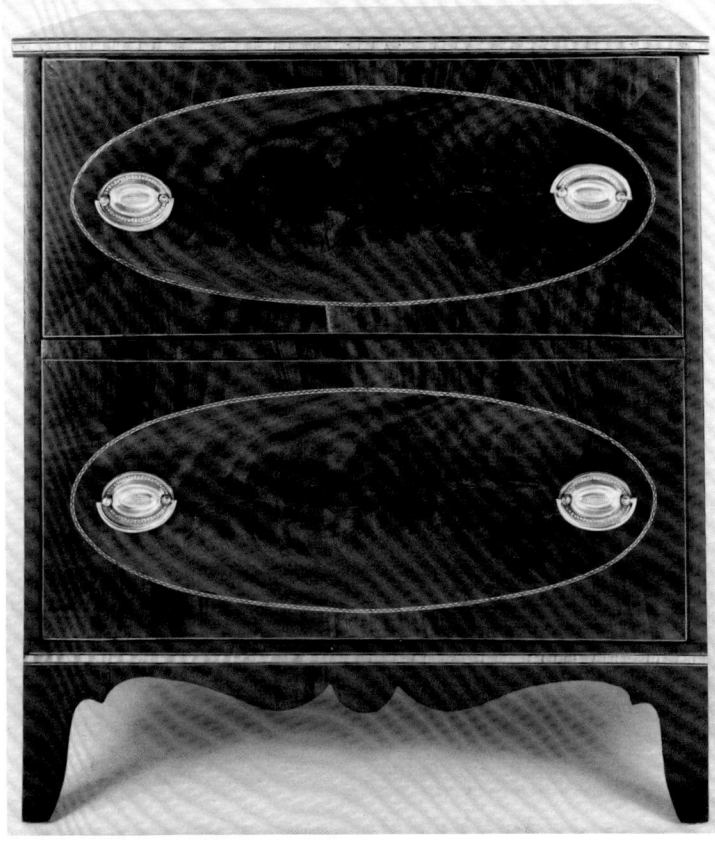

Fig. 12. *Night table*. American, Baltimore, Md., 1790–1810. Mahogany; poplar and white pine. H. 27½ in (69.8 cm), W. 29⅜ in (74.5 cm), D. 18 in (45.7 cm). Maryland Historical Society, Baltimore, gift of Mrs. Ludlow H. Baldwin (Anne Gordon Boyce) in memory of her mother Mrs. Herbert J. Johnston (Anne Gordon Thom), 79.46.8.

the tops of most Baltimore card tables are not as ornate as those illustrated in Hepplewhite's plate 61, the frequent use of elaborate pictorial inlays in half-round panels is an attempt in this direction (fig. 11). Similarly, the typical Baltimore oval Pembroke table, though not as ornamented on the top, resembles in all other respects the example at the bottom of Hepplewhite's plate 62.

The three most typical forms of Baltimore federal chests of drawers (straight, bow, and serpentine front) are related to those in the *Guide*, particularly in the use of the "cupid's bow" skirt with inlaid central scallop and flaring French feet (pl. 76). The related fall-front secretary with flat-top bookcase was very popular in Baltimore. Several local examples imitate the secretary over two doors, similar to Hepplewhite's plate 43, and over three graduated drawers (pl. 44). Even the simplest forms of case furniture made in Baltimore were based on Hepplewhite's designs. A sizable group of commodes in the form of small chests, called "night tables" in Hepplewhite's *Guide*, has survived (fig. 12). Virtually all are based on the two examples shown in plate 82 of the *Guide*.

Sheraton's and Shearer's designs were the ones usually referred to by Baltimore cabinetmakers for the more elaborate, custom-made furniture. Most notable are the extraordinary cabinet desks and dressing tables, all

Baltimore Federal Furniture   267

Fig. 13. *Pier table.* American, Baltimore, Md., or Philadephia, Pa., 1802–10. Mahogany. H. 36¾ in (93.3 cm), W. 45⅛ in (114.6 cm), D. 22 in (55.9 cm). The Henry Francis du Pont Winterthur Museum, Winterthur, Del., 57.779.1.

unique examples, that are based on several of Sheraton's plates. The cabinet desks attributed to Camp have already been mentioned (cat. no. 108; figs. 6, 7, 8). Perhaps the latest and most exuberant of the group is the "sister's" cabinet secretary and bookcase (fig. 8) at the Metropolitan Museum. Made, possibly by Camp, for Robert Oliver's daughter Margaret in 1811, it is derived from plate 7, "A Sister Cylinder Bookcase," of Sheraton's *Cabinet Dictionary*, published in 1803 in London.

With the exception of the cabinet desk (cat. no. 108), all of these pieces feature the use of *verre églomisé* (reverse painting on glass) panels, some designs of which are also based on illustrations in Sheraton's or Shearer's works. Other fine pieces of custom-made Baltimore furniture that have *églomisé* panels and derive from design books are the distinctive corner tables and matching pier tables, such as those at Winterthur (fig. 13). A few other rare and unusual examples, for instance the highly ornamented pier table at the Baltimore Museum of Art (cat. no. 113), and a pair of elegant pier tables with arched stretchers (fig. 14), all based on Sheraton's plate 4 (cat. no. 115), are extremely English in character (cat. no. 114).

Shearer's plates were the source for some major custom-made case pieces. A group of large Baltimore wing wardrobes, some with satinwood panels and having the distinctive Shearer Gothic arch cornice (fig. 2), are based on plate 3. The large Etting family library

Fig. 14. *Pier table*. American, Philadelphia, Pa., 1800–1810. Attributed to Joseph B. Barry. Mahogany; poplar. H. 39 in (99 cm), W. 35¾ in (90.8 cm), D. 19¾ in (50.17 cm). Courtesy Bernard & S. Dean Levy, Inc., New York.

secretary and bookcase (fig. 3) at the Maryland Historical Society derives from plate 1. Both of these pieces were made around 1804–6.

Just how closely did Baltimore's cabinetmakers follow the designs printed in the pattern books? In some cases the copy was virtually exact. For example, the shield-back side chair (cat. no. 106), based on plate 5 of Hepplewhite's *Guide* (cat. no. 107), shows only very slight differences from the plate in the execution of the legs, but these are virtual copies of those seen on plate 6. Similarly, the backs of the Charles Carroll set of shield-back side chairs (fig. 10) are a careful translation of chair back number 5 on Sheraton's plate 36. Interestingly, the former and the latter chairs may have been made in the same shop; the same source (Hepplewhite's pl. 6) was used for the legs of both. Other relatively straightforward pieces, such as the night table (fig. 12), also carefully follow published designs.

More complex and elaborate pieces tend to show greater variation from the inspiring illustration, as seen in the group of cabinet desks. Though Sheraton's designs were unquestionably the source of inspiration, local Baltimore cabinetmakers used his plates only as a starting point for variation. In the case of the "sister's" cabinet secretary and bookcase (fig. 8), Sheraton's highly complex design of a double cylinder desk was somewhat simplified into a single fall-front design, though the striking overall form with its tall towers and trap-

Fig. 15. *Dressing cabinet*. English, about 1790. Satinwood, painted and inlaid. H. 76 in (193 cm), W. 47 in (119.4 cm), D. 25½ in (64.8 cm). Courtesy of Sotheby's.

ezoidal bases was retained. The lady's cabinet dressing table shown in figure 5 is a true American variant of the English theme. The top is ornamented with an eagle, and the bottom is essentially the form of a typical Baltimore federal sideboard with the addition of a dressing drawer.

Another example of a unique and truly magnificent piece is the serpentine chest-on-cabinet (cat. no. 116), again made for the Solomon Ettings. Although the intricate patterns of the veneers are derived from English sources, particularly Shearer, and are related to other Baltimore work, no precise precedent for this piece is known. Owners of several other important pieces (the lady's cabinet dressing table, the library secretary and bookcase, and a pair of corner tables),[26] the Ettings typically commissioned furniture that, although based on the best English taste, showed the originality and vitality of Baltimore adaptations.

270 Gregory R. Weidman

The work of English cabinetmakers, who also copied pattern-book designs, is often quite different from the results of their Baltimore counterparts. An impressive satinwood dressing cabinet (fig. 15), also inspired by Sheraton's plate 49, illustrates some of these differences. Overall, the piece is larger and flashier in its use of fancy wood. It is also closer in detail to the design, including the extensive use of painted decoration. Similar differences can be seen between the Baltimore and English interpretations of more standard pieces such as chairs and sofas. The typical English cabriole sofa (cat. no. 111) is not necessarily closer in detail to the Hepplewhite plates but usually does feature more intricate carving and molding. Naturally, the English sofas are often larger in scale, to better suit their surroundings. English chairs, though not necessarily bigger overall, tend to be more horizontal in proportion. Elaboration and a multiplicity of decorative elements characterize English pieces but are not usually seen on Baltimore examples (see cat. no. 110).

Conclusion

In spite of the paucity of English immigrants among either patrons or furniture craftsmen in late eighteenth-century Baltimore, the furniture of the time shows close adherence to English prototypes. The very newness and vitality of federal Baltimore, combined with the pre-Revolutionary heritage of mostly British goods for the upper classes, the desire of newly wealthy tradesmen to be part of the establishment, and ready access to pattern books, contributed to the production of quantities of fashionable and elegant English-style furniture.

Baltimore federal furniture, however, was not made in slavish imitation of English designs. Local craftsmen often modified English ideas to produce truly American interpretations. The chest-on-cabinet (cat. no. 116) is a particularly good example: although related to published English designs for serpentine chests, its chest-on-cabinet form has no English precedent. In its bold conception and beautiful execution it is a great statement of the best in the American decorative arts.

NOTES

1. Raphael Semmes, *Baltimore as Seen by Visitors* (Baltimore: Maryland Historical Society, 1953), p. 27.
2. Ibid., p. 2.
3. Ibid., p. 3.
4. Thomas W. Griffith, *Annals of Baltimore* (Baltimore: W. Wooddy, 1834), p. 113.
5. Ibid., p. 118.
6. Semmes, *Baltimore Seen by Visitors*, p. 3.
7. Ibid., p. 27.
8. After Irishman Isaac Weld visited Baltimore in 1796, he noted with considerable pride that his countrymen were the most numerous group and counted many of the principal merchants among them. Some of the significant names in this group are Patterson, Oliver, O'Donnell, Buchanan, Smith, Gilmor, Dugan, Purviance, and Wilson—all founders of great Baltimore fortunes and families.
9. Semmes, *Baltimore Seen by Visitors*, p. 12.
10. Gary Browne, "Federalism in Baltimore," *Maryland Historical Magazine*, Spring 1988, p. 51.
11. The example of a leading Republican figure is typical: Robert Smith was a member of a very prominent Scots-Irish mercantile family. He served as secretary of state under President Madison. One surviving piece of his furniture, an unusual alcove table with bellflower inlay, shows his buying standard—English-looking Baltimore furniture. Indeed, in later years when he chose to purchase empire furniture in the French taste, he was obliged to find it in New York.
12. In 1807 William Camp, a renowned Baltimore cabinetmaker, advertised in the August 14 edition of the *Baltimore American* for the return of his lost copy.
13. Maryland Historical Society Library, Genealogical Collections, G5025, Book 4. Shoemaker's name is incorrectly quoted in William Voss Elder and Jayne Stokes, *American Furniture, 1680–1880, from the Collection of the Baltimore Museum of Art* (Baltimore: Baltimore Museum of Art, 1987), p. 28.
14. The established families were the Goughs, Ridgelys, Dorseys, and Bowlys. The newly wealthy clients included Hugh Thompson, Cumberland Dugan, John O'Donnell, Alexander Brown, and General Sam Smith.
15. *Maryland Journal*, August 29, 1786, and June 17, 1788.
16. Johnston Family Papers, Maryland Historical Society Manuscripts Collection, no. 2500. After Lawson's departure, Bankson was joined by Robert Wilkinson, previously an apprentice of William Askew's. Wilkinson continued the firm in turn after Bankson's departure, with William H. Smith until 1797 and then on his own until 1799. Accounts of the firm of Wilkinson and Smith from 1795 show the very elaborate and sophisticated furniture coming from this shop, including dozens of oval- and heart-back chairs and veneered and banded serpentine sideboards.
17. Herbert Cescinsky, *English Furniture from Gothic to Sheraton* (Grand Rapids, Mich.: Dean-Hicks Company, 1929), p. 365.
18. Ibid., p. 404. For Baltimore sideboards, see Edgar G. Miller, *American Antique Furniture* (Baltimore: Lord Baltimore Press, 1937), 1:527, nos. 953, 954.
19. Among those owing debts to Barrett's estate were John Alexander, William Brown, Coleman and Taylor, Combs and Jenkins, Walter Crook, James Davidson, John Dougherty, William Faris, Hopkins and Harris, Nathaniel Hynson, Isaac Johns, Anthony Law, James Martin, Henry Purcell, William Singleton, Levin S. Tarr, and Moses Ward.
20. *Baltimore American*, November 22, 1800.
21. Illustrated in *Baltimore Furniture: The Work of Baltimore and Annapolis Cabinetmakers from 1760 to 1810* (Baltimore: Baltimore Museum of Art, 1947), no. 4.
22. Patterson Account Book, MdHS MS. 111.
23. Camp's ownership of the 1793 edition of this pattern book has already been noted (see note 12).
24. Elder and Stokes, *American Furniture*, p. 42, no. 27.
25. Ibid., p. 37, no. 22, and p. 38, no. 23.
26. Gregory R. Weidman, *Furniture in Maryland, 1740–1940* (Baltimore: Maryland Historical Society, 1984), nos. 148, 97, 149.

Catalogue Objects

106. *Side chair*
American, Baltimore, Md., 1790–1810
Mahogany; oak
H. 37½ in (95.3 cm), W. 21 in (53.3 cm), D. 21⅛ in (53.7 cm)
Maryland Historical Society, Baltimore, gift of Mrs. Francis Tazewell Redwood, XX.4.183

106. Side chair / 107. Side chair design

This chair is as thoroughly English in design and execution as any produced in federal America. The design for the back is closely copied from plate 5 of Hepplewhite's *Guide* (1788, 1794), and the legs are based on those shown in plate 6 of that highly influential publication. Even the details of the carving, such as the half-daisy carving at the base of the splats and the top of the legs, are very similar to those suggested by Hepplewhite. Other elements of the design, such as the broad rounded shape of the shield back and the double-

107. *Side chair design*
George Hepplewhite, *The Cabinet-Maker and Upholsterer's Guide* (London, 1788), plate 5
Photograph courtesy of The Winterthur Library: Printed Book and Periodical Collection

beaded edges, are like those seen on English chairs of the period.

Baltimoreans, whether members of the landed gentry or newly rich merchants, seem to have preferred this very English type of furniture. This chair was owned by the Dorsey family, and closely related ones were owned by the Carrolls, both old established families. The survival of at least four other sets of chairs of similar design point to the great popularity of Hepplewhite's work in federal Maryland.

108. *Lady's cabinet desk*
American, Baltimore, Md., 1800–1820
Possibly William Camp, born Newark, N.J. (1773–1822)
Mahogany, ebony, and satinwood (with gilding); mahogany, poplar, chestnut, white pine, and yellow pine
H. 56 in (142.2 cm), W. 44 in (111.8 cm), D. 21⅜ in (54.3 cm)
Maryland Historical Society, Baltimore, bequest of James Wilson Leakin, 23.17.10

108. Lady's cabinet desk
109. Cabinet desk design

The most important surviving group of Baltimore federal furniture comprises several very elaborate lady's cabinet desks and dressing tables, all with related designs based on the published drawings of Thomas Sheraton. This desk, one of the latest of the group, is actually derived from two plates in Sheraton's *Drawing-Book* (1793). The desk section is copied with very little modification from plate 48 (cat. no. 109); the top is more loosely based on plate 50. The Baltimore cabinet-maker further showed his ability to adapt and expand on English ideas by adding mirrors, gilding to the domes and turnings on the base, and satinwood corner columns. Other aspects of Baltimore federal cabinet-making that relate it to English work, the frequent use of exotic woods and the use of mahogany as a secondary wood, are also seen in this piece. The selection of highly figured mahogany veneers, set off by extraordi-

274   Gregory R. Weidman

109. *Cabinet desk design*
Thomas Sheraton, *The Cabinet-Maker and Upholsterer's Drawing-Book* (London, 1793), plate 48
Photograph courtesy of The Winterthur Library: Printed Book and Periodical Collection

nary eighth-inch crossbanding on all drawers and doors, is further testimony to the skill of the craftsman.

This desk may have been made in the shop of Baltimore's most prestigious cabinetmaker, William Camp (active 1801–22). The work produced in that shop, the largest in Baltimore, was renowned even at the time. Camp was familiar with and was documented to have used all three major English design sources (Hepplewhite's *Cabinet-Maker's and Upholsterer's Guide*, Sheraton's *Drawing-Book*, and Shearer's plates for *The Cabinetmaker's London Book of Prices*). His trade card illustrates several plates from the *Drawing-Book*, including one for a lady's cabinet dressing table which was the basis for a piece closely related to the cabinet desk seen here. The desk also shares features of drawer and case construction with pieces both documented and attributed to Camp's shop. Whoever its maker, the lady's cabinet desk is the summation of Baltimore federal cabinetmaking, reflecting the richness and sophistication of that thriving city.

110. Sofa / 111. Sofa / 112. Sofa design

Baltimore was the fastest growing city in the country during the federal era. Immigrants flocked to the city to make their fortunes, and on achieving success, often built both substantial town houses and country residences. The sofa pictured here (cat. no. 110) was one of the original furnishings of one of Baltimore's finest neoclassical country houses, Druid Hill, built northwest of the city in 1801. The house was designed by its owner, Colonel Nicholas Rogers IV (1753–1822), a wealthy merchant and landowner who was also an amateur architect. Rogers may well have been familiar with Hepplewhite's *Guide* (1788, 1794), the source of this sofa's elegant design, since the book was then available among the volumes in the collection of the Library Company of Baltimore.

Although plate 24 in the *Guide* (cat. no. 112) is clearly the inspiration for the Druid Hill sofa, this Baltimore cabinetmaker did not copy so precisely as did the one who made the shield-back chair (cat. no. 106). The lovely serpentine cabriole shape of the sofa is the same, as is the continuous molding around the back and arms.

Hepplewhite's design, however, suggests a carved crest at the top and carved ornament at the base of the arms and on the legs. The Baltimore cabinetmaker chose to decorate those areas with pictorial inlays and to upholster the seat half over rather than completely over the front rail. This variation from the published design still shows Baltimore furniture's close adherence to English practice, since pictorial inlays and half-upholstered seats are typical of English cabinetwork.

Although both the Baltimore sofa (cat. no. 110) and the English sofa (cat. no. 111) are based on plate 24 in Hepplewhite's *Guide*, there are clear differences in the way the published design was interpreted. The English sofa is embellished principally with carved ornament as Hepplewhite's drawing suggests, the chains of bellflowers on the arms, the rosettes over the legs, and the guilloche molding of the seat rail being particularly close to the drawing. The unusual stepped feet, not found on American furniture, can be seen on other plates in the *Guide* (e.g., pl. 11). The overall fussiness of the English sofa when contrasted with the Baltimore example is

110. *Sofa*
American, Baltimore, Md., 1800–1805
Mahogany; poplar and chestnut
H. 38⅜ in (97.5 cm), W. 78¼ in (198.8 cm), D. 32 in (81.3 cm)
Maryland Historical Society, Baltimore, gift of Mrs. Van Santvoord Merle-Smith and Mrs. Thomas M. Weaver in memory of their parents, Mr. and Mrs. Edmund Law Rogers Smith, 77.23.1

111. *Sofa*
English, 1790–1800
Mahogany; poplar
H. 38 in (96.5 cm), W. 79½ in (201.9 cm), D. 27½ in (69.9 cm)
Collection of Mr. and Mrs. Benjamin Ginsburg

112. *Sofa design*
George Hepplewhite, *The Cabinet-Maker and Upholsterer's Guide* (London, 1788), plate 24
Photograph courtesy of The Winterthur Library: Printed Book and Periodical Collection

heightened by its upholstered arm rests and the triple serpentine shaping of the front seat rail, features not found in the Hepplewhite design.

Despite these differences, there are several similarities. Both sofas have continuous wood molding around the back and are not fully upholstered over the front rail. They are also similar in size and proportion, which is unusual, since many English sofas are larger in scale than their American counterparts.[1] Overall, however, the two sofas show the different approaches of the two cabinetmaking schools.

1. The seat of the Baltimore sofa is unusually deep, though some other examples produced in that city also have this feature.

Baltimore Federal Furniture 277

113. *Pier table*
American, Baltimore, Md., 1800–1810
Mahogany and satinwood; white pine and tulip poplar
H. 34½ in (87.6 cm), W. 39¾ in (101 cm), D. 20⅛ in (51.1 cm)
The Baltimore Museum of Art, anonymous gift, 1982.143

114. *Pier table*
English, 1780–90
Satinwood; pine
H. 36 in (91.4 cm), W. 64 in (162.6 cm), D. 23 in (58.4 cm)
Victoria and Albert Museum, London, W5-1966

113. Pier table / 114. Pier table
115. Pier table design

The heavily ornamented English pier table (cat. no. 114) typifies the exuberant extremes to which English furniture decorators carried the style of fancy furniture in the late eighteenth century. The craftsman may have been inspired by Hepplewhite's description of a pier table as "an article of much fashion; and not being applied to such general use as other tables, admit, with great propriety, of much elegance and ornament."[1] Even the richly colored West Indian satinwood is almost obscured by the multiplicity of ornament. Hepplewhite illustrates elaborately decorated tops for pier and other tables and comments that they may be "inlaid, or painted and varnished."[2] The suggested motifs, however, tend to be neoclassical, with chains of bellflowers or stylized rinceaux being favored over the naturalistic floral festoons and vines seen here. Many wealthy Baltimoreans continued to import pieces such as the painted pier table throughout the 1790s, giving rise to the fashion for richly decorated fancy furniture that became enormously popular in Maryland after 1800.

English tables of this type, though not copied precisely, nevertheless were the inspiration for a great deal of Baltimore federal furniture, both inlaid and painted. Without the confirming evidence of native American woods in the frame, one might attribute this very elaborate Baltimore table (cat. no. 113) to England. The de-

Gregory R. Weidman

sign is derived from plate 4 of the appendix of Sheraton's *Drawing-Book* (1793) (cat. no. 115), notably the shape of the top, the concave stretchers, and the half-round platform that connects the front and rear stretchers. Typical of Baltimore furniture of this time, however, the influence of Hepplewhite's *Cabinet-Maker's and Upholsterer's Guide* (1788, 1794) is discernible in the pattern of the veneering on the top (see pls. 64–66) and in the use of inlaid square tapered legs rather than the turned legs suggested by Sheraton.

Other elements of this table's design also demonstrate its close connection to English neoclassical furniture. The rich use of intricate pictorial inlays is a hallmark of the best Baltimore federal furniture in the English tradition. This table has the particularly distinctive large shaded conch shell and half blossom, plus a basket of flowers, single flowers in pots, and a dogwood blossom and bellflowers on the legs. Another key element of the pier table's design, the extravagant use of exotic veneers, is a further mark of its English derivation.

Despite the overall English impression of this Baltimore table, its American origin is apparent from more than the secondary woods alone. The substantial quality of the construction and use of a medial brace are American features, as are the proportions. The particular designs of the pictorial inlays and patterned stringing and their placement on the table are typical of Baltimore cabinetwork. While closely following English precedents to suit the Anglophilic Baltimore patron, the American cabinetmaker was nevertheless able to make a distinctive statement.

1. George Hepplewhite, *The Cabinet-Maker's and Upholsterer's Guide* (London: I. and J. Taylor, 1794), p. 12.
2. Ibid. See also pls. 59–66.

115. *Pier table design*
Thomas Sheraton, *The Cabinet-Maker and Upholsterer's Drawing-Book* (London, 1793), Appendix, plate 4
Photograph courtesy of The Winterthur Library: Printed Book and Periodical Collection

116. Chest-on-cabinet

If most other pieces of Baltimore federal furniture show close adherence to English design sources, this one demonstrates the great creativity and independence of the city's cabinetmakers. A tour de force of design and craftsmanship, this wonderful piece is unique in American furniture. Although clearly within the standard English idiom, as shown by the patterns of the veneering, the chest-on-cabinet form is not found in either British published designs or known prototypes. The boldness of the conception is heightened by the deeply serpentine shape and the contrasting shades of the richly figured veneers.

This chest reflects not only the skill of the cabinetmaker but also the sophistication and taste of the clients. It was made for Solomon and Rachel Gratz Etting, members of federal Baltimore's mercantile elite. Other surviving examples of their furniture, the extraordinary lady's cabinet dressing table and a pair of *verre églomisé* (reverse-painted on glass) inlaid corner tables, further testify to their selecting the very best in locally manufactured goods. Those pieces, like this magnificent chest, are based on English designs but go beyond them to become uniquely American objects.

116. *Chest-on-cabinet*
American, Baltimore, Md., 1795–1810
Possibly William Camp, born Newark, N.J. (1773–1822)
Mahogany; poplar and yellow pine
H. 91¼ in (231.8 cm), W. 52¾ in (134 cm), D. 25½ in (64.8 cm)
Maryland Historical Society, Baltimore, The Eleanor S. Cohen Collection, XX.3.114

Baltimore Federal Furniture 281

Contributors to the Catalogue

Michael Conforti is chief curator and Bell Memorial Curator of Decorative Arts and Sculpture at The Minneapolis Institute of Arts.

Wallace B. Gusler is director of conservation at The Colonial Williamsburg Foundation, Williamsburg, Virginia.

Morrison H. Heckscher is curator of American decorative arts at The Metropolitan Museum of Art, New York.

Graham Hood is Carlisle H. Humelsine Curator of The Colonial Williamsburg Foundation, Williamsburg, Virginia.

Gary B. Nash is professor of history at the University of California, Los Angeles, and associate director of the National Center for History in the Schools.

Arlene Palmer is an independent scholar and dealer. She was formerly curator of glass and ceramics at The Henry Francis du Pont Winterthur Museum, Winterthur, Delaware.

Donna L. Pierce is a research associate at the Museum of New Mexico, Santa Fe.

Francis J. Puig was formerly curator of decorative arts and sculpture at The Minneapolis Institute of Arts. He is now an independent scholar and dealer of contemporary crafts.

Robert F. Trent is curator and in charge of furniture at The Henry Francis du Pont Winterthur Museum, Winterthur, Delaware.

Barbara McLean Ward is director of interpretation and publications at the Essex Institute, Salem, Massachusetts.

Gerald W. R. Ward is curator of Strawbery Banke, Portsmouth, New Hampshire.

Gregory R. Weidman is curator at the Maryland Historical Society, Baltimore.

Index

Adobe, 190
Affleck, Thomas, 7, 93, 95, 96, 99, 103–4
Agriculture
   Connecticut, 116
   Santa Fe, N.M., 181
Allen, James, 67, 68
Allen, John, 67, 68, 75n, 80–81
Allen, Stephen, 11
American China Factory, 240–46
American Indians. *See* Native Americans
Andrews, Samuel, 140
Andros, Edmund, 67
Anglicization, xvii, xix
   Baltimore, xvii
   Mississippi River valley, 166
   See also English influence
Anglo culture. *See* Anglicization
Anthony, Isaac, 90
Antiquarianism, xiii
Antiques magazine, 52
Apprentice
   defined, 2–3
   family, 182
   guild, 179
   hierarchy, 1
   income, 2
   vs. journeyman, 16
   vs. master, 16
   records, 241
   skills, 16
   Williamsburg, Va., 53
   See also Journeyman, Master
Architectural history
   terms, 112
Architecture
   French influence, *155*, 155–57
   Mexican, 181
Aristocracy
   lack in America, 16
Arkell, Peter, 120
Armoires
   French, *179*
   Mississippi River valley, *156*, 157, *159*, *160*, 161–62, *163*, *164*, 165, *174*, *175*, *176*
   Philadelphia, 168
   See also Wardrobes
Art of Making Money Plenty in Every Man's Pocket, 2
Artisans. *See* Craftsmen

Assimilation, xix, xiii
   Associators, 5

Bacon, Pierpoint, 116
Baltimore, Md.
   commercial center, 1, 256
   English tradition, xvii
   federal-period, 19–20, 256–81
   furniture, 256–81
   mechanics, 11
   population, 257
Barnes, Abraham, 69
Bartlem, John, 246, 247n
Bartram, John, 92
Beach, Abigail, 140
Beakers
   silver, 70, 141
Beer glasses, 217
Belcher, Andrew, 4
Bell, Phillip, 42
Bentley, William, Reverend, 23, 29
Bernard, Nicholas, 93, 96, 100, 104–5
Bespoke work, 4, 74
Biddle, Owen, 7
Bisson, Joshua, 26
Blanck, Jurian, 138
Boas, Franz, xxn
Bogardus, Everardus, 137
Bonnin, Gousse, 241
Bonnin, Henry, 241
Bonnin and Morris porcelain factory, xviii, xix, 241–55 passim
Book of Cyphers, 139
Booker, Richard, 53
Boston, Mass.
   artisan property owners, 9
   artisan status, 15
   cabinetmakers, 29, 34–35
   commercial center, 1, 27
   economics, xvii, xix, 4, 70, 74–75
   Edwards family, 66–75
   goldsmiths, 74–75
   silversmiths, xvii, xix, 66–91 passim
   woods, 43
Boston Massacre
   engraving, 7
Boston Tea Party
   last surviving member, 3
Botetourt, Lord, 52
Bottles
   English, 226–27, *227*

green glass, 204–5, 222, *226*, 226–27
pocket, 214, *214*, 230, *230*, *231*
Boutet, Peter, 69
Bowls
    bases, 220
    brandy, 138
    china, 243, 255, *255*
    Dutch, 146–147, *147*
    Kierstede, 138, 140 passim, 146–47, *146*, *147*
    lemon, 216
Boycott
    British goods, 6–7, 240
Boyer, James, 69
Brasher, Abraham, 7
Braudel, Fernand, xix
Bridenbaugh, Carl, 7
British Architect, 96
Brittain, Lionel, 2
Brody, David, 9
Broutin, Ignace François, 168n
Brown, William, 26
Bucktrout, Benjamin, 44, 49, 52–54, 55n, 58, 59
Buffington, Thomas and Sarah
    cabinet, 34–35, *37*
Buildings
    changing colonial culture, xiii
Bulkeley, Eliphalet, 113, 119, 120, 123, 128
Bulkeley, Houghton, 114
Bulkeley, John, Reverend, 128
Burnham, Benjamin, xviii, 113–18, 119, 120–21, 125–30
Burnham, Catherine Trumbull, 113, 128
Burnham, Griswold, 113
Burnham, Joseph Trumbull, 113
Burr, Aaron
    trial, 53
Burt, John, 72, 74
Byrd, William, III, 52

Cabinet and Chair-Makers in the Federal Procession, 95
Cabinet-Maker and Upholsterer's Drawing-Book, 258, 262–71, 274–75, 278
Cabinet-Maker and Upholsterer's Guide, 257, 262–63, 266–73, 275, 276, 279
Cabinetmaker's London Book of Prices, 258, 262, 275
Cabinetry
    Baltimore, 256, 258
    Canadian, 169–75
    Colchester, 112–18
    Boston, 29, 34–35, *37*
    Colchester cabinetmakers, 116
    emergence of cabinetmakers, 29
    French cabinetmakers, 258–59
    London influence, 42, 46, 258
    methods, 42
    New Mexico, 188, *189*
    Philadelphia style, 92–111, 115
    production responsibility, 161
    simple, xviii
    Symonds, 34–35, *35*
    technologically advanced, 43

Caddow, William, 69, 84n
Cadwalader, John, 93, 96, 100
Cadwalader, Thomas, Dr., 4
Camp, William, 259, 275, 280
Campbell, R., 14–16
Candlemolds
    glass, 208, *209*
Candlestands
    Hay, 42
Candlesticks
    Kierstede, 139, 143–45, *143*, *145*
Canns, Glass, 215, *215*
Capen, Nathaniel, 26
Caribbean influence, 175
Carpenters
    Native American, 180
    New Mexico, 182
    strike, 9
Carvers, 96
Case furniture, 44, *45*, *47*, 60–61, 113–15, 117, 269
Cats, Jacobus, 139
Cavelier, René-Robert, 153, 154
Ceramics
    colonial life interpreted, xix
    European norm, xvi
Chairs
    Baltimore, 259, 269, *272*, 272–73
    butaca, *165*, 165–66
    Camp, 262, 263, *263*, 266
    capitol, 50, 56, 62
    ceremonial, 42, 49–50, *50*, 54, 56
    Chippendale, 59
    Colchester, 134–35, *134*, *135*
    English, *41*, 41, 58–59, *58*, *59*, 62–63, *63*, 272–73, *273*
    French, 169, *169*
    Hay, 46, *48*, 48–50, *50*, 54, 56–59, *57*, *58*, *63*
    Mississippi River valley, 169, *169*
    New Mexico, 185–188, *186*, *187*, *198*, *199*
    Philadelphia style, 94, *97*, 102–4, *102*, *103*, *104*
    Salem, 27
    simple, xviii
    Spanish, 180, *198*, *199*
    speaker's, 56
    Symonds, *40*, 40–41
    upholstered, 28, 40–41
Chamber table
    luxury item, 28
Champion, Epaphroditus, 114
Champion, Henry, Jr., 114
Chapin, Eliphalet, 18–19
Charleston, S.C.
    cabinetry, 29
    commercial center, 1, 10
Chests
    Camp, 280, *281*
    Chippendale, 112
    Colchester, 114–15, 128–30, *129*
    high, 96, *97*, 98, *98*, *99*, 106–10, *107*, *109*, 112–15, 128–30, *129*, *131*
    London, 33, 33–34
    Michoacán, 196, *197*
    New Mexico, 183–85, *184*, *185*, 193–96, *193*, *195*, *197*

Philadelphia style, 94, *96*, *97*, 98, *98*, 99, 106–10, *107*, *109*, 112, 113, 130, *131*
Salem, 26
Spanish, 180, 193–96, *194*, *195*
Symonds, 31–32, *32*
Chests of drawers
Baltimore, 267, *267*
Boston, *39*, 39–40, 170–73, *172*
Colchester, 125–30, *126*, *127*
labor-intensive, 28
Symonds, 38, *38*
Chests-on-chests, 20, *21*, 95, 120–25, *121*, *122*, *124*, 188
Chests-on-stands
predecessor of highboy, xvii
Chew, Samuel, Attorney General, 92
China
American, 240–46
dining sets, 243
glaze, 244
marks, 244
vs. other trades, 240
quality, 244
tea sets, 243
See also Porcelain
Chippendale, Thomas, 42, 44, 58, 59, 61, 93, 104, 110, 111, 112
Chippendale's *Director*. *See* Gentleman and Cabinet-Maker's Director
Chocolate pot
Coney, 69, 70, 77–79, *78*
Dighton, 77–79, *78*
Chouteau, Pierre, 161, 162, 165, 175
Churches
furniture, 179
Gothic, 179
religious objects, 182
silver, 136–37
Class differences, xv
Classical proportion
English cabinetry, 46
Symonds teaching, 25
Claypoole, George, 95
Clearcutting, 43
Clifton, Henry, 96, 98
Clothespress
Chippendale, 61, *61*
Hay, 46, *60*, 60–61
Coates, Thomas, 2
Coburn, John, 87
Coffee pots
Edwards, 72, 87, *88*
English, 87, *89*
Coffins
Evans, 95
Hay shop, 52
Colchester school, 112–35 passim
Cole, Joseph G.
portrait by, 3
Colman, Benjamin, Reverend, 78–79
Commerce
Philadelphia, 92–93
Commercialism
New England, 27
Commode
Canadian, 170–73, *171*

Mississippi River valley, *161*, 161–62
New Orleans, 170–73, *173*
Common Sense, 10
Community
vs. capitalism, 6
craftsman protecting, 5, 6, 8, 11
and individual, 6
Conant family
chest, 31
Coney, John, 69, 71, 77–78
Connecticut
agriculture, 116
furniture, 113–35 passim
Connell, James, 96
Connell, William, 95
Conservatism
colonial, xiv
Constitution (U.S.)
ratification, 10, 11, 15
Conyers, Richard, 68, 75n
Cooke, Elisha, Jr., 4
Cooperative workshop. *See* Labor
Copies
old master, 20
Copley, John Singleton
portrait by, 3
Council of Revision, 10
Courtenay, Hercules, 96, 110
Cowell, William, 72
Craftsmen
clientele, 1
Dutch-American, 137
English-trained, 44, 93–96, 210, 242
family, 182
French-trained, 162
history, 1–14
London-trained, 44, 93–96
milieu, 1
mobility, 42
opportunities, 70
political involvement, 1, 4–6, 7
respect, 3
specialization, 1
Cream jugs
Greiner/Stiegel, 216, 232, *232*
English, 232, *232*
Creativity, 14, 16–19, 20
Crèvecoeur, Hector St. John de, 2
Crucibles, 242
Cruets
glass, 216
Crump, John, 53
Crystal. *See* Lead glass
Culture
spread, xv, 165
underlying system of thought, xv
upper-class, xix, 43, 92, 257
See also Colonial culture, European culture
Cupboard
Spanish, 180
Symonds, 36, *37*
Cups
silver, 66, 69, *69*, 70, 72, 73, 77, 77–79, 138, 140
See also Mugs; Porringers; Tankards

Index 287

Darling, Thomas, 140
Davenport, William, 53
Davis, David, 52, 53
Decanters
  glass, 216, 219
Delancey, James, 7
Dell, Samuel, 139, 150–51
Deming, Jonathan, 114, 115, 117, 120, 123, 134
Denman, Peter, 84n
Denny, William, 69
Denting, Bastiaan, 138
Depreciation
  currency, 8
Depression, post-1760, 5
Deshler, David, 95
Design
  conservative, 70
  new ideas, 16–19, 27, 68, 70, 72, 117, 166
Desks
  Camp, 263, *264*, *265*, 268, *274*, 274–75
  Colchester, 113–14, *119*, 119–20
  Connecticut, 113–16
  English, 268, 269, 274–75, *275*
  Philadelphia style, 110, *110*, *111*
de Vries, Hans Vredeman, 24
Dickinson, Edmund, 44, 50, 52, 53, 54, 59, 64–65
Dickinson, John, 96
Dighton, Isaac, 77, 79
Director. *See* Gentleman and Cabinet-Maker's Director
Display of Heraldry, 72, 139
Distribution. *See* Merchandising
Dixwell, John, 71, 72
Donald, George, 52, 59
Dowdney, Nathaniel, 95
Drawer construction, 43, 162
Druid Hill, 276
Dummer, Jeremiah, 68, 69, 75n, 80–81
Dunlap, John, Major, 20
Dutch influence
  silver, 136–41, 146–47, 149

Early Furniture of French Canada, 178
Economics
  Baltimore, 256, 257
  Boston, xix, 4, 70, 74–75
  bourgeois orientation, 6
  classes, 21
  colonial conditions, 14
  Connecticut, 116–17
  craftsman's role, 15
  effect on furniture style, xviii
  Mississippi River valley, 153, 154, 161
  New Mexico, 181, 182
  New Orleans, 165
  Pennsylvania, 202
  Philadelphia, 241
  as social, 6
  urban, 1, 4, 11, 93
  wartime, 7, 8
Edict of Nantes revoked 1685, 138
Education. *See* Training

Edwards family
  silver, 66–91 passim
Edwards, Elizabeth, 68
Edwards, John, 19, 66–75, 77, 78, 80–84, 87, 91
Edwards, Joseph, 72, 91
Edwards, Samuel, 66, 71–74, 76n, 82, 87, 88, 90, 91
Edwards, Thomas, 66, 71–74, 76n, 84–85, 87, 91
Elliott, John, 95, 96
Embargoes, 11
Emulation, English. *See* English influence
Endicott family
  chest, 31
Enfield, Conn.
  woodworking, 26
English influence
  acceptance of, 112, 118
  Baltimore, 256–62 passim, 269–73 passim
  Boston, 67, 68, 70
  china, 240, 244, 246
  glass, 203–4, 210–11, 212–15, 217, 218, 220, 226, 236
  Hay shop, 42–65 passim
  household goods, 66
  joinery, 24, 25, 27
  Mississippi River valley, 161, 162, 175
  New England government, 66
  New Orleans, 165
  Philadelphia style, 93, 95–96, 98, 99
  porringers, 90–91
  silver, 136–41, 143
  Virginia, xvii
Engraver, 218–19, 236
Engraving
  Heraldic, 85
  tradition, 219
Entrepreneurs
  new breed, 9
Environment
  colonial craftsman's, 14, 23, 66
  Essex County, Mass., xvi, 23–41
  cupboards, 36, *37*
Etat et description de la ville de Montpellier fait en 1768, 15, 20–21
Ethnicity. *See* Tradition
Etting, Solomon and Rachel Gratz, 280
European culture
  colonies as extension, xiii
European influence, 14–22
  adaptation of, 16
Evans, David, 95
Evans, Edward, 95

Fall of British Tyranny; or, American Liberty Triumphant, 7
Faneuil, Benjamin, 87
Faneuil, Peter, 72, 87
Faneuil family
  coat of arms, 87
Fashion, 15, 27, 29, 43, 44, 68 passim, 72, 112, 158, 216
  See also specific influence (e.g. English influence); Style

Father Abraham's Speech, 2
Fauquier, Governor
    coffin, 52, 59
Federalism, 10
Fisher, Sarah Logan, 103
Fishing
    Salem industry, 24
Fitch, Isaac, 117, 132
Fleeson, Plunkett, 7
Flint glass, American
    Stiegel, 202, 210–11, 212, 214, 218, 219, 220, 222
    See also Lead glass
Flour merchants, Scots-Irish, 256, 257
Flowerer. *See* Engraver
Focillon, Henri, xv
Folk art, New Mexican, 182
Food shortage, 8
Forman, Benno M., 29, 99
Foster, John, 71
Franklin, Benjamin, 2, 3, 5, 6, 92, 242, 244
French and Indian wars, 116–17
French influence
    Mississippi River valley, 152, 154, 155, 157, 158, 161–62, 172, 175
    New Orleans, 162, 165
Frontier theory, 23
Fruitbasket, Porcelain, 244, 252, *252*, *253*
Fruits of Abitrary Power; or, The Bloody Massacre, 7
Furnishings
    Salem house, 26
    17th-century shift, 27
Furniture
    Baltimore, 256–81 passim
    Burnham-Loomis, 113–18
    church, 179
    colonial life interpreted, xix, 152
    Connecticut, 113–35 passim
    construction by housewrights, xviii, 159
    development in Williamsburg, Va., 43, 44
    domestic Spanish, 179
    English standards, xvii, 259
    federal, 256, 259–81
    French Canadian, 178
    Massachusetts, 23–41 passim
    Michoacán, 196, 197
    Mississippi River valley, 152, 159
    New Mexican construction, 190
    Philadelphia style, 92–111
    plain vs. decorated, 113
    production, 161
    regency style, 9
    scholars, 112–13
    Spanish construction, 182
    Spanish portable, 180, 188
    Symonds's forms, 26, 28, 29
    See also specific object
Fussell, Solomon, 94, 99, 102

General Society of Mechanics and Tradesmen, 10
Gentleman and Cabinet-Maker's Director, 46, 49, 52, 58, 61, 95, 98, 99, 100, 104, 110, 135

George, John, 79
George III, King, 7
German influence
    glass, 202–4, 205, 212–13, 214–15, 220
Gibbs, Daniel, 69
Gillingham, James, 95, 96, 99
Glass
    colonial life interpreted, xix
    enameled, 212–13, 234–35
    English glassblowers, 202, 211, 212, 216
    European norm, xvi
    German glassblowers, xvi–xvii, 202, 203, 212, 214
    glassblower's mold, 20
    glassmakers' parade, 208
    glassmaking history, 202
    Greiner, 205
    horn, 207–8, *208*
    import duties, 209–10
    import records, 216
    manufacture, 202
    Venetian, 202–3
    white, 205, 210, 213, *213*, 216
    window, 205, 222
    See also Flint glass, American; Lead glass
Glasscutter. *See* Engraver
Glover, Jose and Elizabeth, 66
Goblets
    glass, 220, 222, 234–235, *234*, *235*, 236–39, *237*, *238*
Goddard-Townsend shops, 113, 126–27
Gostelowe, Jonathan, 95
Gold
    Boston goldsmiths, 72
    immigrant goldsmiths, 68, 69
Gordon, Adam, Lord, 92
Government
    New England, 66
Grafton, Nathaniel, 27
Graing, Roger, 75
Great Yarmouth, Norfolk, 23–24
Grendey, Giles, 42, 44, 50, 54n
Grignon, René, 69, 75n
Guild system
    carpenters', 179
    English, 21
Guillim, John, 72, 139

Hains, Adam, 95, 152
Hamilton, George, 50, 52
Hamilton, James, 64–65
Hamminck, Arent, 137, 146–47
Hancock, John, 7, 84
Hancock, Thomas, 72
Hardwoods. *See* Woods
Harland, Thomas, 116, 125
Harpsichords
    Bucktrout, 54
Harrocks, Richard, 53
Hart, Thomas
    cabinet, 34–35
Hay, Anthony, 42–54
Hay, Charles, 53
Hay, Elizabeth, 53

Hay, George, 53
Hay, Joe, 52
Hay, Thomas, 52
Hay shop, 42–65
   armchair, 56–57, 57
   card table, 62, 62–63
   china table, 64, 64–65
   clothespress, 60, 60–61
   London influence, 42
   Masonic master's chair, 58, 58–59
Hazzard, Ebenezer, 43
Hebard, Nathaniel, 134
Heckscher, Morrison, 119
Hepplewhite, George, 165, 188, 272–73, 276–77, 278–79
Hepplewhite's *Guide*. *See Cabinet-Maker and Upholsterer's Guide*
Herrick, Ephraim and Mary
   cabinet, 34–35
Herrick, George, 28, 40
Hewes, George Robert Twelves
   Cole's portrait of, 3
Hierarchy
   American vs. European, 20
   clientele, 42
   craft, 1, 10
   economic, 21
   English cabinet industry, 42
   social, 14, 66
   trade, 1, 4, 5, 6, 15, 20
Highboys
   symbol of elegance, xvii
Hillhouse, Mary, 140
Honey, James, 53
Hornor, William Macpherson, 95
House of the Seven Gables, 28
Household goods
   English, 66
   Spanish, 179
Housewrights
   furniture construction, xviii, 159
Hughes, Hugh, 5
Hughes, John, 5
Hull, John, 69
Hunt, Samuel, 132–33
Huntington, Ebenezer, 120
Huntington, Felix, 116, 126, 134
Hurd, Jacob, 72–74, 76n, 84, 87
Hurst, Henry, xvi, 18, 68, 139
Hutton, John Strangeways
   Peale's portrait of, 3

Ince, William, 44
Income. *See* Wages
Incorporation
   craftsmen involvement, 10, 11
Independence
   craftsman's goal, 3
Individual
   and community, 6
   vs. tradition, xiv
Industrial age, xvi
Inflation
   in 18th-century Boston, 70, 74
Innovation, 19–20, 68, 140, 152
Inventor
   defined, 19

Inventory
   Bolduc's, 157–58
   Carpenter's, 239
   Deming's, 114, 115
   18th-century New Orleans, 162
   Glover's, 66–67
   Lupien's, 159
   New Mexico, 183
   Putnams's, 36
   17th-century Salem, 27–28, 36
Isaac, Lazarus, 236
James, Edward, 95
Jefferson, Thomas, President
   Hay appointment, 53
Jelly glasses, 217–18
Jesse, David, 68, 75n
Johnson, Thomas, 98, 110, 111
Johnston, Thomas, 84, 87n
Joinery
   agricultural communities, 25, 159–60
   Chinese, 62
   English, 24, 25, 27
   in agricultural communities, 24
Jones, E. Alfred, 75n
Journeyman
   vs. apprentice, 16
   18th-century ads, 53
   guild, 179
   hierarchy, 1
   immigrant, 68
   income, 2, 74
   vs. master, 6, 9, 21, 68
   postwar, 8–9
   respect, 2–3
   strikes, 9
   See also Apprentice, Master
Jugiez, Martin, 93, 96, 100, 104–5

Kammen, Michael, 137
Keels, Newfoundland
   furniture, 20
Keith, William, 4
Kendall, Joshua, 52
Kennedy, William, 52, 53, 59
Kierstede, Cornelius, xvi, 136–50
Kip, Benjamin, 137
Kip, Jesse, 137
Kirk, John T.
   European tradition, xxn
Knowles, Charles, Governor, 4, 72
Kubler, George
   anthropological perspectives, xv, xix, 19

Labor
   as capital, 8
   cooperative workshop, 3
   early American belief in, 1–2
   factory wage, 11
   relations, 9
   scarcity, 28, 42
   skilled, 1, 52
   See also Skill
Lacquerware, 184–85, 196
Language
   colonial culture, xiii, xix
   loss, xiii
Lannuier, Charles-Honoré, 152, 259

LaSalle, René-Robert Cavelier, sieur de, 153, 154
Laughton, John, 7
Leacock, John, 7
Lead glass, 203, 210–11, 212, 217, 218
Learned professions
    defined, 14
Learning, 14
Leather Apron Club, 4
Légaré, Francis, 69
LeRoux, Bartholomew, 74
LeRoux, John, 74
Lewis-Byrd families
    china table, 65
Liberal arts
    defined, 14
Library Company of Baltimore, 276
Library Company of Philadelphia, 99
Linnel, John, 42, 44
Literature
    changing colonial attitudes, xiii
    popular, xiii
Little, Peter, 11
Lloyd, Elizabeth, 93
Lockwood, Joshua, 7
Logan, William, 103
London influence. *See* English influence
London Tradesman, 14
Loomis, Samuel, 114–18, 119, 120–21, 123, 125–30, 134
Lord, Epaphras, 114, 128
Lord, Richard, 128
Lottery
    Stiegel, 222
Lumber
    cutting, 159
    Salem industry, 24, 28

M. T. 1700/1701 chest, 31
MacCollough, Thomas, 69
Mannerism, 24, 36
Manufacturing
    beginnings, 8, 240
    British goods, 208–9
    Philadelphia, 93
Marine Society, 15
Market. *See* Trade
Marot, Daniel, 149
Mason, Ralph, 27, 39
Masonic chair, 48, 58, 58–59
Masonic master's chair, 49, 58, 58–59
Mass production, 240
Massachusetts
    furniture, 23–41
Master
    vs. apprentice, 16
    goal, 3
    guild-certified, 179
    hierarchy, 1
    income, 2, 242
    vs. journeyman, 6, 9, 21, 68
    native, 68
    postwar, 8
    status, 2
    See also Apprentice, Journeyman
Mather, Cotton, 67
Mather, Increase, 67

Matlack, Timothy, 7
Mayhew, Edgar DeN., 114, 119, 120
Mayhew, John, 44
McIntire, Samuel, 17
McKinsey, Kristan, 137
Mechanical arts
    defined, 14
Mechanics Committee, 6
    See also Sons of Liberty
Mensuration, 10
Merchandising, 73, 74
Merchant-mechanic coalition, 10
Meredith, Samuel, 10
Messinger, Henry, 27, 39
Metal
    Hispanic, 180
    scarcity, xviii, 70
    See also Silver
Metropolitan Museum of Art
    Star Hotel paneling, 24
Mexican influence
    furniture, 179–201
    originality, 17
Mickle, Samuel, 94
Milk jugs
    glass, 216
Mississippi River valley, xvii, xviii, xix
    early furniture, 152–78
Moller, Henrik, 139
Monroe, Eliza, 53
Monroe, James, 53
Moody, Matthew, 53
Moorish influence, 179–80, 190, 193, 195, 199
Morgan, John, Dr., 7
Morphology, xv
Morrell, Richard, 139, 143, 145
Morris, George Anthony, 241
Morris, Robert, 8
Moulton, Jeremiah, Colonel, 83
Mugs
    glass, 205, *206*
    silver, 70–71,
    See also Cups; Tankards
Myers, Minor, Jr., 114, 119, 120

Nash, Gary, 15
Native Americans
    carpentry, 180, 190
    colonist contact, xvi
    Mexico, 180
    Mississippi River valley, 152
    New Mexico, 182
New Book of Ornaments, 110
New Hampshire
    furniture, 20
New London County Furniture, 1640–1840, 120, 132, 134
New Mexico
    furniture, 179–201
    wood, 193
New Orleans, 152–79 passim
New York City
    commercial center, 1
    journeymen strikes, 9
    mechanics, 10–11
Newman, Antipas, 68

Newman, Sybil, 68
Nonimportation, 210, 211, 240, 242–46 passim
Norris, Charles, 95
Norris, Isaac, 4
North-American Almanack
    Revere's frontispiece, 7
North Briton
    Wilkes on King George, 7
Nouveaux riches
    Baltimore, 257

Objects. *See* Imported objects; specific object
Observer, Raleigh
    on Bucktrout, 54
Onckelbag, Gerrit, 137, 138
Oriental influence, 180, 181
Ormeston, John, 53
Osborne family
    chest, 29, 31
Overing, Charles, 71, 83

Paine, Tom, 10
Palardy, Jean, 178
Palmer, John, 2
Patent
    Bonnin, 242
Patronage, 4, 16, 136–37, 138, 257, 271
Paz, Octavio, xxn
Peale, Charles Willson
    portrait by, 3
    Revolutionary leader, 7
Pease, John, 26
Peaston, William, 84, 86
Pemberton, James, 93
Penn, John, Governor, 93, 95
Penn, William, 92, 93
Perley, Sidney, 23, 29
Philadelphia, Pa.
    artisan success, 2–3, 5
    carpenters' strike, 9
    commercial center, 1, 241
    furniture, 92–111 passim
    recession, 4
    woods, 43
Philipse, David, 7
Phillips, John Marshall, 75n, 136
Phips, William, Sir, 67
Phyfe, Duncan, 9
Pianos. *See* Spinets
Pieceworkers, 74
Pioneer Village, Salem, Mass., 23
Plantation houses, 43
Pocius, Gerald L., 20
Pokal, German, 220, *221*
Politics
    American Revolution, xviii
    anti-Britain, 6–7, 100, 202, 210, 241
    colonial-Anglo ties, xix, 112, 240
    craftsman involvement, 1, 4–6, 7, 11
    Mississippi River valley, 152–53, 154
    17th-century Boston, 67
Pompadour, Madame, 108
Population shift
    Mississippi River valley, 154

New Mexico, 182
New Orleans, 162
Porcelain
    Bonnin, 242
    Chinese export, 243
    hard-paste, 241, 245
    production/marketing, 240
    See also China
Porringers
    Edwards, 70, 71, *90*, 90–91
    English, 90–91, *91*
    as icon, xviii
    popularity, 90
    silver, 70, 71, 90
Portraits of artisans, 3
Potpourri dish, porcelain, 244, *254*, 254–55
Powell, Samuel, 92, 93, 96
Prevereau, Moses, 69
Pricing
    controls, 8
    fair, 6
Priest, William, 72, 89
Prior, Matthew, 49
Privateering, 117
Production
    Boston silver, 73
    early 18th-century furniture, 161, 166
    late 18th-century, 21
    post-Revolution reorganization, 9
    schools, 113
Prothero, I. J., 3
Putnam, Benjamin, 36
Putnam, Daniel, Colonel, 116
Putnam, Stephen, 36
Putnam family
    cupboard, 29, 38
Pye, David, 19

Queen Anne's War, 70
Quick, Abraham, 9
Quick, Theunis Jacobsen and Vroutje, 138

R. L. chest, 31–32
Raleigh *Observer*
    on Bucktrout, 54
Randolph, Benjamin, 95, 96, 99
Randolph, Edmund, 53
Randolph, Peyton and Betty Harrison, 84
Reese, Thomas, xxn, 17
Religion
    Baltimore, 257
    Dutch emphasis, 137
    effect on furniture style, xviii, 112
Rensselaer, Killian Van, 143
Retail. *See* Merchandising
Retzel, Fredrich, xxn
Revere, Paul
    Copley's portrait of, 3
    political graphics, 7
Reynolds, James, 1–3, 96
Richardson, Joseph, Jr., 2
Riegl, Alois, xv, xxn
Rittenhouse, David, 7, 92
Riving, 28–29

Roberts, Aaron, 122
Rococo style. *See* Style
Rogers, Nicholas, IV, 276
Roode, Alexander, 75n
Rose, Alex, 95
Rouse, William, 68, 141
Rush, Benjamin, 240, 242
Russell, Moody, 71

St. Monday, 2
Salem, Mass., 24, 26, 27, 28, 29
Salts
    glass, 205, 218, *218*
    standing, 80–81, *80*, *81*
Salvers
    silver, 72, 84–87, *85*, *86*
Sanderson, Robert, 69
Santo Domingo, 168n, 175
Sauceboat, Porcelain, 244, *250*, 251, *251*
Savery, William, 93, 94, 99, 100, 102–6
Sawyers
    English, 29
Schlereth, Thomas J., xxn
Schuyler, Johannes and Elizabeth, 139, 143
Scott, John, 55n
Scott, Peter, 44, 52, 53, 54, 65
Second Continental Congress, 7
Sehl, Ferdinand, 139
Semper, Gottfried, xv, xxn
Seven Years' War, 5
Shaw, William, 72, 89
Shearer, 275
Sheraton, Thomas, 165, 188, 274, 278, 279
Sheraton's *Drawing-Book*. *See Cabinet-Maker and Upholsterer's Drawing-Book*
Shipbuilding
    Philadelphia, 93
Shippen, Edward, Jr., 95
Shippen, Joseph, Jr., 243–44
Shipping
    Salem industry, 24
Shoemaker, Jonathan, 95
Sideboard, Baltimore, 259, *260*
Silsbee, Nathaniel, 26
Silver
    availability, 70
    Boston silversmiths, 68
    colonial life interpreted, xix, 140–41
    Hispanic, 180
    luxury trade, 40, 67
    settlers ownership, 67
    17th-century forms, 70
    traditions, 136, 137
    See also specific forms
Skaats, Bartholomew, 137
Skerry, Ephraim, 27
Skill
    apprentice, 16
    form of property, 8
    See also Labor
Slaves
    in furniture industry, 53
Smelling bottles, 218, *219*
Smith, Elizabeth Storer, 87
Smith, Isaac, 76n

Smith, William P., 84
Smithsonian Institute
    china table, 65
Snuffer stand, Kierstede, 139
Social customs
    adaptation, xiii
    bed hangings, 66
    effect on furniture style, xviii, 256
Sofas
    Baltimore, 266, *276*, 276–77
    English, 276–77, *277*
Sons of Liberty, 5, 6, 7
Spanish influence
    Mexico, 180, 181
    Mississippi River valley, 165–66
    New Mexico, 182
Spicer, Oliver, 116
Spiers, James, 44, 53
Spinets, Bucktrout, 54
Sprats, William, 117, 132
Stamp Act of 1765, xviii, 101n, 240
Star Hotel, Great Yarmouth
    paneling, 24, 25, 26, 28, 34, 35, 36
Stark, John, General, 132
Stedman, Charles, 92
Steuart, Robert, 11
Stiegel, Henry William, xvi, xviii, 202–40 passim, 247n
Stoddard, Solomon, Reverend, 81
Stoneware, English, 243, 246
    See also Wedgwood Queensware
Stoughton, William, Lieutenant Governor, 77
Strong, Caleb, 132
Style
    advanced, 44
    baroque, 180, 193
    Chippendale, 7, 92
    Colchester, 112–35
    Corinthian, 24, 25
    economic and social forces, xvii-xviii
    18th-century London, 42, 257
    Gothic, 178–79, 190, 193
    high vs. popular, 112
    Hispanic, 180
    longevity, xix
    Louis XIII, 199
    Louis XIV, 199
    Louis XV, 175
    neoclassical, 181, 259, 278
    Philadelphia, 92–111
    Queen Anne, 102
    Renaissance, 180
    rococo, 46–47, 52, 56, 64, 72, 92–111 passim, 112, 115, 181, 185, 199, 216, 219, 220, 236
    transfer, xvi, 18, 70, 166
    urban/rural, 112
    See also Design; specific influence (e.g. English influence)
Sugar bowls, Glass, *206*, 206–7, 216, 228–29, *228*, *229*, 233, *233*
Swan, Abraham, 96
Sweetmeat dish, Porcelain, 244, *248*, 248–49, *249*
Symmes family
    silver coffeepot, 87

Symonds, James, 26, 28, 31, 37, 40
Symonds, John, xvi, xviii, 23–29, 36
Symonds, Joseph, 29
Symonds, Samuel, 26, 31
Symonds, Thomas, 26, 29
Symonds shop, 23–41
    cabinets, 34–35, *35*
    chests of drawers, *38*, 38, *39*
    chests with one drawer, 31–32, *32*
    cupboards, 36–37, *37*
    serge chairs, *40*, 40–41
    upholstered chairs, *40*, 40–41
Sympson, Joseph, 139

Tables
    Baltimore, 263, *263*, 266–67, *267*, *278*, 278–79
    Canadian, 158, *158*
    china, 42, 50–52, *51*, *64*, 64–65
    Colchester stand, 132–33, *133*
    Dickinson-Hamilton, 65
    English, 268, 270, *278*, 278–79, *279*
    French, 158, *158*, 178, *178*
    Hay, 46, 49, 50–52. *51*, *62*, *64*
    Mississippi River valley, 157–58, *157*, 165
    New Mexico, *200*, 200–201
    New Orleans, 165, 178, *178*
    simple, xviii
    Spanish, 180, 188, 200–201, *201*
    tea, 100, 104–5, *105*
Tailer, Sarah Byfield, 77
Tailer, William, 77
Tankards
    Dutch, 150–51
    Edwards, 70–71, *82*, 82–84
    English, 82–84, *83*, 139, *151*
    flat-top as icon, xviii
    Hurst, 18, *18*
    Kierstede, 139, 140, *150*, 150–51
    popularity, 70
    silver, xvi, 70–71, *71*
Tariff protection, 10
Teakettle
    Kierstede, 138, *148*, 149
    See also Water kettle
Technology
    advanced, 43, 44, 46
    bottle glass, 226
    18th-century London, 42
Ten Eyck, Koenraet, 137, 143
Ten-hour day. *See* Working hours
Textiles
    in colonies, 66
    Connecticut mills, 116
    imported, 117
Texts. *See* Literature
Thompson, E. P., 21
Timber. *See* Lumber; Woods
Tools
    Cambas's cabinetmaking, 159
    crude, xviii, 193
    Mexican, 182
    New Mexican, 182
    Spanish, 182
Townsend, John, 113
Townsend, Thomas, 74, 76n

Townsend Acts, xviii, 7, 101n, 208–10, 111, 240
Trade
    Baltimore, 256, 258
    coastal, 98
    export, 8, 9, 42
    inter-trade relationship, 15
    maritime, 15
    Mississippi River valley, 153
    New England, 92, 222
    New Mexico, 182
    New Orleans, 162
    Pennsylvania-German, 222
    Philadelphia, 92–93
    post-Revolutionary, 220
    regional, 8
    schools in Canada, 159
    Spain-Mexico, 180, 196
Tradition
    accepting new, xix–xx
    ethnic, xvi passim, xix, 136, 137, 154, 202
    vs. individual, xiv
Training
    craftsman's, 16, 159, 179, 258
    retraining, 43
Trappers, French fur, 153–54
Trask family
    chest, 29, 31
Trent, Robert F., 120
Trott, George, 7
Trotter, Daniel, 95
Trueman, Constant, 4
Trumbull, David, 132
Trumbull, Jonathan, Governor, 117, 132
Tufft, Thomas, 95
Tumblers
    glass, 215, 220, 234–35, *235*
Turner, John, 28
Tyng, Edward, Commodore, 72

Umbrella repair
    Bucktrout, 54
Undertaking
    Bucktrout, 52
    Hay shop, 52
    See also Coffins
Union
    cross-craft, 6
    journeymen's, 9
Upholstery
    chairs, 28, 40–41
    Hay shop, 52
    luxury trade, 40
Upper-class culture
    American Revolution, xix
    Philadelphia, 92
    Virginia, 43
Urban growth
    Baltimore, 256–57

Valdez family, 183, 192n, 195
Valois, Gabriel, 96
Values
    colonial, xiv
    cultural, xv
    Dutch, 137
    labor, 1

Van Beest, Hendrik, 149
Van der Burch, Cornelius, 139
Van der Spiegel, Jacob, 137
Vargueño, 183–84, 190, *195*, 195–96
Veren, Hilliard, 27–28
Vernon, Samuel, 71
Verre églomisé, 268
Vile, William, 42
Virginia
   case furniture, 68
   English gentry, xvii, xix
Virginia Gazette
   ads, 47, 49, 53

Waddill, William, 52
Wages, 2, 10
   controls, 8
   fair, 6
   vs. hours, 2
   incorporation, 10
Walker, Benjamin, 68, 72
War of 1812, 9
War of the Austrian Succession, 5
Warder, John, 2
Wardrobes, Baltimore, 260, *261*, 262, *262*, 269
   See also Armoires
Warren, William L., 120, 132
Washington, George, President, 15, 42, 46, 50
   table, 50, 52, 65
Washington Benevolent Society of New York, 11
Water kettle
   Dutch, 149, *149*
   See also Teakettle
Way to Wealth, 2
Wayne, William, 96
Webb, Edward, 69
Wedgwood, Josiah, 242–43, 246, 247n
Wedgwood Queensware, 241, 246
Weidman, Gregory, 19
Wells, Amos, 113, 116

Weyman, Edward, 7
Wickes, George, 72, 84
Widdatch and Drummond, 53
Wilkes, John, 7
Williamsburg, Va.
   Hay shop, 42–54
Wilson, James, 44, 47, 52, 56, 62, 63
Wiltshire, 52, 53, 54–55n, 59
Wineglasses, 216, *217*, 220
   wine-and-water glasses, 216
Winslow, Edward, 69, 71, 80, 90
Winthrop, Governor, 66–67
Witch hunts, Salem, 36
Woods
   Australian, 260
   availability, 43, 182
   cherry, xviii, 162
   French Canada, 167n
   Hay shop, 53
   mahogany, xviii, 96, 165, 166, 260–61
   maple, xviii
   oak, 43
   pecan, xviii
   Philadelphia, 43
   pine, xviii, 162, 165, 193
   red cedar, 162
   satinwood, 260, 278
   South American, 260
   Symonds chests, 32
   walnut, 162, 165
   zebrawood, 261
Woodward, Abishai, 116
Woodworkers
   Native Americans, 180
   London, 99
   settlement patterns, 24
Working hours, 9
Workmanship, 19, 20, 46
Wynkoop, Benjamin, 137

XYZ Dialogue, 5

Young, Alfred, 11

Photograph Credits

Gavin Ashwolt: cat. no. 90
David Bohl: cat. no. 5
Joel Breger: cat. no. 113; fig. 9, p. 266; fig. 11, p. 267
brt Photographic Illustrations: cat. no. 96
Mary Anne Burns: fig. 3, p. 156
Richard Cheek: fig. 1, p. 94; fig. 3, p. 97
Blair Clark: cat. nos. 74, 78; fig. 2, p. 185; fig. 4, p. 187; fig. 5, p. 187; fig. 7, p. 189
P. Richard Eells: cat. no. 6
Christine Guest: cat. no. 66
Don Johnson: fig. 9, p. 217; fig. 10, p. 218
Hans E. Lorenz: fig. 4, p. 97
Gary Mortensen: cat. nos. 30, 52, 67, 80, 88, 101
Mary Peck: cat. no. 79
Robert Reck: cat. no. 81
Han van Senus: cat. no. 61
James Zietz: cat. nos. 70, 72, 73

Designed and produced by
Kachergis Book Design, Pittsboro, North Carolina.
Composed by Marathon Typography Service, Inc.,
Research Triangle Park, North Carolina.
Printed by Eastern Press, Inc., New Haven, Connecticut